Center for Basque Studies
University of Nevada, Reno

Basque Politics Series, no. 7

The Basque Fiscal System

History, Current Status, and Future Perspectives

Edited by Joseba Agirreazkuenaga and Eduardo Alonso Olea

Basque Politics Series, no. 7

Center for Basque Studies
University of Nevada, Reno

This book was published with generous financial support from the Basque Government

Translation funding for this book was provided by the Documentation Centre of the Economic Agreement and Foral Treasuries at the University of the Basque Country (Leioa), in agreement with the Foral Deputation of Biscay

Basque Politics Series, no. 7
Series editor: Xabier Irujo

Center for Basque Studies
University of Nevada, Reno
Reno, NV 89557
www.basque.unr.edu

© 2014 Center for Basque Studies
All rights reserved. Printed in the United States of America

Translation by Robert Forstag
Book and cover design by John Coleman
Cover illustration: photograph by Joseba Agirreazkuenaga of *Gaztelu*, a sculpture by Remigio Mendiburu. On loan to the Center for Basque Studies by Rámon Cengotitabengoa and Gema Egaña

Library of Congress Cataloging-in-Publication Data

The Basque fiscal system : history, current status, and future perspectives / edited by Joseba Agirreazkuenaga and Eduardo Alonso Olea.
pages cm. -- (Basque politics series ; no.7)
Includes bibliographical references and index.
Summary: "Collection of articles exploring the history, development, and current policy of the Basque taxation agreements with the Spanish government"-- Provided by publisher.
ISBN 978-1-935709-46-6 (pbk. : alk. paper) 1. Taxation--Spain--País Vasco. 2. Taxation--Law and legislation--Spain--País Vasco. 3. Finance, Public--Spain--País Vasco. I. Agirreazkuenaga, J. (Joseba) II. Alonso Olea, Eduardo J.

HJ2849.P35B37 2014
336.200946'6--dc23

2013040389

Contents

Foreword

Acting in my capacity of Foral Deputy of Treasury and Finances in the Foral Deputation of Bizkaia, I am thoroughly pleased to introduce this book, result of the collaboration between the Center for Basque Studies of University of Nevada in Reno and the Centre of the Economic Agreement Documentation and of the foral Treasuries.

For many years, now, the Foral Deputation of Bizkaia made the decision to diffuse, in a broad sense, the history, contents and significance of our most genuine self-government legal instrument: the Economic Agreement. No effort has been spared to achieve this goal and, as a fruit of this determination, Ad Concordiam Association was set up by the Foral Diputation of Bizkaia, along with the University of the Basque Country (UPV-EHU) and Deusto University in 2000. Ad Concordiam is a not-for-profit private organization, which aims at diffusing and studying issues concerning taxation and public treasury, with special reference to the aspects related to the legal and institutional particularities in force in the historical territory of Bizkaia. In order to pursue these aims, the association carries out various tasks, such as research studies, conferences, seminars, expositions and, in general, any kind of diffusion and educative activities within the purpose of the association.

Complementing the abovementioned initiative, in May 2007, the Foral Deputation of Bizkaia and the UPV/EHU signed a collaboration agreement in order to set up the Center of the Economic Agreement Documentation and of the Foral Treasuries. Its purpose is to organize a Centre and Documentation Service, within the Department of Contemporary History at the UPV-EHU, in order to diffuse the past, present, and future information concerning the Economic Agreement and the Foral Treasuries, to institutions, the academia, professionals, and the general public. This information platform will be useful not only for researchers but for anybody interested in the economic regime of the Basque Country, as it also intends to cooperate with any interested institution in the diffusion of the Economic Agreement regime.

All these collaboration activities between academic institutions and the public administration try intensively to foster and focus the diffusion and knowledge of the Economic Agreement, as a recognized fiscal federalism model, at an international level, moreover since the European Court of Justice (CJEU) regarded as fully compatible with the European law in 2008.

The Economic Agreement regime assigns the capacity to establish and regulate their own tax system as well as the capacity to administer and collect the taxes within it to the historical territories. In return, the historical territories must finance the four levels of government in the Basque Country (the central government, the Basque government, the Foral Deputations and the municipalities). This leads to a complex scheme of transfers that redistributes tax revenue from the Foral Deputations to the other tiers of government. From this viewpoint, the Economic Agreement should be one of the models to be looked closely by regions in a comparative approach. Thus, we believe in the relevance and benefits of the diffusion in international academic and institutional fields.

In order to do so, it is necessary to overcome one of the main obstacles this task has come across so far, this is, the shortage of academic papers and contributions in English and the particularities of the concepts and terminology regarding the Economic Agreement, which are not easily included within the historical and legal categories used by other countries.

This book, joint venture of the Center of the Economic Agreement Documentation and the University of Reno, comprises excellent papers by well-known professionals of the institutional, social and university field. Their contributions offer a multidisciplinary approach to our unique financing model and contribute enormously to its better knowledge and understanding.

I profusely thank the University of Nevada and the University of the Basque Country for their intense and effective work and efforts, which have made this book a precious reality and which I hope it becomes a landmark in the long path of future fruitful collaboration.

—Jose Maria Iraurizarraga
Foral Deputy of Treasury and Finances,
Foral Deputation of Bizkaia

Foreword

The "Economic Agreement" or Basque Fiscal System, Guarantee for the Self-Government of Euskadi

This is something that has always been absolutely clear to me. And yet, however obvious the importance of this highly distinctive instrument of self-government might be for those of us who love our land, the latest *Sociómetro* survey released by the Sociological Research Department of the Basque Government reveals that 45 percent of our fellow citizens have stated that they have never heard of the Economic Agreement.

It is shocking that the existence of a tool that has been so treasured by some, and so vilified by others—a tool that, as Mario Fernández says, in this book, empowers our institutions to make decisions regarding the great issues that face our society, such as the design of our tax system, proper tax levels, and the variable application of taxation to different citizens—is completely unknown by nearly half of these selfsame citizens.

The Foral Deputation or regional government of Bizkaia has generated, and is currently sustaining, a number of initiatives that have the purpose of disseminating information about the Agreement to different segments of the population. These initiatives have taken into account the different characteristics, and specific needs, of the targeted populations.

During the past ten years, we have been proactive in this regard, with policy initiatives forged in the Juntas Generales or Bizkaia Assembly and in the Basque Parliament aimed at reinforcing and given continuity to the "Economic Agreement."

In part, our efforts have involved legal initiatives in the Spanish Parliament and European courts aimed at defending our authority to collect taxes. Other actions have involved academic initiatives and information campaigns. One example of these efforts is these publication that forms part of the series published by the Ad Concordiam Association.

Since December, 2000, the Foral Deputation of Bizkaia has financed and participated in the various activities of the Association for the Promotion and Dissemination of the Economic Agreement in the Ad Concordiam. This association, which links the Foral Deputation of Bizkaia, on the one hand, and the University of Deusto and the University of the Basque Country (UPV-EHU) on the other, has been dedicated to actions aimed at assuring that the "Economic Agreement" does not remain as unknown as it appears to be today.

In addition, the Foral Deputation took an important step six years ago in signing an Agreement with the UPV-EHU to create the Center for Documentation of the Economic Agreement and the Foral Treasuries. The purpose of creating this Center was to gather knowledge and disseminate information to the academic community in particular and the public in general.

This book explains the "Economic Agreement," or Basque Fiscal System, and the historical background of the foral regulations, as well as the well-known efforts to safeguard it legally. The truth of the matter is that all of us who work in the deputations and universities would like to turn matters around with respect to the *Sociómetro* survey data.

Our most earnest wish is that the Economic Agreement be recognized for its inherent worth in general, for its capacity to resolve problems, for its ability to reconcile distinct interests and, above all else, for its supreme role in the construction of our society and our country.

I hope that we can all learn a little more about the importance of its value and—what is most important of all—that we can come to act as a driving force to ensure that the Agreement becomes better known and more respected in the future.

Let me conclude with one final thought. Normally, discussions, diatribes, and confrontations regarding the Agreement have a high public impact, and nowadays we typically focus on what is going on with respect to corporate income tax, the current state of affairs with respect to regulatory capacity, and other matters.

I would like now to make an observation in a more long-range and historical vein.

Those working in the Foral Deputation of Bizkaia including the general secretary responsible for Legal questions, have never lost sight of the fact that, in addition to dealing with the safeguarding of the "Economic Agreement," are also committed to the defense of the foral tradition. I wanted to remind all of you that, around the end of 2004, the Supreme Court of the Kingdom of Spain issued a ruling in which it more or less stated that any kind of assessed rate of corporate tax below the state rate was considered by that body to constitute state aid, and that this was incompatible with EU treaties. At that time, within the context of the legal and institutional system of the Kingdom of Spain, the "Economic Agreement" was a dead letter. It was a dead letter because the regulatory capacity of the foral institutions within the Basque Autonomous Community had been rendered ineffectual by a ruling of the Supreme Court.

In the wake of this ruling, the Foral Deputation of Bizkaia responded by initiating two long-term and strategic approaches that I believe are fundamentally important, and that have yielded important results. The first of these, which was instituted following a debate in the Juntas Generales, involved working toward institutional reform of two organic laws: the Organic Law of the Judiciary and the Organic Law regulating the constitutional court. The purpose of these reforms is to secure the legal underpinning of the foral tax regulations in order to protect them from various jurisdictional, legal and other challenges. The objective of these safeguards is to afford the foral regulations constitutional, rather than merely legal, protection in the Kingdom of Spain.

On the other hand, at the Foral Deputation of Bizkaia—and I say this from a historical perspective—we began instituting a rather risky procedure: putting the Economic Agreement to the acid test in European courts and parliaments. The Foral Deputation was thus faced with a pretrial question about which many expressed skepticism. On more than one occasion, we indeed were told that it involved communal institutions legally safeguarding the "Economic Agreement." We arrived at the Court of Luxembourg, which endorsed the tax system of the Basque historical territories within the Kingdom of Spain fully and completely.

These two achievements—securing the modification of the Organic Laws in order to ensure that the foral tax regulations have constitutional rather than legal force, and submitting said regulations to the acid test of the European Court in Luxembourg, mean that the Economic Agreement has been assimilated and endorsed—and that it is respected by—the Supreme Court of Luxembourg. I believe that a historical perspective of the Economic Agreement over the course of its existence has allowed us to achieve a definitive endorsement, assure its place within the regulations of the European Union, and has also permitted the safeguarding of the foral tax regulations in order to guarantee their constitutionality—and not merely their legality—as laws that are material rather than formal in nature. This is a position that we have upheld over the course of many years.

In conclusion, I believe that, with this historical perspective during the past ten years, those who follow us over the next twenty or fifty years will be able to look back and see this as a critical juncture during which the Economic Agreement was saved, and that Mario Fernández and Pedro Luis Uriarte were key players in that process. But I also think they will be able to recognize another historic moment, one that witnessed the consolidation of the Economic Agreement system, both at the level of the constitutional regulations of the Kingdom of Spain, as well as in terms of its definitive acceptance by the European Union. I believe that these two events will come to be seen, in the long term, and within the context of the modern history of the "Economic Agreement," as critically important. I am certain that they will be continually referred to in years to come.

—Jose Luis Bilbao
General Deputy of the Foral Deputation of Bizkaia

Preface

During the nineteenth century the scale of public finances increased in line with the debts that had been accumulated by the public institutions in the course of different wars. But far from ceding the management of the enormous debt to a higher entity like the new Spanish nation-state, the Basque Foral Deputations aspired to manage them directly, and introduced channels for their settlement and for fomenting the economy, without ceding or transferring responsibility to nation-state. This finally generated a strengthening of the institutions and resulted in a growing capacity of resilience. The abolitionist crisis of the Foral constitutional Law in1876 was a new legal challenge and, in spite of political-juridical weakness, the inertia of the management of public finances prompted the provisional and transitory agreement in taxation for their integration in the Spanish Concierto Ecónomico (hereafter in this book, this is translated as "Economic Agreement"). But the "Agreement" became a new category for regulating the fiscal agreement between the state and the Basque provinces. In the final third of the nineteenth century the public economy acquired even greater relevance in society as a whole.

In the midst of the financial crisis, (2010) we at the Documentation Centre for the Economic Agreement and the Foral Treasuries (UPV-EHU) are presenting an overall reflection on the system of the Economic Agreement and the management of the Foral Treasuries over the last 30 years, since their recovery. We wanted to gain a deeper understanding of the process of their recovery and the generation of a Basque public sector. That is why, as well as dealing with the "Economic Agreement" in itself, the purpose of this book is also concerned with the Basque Treasuries. The contributions brought together in this volume try to answer questions raised in both the academic field and in society. That is why we situate this volume, also in the field of "public history," that is, our aim is to address society beyond the scientific community. The "Economic Agreement" is a category that represents the desire for self-government of the public patrimony and finances. Consequently we have proposed three sections: a long-term view on the one hand, in which the desire for self-management emerges as the practice that foments the capacity for resilience. On the other hand, we provide an approach to what public management has meant, an analysis of 30 years of self-management. Finally, the juridical and political challenges in both the Spanish state and the European Union are dealt with from a juridical point of view. We have also incorporated analyses of public opinion, which show us how, in spite of the fact that the "Economic Agreement" is a basic element in the self-government of the Basque Country, a work of diffusion and communication remains to be done in order to provide society with information about it.

But the dimension of the "Economic Agreement and the Foral Treasuries" is not restricted to the Basque Country nor even to Spain, as it is currently being examined in the European courts and in the studies of comparative fiscal federalism, precisely in the international lingua franca. It seems inevitable and obligatory that the literature concerning the "Economic Agreement" should also be cultivated in English from now onwards. That is why we at the Documentation Centre must thank the Center for Basque Studies of the University of Nevada in Reno for agreeing to become involved in publishing this book. This publication will fill a gap in the qualified and excellent collection of publications in English published by the Center for Basque Studies. Fiscal culture and its practice inundate the daily activity of society and that is why it is a fundamental element of Basque political culture. In the near future we hope to be able to continue this collaboration by cultivating new focuses and analyses on a series of questions of general as well as academic interest in areas relating to fiscal federalism and complex political unions such as that represented by the European Union.

—Joseba Agirreazkuenaga and Eduardo Alonso
Documentation Centre for the Economic Agreement and Foral Treasuries, University of the Basque Country
September 23, 2013

Part 1
Origins and History of the Economic Agreement

1
Resilience of the Foral Tax Systems during the Liberal Revolution (1793–1937)

Joseba Agirreazkuenaga Zigorraga

The Representative Assemblies or *Batzar Nagusiak*–Juntas Generales of Araba (Álava), Bizkaia (Vizcaya), and Gipuzkoa (Guipúzcoa), agreed to a "general" tax system in those territories in order to assure their efficient general administration of the territory: For instance, between 1629 and 1640, the Juntas Generales of Bizkaia agreed to impose taxes of a general nature within that territory.[1] This was the beginning of the *General Treasury System,* which in the nineteenth century came to be called the *Foral treasury systems* (in contrast to the *Provincial Tax System,* which was the constitutionally mandated system for the majority of Spanish provinces). Until 1640, the most important tax systems were those of the local authorities. By the end of the eighteenth century, as a consequence of expenses generated from financing the War of the Pyrenees (1793–1795) and paying for road infrastructure, the representative assemblies faced a serious challenge. Namely, they had to approve a system that would manage the financing of accumulated debt by means of their own tax system. At the same time, new forms of organizing public financing were emerging within the context of the liberal revolution, as well as through the establishment of direct taxes on estates and other property. During the course of the nineteenth century, the general Treasury and tax systems, which were dependent on the Basque representative assemblies, grew stronger. These general Treasury, which functioned at a level in between the local or municipal tax authorities and the national system of the new Spanish nation, gained widespread recognition for the efficiency of their management and the political will of the leaders of the Juntas Generales.

"We need to correct the historical view, created by diligent functionaries and bureaucrats, which holds that the guarantee of equality, solidarity, and social progress is strictly tied to the process of the bureaucratic and political centralization of the state."[2] When, in 1812, the Constitution of Cádiz was proposed to the Juntas Generales of Bizkaia, it was adopted with the inclusion of a reserve clause that implied the recognition of a double constitution: The "Foral Constitution" of Bizkaia and "the Constitution of the Spanish nation."

Beginning in 1812, however, successive Spanish constitutions interpreted the new Spanish nation-state in terms of a single nation, rather than as a composite monarchy. Until 1877, the foral institutions developed within the framework of the Constitution. Afterward, these institutions were abolished, although the Economic Agreement or Fiscal Tax Agreement survived as a result of inertia under different legal and political forms until 1937. This survival is evidence of the adaptive capacity of the elite governing class of the Basque Country within a context of continual disturbances of the ongoing process of liberal revolution—a context characterized by successive civil wars. This resilience reflects a capacity to cope with the changes and disturbances that were occurring in a way that assured continual progress. It is useful in this connection to recall the definition of the word "resilience": "the capacity to change and develop."[3] In the present chapter, we will show that the political leaders responsible for managing public resources of the Foral treasury systems in the Basque Country demonstrate a high degree of resilience.

Absolute Monarchy and Liberal Revolution (1793–1720)

The process of reinforcing the royal authority and the scope of its sovereignty through the expansion of a direct administration that was dependent on the royal court was consolidated in the eighteenth century. At that same time, the Representative Assemblies, the Juntas Generales, and their lawyers secured the legitimacy of the power of self-government within the territories where they exercised jurisdiction. The underlying principle of this schema was the concept of a composite Spanish monarchy. At the beginning of the nineteenth century, the Spanish monarchy was a composite monarchy, given that the kingdom of Navarre (Nafarroa in Basque; Navarra in Spanish) conserved its status as a kingdom for all practical purposes, even though formally united to the Spanish crown. Ferdinand VII was also known as Ferdinand III of Navarre.

During the course of the liberal revolution, a new political category was born: that of the people or nation, which was conceived as the source and repository of sovereignty, and whose recognition was implicit in the new legal text *par excellence*: the new constitution. This was in opposition to the historical constitution, *Novísima Recopilación* (1804) which involved the absolute sovereignty of the Crown. But according to the "legal pact " between the king and the Representative Assemblies and in the case of Navarre, the kingdom of Navarre, the Monarch's absolute sovereignty in these territories was limited.

The representatives of the three Juntas Generales of Araba, Bizkaia, and Gipuzkoa, who met from October 30 to November 2, 1793, in one of their joint conferences, agreed to improve "the Constitution of the 'pays' (the common Basque territory) and harmonize their political action."[4] In the War of the Pyrenees (1793–1795), the French had the upper hand, and the Juntas Generales of Gipuzkoa decided in 1794 to change the historical pact with Castile and become voluntarily incorporated into the French Republic, even though the French simply thought of the Basque province as territory that had been won by conquest.

However, the turning point really occurred in Bayonne, where Napoleon prepared the establishment of a new political constitution for Spain, the first public debate about the *fueros* and the liberal constitution within the framework of the situation in Spain. The representative of the Juntas Generales of Bizkaia at the Bayonne Assembly, J.A. Yandiola, delivered an unforgettable defense of the constitution of Bizkaia, explaining it in terms of liberal principles, and for this reason denying any contradiction in advocating that it be continued under the new constitution. The representative of Araba, the Marquis of Montehermoso, referred to the "Foral Constitution" as a source of happiness, while the representatives of Gipuzkoa and Navarre also each spoke in defense of the foral constitutions.[5] Finally, the text of the new Spanish Constitution that was in effect during the Bonaparte dynasty, explicitly stated that any discussion of the future of the foral systems would be postponed, a statement that implicitly guaranteed their survival.

Both the War of the Pyrenees and the war against Napoleon (or War of Independence) generated enormous public debt. Both contending armies demanded that municipalities both pay for rations and provide funds to finance the armies. Guerrilla forces did the same, and public administrations also placed themselves on a war footing, and therefore contracted loans at 3–5 percent interest, with payment on this interest required as part of the terms. For these payments, the foral institutions needed to legalize new sources of revenue through the approval of new taxes, the majority of which were on consumer goods or traded products. In addition, there were direct taxes on income and real estate. This gradually enabled the liquidation of debt, and also facilitated the exponential growth of the foral tax systems. In addition, the foral tax systems began to finance and manage the construction of road infrastructure.

During the period of Napoleonic domination and the "Government of Bizkaia" (1810), formed in the Basque Country to replace the foral institutions and dependent on Paris, the new French administration applied a direct progressive fiscal system to owners and rent collectors, a system that was responsive to the economic reality of the place and time. It was definitely a modern experience and one that helped ensure that the new public administrations would have important resources at their disposal that were based on a progressive tax system.

Despite the fact that the Constitution of Cádiz modified the institutional political system, the inertia of political practice and the traditional management of the ruling classes of the Basque foral territories led this system to go beyond the merely administrative functions that the constitution had assigned the provincial Deputations. In this way, when the government of the Spanish Regency became established, political conflicts immediately became an issue—especially regarding the tax system. The General Revenue Office thus drafted a plan that called for the transfer of customs duties to the coast.[6]

When Ferdinand VII returned from France to assume the throne of Spain in 1814, he abolished the liberal Constitution and re-established the foral system in its entirety with the framework of the absolutist monarchy. Within this context of political and institutional instability, the Court created the Board for Addressing Abuses of the Royal Tax System of the Basque Provinces, which issued a report in 1819 that established a precedent for the actions of the Spanish public tax collection system vis-à-vis the public foral tax systems throughout the remainder of the nineteenth century. The argument of this report was based on the principles of the commissions created by Godoy and were historically grounded in the postulates of Llorente. The following text will serve as an example:

> *Many centuries have passed during which the sovereign authority of Your Majesty was subject to frequent affronts and highly obstinate resistance. . . . It is beyond doubt that, in those parts, everything is seen as prejudicial to the fueros if it does not arise from a dictate or order from the native authorities of the country. . . . What does that region have in common with the other Spanish provinces? Absolutely nothing. The laws are different, the government has its own peculiar characteristics, no taxes are collected, trade is conducted without rules or duties, and the customs offices are non-functional. What do these provinces contribute to the state (from which they receive the protection of their trade, the administration of justice, and many other favors and benefits)? They are even free of the obligation of military service....* [7]

We see here a certain degree of exaggeration to heighten the expression of disapproval. In sum, the *Junta*, by the time it concluded its work in 1819, proposed the following four measures: (1) transfer of customs duties to the coast and Pyrenees, with the consequent suppression of the "contraband courts"; (2) the provincial Deputations and other authorities and courts of the exempt provinces would not be ever able to meddle in matters dealing with revenues or trade, or to in any way obstruct either the free exercise and administration of customs or the jurisdiction of those employed by the king, under threat of rescission of the *fueros*; (3) state monopolies on tobacco and salt would continue; (4) as a consequence, iron and other industrial products could freely enter the ports and cities of the monarchy without being subject to any surcharge.[8]

The report proposed a limitation on the political and fiscal powers of the Juntas Generales of Araba, Bizkaia, and Gipuzkoa. The successive royal orders of January 18, 1816; April 2, 1817; August 13 and November 6, 1818; and January 6, 1819—all relative to the extension of jurisdiction of the judge of the contraband courts and the establishment of a Records Office in Bilbao—were the expression of the absolutist government's attempt to exercise control. In addition, high duties were applied by the customs office of Castile and Aragon, and tanned leather destined for the interior of Spain was also taxed. It should be added that duties were placed on iron bars, iron works, and nails from Bizkaia by the maritime customs offices of the peninsula. A tax on products of consumption, which was construed as a foreign product, was also introduced. By means of these measures, the public tax system attempted to prejudice the interests and benefits of tradesmen and industrial merchants in order to increase tax revenues. Through this "tariff siege," this system aimed at indirectly collecting liquid monies that the provinces had declined to pay to the general Treasury system of the monarchy.

In the face of this policy of the absolutist monarchy, the ties of solidarity among the Basque provinces grew stronger in an effort to organize a formidable and united opposition. Because the adverse measures also affected Navarre, representatives of that province were invited to the meeting held on December 7, 1817, for the purposes of including it in a united front. That initiative was apparently unsuccessful. The authorities of the three provinces sensed that a new phase was beginning in relations with the central power. This could be discerned specifically from the communication sent to Gipuzkoa in 1817, which stated that the validity of the *fueros* was being confirmed "without prejudice to the general interests of the nation, and of the system of unity and order." The representatives of the General Deputations (Francisco Zabalburu, for Bizkaia; José Sola, for Gipuzkoa; and Diego Arriola, for Araba) responded in a meeting held in Vitoria in December 1817: "The united system can hardly be called compatible with a monarchical government that essentially demands classes, distinctions, and privileges. It cannot coexist with or consent to the diversity of character and laws. . . ."[9]

Constitutional Homogeneity: 1820–1823

In 1820, when the Spanish Constitution of 1812 was once again instituted, the Juntas Generales of Bizkaia requested that their political and administrative system be continued (or, in the absence of such continuation, that they at least have freedom over the management of their public finances): "The nation seeks to arrogate unto itself all of the debts contracted in order to receive access to services, expenses, and public works to which it must attend as a state separated from others of the Peninsula, and ruled by its own particular Constitution." But the response of the new constitutional power was negative: "Any exception which a province enjoys over all others in effect makes it into a separate republic unto itself." This argument was based on the following reasoning, in accordance with the unifying vision of the nation-state:

> It is no longer relevant to speak of reasons, the right to co-existence, or the prejudices that may result if the provinces continue to be exempt from their privileges, or if they become subject to the same obligations as those of the monarchy.... This is because national representation is of a single character, and there is one king and one set of laws that apply to all. Thus the rights of obligations of all who have thus far believed themselves exempt from such must also be the same. The resident of those nations that have almost felt themselves foreigners.... should now begin to enjoy the benefits of union.... [10]

The aforementioned report insisted that there could be no compromise regarding "the attributes of sovereignty" exercised by the Basque provinces, especially their tax system. According to the Customs Inspector of Cantabria, abuse and fraud were on the rise, and the Deputations were rejecting his authority "because their laws were rejected if they did not meet with the veto approval of the Deputations." In his opinion, there was smuggling of tobacco and textiles going on, along with a process of de-capitalization due to the flow of monies out of the country. As a result, the new central government began to transfer customs duties to the coast and to locations along the Pyrenees mountain range.

The provincial Deputation of Bizkaia, in a document sent to the king on April 28, 1821, summed up as follows the impact of the constitutional system: "One of the difficulties that has stood in the way of enforcing the constitutional system throughout that district has been the liquidation of public debt that the province had acquired, and the way it later attended to paying off that debt. For it was not fair that Biscay, which formed a part of the greater Nation, suffer by itself the weight of an enormous debt that it felt responsible for as a result of the peculiar government that had previously ruled its territory."

An attempt was made to reach a bilateral agreement for managing the debt, but instead the state assumed the debt and, in 1821, applied the fiscal system of the constitution in its entirety. At a meeting held by the three Deputations,[11] an agreement was reached regarding the following distribution of direct and consumer tax payments

Table 1.1. Distribution of Direct and Consumer Tax Payments

	Territorial tax	Tax on consumption	Total
Gipuzkoa	1,089,000 (32.3%)	936,107 (30.4%)	2,025,107
Bizkaia	891.000 (26.4%)	1,353,107 (44%)	2,244,107
Alava	1,388,887 (41.2%)	780,107 (25.4%)	2,168,994
Total	3,368,887(100%)	3,069,322 (100%)	6,438,209

that had been demanded, as seen in table 1.1.

A similar policy was also applied in Navarre, where the autochthonous political institutions of the kingdom of Navarre were abolished and the state assumed its public debt. However, the central state had neither the time nor the means to pay interest on the debts of the foral territories. This failure to meet debt obligations had a decisive effect on the behavior of the liberal elite of the Basque Country. During the following decade, this liberal elite continued to defend the continuity of self-government—in terms of both politics and also (and especially) in terms of the public tax system of the foral territories—within the framework of the liberal constitution.

Absolute Monarchy and Anti-liberalism: Establishment of the Regular Quota, 1824

In 1823, when the absolutists returned to power, they began persecuting and purging the liberals. The following year, in response to the needs of the monarchy, they demanded an annual contribution quota to the Finance Ministry of the monarchy (López Ballestereos; February 16, 1824). The Deputations initially were opposed to this demand because they did not want the contribution to be instituted as a regular annual obligation.

In 1825, the establishment of customs offices along the Ebro was the subject of debate. At the same time, tradesmen began clamoring for the transfer of these offices to the coast. In 1827, the Council of Ministers agreed to send a military force to collect the corresponding quota. Finally, the Deputations decided to make a partial contribution, to be conceived under the traditional category of a "donation" of 7 million reales. The agreement for the distribution of this obligation, in terms of payment and percentage, was as follows:

- Bizkaia: 2,658,000 reales (37.9 percent)

- Gupuzkoa: 2,408,000 reales (34.4 percent)
- Araba: 1,934,000 reales (27.6 percent)12

Later, at the conferences in Vitoria on October 4–5, 1830, a decision was made to contribute 100,000 reales at a time when there was a threat of a liberal invasion. The division of this contribution was as follows: Bizkaia, 38,391; Gipuzkoa, 35,723; and Araba, 25,885. At that same conference, a decision was made to provide "a foral naval force." Simultaneously, there was a prevailing fear of an armed intervention on the part of the government to enforce payment of the agreed contributions. Within this social and political climate, Ferdinand VII died in 1833, leading to the outbreak of the First Carlist War.

Law of October 25, 1839: Recognition of the Foral Constitution and the Basque Political Identity.

Among historians of modern Basque history, there are contradictory perceptions and interpretations regarding the law of October 25, 1839, which was approved by the Spanish Parliament. The Marquis of Viluma wrote, in reference to the proposal that the Foral Constitution and Spanish Constitution (of 1837) be reconciled, that the law "contains two contradictory and incompatible provisions." But how did this law come to be, and what did it hope to achieve? The Spanish government proposed the law ten days following the Bergara Agreement of October 10, 1839, which was a military agreement between a number of high-ranking officials of the Carlist army and the leader of the liberal armies. The preamble of the law indicated that its purpose was "to promote general peace" during the Civil War. Article 1 declared that "the *fueros* of the Basque Provinces and Navarre are hereby confirmed." Article 2 then declared that these *fueros* would be modified only to the minimal extent necessary. This project of reconciling the *fueros* (or the Foral Constitution) with the liberal Spanish Constitution was debated in the British Parliament in 1837. British Prime Minister Palmerston supported a recognition of the Basque laws within the framework of the liberal Constitution. Lord Hay, representing the British government, assisted Joaquín Marcos Satrústegui in the drafting of the Bergara Agreement that ended the Civil War in the Basque Country. The war continued in Catalonia until 1840.

From the legal and administrative point of view, the Constitution of 1837 reflected a centralist and uniform conception of the Spanish nation-state. One year earlier, the General Deputation of Bizkaia, in the midst of the Civil War and under siege from Carlist forces, asked the Regent María Cristina on May 5, 1836, to conserve the foral institutions, citing the example of the nationalities of the United Kingdom who lived under a united monarchy. For this reason, the Deputation criticized the Constitution of Cádiz for "stripping the Basque provinces of their nationality and fundamental laws, and prejudicing their social freedoms." However, given the uniqueness and the strength of the foral institutions of the Basque Country, on September 16, 1837, the Spanish Parliament approved *ex professo* a law to abolish the foral institution (this despite the fact that the Constitution of 1837 was still in effect without recognition of the foral system). As a result, provincial Deputations were established in accordance with the Constitution. Two years later, another law (of October 25, 1839) and a decree (of November 16, 1839) re-established the Juntas Generales, charging this body with the task of reconciling the *Foral Law* to the Spanish constitution (instead of to the principles of the absolutist monarchy).[13]

The law of 1839 was approved after overcoming a certain degree of resistance in Parliament, and with several amendments to the original text. Some wanted to limit the *fueros* to the economic, administrative and municipal spheres. Others wanted to invest them with political power. This resulted in a certain ambiguity that led to different interpretations and claims. The City Council of Bilbao presented a petition signed by nine hundred residents calling for the confirmation of the *fueros*. Bilbao was something of a liberal icon, given that it had resisted the Carlist sieges. On the other hand, a group of Basque liberals residing in Madrid declared that "the *fueros* have created a Navarran and Biscayan nationality that we carry within our hearts."[14] Approval of the law was celebrated in Bilbao and Vitoria because it was interpreted as a re-establishment of the foral institutions of self-government. Later, the Juntas Generales of Bizkaia and Gipuzkoa interpreted the law as having implicit additional meaning and understood it as forming an integral part of the Spanish Constitution itself. The new law of 1839 confirmed that the foral provinces constituted an exception with respect to political institutionalization, as well as from the standpoint of the public tax system. As a result of both its past *fueros* and a new liberal discourse, "the general will" expressed in the Juntas Generales, an appeal was made to a national distinctiveness. The leaders of the Juntas Generales proposed that "political existence" or Basque political identity be guaranteed. The survival of the "Foral Constitution" and its adaptation became a legal means according to the Spanish Constitution.

In order to enact the reform of the Foral Constitution mandated by the law, representatives of the four foral territories were elected in an attempt to attain a common negotiating position. While the representatives of Araba, Bizkaia, and Gipuzkoa defended the preservation of the *fueros* in their entirety, Navarre negotiated a reform that helped consolidate the liberal regime, and involved legal recognition of the purchase of church assets by liberal elites and the state's assumption of public debt. Furthermore, Navarre limited the continuity of its foral system to the economic and administrative fields (i.e., it conserved control of its tax system).

For its part, the central government wanted to extend the foral reform model that had been established with Navarre to the rest of the foral territories and took this initiative on January 5, 1841. By decree it abolished the "foral veto" (i.e., the right of veto previously enjoyed by the Juntas Generales to organize their own government). Later, and exploiting the rebellion and subsequent defeat of the moderate liberals, Joaquín Baldomero Espartero, the Spanish president of government and regent during the minority of Queen Elizabeth II signed a decree on October 29, 1841, that transferred the customs offices of the interior to the coast, incorporated the foral provinces within the national market, abolished the Juntas Generales, and established a system of common justice. In 1844, the Juntas Generales were reestablished and Basque liberals embraced a new foral doctrine that advocated preservation of political self-government and therefore the public foral tax system. As an example of these new ideas, the Juntas Generales of Bizkaia, along with the liberal political leaders of Araba and Gipuzkoa, declared in 1850 that "The Basque provinces find themselves today in one of those grave and solemn situations that determine the long-term future course of a people, either conserving or destroying its nationality." V.L. Gaminde, leader of the progressive liberals, wrote in 1852 that "it would be entirely appropriate to focus on the letter of the law and the Basque nationality that we have embraced [...]. The Confirmation of the fueros, according to the law of October 25th, is the equivalent of a proclamation that the Basque provinces are, as a result of an annexation agreement, allied with Spain, bound by an alliance of mutual help. Yet, except in cases of emergency, they remain independent states—as they should in fact be, and as they are."[15]

In sum, the law of 1839 launched a new political and legal discourse that contributed to the consolidation of Basque political power, and that even came to include new competences or powers in 1853. The Basque liberals interpreted the institutionalization of the *fueros* as an expression of Basque nationality, but at the same time denounced an elimination of foral competences instituted without the approval of the Juntas Generales, proposing the creation of a "Basque Constitution."

The Tax Reform of Mon and Santillán of 1845: The Foral Treasury in the Constitutional Unity of Spain

Casimiro Loizaga, Adjunct Counsel of the Juntas Generales, drafted an initial bill in December, 1839 aimed at harmonizing the *fueros* with the Spanish Constitution. He intended that this draft bill should serve as a basis for negotiation. Articles 3 and 9 respectively read as follows:

> It is the responsibility of the Juntas Generales of Bizkaia to impose, with Royal approval, the direct and indirect tax payments that are to be collected in its territory for the purpose of meeting its provincial tax obligation. . . .
>
> The Deputation of Bizkaia will convey to the Central Treasury of the Nation the amount designated, and representing all of the various kinds of tax payments assessed or that may be assessed in the future, in accordance with the Junta General that convenes beneath the Tree of Gernika.[16]

Thus, it was agreed that it would be appropriate to contribute periodically to the general expenses of the state, given the likelihood that the monarchy would demand fixed contributions at regular intervals. Article 7 of that same document indicated that provisions related to religious matters and the clergy, educational institutions, charitable organizations, prisons, road construction and maintenance—in short, the social and educational expenses assumed by the state in the middle of the nineteenth century—would "not be subject to any levy whatsoever on the part of the national treasury."

The project for modifying the power of the central government, which had been applied in Navarre, was limited to fiscal matters, and the transfer of customs offices was a nonnegotiable issue: "Give me the customs offices on the coast, and you can have the rest" is a saying attributed to Minister Mendizábal in relation to the modification of the *fueros*. In reality, this transfer did greatly benefit the state Treasury, given that it resulted in an increase in annual revenues from 6 million to 25 million reales, as in the case of San Sebastián-Irún.

The 1842 bill to reform the Foral Constitution was more restrictive in every respect. It called for the Basque provinces to pay, as a single direct annual contribution, the sum of three million reales. The Deputations were given the discretion of instituting a system for contributing to the military defense of the state. The bill called for the consumption of salt and tobacco to be free from taxes, but at the same time regulated by the government. Expenses for religion and clergy (about six million reales per year) were to be the responsibility of the Deputations (while such expenses were assumed by the monarchy in the rest of the state).

The year 1845 witnessed a crowning moment for the ambitious aspirations of the liberal revolution in Spain: the tax reform promoted by Alejandro Mon and Ramón de Santillán. The aim of this reform was to adjust state finances to the new sociopolitical needs. However, the collection of 50 to 60 percent of monies came from traditional taxes, especially tobacco and customs. The remainder came from a group of five new taxes in the following categories (which replaced provincial revenues): construction of properties, crops and livestock, and industrial and commercial subsidies. But the direct contribution for agricultural wealth and real estate was instituted without the benefit of a cadastre. Town governments paid their quotas, which may have been collected for other purposes, in such a way as not to harm the interests of the major property holders who controlled the institution. Thus, there was a certain inequity in the distribution. Yet, according to J. Fontana, this reform tripled state revenues within thirty years.

As regards the foral tax systems, the commissioners told Mon on January 14, 1845, that "there is currently rapid progress toward a leveling centralization of the institutions of our nation."[17] The reports drafted by José Sánchez Ocaña of the Administrative Offices of the state Treasury reflected one key idea: that no contributions had been made since 1824 and that the total unpaid monies during the period 1835–1845 for the following categories was 56,896,972 reales: annual donations; special contributions of 1838 (i.e., the 600 million reales mandated by the law of June 30, 1838) and of 1840 (the 180 million reales mandated by the law of July 30, 1840) and the law of August 14, 1841, for religion and clergy.[18] In the opinion of the bureaucrats and politicians of the central tax authority, the objective of this report was "to goad those provinces toward the path taken by Navarre."[19] The terms of negotiation were thus clearly established.

The Basque authorities of Bizkaia, Gipuzkoa, and Araba, who met on August 13, 1846, in order to analyze the consequences of the reform of the Foral treasury systems, were opposed to the contribution amounts that had been assigned. In addition, they were not in agreement with the new direct taxes on properties, commerce, and industry. The main argument of the Deputations was that they were assuming responsibilities that, in the rest of the monarchy, were duties of the supreme government of the kingdom. According to the foral Deputations, the annual expenses of the three provinces were as follows:

- 6,000,000 reales for expenditures pertaining to religious matters and clergy (although the state had calculated such expenses as totaling 2,072,000 reales)
- 1,500,000 for interest on debt contracted during the War of the Pyrenees (1793–1795), the War against Napoleon (1808–1814), and the Royalist War (1822–1823)
- 1,200,000 for capital interest for general road construction. The total calculated investment in this category was some 200

million reales

- *Renta de Cruzadas*. Nearly 2 million reales were contributed in this category

The provinces satisfied expenses that the government established for teaching, charitable works, nursing and educating foundlings, emergency relief for prisoners, expenses for trial courts, and equipment and supplies for the army.

However, the majority of the analysts in the Spanish Finance Ministry during those years limited themselves to denouncing the exceptional status of the Basque provinces as adverse to administrative unity. The 1841 statement of Pita Pizarro was reprinted in treatises published in later years, and came to be embraced by successive central governments:

> A small proportion of the contributions of Navarre to the public treasury of the kingdom, since it was absorbed by the latter, has been in the form of a voluntary subsidy, and has totaled four and a half million reales.
>
> The Basque provinces have made a similar kind of contribution, the amount of said contribution being some three million. Thus, while in proportion to their inhabitants, these provinces, along with Navarre, should be contributing 50 percent of expenses to the state, they instead contribute only 7.5 percent, as a result of their fueros and privileges that give them the character of political entities that are fundamentally distinct from the Spanish monarchy, while they continue to enjoy the support, protection, employment, benefits and favors provided by the latter.
>
> This simple consideration ought to be enough to justify putting an immediate end to such an irregular and anomalous state of affairs, which is inherently unjust, like any political and economic distinction among provinces and peoples comprising the same monarchy. It is improper that those provinces enjoy their exemptions, which result from fueros and privileges held to be inviolate. Everything they have has been a gracious and temporary concession on the part of the kings, and can thus be revoked by the king's will, or that of his successors.[20]

When negotiations began in 1846, a request was made that the state authority for direct contributions immediately enter a legally sanctioned debit for the second half of 1845 that totaled 1,719,000 for Bizkaia. Added to the debit of 1,424,000 for the first half of 1846, this resulted in a total amount due of 3,153,000 reales.

After holding a number of different conversations, Mon became convinced of the need to draft a bill to address "dealing with the *fueros*" in accordance with the law of October, 1839, in order to legally extend the tax reform to the Basque provinces.

In accordance with the law of May 23, 1845, the contribution with respect to property, crops, and cattle would be distributed as follows (in terms of reales): Araba, 1,836,000; Gipuzkoa, 2,328,000; Bizkaia, 2,808,000; total, 4,336,000. The contribution for the industrial and trade subsidy, mortgages, and consumption, would be as follows: Araba, 795,000; Gipuzkoa, 1,357,000; and Bizkaia, 1,468,000.

Factoring in the expenses for which the Deputations were responsible as regards religious matters and clergy (i.e., Araba, 2,445,083; Bizkaia, 1,971,336; Gipuzkoa, 1,914,629) as well as other departmental expenses (906,984), the real contribution of each province was as follows according to the Spanish government: Araba, 721,067; Gipuzkoa, 405,016; and Bizkaia, 1,457,680.

In addition, the import quota for tobacco and salt was regulated. As previously indicated, this was one of the other distinctive preferences of the state. In sum, the provinces were obliged to pay 10,652,000 reales but, given that they had been credited 8,652,000, their net annual contribution would be two million reales (AFB, Foral Regimen).

The reaction of the committee members, among them P. Novia Salcedo, was one of energetic opposition. In their response, they added interest to be paid annually for roads and war debt. In addition, since they proposed a donation of 1,500,000 reales, they concluded that a payment of 48,000 over and above the indicated amount was in fact due. It does not appear clear in their document that the "donation" of one and a half million was to be an annual contribution. In the administrative realm, it would seem that the differences with Minister Pedro José Pidal could have easily been resolved.

In the meantime, ministers Alejandro Mon and Pidal were no longer in office, and in 1848, the controversy arose once again. The representative of Gipuzkoa, Ignacio Ascensio Altuna, assigned the counsel of Araba, Blas López, the task of drafting an outline that would serve as a definitive basis for the *fueros*. This document was approved by Araba and Gipuzkoa. In 1848, Araba political leaders Pedro de Egaña and Blas López drafted a bill to modify the *fueros*, taking the initiative from the central government and defining the fundamental features of the new foral system that would function under the protection of the Spanish constitution. As regards relations with the central tax authority, the text drafted by Blas López, and the justification he offered, reflected the opinion of the liberal elite that was in charge of the foral institutions:

> The Basque provinces and their general Deputations will support the public needs of the state with an annual donation of one and a half million reales, to be proportionally distributed among them, as has been the case until now. This agreement will be regulated and renewed between their peoples in the most equitable manner pos-

> sible, as defined by the fuero and by custom. These million and a half reales will include the excise taxes and other fees that could otherwise be paid in a number of the towns, but that will be abolished. These million and a half reales will be collected by the Treasury, and the Juntas and Deputations will assume responsibility for the costs and expenses necessary for their imposition and distribution, as well as for the administration of associated fees.[21]

In sum, it seems that the conditions established by Mon began to be accepted by those Basques advocating the foral system. This bill accepted the transfer of customs offices, although it did allow two products, tobacco and salt, to be freely introduced and traded. The balanced budget of the foral tax system was founded on income earned from taxes on tobacco.

This bill, which was supported by the Juntas Generales of Araba and Gipuzkoa, was rejected in 1850 by Bizkaia, which requested the re-establishment of the foral system. Araba and Gipuzkoa did not embark upon separate provincial negotiations and, once again, the undefined legal status of the *fueros* was at the forefront of discussion. One segment of the elite of Bizkaia had proposed as a condition to considering its later modification, the restoration, in its entirety and to its fullest extent, of the foral system. The truth is that a competition arose between legality in terms of the *fueros* on the one hand, and its centralist constitutional conceptualization, on the other. Within this context, Ramón Ortiz de Zárate introduced a new political discourse: the defense of what he called a "Basque politics" that transcended ideological differences.[22]

In 1852, Spanish President Juan Bravo Murillo proposed a new project for changing the foral institutions according to the Law of October 25, 1839. This was centralist in orientation, and perhaps the most reductionist of all the different possible foral arrangements that had been studied. Article 6 of his proposal indicated that "the government could suspend or annul any agreement that, in its judgment, was manifestly harmful to the Basque Country or the other peoples and provinces of the kingdom."

This project was categorically rejected by, among others, P. de Egaña, B. López, and V.L. Gaminde. The fall of Bravo Murillo ended all possibility of its being approved. In any event, by 1850, the three provinces were contributing one million reales, which was termed "a donation," and which the central government used to fund the army units stationed in the Basque provinces.

In addition, the state periodically collected other taxes. The Ministry of Finance had sent an inspector or representative (in the terminology of the time) who reported on the progress of both revenue generation and the material, economic, and agricultural state of affairs.

In 1853, one inspector wrote: "The fact that these provinces were exempt from the contributions and revenues of others of the kingdom means that the responsibility for the collection and administration of revenues other than customs falls mainly on the Foral Deputations. Your Majesty therefore realizes that such activity does not depend on the government administration, or on how high or low its values are (with the exception of the state farms, which we are responsible for, and the insignificant revenues from tobacco)." The customs brought in revenues of about 25 million reales per year to Bilbao. In addition, direct tax payments were collected (purchaser's obligations, matching funds, progressive tax on salaries), income from government monopolies (sales of gunpowder and stamped paper for paying fines), the postal authority branch of the Ministry of the Interior, and development. The public finance inspector indicated that, during the months of January, February, and March of 1853, 755,212; 1,153,890 and 931,905 reales had been collected. If revenue from customs is subtracted, the result is as follows: 62,510; 97,545 and 62,200 reales. These figures allow us to conclude that, aside from customs, in Bizkaia the state collected about 900,000 reales, not an insignificant figure, in terms of the proposed tax contributions. As regards smuggling, this same inspector indicated that such activity decreased to less than a third of what it had been in 1849 as a result of the customs provisions, the quality of local products, and intense vigilance. In 1853, the Deputations of Gipuzkoa and Bizkaia assumed control of the budgets of local governments, under the leadership of Interior Minister of Spain, P. de Egaña.

The following statement is recorded in a Statistical Manual published by the state tax authority during the period of liberal progressive government:

> The amount of 12,400,000 reales has been assessed to the Basque provinces and Navarre to support the services of religion and clergy. The upper-level administration has not been able to nullify this arrangement—something that the administrative unit in general is calling for—because it is a matter that involves the political issue of the arrangement of the fueros of these aforesaid provinces.

The contribution for properties, crops, and livestock of the three Basque provinces was estimated at 9,197,220 reales, in accordance with the law of March 26, 1858. Later, however, in response to the outbreak of the Hispano-Moroccan War in 1859, these Deputations contributed four million reales and three thousand battle-ready soldiers to the war effort. Consequently, direct taxes were instituted on territorial wealth, industry, and commerce to raise these needed revenues. When, in 1870, Bizkaia, Gipuzkoa, and Araba were asked to make a contribution of 2,529,235 *pesetas*, the foral provinces expressed opposition on the basis of a reinterpretation of the Act of 1839. In 1870 this Act represented the confirmation of the foral system, ignoring the pending reform. On the same grounds, the three provinces opposed a tax of 10 percent on travelers' fees and registration cards. On the other hand, on August 7, 1868, the Deputations assumed the defense of the interests of the Banks of Bilbao, San Sebastián, and Vitoria in the conflict surrounding the Royal Order of June 15, 1868, which executed the prior Royal Order of March 3 that called for a tax of 5 percent on banks, trading companies, and similar entities. The Deputations argued that the central government did not have the legal authority to demand such taxes. However the central government imposed the law on a de facto basis, taking advantage of the legal ambiguity regarding the matter, applying and extending the indirect tax system to the Basque provinces. The Deputations produced a report in 1875 regarding what it considered the following state violations of the foral self-government: the demands for war stamps per the decree of October 2, 1873; a tobacco monopoly for sales to the army; a tax of 5 percent on the profits of banks and trading companies; a tax of 10 percent on travelers' tickets, private charitable organizations, and personal registration cards; the abolishing of agricultural, industrial, and commerce committees and the stripping the Deputations of legal and administrative authority; the capacity to seize private property and sell common lands and create rural civil law enforcement bodies; a tax on the salaries of doctors administering mineral baths; the taxing of official paper required for use in treasury offices, and taxes on colonial articles imported as of 1862.

An overall picture thus emerges of an institutionalization of self-governing "state entities" operating in a framework of increasing industrialization, but at the same time with a weak legal and constitutional basis, and basing their legitimacy more on their political will and self-confidence.

This took place amid the outbreak of another civil war, instigated by the Carlists, that saw the liberals defend the constitutional state. It was at this point that the foral system was modified by Cánovas de Castillo by means of the law of July 21, 1876. This law eviscerated the foral institutions of their political dimension while, economically, the Agreement instituted was nothing more than the culmination of a an aspiration on the part of the state—an aspiration that went back to 1814—to establish both a tax quota and a military draft quota for the Basque territories. In 1876, the central government directly administered the assessing of revenues and taxes such as customs duties, postal services, lotteries, and taxes on gunpowder, mineral iron, and identification cards. From that time forward, these matters would be directly administered by the state, without any type of joint administration.

It is beyond question that the dilution of the "reform of the Foral Law" generated a culture of ongoing bilateral negotiation between the central government and the institutions of the Basque Country that contributed to the political recognition of Basque political identity. In the short term, and from the standpoint of both the economy and the contribution to the general budget of the state, this situation was politically and economically advantageous to the foral institutions. In the end, however, this dynamic did not result in any formal legal and political sanction of said institutions. Yet by 1877 this state of affairs strengthened the Foral treasury systems in such a way as to enshrine these systems as a de facto reality, one difficult to undermine even for a state that declared Spain to be "a single nation." Thus, despite the legal and political abolition of the Foral Law in 1876, the decree of 1878 that was meant to be a transition toward integration into a centralized system in fact led to the Economic Agreement. And that is why we view this phenomenon as singular evidence of fiscal and political resilience.

Management of the Public Budgets of the Foral Treasury Systems

The foral treasury systems had two key aspects: their relationship with the central treasury and the management of the revenues paid by taxpayers. As a consequence, and in the same way as the Spanish state, the foral treasury systems promoted the creation of a bureaucratic and administrative apparatus aimed at guaranteeing revenues and budgeting expenses. The defense and the implementation of the foral treasury systems became the key element of the new Basque political issue together with the management of the resources in order to strengthen public finances. In table 1.2 we see a series of graphic representations of the structure of revenues and expenses at two different historical moments: at the time of the fall of the absolute monarchy and when the development of liberal institutions at the dawn of the industrial revolution was in full force.

The situation in Navarre has been addressed in a book in which the evolution of its tax system during the nineteenth century is described. Developments in Navarre were similar to those described above in Alava, Bizkaia, and Gipuzkoa.[23] Thus, an analysis of the available data reveal the consolidation of a number of different political communities, each having their own representative political body (i.e., the Juntas Generales) with autonomous fiscal authority. Both contributions to the Treasury, as well as "donations" or the quota were infrequent, at least in any direct form. However, the payment of the contribution for matters involving religion and clergy, which in the rest of the state

Table 1.2. Structure of Revenues and Expenditures at Two Historical Moments (Annual Averages, in Thousands of Reales and Percents)

Income						
	Alava		Gipuzkoa		Bizkaia	
Years	1815–19	1865–67	1828–30	1865–67	1816–20	1864–67
Direct taxes	1,066 45%	857 16%	23 1%	0 0%	32:14%	460 5%
Indirect taxes	591 25%	1,875 36%	1,094 57%	4,355 60%	1,2 56%	6,279 62%
Tolls	320 14%	601 12%	274 14%	479 7%	10 1	2,067 20%
Loans	183 8%	1,200 23%	392 20%	1,705 24%	52(21%	1,054 10%
Others	182 8%	672 13%	145 8%	66 9%	18‹8%	314 3%
	2,342	5,205	1,928	7,203	2,333	10,174
Expenditures						
	Alava		Gipuzkoa		Bizkaia	
Years	1815–19	1865–67	1828–30	1865–67	1816–20	1864–67
Admin.	588 24%	1,226 25%	682 32%	1,575 21%	586 23%	1,510 14%
"Donations" Quot	620 25%	14 1 1%	412 20%	74 1%	807 32%	86 1%
Investments	405 17%	1,251 25%	247 12%	3,386 46%	56 3%	5,374 52%
Social expenses	0 0%	946 19%	394 19%	892 12%	187 7%	1,439 14%
Debt service	829 34%	1,514 30%	361 17%	1439 20%	895 35%	1,979 19%
	2,443	4,951	2,096	7,366	2,531	10,388

Sources : J. Agirreazkuenaga, *Vizcaya en el siglo XIX : Las finanzas públicas de un Estado emergente* (Bilbao, 1987); J. Ortiz de Orruño, *La Hacienda foral alavesa en la crisis del Antiguo Régimen (1850–1876)* (Vitoria, 1987, doctoral thesis); *Registro de las Juntas Generales de Gipuzkoa;* J. Agirreazkuenaga and J. M. Ortiz de Orruño, "Las haciendas forales de Alava, Guipuzcoa y Vizcaya entre 1800 y 1878," *Ekonomiaz,* 9–10 (1988): 69–92.

was subsumed under the general budget, became the responsibility of the Foral treasury system. In Navarre, the monies of the quota did not end up in the Treasury, but instead were used to liquidate the public debt of the foral province, and which the state had formally assumed under the 1841 law that modified the *fueros.*

The extensive road network, its quality, railroad infrastructure, and teaching establishments are some of the most important fruits of the efforts undertaken. In sum, a number of solid "partials elements" of a structure had been consolidated in which the Deputations exercised a series of functions characteristic of the new liberal state. Social cohesion in these political communities had increased under the hegemony of a land-owning nobility and a commercial bourgeoisie that were prepared to promote a process of industrialization.

Revenues were for the most part generated from excise taxes on products of consumption. Taxes on tobacco played an especially decisive role in allowing the budget to be balanced. In 1859, agreement had been reached in Bizkaia regarding the creation of a strengthened bureaucratic and administrative structure of the foral tax system. The ideological architect of this plan was V.L. Gaminde, who used the United States as his model.

Law of July 21, 1876, of the Spanish Parliament and Decree of 1878

The frustration resulting from the 1876 law that abolished the *Foral Law* can be better understood by considering the wider context of the management of public resources. Given the strength of the system that took shape during the first liberal period (despite attempts by the central government to impose limits on and abolish the autonomous system of administration and the Foral treasury system) the system of Economic Agreements, at first conceived as a temporary measure, became instead a fixed institution. This represented continuity within the fiscal context, because the management of said system was under the exclusive jurisdiction of the new provincial Deputations and beyond the "parliamentary" control that the Juntas Generales had exercised in the past. On the one hand, there was a loss of legal and political legitimacy. On the other hand, the government of Antonio Cánovas del Castillo approved a provisional decree to remain in effect for eight years, which served as the legal basis of the Economic Agreement or Fiscal Pact. This agreement was extended as a result of an accord between the two sides: In 1906, the Economic Agreement was approved for a period of twenty-five years. In 1919, Jose Orueta proposed a new formula: the definition of a general quota and the abandonment of partial negotiation over taxes.

Cánovas del Castillo took the initiative regarding modification of the Foral Law abolishing the representative Juntas Generales and establishing a new framework for tax arrangements that would allow the Basque provinces, according to the decree of February 28, 1878, to "enter into the economic system of the Spanish nation." This was to be accomplished through the payment of a quota as well as through the "blood contribution" (i.e., military service obligations). This arrangement was of a provisional nature because the foral treasury system had, due to the strength it had attained both administratively and fiscally, been able to meet the needs of the population. The Deputations had replaced the public and social services that the constitutional was deploying in other provinces. For this reason, a transition period was necessary, and this period eventually served as the basis for a process of consolidation of the new provincial Deputations within a fragile legal foundation for the Economic Agreement. Pablo Alzola, president of the Deputation of Bizkaia wrote the following in 1890: "In recent years, the Economic Agreement has gained increasing stability and administrative autonomy has become consolidated. Recently, however, a concern has arisen regarding municipal budgets... but administratively, and for a number of rather complex reasons, it has not been possible to collect everything—leaving aside for the moment the claiming of historical rights—that justly belongs to the Basque Country."[24]

The Economic Agreement marked a turning point. At first, it was seen as nothing more than crumbs by the most hardline *fueristas*, who were in favor of Foral Law, led by F. Sagarminaga. Yet, in the course of time, the Economic Agreement attained the status of a "historical right."

The Economic Agreement was defined as a governmental provision (one that generally never held a status beyond that of a royal decree) that set the annual lump sum (or "quota") that each Basque Deputation was to hand over to the Ministry of Finance and that represented the collection of certain taxes (so-called "arranged taxes") that the state had renounced the right to collect. The Deputations made good on their obligations to turn over these monies on the basis of resources gathered from mechanisms of exaction or their own revenues that were not directly related to the arranged taxes, with the only exception (as of 1906) being that of international agreements. Logically, these arrangements were limited to those taxes that were identified in the agreement. The agreement in general would over the course of time be renewed for varying terms, from the eight years of the original 1878 accord to the twenty-five years stipulated for that of 1926.

One basic feature that differentiated the agreement from other formulas is that the Deputations were under no obligation to collect the arranged taxes. For this reason, the Deputations did not function as mere proxies or delegates of the Ministry of Finance. Instead, they financed the collection of the agreed quota from their own revenues. They had the right to collect or not collect the arranged taxes and also to apply any additional fees that they saw fit. Each Deputation chose its own financing model (within the common framework of the nation). Each of these models was not only separated from the Ministry of Finance, but from the other two historical territories as well.

On the other hand, the Economic Agreement not only contained fiscal accords. In addition, it legitimized the economic and administrative authority that the Deputations had already been exercising. Such authority was never clearly defined, and this lack of specification was at one and the same time both a problem and an advantage. It was a problem in that there was no legal text to refer to in the case of questions or disputes between the distinct spheres of the administration. It was an advantage because it was always possible to argue that a competence or power—any competence at all—had been exercised by a Deputation or a local government from time immemorial. Thus, both fiscal and administrative conflicts ensued between the Deputations, on the one hand, and the different authorities of the Spanish central government, on the other.

In contrast to the Economic Agreement for Navarre, the renewals of the Economic Agreement of the Territories resulted from two different causes. In some instances, renewals resulted from the expiration of the previous agreement (1887, 1906, and 1926) or modifications in tax regulations (1894). On other occasions, partial modifications were made that did not introduce any essential difference in the content of the agreement other than the amount of the quota, either as a result of regulatory changes (1898, 1900, 1904) or as a result of previously scheduled changes (1916). Increases in the quota often resulted in total or partial differences in the arranged taxes. In 1900, for example, as a result of the reform of Villaverde, the fees for the industrial contribution became subsumed under the new tax on profits. This meant that the quotas needed to be modified to include these new fees and to include still other fees that were part of the new tax. Thus, with each new partial modification and renovation, the number of arranged taxes (and, logically, the amounts collected) increased. The negotiations for the renewal of the agreement clearly show that the system became definitively consolidated in 1906, when it was renewed for a period of twenty years. In reality, the negotiation of the various renewals over the years centered mainly on the amount of the quota, as well as on the taxes subject to the agreement—but not on the system per se. As the expiration date for each agreement neared, these negotiations led to a certain instability, and at times to outright conflict. For this reason, different formulas were proposed on a number of occasions to ameliorate the resulting tensions. Thus, in 1919, J. Orueta proposed the establishment of a fixed quota and the abandonment of partial negotiation of taxes in favor of a system proportionate to the budget at any given time. From the standpoint of the state, this formula was finally embraced when the new constitutional system, which included recovery of autonomy, reformulated the agreement for the three historical territories.

In 1937, Francisco Franco abolished the civil system of arranged taxes for Gipuzkoa and Bizkaia as punishment for their resistance during the Civil War against his Nationalist forces. However, the specific system of administering taxes according to an agreement or accord survived in both Araba and Navarre during Franco's dictatorship. This same system was reinstituted in 1981 in Bizkaia and Gipuzkoa on the basis of new theoretical principles.

Conclusion: An Example of Institutional Resilience

The theory of the Foral treasury system, which directly led to the solution of the Economic Agreement, was formulated in part during the period of liberal revolution. It is also possible to interpret the agreement as a consequence and specific expression of the previously mentioned theory, albeit with the obvious element of legal delegitimizing in the case of the Basque territories, since Antonio Cánovas del Castillo's dissolution of the Representative Assemblies meant that these bodies did not sanction the accord. In spite of his unifying zeal, Cánovas del Castillo finally agreed to an economic-fiscal agreement, in part because the presence of the Spanish state administration was in fact weak and unpopular in the Basque territories in 1877–78. On the other hand, Cánovas de Castillo attempted to expand his social and political base of support among the new Basque industrial bourgeoisie. This fact notwithstanding, the agreements for the provinces of Araba, Bizkaia, and Gipuzkoa, along with the amending of the Economic Agreement for Navarre—agreements that, once again, were seen by hardline *fueristas* as nothing more than "crumbs"—gradually evolved into a historical right. In fact, the Agreement contributed to eventual fiscal sovereign plurality, a notion that had only a fragile legal basis, except in Navarre (thanks to the 1841 law modifying the *fuero* in the latter province). At present, we do not have customs or a military quota, but we do face new challenges from another kind of political union—the European Union—at a time when the winds of uniformity once again appear to be blowing strong within the Spanish political union. The strengthening of the foral tax systems in the nineteenth century reflects a resilient structure, not only in terms of the will to self-government, but also because of their management capacity and the benefits gleaned by those paying into the systems. In the nineteenth century, the Juntas Generales defended the policy of a double constitution: a "foral constitution" and the Constitution of the Spanish nation. Underlying this vision was the notion of a combined monarchy. Beginning in 1876, it was the discourse of a "single nation" that prevailed and, during the subsequent period of crisis—a time of profound change—Basque political leaders and Basque society, in the process of adapting to the newly established legal limits, successfully instituted an autonomous model for administering its public finances.

Endnotes

1. R. Lopez Atxurra, *La administración fiscal del Señorío de Vizcaya (1630–1804)* (Bilbao: Diputación Foral de Bizkaia/ Instituto de Derecho Histórico de Euskal Herria, 1991).
2. Josep Fontana, *Modernización y progreso: Política y hacienda del Despotismo Ilustrado,"* in *Haciendas forales y hacienda real: Homenaje a D. Miguel Artola y Felipe Ruiz Martín*, ed. R. Fernandez de Pinedo (Bilbao: University of the Basque Country, 1990).
3. Brian Walker and David Salt, *Resilience Thinking: Sustaining Ecosystems and People in a Changing World* (Washington, DC: Island Press, 2006), 6
4. Joseba Agirreazkuenaga, *La articulación político-institucional de Vasconia: Actas de las "Conferencias" firmadas por los representantes de Alava, Bizkaia,Gipuzkoa y eventualmente de Navarra (1775–1936)* (Bilbao: Foral Dep-

utations of Bizkaia, Gipuzkoa, and Araba: 1995) I: 120

5. *Actas de las Juntas de la Diputación General de españoles que se juntó en Bayona el 15 de Junio de 1808 en virtud de convocatoria expedida por el gran duque de Berge como Lugar-teniente general del Reino y la Junta Suprema de Gobierno con fecha 19 de mayo del mismo año* (Madrid: Imprenta y fundición de J.A. García, 1874), 109.

6. Joseba Agirreazkuenaga, "The Debate on the Constitution of Cádiz in the Basque General Assemblies: The Constitution of Biscay and Reservations about the Unconditional Oath (1812)," in *Las Cortes de Cadiz y la Historia Parlamentaria,* ed. D. Repeto. (Cadiz: University of Cadiz, 2012).[AU: Please provide page range.]

7. *Copia del informe de la Junta de Reforma de Abusos de Real Hacienda de las Provincias Vascongadas creada en Real Orden de 6 de noviembre de 1815* (Madrid: Oficina de Don Tomas Jordan Impresor de Camara de S.M., 1839), 5–7.

8. Ibid., 143–44

9. Agirreazkuenaga, *La articulación,* I: 200–210

10. National Archives, Archivo Histórico Nacional (AHN), Consejo de Regencia, August 19, 1820, 96.

11. Agirreazkuenaga, *La articulación,* I: 223.

12. Agirreazkuenaga, *La articulación,* I: 229; determined at conference held in Bilbao by the Representatives of Bizkaia Araba and Gipuzkoa, on June 12, 1824.

13. Agirreazkuenaga, *The Making of the Basque Question. Experiencing Self-Government, 1793–1877* (Reno: Center for Basque Studies–University of Nevada, 2011), 173–83.

14. *Representación de los vascongados y navarros residentes en Madrid pidiendo la conservación de los fueros de sus provincias* (Madrid: Imprenta de la Compañia Tipográfica, 1839), 12

15. Victor Luis Gaminde, *Impugnación al proyecto llamado Arreglo de los Fueros de las Provincias Bascongadas presentado por la Comisión del Gobierno a las de las mismas Provincias* (Bilbao: J.E. Delmas, 1852), 14–15.

16. See Joseba Agirreazkuenaga, "'Casimiro Loizaga': La definición de los principios del Régimen *Foral* o del régimen constitucional en el marco de la Constitución española de 1837 para lograr su articulación y compatibilidad (1782–1841)," *Notitia Vasconiae* 1 (2002): 219–49.

17. Joseba Agirreazkuenaga, "Haciendas forales en tiempos de revolución liberal: La reforma tributaria de Mon-Santillán y su proyecto de aplicación en Araba, Bizkaia y Gipuzkoa (1845–1846)," in *Josep Fontana: Història i projecte social; Reconeixement a una trajectòria* (Barcelona: Crítica, 2004).

18. AGA (General Archive of the Administration), file box 103.

19. Ibid.

20. Pio Pita Pizarro, *Examen económico histórico critíco de la Hacienda y deuda del Estado, proyecto de su reforma general y la del Banco* (Madrid: Imprenta Narciso panchiz, 1840).

21. Pedro de Egaña, *Breves apuntes en defensa de las libertades vascongadas / escrito leído a la llamada Comisión de arreglo de Fueros nombrada por Juan Bravo Murillo en 1852 (*Bilbao: Imprenta Juan E. Delmas, 1870).

22. Ramón Ortiz de Zárate, *Escritos de Don Ramón Ortiz de Zarate,* vol. 1 (Bil-

bao: Biblioteca Bascongada de Fermín Herran, 1899–1900), 205.
23. Joseba Torre, "Hacienda foral y crecimiento económico en Navarra durante el siglo XIX," in *Navarra siglo XIX: Cien años de Historia* (Pamplona: Caja Laboral, 1994).
24. Pablo Alzola, *Discurso pronunciado por el Sr. D. Pablo de Alzola presidente de la Diputación de Vizcaya en la sesión celebrada el 29 de diciembre de 1890* (Bilbao: Imprenta provincial, 1890).

Sources and Bibliography
Archives
Archivo Foral de Bizkaia: (AFB) Bilbao. Régimen Foral: 21 Registros.
Archivo Histórico Nacional (AHN) (Madrid) Estado, legajo 96
Archivo General de la Administración. A.G.A (Alcalá de Henares) Presidencia del Gobierno, box 11, Actas del Consejo de Ministros. A 1/4. folio 298.). Box 103.

Bibliography

Actas de las Juntas de la Diputación General de españoles que se juntó en Bayona el 15 de Junio de 1808 en virtud de convocatoria expedida por el gran duque de Berge como Lugar-teniente general del Reino y la Junta Su prema de Gobierno con fecha 19 de mayo del mismo año. Madrid: J. A. Garcia, 1874.

Agirreazkuenaga Joseba, ed. *La articulación político-institucional de Vasconia: Actas de las "Conferencias" firmadas por los representantes de Alava, Bizkaia,Gipuzkoa y eventualmente de Navarra (1775–1936)*. Bilbao: Foral Deputations of Bizkaia, Gipuzkoa, and Araba, 1995.

———. "'Casimiro Loizaga': La definición de los principios del Régimen *Foral* o del régimen constitucional en el marco de la Constitución española de 1837 para lograr su articulación y compatibilidad (1782–1841)," *Notitia Vasconiae* 1 (2002): 219–49.

———. "Haciendas forales en tiempos de revolución liberal: La reforma tributaria de Mon-Santillán y su proyecto de aplicación en Araba, Bizkaia y Gipuzkoa (1845–1846)." In *Josep Fontana: Història i projecte social: Reconeixement a una trajectòria*. Barcelona: Crítica, 2004.

———. *Vizcaya en el siglo XIX: Las finanzas públicas de un estado emergente*. Bilbao: University of the Basque Country, 1987.

Agirreazkuenaga Joseba, and Ortiz de Orruño José, "Las Haciendas forales en Alava, Guipúzcoa y Vizcaya entre 1800 y 1878." *Ekonomiaz* 24 (1988): 69–92.

Agirreazkuenaga, Joseba, Eduardo Alonso, and Mikel Urquijo. "Representative Assemblies and Taxes: The Making of the 'Taxation

Agreement' ('Concierto Económico') of the Basque Country (1839–1937)." In *Assemblee rappresentative autonomie territoriali culture politiche: Representative Assemblies Territorialautonomies, Political Cultures,* edited by A. Nieddu and F. Soddu, 503–510. Sassari: Ed. Democratica Sarda, 2011.

Alonso Olea, Eduardo. "Para repensar el Concierto Económico: De "migaja" a Derecho Histórico." *Historia Contemporánea* 16 (1996): 431–64.

———. *Continuidades y discontinuidades de la administración provincial en el País Vasco, 1839–1978: Una "esencia" de los Derechos Históricos.* Oñati: IVAP, 1999.

———. *El Concierto Económico (1878–1937): Orígenes y formación de un Derecho histórico.* Oñati: IVAP, 1995.

Alzola, Pablo. *Discurso pronunciado por el Sr. Pablo de Alzola, Presidente de la Diputación de Vizcaya el 29 de XII de 1890.* Bilbao: Provincial Government Press, 1991.

Barahona, Renato. *Vizcaya on the Eve of Carlism: Politics and Society, 1800–1833.* Reno: University of Nevada Press, 1989.

Castells, Luis, and Arturo Cajal. "La negociación imposible: Cánovas y el fuerismo vasco en 1876," *Hispania* 65, no. 220 (2005): 601–42.

Comin, F., and Rafael Vallejo. "La reforma fiscal de Mon-Santillán desde una perspectiva histórica." *Hacienda Pública Española* (1996): 7–20.

Pedro de Egaña, *Breves apuntes en defensa de las libertades vascongadas / escrito leído a la llamada Comisión de arreglo de Fueros nombrada por Juan Bravo Murillo en 1852.* Bilbao: Imprenta Juan E. Delmas, 1870.

Estecha, José María. *Régimen político y administrativo de las Provincias Vasco-Navarras: Colección de leyes decretos,* Reales *Ordenes y resoluciones del Tribunal Contencioso administrativo relativos al País Vasconavarro.* Second edition and appendices 2 and 2. Bilbao: Diputación Foral de Bizkaia/ Instituto de Derecho Histórico de Euskal Herria, 1997. Reedited facisimiles.

Fontana, Josep. "Modernización y progreso: Política y hacienda del Despotismo Ilustrado." In *Haciendas forales y hacienda real: Homenaje a D. Miguel Artola y Felipe Ruiz Martín,* edited by E. Fernandez de Pinedo. Bilbao: University of the Basque Country, 1990.

Gaminde, Victor Luis. *Impugnación al proyecto llamado Arreglo de los Fueros de las Provincias Bascongadas presentado por la Comisión del Gobierno a las de las mismas Provincias.* Bilbao: J. E. Delmas, 1852.

Herb, M. "Taxation and Representation." *Studies in Comparative International Development* 38, no. 3 (Fall 2003): 3–31.

Howland, Douglas, and Luise White, ed. *The State of Sovereignty.* Bloomington: Indiana University Press, 2009.

Lopez Atxurra, Rafael. "La foralidad en la historiografía vasca." *Ernaroa* 3 (1989): 117–171.

———. *La administración fiscal del Señorío de Vizcaya (1630–1804).* Bilbao: Diputación Foral de Bizkaia/ Instituto de Derecho Histórico de Euskal Herria, 1999.

Novia de Salcedo, Pedro. *Defensa histórica legislativa y económica del Señorío de Vizcaya y provincias de Álava y Guipúzcoa contra las Noticias histórica de las misma que publicó d. Juan Antonio Llorente y el informe de la Junta de reformas de abusos de la real hacienda en las tres Provincias Bascongadas.* 4 vols. Bilbao: J. E. Delmas, 1851.

Ortiz de Zarate, Ramón. *Escritos.* 2 volumes. Bilbao: Fermin Herran, 1899, 1900.

Perez, Javier. *La Diputación foral de Vizcaya: El régimen foral en la contrucción del Estado liberal (1808–1968).* Madrid: Centro de Estudios Constitucionales, 1996.

Pita Pizarro, Pio. *Examen económico histórico critico de la Hacienda y deuda del Estado, proyecto de su reforma general y la del Banco.* Madrid: Imprenta Narciso Sanchiz, 1840.

Rull Sabater, Alberto. *Diccionario sucinto de Ministros de Hacienda (Siglos XIX y XX).* Madrid: Instituto de Estudios Fiscales, 1991.

Torre, Joseba. "Hacienda foral y crecimiento económico en Navarra durante el siglo XIX." In *Navarra siglo XIX: Cien años de Historia.* Pamplona: Caja Laboral, 1994.

Vazquez de Prada, Mercedes. *Negociación sobre los Fueros entre Vizcaya y el poder central 1839–1877.* Bilbao: Caja de Ahorros Vizcaína, 1984.

Vidal Abarca, Juan, Federico Verastegui, and Alfonso Otazu. *Fausto de Otazu a Iñigo Ortés de Velasco: Cartas 1834–1841.* Vitoria-Gasteiz: Diputación Foral de Araba, 1995.

Walker, Brian, and David Salt. *Resilience Thinking: Sustaining Ecosystems and People in a Changing World.* Washington, DC: Island Press, 2006.

Zabala Allende, Federico. *El Concierto Económico: Qué ha sido, qué es, qué debe ser.* Bilbao: Ed. Vizcaína, 1998 [1927, facisimile reproduction].

2
The Economic Agreement in the Context of the Nineteenth-Century Spanish Treasury

Miguel Martorell Linares

Following the signing of the Constitution of 1876 and the end of the Carlist War, the law of June 21, 1876, authorized the state to extend tax obligations and military service to the Basque provinces. This reflected an effort to establish a territorially unified tax system that the liberal tax reform of 1845 had not managed to achieve. In compliance with this law, the Royal Decree of February 28, 1878, which was enacted following arduous negotiations with the important political forces of the region, established an Economic Agreement with the Basque provinces, which involved the provincial Deputations assuming responsibility for the collection of territorial and industrial taxes, as well as of royal fees, the tax on products of consumption and salt, and part of the stamp tax for official paper. In addition, the agreement called for the Basque provinces to provide the state with an agreed amount or quota, which would be discounted between 33 and 40 percent for each province, in order to cover collection costs and other expenses. The state would collect all remaining taxes, with the express mention of the categories of mines, personal registration cards, and transportation. In addition, the tobacco monopoly was extended to all of Basque territory, which had previously been exempt from it. Following application of the discounts, the amounts collected by the state (in *pesetas*) were as follows: Araba, 529,634; Gipuzkoa, 655,777; and Bizkaia, 857,765.[1]

The agreement reached in 1878 was consistent in some respects with the prevailing Spanish tax system, some of whose main taxes were applied through the assigning of a quota to local administrations, which took responsibility for collecting them. This can be seen in the following pages, which address the construction of the Spanish tax system, its evolution during the period 1845 to 1878, and the structures of its primary taxes.

Evolution of the Tax System, 1845 to 1874

The Restoration inherited the tax system approved in 1845 by the

Spanish Parliament, as later modified at the insistence of Alejandro Mon, Minister of Finance in the Narváez government. It should be noted, however, that during the thirty years prior to the Putsch of Sagunto, which restored the throne to the Bourbon dynasty, the system had been modified in important ways. Historians of the tax system have insisted on the collective authorship of the system, given that the bills that Mon defended before Parliament reproduced reports that had been drafted by a commission for the reform of the tax system created in December 1843 and presided over by Javier de Burgos and that included, among other notable politicians, Mon himself as well as Ramón Santillán, the main promoter of Mon's initiatives. The work coordinated by Mon and Santillán represented the culmination of a long reformist tradition that went back to the *Cortes* of Cádiz and the liberal triennium of 1820–1823, which had been inspired by the French tax system. Mon's tax system was made possible by a climate of social calm following three decades of military conflicts. The initiative was also related to a broader process of consolidation of the liberal-moderate state, two of the landmark achievements of which—the constitution and the municipal law—were also enacted in 1843. The tax reform contributed to this labor of state building the unification of a tax system throughout the entire national territory, with the exception of the Basque Provinces and Navarre.[2]

The French tax system, which combined indirect taxes with direct taxes on products, was the main reference of the liberal creators of tax policy in Spain, Italy, and Portugal during the first half of the nineteenth century. For this reason, the organization of the set of taxes adopted by these countries during the consolidation of liberal regimes is commonly called "the Latin tax system." The categorization of taxes into two large groups—direct and indirect—goes back to the French Constituent Assembly of 1790 and has been frequently called into question, but its use continues to be widespread even today. Indirect taxes are those assessed on imports, purchases, sales, and transportation of merchandise, or on the provision of services, as well as on exactions derived from the formalizing and public recognition of particular legal documents. Direct taxes, on the other hand, involve a direct and ongoing tax on income or wealth, and are applied to individuals and their properties on the basis of fiscal and territorial records that are individual in character. Direct taxes, in turn, are divided into two groups. "Real taxes" (or product taxes) are assessed on returns on property, estates, or capital, without considering the economic or personal situation of those who possess said goods or receive income. Thus, all taxpayers are assessed the same rate, independently of their incomes. Personal taxes, on the other hand, are always assessed to a specific individual taxpayer, on the basis of that individual's wealth or income.[3]

Latin tax systems are not particularly rigid, given their important emphasis on direct taxes on products. The majority of these taxes were administered through the quota system, which involved the *Cortes* assigning a predetermined amount that the state needed to collect each year, with the tax base not being calculated either according to the sworn declaration of the taxpayer or on the basis of the examination of accounting records, but rather on the basis of external factors (e.g., the area where a business or property was located, the extension or quality of a property, or the number of steam engines used in a particular industry). This was a mode of assessment that did not adjust for economic growth and that was conducive to fraud. In addition, given that collection of taxes under this system was disconnected from economic growth, political institutions had to increase quotas periodically in order to boost revenues. In addition, legislation for each separate tax category had to be reformed in order to take into account new kinds of professional activities.[4]

Broadly speaking, the strategy of those formulating Spanish tax policy in 1845 consisted of adapting some of the tax principles that were at that time in effect in France, where a large number of the exactions of the *ancien régime* had been retained. In 1845, the Spanish Parliament approved the taxation of the following categories: real property, crops, and livestock; industry and commerce; mortgage fees (which would later be called *tax on real property rights*); tenants' tax; and a tax on specific animal products (which would later be known as the *contribution* or *tax on products of consumption*). A number of holdovers from the *ancien Régime* completed the 1845 tax system, among them customs revenues, a tax on official paper (precursor of the stamp tax), a series of taxes on the transportation and trading of merchandise (among them a toll-gate tax), as well as various taxes on mining activities. Finally, Mon and Santillán also preserved the state monopolies on tobacco, salt, gunpowder, and lotteries. The reform of 1845 was fundamentally modified in the following years. In 1846, Francisco Orlando abolished the tenant tax ("a remote but clear precursor of the personal tax," in the words of Enrique Fuentes Quintana). One year later, Santillán himself introduced a regressive modification of the industrial tax. In 1845, the latter tax consisted of two fees, one fixed (which was applied to all individuals and companies that exercised any kind of industrial, mercantile, professional, or financial activity listed among taxable activities) and a complementary proportional quota, that consisted of 10 percent of the income of tradesmen and those operating industries. In the face of taxpayers' protests, Santillán (who at that time was minister of finance) abolished the proportional quota and, even more importantly, assigned the collection of the fixed fee to guilds comprising tradesmen and those operating industries, an action which led to increased fraud and stagnation in terms of the taxes collected.[5]

In 1854, with the initiation of the two-year progressive period, the revolutionary *juntas* abolished the tax on consumption, and the government of Espartero was faced with a fait accompli. Although the progressives included the abolition of the tax on consumption in their program, José Manuel Collado, Prime Minister of Finance of the new government, regretted such a hasty decision. Given "the large and permanent deficit," he said in Congress, "the government was obliged to reestablish those taxes that had been legally established previously." However, despite the reluctance of the ministers of finance, the *Cortes* ended up ratifying the decision of the *juntas*, and the tax was abolished on January 1, 1855. The abolition only lasted a short time because, the following year, the moderates, having once again assumed power, reinstituted it. There were no further significant modifications of the structure of the tax system until the economic crisis that began in the middle of the following decade laid bare the system's extraordinary degree of rigidity. In the face of a drastic drop in collected taxes, the ministers of finance had to work hard to find new sources of revenue. In 1861, the deficit reached 146 million pesetas, a figure that represented 22 percent of state expenses (calculated at 652 million pesetas). Three years later, in 1864, the deficit reached 200 million (28 percent of expenses). The need to procure other resources required both the creation of new taxes and the reformation of existing taxes. In 1862, the first tax on sugar was introduced and, in 1864, the first tax on railroad transport was imposed, which consisted of a simple ten percent surcharge on the face value of tickets. More important was the reform of the mortgage fee. In 1845, the latter had only been applied to the transfer of real property. Between 1864 and 1867, its application was expanded to movable assets, and was relabeled *tax on transfer of domain*. In addition, the section of mortgage fee that taxed inheritance was extended in 1867 to cover inheritance by immediate family members, who had been exempt since 1845. In 1867, Manuel García Barzanallana reintroduced the tax that had been created by Juan Bravo Murillo in 1852, but revoked four years later: the contribution of salaries and allowances, a levy of 5 percent on all income, salaries, and allowances paid by public administrations.[6]

Two opposing tendencies characterized the six-year period of democratic government. During the first phase, Laureano Figuerola tried between 1868 and 1870 to introduce into the Ministry of Finance what Martín Niño characterized as the tax program of individualist liberalism. The target of Figuerola's reforms were indirect taxes. The progressives called for the elimination of these indirect taxes because they impeded free trade and the circulation of wealth. Figuerola legally sanctioned the abolition of the tax on products of consumption that, as had occurred during the two-year progressive period, had already been revoked in practice by the revolutionary *juntas*. In addition, he abolished the toll-gate tax and other minor imposts, such as the tax on sugar. Furthermore, Figuerola lowered the tax on official paper, ended the salt monopoly, and followed a customs policy that tended toward free trade (though modified by the need to reach agreement on minimum rates with defenders of a protectionist policy). In order to compensate for the decrease in collected taxes, he proposed to the *Cortes* a direct tax on family wealth estimated on the basis of rent paid for one's home, and the number of individuals within a family. However, this tax ended up not being strictly enforced, given the difficulties involved in collecting it. In 1870, the government assigned its collection to municipalities in order to compensate for the discontinuation of the tax on products of consumption but the municipalities, in part because of technical deficiencies, and in part because of refusal by municipal oligarchies to enforce it, chose instead to gradually reintroduce the tax on products of consumption.[7]

Figuerola's reform provoked the opposition of a segment of the liberal ranks that supported the democratic adventure, because it was worried by the spiraling deficit. Between 1867 and 1870, expenses increased 111 million pesetas, while revenues, thanks to Figuerola's reform and the political and administrative disorder of the six-year democratic period, fell by 102 million *pesetas*. The deficit rose in 1870 to 332 million, almost triple that of 1867, and represented 40 percent of the budget (of 804 million). For this reason, between 1871 and 1874, the finance ministers struggled to revise the work of Figuerola and secure new resources in order to combat the deficit, and to finance military operations aimed at suppressing the struggle for Cuban Independence, a Carlist insurrection, and regional unrest within Spain. The first major step toward rectification in this regard was taken by Finance Minister Servando Ruiz Gómez who, in the 1872–1873 budget, expanded the scope of two existing taxes to encompass various capital revenues. On the one hand, the tax on transfer of domain was renamed the tax on real property rights and was extended to all kinds of transfers of funds of assets, including inheritance by immediate family members (which had been exempted by Figuerola), mortgages, movable property assets, and liquid capital contributions. On the other hand, the stamp tax and official paper tax were expanded beyond their original function of a levy assessed for public services to tax certain income derived from movable property assets. In addition, Ruiz Gómez not only restored the tax on sugar and established new surcharges for the tax on railroad tickets, but also assessed a tax for

Grandee and noble titles.[8]

Inadequate revenues forced the Spanish government to incur debt, and to request help from the Banco de España, which, in exchange, received a monopoly on the issuing of rail tickets in March, 1874. Two years earlier, for the same reasons, a monopoly for the issuing of mortgage certificates had been granted to the Banco Hipotecario. As Francisco Comín Comín has pointed out, given that the majority of national assets resulting from property seizures had been sold, all the state had left to sell were nonmaterial assets, such as issuing monopolies. Even previously, at the time of the Republican dictatorship of General Serrano, Juan Francisco Camacho had restored the tax on products of consumption, which he expanded to include salt (in order to compensate for the discontinuation of the monopoly on this product in 1869), cereals, and coal (and which, because it had a disproportionate impact on the lower classes, highlighted the unfairness of the tax). Camacho also created two new taxes: the sales stamp (which was abolished three years later) and the tax on personal registration cards, a rare exception within the tax system of a progressive exaction that arose due to the introduction of changes to residence cards, which were police identification documents that had been created in 1854 to replace passports.[9]

In 1850, territorial tax payments contributed 22 percent of regular revenues to the state, followed by customs revenues (13 percent), the tobacco monopoly (14 percent), the tax on products of consumption (12 percent) and, trailing far behind, the stamp and official paper tax (5 percent), the industrial tax (4 percent), and the mortgage fee, later called the tax on real property (1 percent). By 1874, these percentages had not varied much, although there was a noticeable decrease in customs and tobacco. In the meantime, the tax on salaries and allowances, which had been created in 1867, was contributing 4 percent of regular revenue. However, despite the relative stagnation in the collection percentages between 1850 and 1874, the tax system inherited by the Restoration, which was the work of those in the Spanish tax authority in the year 1845, also benefited from the modest reforms undertaken during the period 1864–1867 to combat the deficit, and in 1872–1874 to correct those reforms of the first governments of the six-year democratic period. The finance ministers during both of these periods established the tax on salaries and allowances, the first direct tax that was not governed by the quota system. These ministers also defined the nature of the tax on real property and the stamp tax, which began to tax movable assets, which had been practically exempt under the 1845 system. They also created the tax on personal registration cards and a personal progressive tax and, in addition, modified the indirect tax with the creation of a tax on sugar (which constituted the first step toward the consolidation of exactions on specific products of consumption) and a tax on rail transport. The fact that these changes did not fundamentally modify the collections structure does not diminish their qualitative significance.

Characteristics of the First Taxes and Problems of the Tax System by 1878

In 1875, 35.8 percent of ordinary state revenues came from direct contributions, 30.1 percent from indirect contributions, and 21.6 percent from fiscal monopolies. The territorial and industrial taxes, as well as the tax on salaries and allowances and the tax on real property, were responsible for 90 percent of direct taxes. The remaining 10 percent came from taxes on personal registration cards, mines, honorary and noble titles, luxury carriages, and municipal revenue. The territorial tax was a product tax on returns generated from rural and urban real estate, and from agricultural and livestock-raising activities. The *Cortes* defined the amount (or quota) that needed to be collected which, once determined, was divided among provinces. The provincial Deputations in turn applied the quota to municipalities, which in turn assessed it to individual taxpayers. Quotas made the tax system less flexible and stifled its development, given the fact that the growth of rural revenues was not reflected in returns generated by the quotas, which tended to remain stagnant. The quota was distributed according to data contained in the *amillaramientos*, municipal registries created by councilmen and primary contributors on the basis of the declarations of taxpayers themselves regarding the lands and head of cattle that they possessed, their intended use, their quality and their productivity. Values were assigned to these properties according to standards established in "assessment cards," which indicated amounts to be paid for each kind of land and type of livestock. In contrast to a cadastre, the *amillaramientos* did not contain records of land parcels determined by surveys. Instead, the ministry simply accepted at face value the declaration of taxpayers, As Finance Minister Gabino Bugalla pointed out, this system amounted to nothing more than "some persons registered in some notebooks who were assigned, without describing their farms or even thinking about them, a particular tax capacity."[10]

The amount that each taxpayer was responsible for was calculated by prorating the quota assigned to the municipality, according to the data on the *amillaramiento*. The assessed wealth, which served as the basis for the distribution of the provincial quota, was estimated on the basis of the sum of the wealth of individuals who lived in that locality. The distribution of this quota through this procedure was associated with a considerable degree of fraud and fiscal injustice, as regards both the distribution of the provincial quota among the municipalities and among taxpayers within each locality. First, the absence of objective real estate records facilitated fraud. In addition, the creation and revision of the *amillaramientos* was the responsibility of the *juntas periciales*, institutions that were composed in equal proportion of the councilmen and the largest contributors of each municipality (who enabled fraud on the part of the local oligarchy). The essence of the system, as Juan Pro Ruiz has indicated, consisted of the negotiation of made-up numbers of taxable wealth, and those who benefited from the system were those with the most political, economic, and social power in each locality. The injustice was aggravated by the fact that the state always collected the total amount of the quota in each municipality, and this meant that those taxpayers who did not commit fraud not only paid their own taxes, but also those of the persons who cheated the system.[11]

The industrial and commercial taxes were assessed on industrial, mercantile, and professional revenues and were required of all individuals or companies who engaged in activities related to any of the five tariffs listed in the Regulation of March 20, 1870. The first tariff included commerce; the second, banks and corporations; the third, factory and manufacturing industries; the fourth, liberal professions and artisans; and the fifth, patents. The amount to be collected was calculated on the basis of a number of external factors that provided the basis of "presumed benefits," such as type of activity, size of the city where the activity was carried out, and the capacity of the establishment where it was conducted. As the basis for determining the quota for each municipality, the state used the information contained in the registry for the industrial tax. This registry contained fiscal data that included the individual taxpayers of a given population. Those operating industries and businesses within a locality were included in guilds according to the taxable activities that they were engaged in, and these guilds shared the distribution among producers, assigning each of them a quota. The state ratified the distribution and, in this way, the guilds of those operating industries and businesses collected the tax without interference on the part of the administration. This was "the most comfortable system from the point of view of the taxpayer," since it did not require a sworn statement or the provision of other business-related data. In addition, this system excluded "agents of the tax authority from intervening in the private accounting of those operating businesses." However, the system was also conducive to cheating: between 1863 and 1893, the number of taxpayers decreased by 18,000 "due to concealment and fraud," according to Raimundo Fernández Villaverde. Given the rigidity of the tax, the Courts had to periodically adjust the tax rates, and new industries and professions only paid taxes when the administration specifically designated them as subject to the tariffs. In sum, as Fabián Estapé has written, the industrial tax was "the greatest failure of the 1845 reform.[12]

The tax on real property was a complex tax that was determined on the basis of the successive incorporation of various different categories and that included different kinds of activities (although mainly focusing on those involving the transfer of assets). Broadly speaking, this tax was divided into two different classifications: the first taxed transfers between living persons, although it also included other actions, such as warnings re attachment of assets, bonds, administrative concessions, and construction contracts. The second classification dealt with the transmission of assets through inheritance (i.e., *mortis causa*). In 1875, the amount of the tax on personal registration cards, a progressive poll tax, was determined either on the basis of the number of inhabitants of the city where the taxpayer resided, or whether or not he paid the direct tax. Two different taxes were applied to mining properties: the "land surface canon" and the tax on mineral exploitation. The first went back to 1825, although it was modified in a number of ways in both 1859 and 1868. This tax required mining concessions to pay a tax that varied according to the mineral exploited on each hectare of land surface. The second consisted of the payment of a percentage of the gross revenues of a concession (understood as the total value of the extracted mineral, calculated on the basis of the sales price). Two sumptuary exactions rounded out the direct taxation: a tax on luxury carriages and horses (later discontinued in 1877) and a tax on honorary and noble titles in Castile (which taxed the inheritance of noble titles, the rehabilitation of expired titles, the concession of new titles, and authorization of Spanish subjects to use foreign titles within Spain).[13]

Some 40 percent of the indirect taxes came from customs revenues, 30 percent from the tax on products of consumption, and another 30 percent from the taxes on stamps, sugar, and transportation. In 1875, the tax on products of consumption was determined by the decree of June 26, 1874. This was a tax on the consumption of various different items, classified into three different groups: salt, alcoholic beverages, and a wide range of different foods, fuels, and other products. There were four different systems for collecting the tax: the contracting of collection; direct administration by the Ministry of Finance; *repartimiento*;[14] and an agreement with guilds representing those producing the items subject to the tax. Little by little, this tax was delegated to municipalities. In 1853, the state collected (either directly or through cession) 53 percent of the tax. In 1905, the state only collected 5 percent of the tax (none of which was obtained directly). Local governments could increase the quota in order to meet municipal expenses: in 1905, local surcharges accounted for 53 percent of the amount collected for products of consumption, and 56 percent of the revenues of local tax authorities (who could in turn either administer the tax directly or assign collection to a third party—the latter option being rather common in large cities). There were two kinds of cession: "exclusive sale" and "free sale." The first only applied to populations of fewer than 5,000 inhabitants and involved granting a concession to the contractor of a monopoly on retail sales. "Free sale," on the other hand, was more common in cities and allowed for free competition among sellers of the taxed items. When direct collection or concession was employed, numerous municipalities collected the tax in special warehouses at the city gates (*fielatos*) designated for this purpose. This system made conducting internal commerce awkward, because in order to guarantee collection, it was necessary to control access to each locality. Local governments could also arrange tax payment for a number of items with guilds or divide the quota among all residents. Division among residents was the most common form of exaction in small municipalities, where there was not a great deal of commercial activity. In this way, the tax on products of consumption functioned in many places as a direct tax on agricultural property, and not as an indirect tax.[15]

There were a number of objections to the tax on products of consumption. From a social perspective, it made life more expensive and provided an unjust division of the tax burden, something that resulted in frequent outbreaks of popular violence. Economically, the *fielatos* constituted an obstacle to commercial activity and led to an increase in smuggling. In addition, municipal authorities excessively taxed foreign products and exercised a kind of local protectionism, while the high costs of the concessions and the high number of guards that were needed reduced net revenues. Furthermore, the system for collecting the tax on products of consumption exemplified municipal corruption, and those granted the concessions represented the epitome of political venality. The abolition of this tax, however, presented serious problems. Many local tax authorities depended on their surcharges on the tax, and it was not easy to find substitute resources. This was due primarily to the resistance of economic and social elites to modifying the division of the fiscal burden. For this reason, whenever the tax was rescinded, many municipalities soon reinstituted it under a different name. Ending the tax on products of consumption required new sources of revenue, the most obvious candidate for which was real property, the economic bulwark of the urban oligarchies. The resistance of property owners was decisive in the 1856 and 1874 conservative restitutions of the tax on products of consumption. On the other hand, the state Treasury, which was deeply in debt, was also not in a position to renounce the tax, which in 1874 represented 12 percent of regular revenue.[16]

The stamp tax of fixed or proportional fee was assessed on all civil, economic, mercantile, and administrative documents by means of sheets of sealed paper and fixed and detached stamps of different classes and values. These elements constituted "the visible seal that represented the State's guarantee of the authenticity of the objects and documents upon which they had been placed." There was a good deal of chaos surrounding the creation of this tax, and the determination of the different fees. This exaction taxed, at different and fixed rates that were determined in an arbitrary manner, a number of different kinds of documents, such as the issuance of checks, rental contracts, university diplomas, and stock shares. Activities that were subject to the tax were divided into to two broad categories. As a tax on transactions, it was an impost on circulation, comparable to that part of the tax on real property applicable to transactions between living persons, with which it overlapped. On the other hand, as a payment to defray the cost of public services, it was a simple administrative rate or fee. The tax on sugar went back to 1862. Rescinded by Figuerola in 1869, it was reinstituted by Ruiz Gómez in 1872, with a single fixed rate for national, colonial, and foreign sugar (although, in practice, national producers were at an advantage, given that they collaborated with the administration regarding collection of the tax). Among the minor exactions on transport, that which taxed railway tickets deserves special mention. This tax originated in 1864, with the taxes on loading and unloading merchandise, and on the embarking and disembarking of passengers on maritime transport, and arose from the combination of various taxes in 1868 and 1874.[17]

By 1878, the tax system could fairly be characterized as rigid, given the weight of direct taxes on products and the use of the quota, the tax base of which was not adjusted to the real income of taxpayers, and the returns of which were not adapted to the increasing diversification of productive activity. These defects required a continual revision of legislation in order to reinforce income and integrate new economic activities. On the other hand, the taxpayers themselves managed the division and collection of the majority of these taxes: directly in the case of those that were collected by means of a standing agreement or collaboration with guilds (e.g., the industrial tax, the sugar tax) and indirectly in the case of those exactions whose division was managed by local governments (e.g., the territorial tax, the division of the tax on products of consumption). This was because the largest contributors of each locality controlled the municipal councils that were responsible for carrying out the division.[18]

The state hardly exercised any control over the major taxes. On the other hand, given the unreliability of their fiscal data, the state also did not exactly know the sources of wealth that ought to be taxed. In this regard, the 1901 statement of José Manuel Piernas Hurtado is compelling: "Direct contributions required data that were not available in 1845 but, fifty years later, we have only been able to gather minimal additional data regarding the notoriously unreliable matter of taxable wealth. And this is worse than haven´t none." The involvement of contributors in the collection and division of the fiscal burden, the stunted development of the tax administration, and the lack of reliable data were all conducive to a high level of concealment and fraud. Of course, not all citizens had the same opportunity to commit fraud, given that the construction of the liberal state on the foundation of hierarchical connections of mutual support meant that fraud was enabled by social and political influence. In the words of Francisco Comín Comín, "taxes were not paid by those who, by virtue of the constitution and tax law, were obliged to pay them, but instead by those who lacked political influence." Under such conditions, it was difficult to combat the deficit and achieve the liberal tax policy ideal of a balanced budget. Governments tended to compensate for the rigidity of the tax system by becoming indebted and resorting to requests for credits from the Banco de España. However, this policy proved counterproductive in the medium term, because it meant having to dedicate an ever-increasing part of the budget to payments on the debt thus acquired, and the inflation resulting from the process of the monetization of the deficit devalued revenues.[19]

Last but not least, agricultural income carried the greatest tax burden, due to the scant revenues generated by the industrial and commercial taxes and the absence of sufficient fiscal pressure on both movable assets (which were reduced to little more than the minor stamp and real property taxes) and on income from labor (limited to the deduction from salaries of government functionaries of the tax on salaries and allowances). An example of this is the fact that, in 1874, the territorial tax contributed 23 percent of regular revenues, while the industrial tax contributed 4 percent. However, the fiscal burden on agriculture was even greater, given that a portion of the products that were subject to the tax on products of consumption were agricultural. Moreover, in many small towns, the latter tax was collected by means of a general division that was determined in a manner similar to that employed for the territorial tax. In 1887, Finance Minister Vicente López Puigcerver recognized that the tax on products of consumption, "because of the prevailing conditions of the majority of the rural population, loses. . . its indirect character, which is something intrinsic to it, and instead becomes a direct tax that often functions as a new charge assessed upon territorial wealth." For this reason, Rafael Vallejo has pointed out that, together with the tax on real estate, the tax on products of consumption represented "a double encumbrance on agricultural production." This imbalance of agricultural and industrial revenues to the contribution of State resources was, on the other hand, a faithful reflection of the weight of the former on economic activity as a whole.[20]

The Economic Agreement in the Context of Spanish Fiscal Policy of the Nineteenth Century

The Basque Economic Agreement of 1878 was a response to common practices in the Spanish tax systems of the nineteenth century. In the face of the absence of an effective fiscal administration, a quota, or lump sum, was assigned to local administrations that assumed responsibility for the collection of a tax. This is what happened with the territorial tax, regarding which the state determined a quota or general quantity that the tax was to supply, and this quantity was then assigned to the provinces, which in turn delegated it to local governments. The same thing occurred with the tax on products of consumption, which in the majority of cases were collected by local governments, which then paid the state a quota estimated on the basis of the number of inhabitants of the locality, and the mean consumption of each product taxed. In addition, given the reality of the lack of development of the fiscal administration, it was also frequently the case that taxpayers themselves managed the collection of certain taxes. This was the case for the industrial tax, which was collected by guilds of tradesmen, businessmen, and owners of industries, and paid as a lump sum to the state. It was also the case for the sugar tax, the total amount of which was agreed upon with sugar manufacturers. In its origins, the Basque Economic Agreement was similarly structured. Because the *fueros* had been in force for centuries, the treasury of the relatively new liberal state had never penetrated the Basque provinces (territories that were, moreover, largely rural in character, sparsely populated, and relatively poor). Thus, the finance ministers opted for a practice that was rooted in the tax system: demanding a quota from local institutions, which would be responsible for collecting the taxes.

With the passage of time, however, the Basque provinces would obtain a clear advantage over the rest of the Spanish nation, as a result of the Agreement coming to be seen as a permanent alliance. The decree of 1878 declared that the system enshrined in the agreement would be provisional, since it had been concluded in the absence of knowledge of the tax base of the Basque territories, which had until then not been subject to the fiscal administration of the state. Thus, it was to remain in force for only eight years. In spite of this, the Agreement was periodically renewed, surviving in Bizkaia and Gipuzkoa until 1937 and in Araba until the present time. On the other hand, the decree of 1878 indicated that any new contribution or tax would also be established in the Basque provinces and that it was the government's responsibility to determine the quantity that was to be contributed, after "first having consulted with the Deputations." However, from the very beginning, the right of consultation was interpreted as the right of veto. Thus, the state did not proceed without the consent of the Deputations, and every negotiation to renew the Agreement, or to extend the effect of the tax reforms to the Basque Country, resulted in a pitched battle between the provinces and the state—a battle from which, in the majority of cases, the Basques emerged victorious. This can clearly be seen in the renewals negotiated by López Puigcerver (1887) and Germán Gamazo (1894). Finally, to the extent that a fixed quantity was handed over, the real contribution of the Basque Deputations notably decreased in times of economic growth or inflation. In sum, as Alonso Olea has written, the Agreement assured the Basque provinces of "a regimen of economic and administrative autonomy of unspecified limits," and this resulted in "a very good deal for the Deputations."[21]

The policy aimed at "establishing fiscal unity throughout Spanish territory" (in the words of Serrano Sanz) was also extended in the Budget Law of 1876–77 to relations of the Spanish State with the province of Navarre. Under the terms of the Partnership Law of 1841, Navarre provided the State a fixed and unalterable quota (or foral contribution) calculated at 1,350,000 pesetas (which the Budget Law of 1877 increased to two million pesetas, to account for the incorporation of the territorial contribution). As in the Basque case, the 1841 law envisaged that the state would consult the provincial Deputation prior to incorporating any new contribution to the quota regimen. Also similar to the State's arrangements with the Basque provinces was the fact that, under the terms of the accord with Navarre, the right of consultation came to be seen as a de facto right of veto. This is something that Germán Gamazo realized in 1893 when he tried to unilaterally add new taxes to the Navarre accord, and found himself forced to resign when his offensive was met with bitter opposition on the part of the *foralistas*. Although it is certainly true that the first governments of the Restoration extended some tax obligations to the old territories of the *fueros*, the fact remains that, in the words of Joseba de la Torre, by the end of the nineteenth century, a Basque or Navarran citizen was paying one-third of the taxes of other Spanish citizens.[22]

Endnotes

1. The text of decree and its renewals can be found in *Intervención General de la Administración del Estado, Estadística de los Presupuestos Generales del Estado y de los resultados que ha ofrecido su liquidación: Años 1890–91 a 1907*, Madrid, Imprenta de la sucesora de M. Minuesa de los Ríos, 1909, 501 ff. For negotiations pertaining to the drafting of the decree and its renewals, see Eduardo J. Alonso Olea, *El Concierto Económico (1878–1937): Orígenes y formación de un Derecho histórico* (Oñati: IVAP, 1995), 81 ff., and Eduardo J. Alonso Olea, "La reforma de Fernández Villaverde y las haciendas concertadas," *Hacienda Pública Española*, no. 1999 (1999). 203–220
2. For the reform tradition, see Josep Fontana, *La hacienda en la historia de España, 1700–1931* (Madrid: Instituto de Estudios Fiscales, 1980), 31 ff. For the collective authorship of the reform, see Fabián Estapé Rodríguez, *La Reforma tributaria de 1845* (Madrid: Instituto de Estudios Fiscales, 1971); Francisco Comín Comín, *Hacienda y economía en la España contemporánea (1800–1936)*, 2 vols. (Madrid: Instituto Estudios Fiscales, 1988); Enrique Fuentes Quintana, *Las reformas tributarias en España: Teoría, historia y propuestas* (Barcelona: Crítica, 1990), 4 ff. Navarre and the Basque provinces were joined in their exceptional status in 1852 by the Canary Islands.
3. For the classification of taxes in France in 1790, see Juan Pan-Montojo, "La imposición indirecta en el sistema tributario de Mon-Santillán," in *Hacienda Pública Española, nº extraordinario, 1996, pp. 101-118*; and Juan Pro Ruiz, "El poder de la tierra: una lectura social del fraude en la contribución de inmuebles, cultivo y ganadería (1845–1936)," in *Hacienda Pública Española, nº. extraordinario, 1994, pp 189-201*. For the classification of direct and indirect taxes, see Francisco Comín Comín, *Historia de la Hacienda pública, I. Europa* (Barcelona: Crítica, 1996), 46 ff., and Fuentes Quintana, *Las reformas tributarias en España*, 364 ff.
4. For the "Latin tax systems," see Fuentes Quintana, *Las reformas tributarias en España,* 353-451. For problems in enforcing the royal tax system, see also Comín Comín, *Hacienda y economía en la España contemporánea (1800–1936)* and Francisco Comin Comin, *Historia de la Hacienda pública, II. España (1808-1995)* Barcelona: Crítica, 1996. For the French influence on the tax system of 1845, see Estapé Rodríguez, *La Reforma tributaria de 1845*; Fuentes Quintana, *Las reformas tributarias en España: Teoría, historia y propuestas*; Pan-Montojo, "La imposición indirecta en el sistema tributario de Mon-Santillán"; and Juan Pro Ruiz, "Las contribuciones de producto 'antiguas'de 1845," in *La reforma de Mon-Santillán, 150 años después, Hacienda Pública Española,* ed. Comín Comín and Vallejo.
5. Fuentes Quintana, *Las reformas tributarias en España,* p. 13. For the influence of the tax system of the *Ancien Regime* on the reform, see J. Zafra, "Inercias fiscales en la reforma de 1845," in *Hacienda Pública Española, nº extraordinario, 1996, pp. 23-39*; J. Zafra, "La Hacienda del Estado liberal y la economía española (1808–1868)" (paper presented at the Ponencia en el Seminario de Historia Económica, Estado, Hacienda y economía en la historia de España: del absolutismo a la democracia actual (siglos XVI–XX), 1999). Among the best studies dedicated in full or part to the tax reform of 1845 are those of Estapé Rodríguez, *La Reforma tributaria de 1845*; Comín, *Hacienda y*

economía en la España contemporánea (1800–1936). Vol. I Fuentes Quintana, *Las reformas tributarias en España*, 4 ff; Francisco Comín Comín and Rafael Vallejo Pousada, "La reforma fiscal de Mon-Santillán desde una perspectiva histórica," *Hacienda Pública Española, nº extraordinario, 1996, pp. 7-20*; and M. Martin Rodriguez, *Análisis económico y revolución liberal en España: Economistas académicos en las Cortes liberales, 1834–1874* (Pamplona: Civitas-Thomson Reuters, 2009). See also Santillán's own memoirs: Ramón Santillán, *Memorias (1815–1856)* (Pamplona: Studium Generale, 1960).

6. For the abolition of the tax on products of consumption of 1855, see J. Martin Niño, "1854: Una fecha en la historia del impuesto de consumos," *Hacienda Pública Española*, no. 69 (1981). For information on Collado, see Comín Comín, *Hacienda y economía en la España contemporánea (1800–1936)*, 450. For taxes on sugar and transportation, see M. Martin Rodriguez, "Del trapiche a la fábrica de azúcar, 1779–1904," in *La cara oculta de la industrialización en España*, ed. J. Nadal and J. Catalán (Madrid: Alianza Editorial, 1994) and, "El impuesto sobre el azúcar de 1899 y su incidencia sobre la industria azucarera," in *Hacienda Pública Española,* nº extraordinario, 1999, pp. 153-164; and Jesús María Valdaliso Gago, "La reforma de los impuestos sobre el transporte," in *Hacienda Pública Española,* nº extraordinario, 1999, pp. 137-152. For the tax on salaries and allowances, see J. Martin Niño, *La Hacienda Española y la Revolución de 1868* (Madrid: IEF, 1972), 199 ff.

7. This is a simple summary of the tax policy during the six-year democratic period. A more detailed analysis can be found in Martín Niño (1972) and Costas (1988, 1996). On the Figuerola duty. See Gabriel Tortella, *El desarrollo de la España contemporánea: Historia económica de los siglos XIX y XX* (Madrid: Alianza, 1994), 171. For the reintroduction of the tax on products of consumption by municipalities, see Gregorio L. de la Fuente Monge, "Las elites políticas ante el conflicto fiscal durante la revolución española de 1868," in *La reforma de Mon-Santillán, 150 años después,* ed. Francisco Comín Comín and Rafael Vallejo, *Hacienda Públia Española*, no. 1996.

8. For the statistics and evolution of the deficit, see Comín Comín, *Hacienda y economía en la España contemporánea (1800–1936)*, 299. For a review of Figuerola's policy, see Martin Niño, *La Hacienda Española y la Revolución de 1868*, and Antón Costas Comesaña, "Las reformas impositivas de la Revolución Liberal de 1868: ¿cambio o continuidad al sistema de 1845?," in *La reforma de Mon-Santillán, 150 años después.*

9. For issuing monopolies, see Rafael Anes Alvarez, "El Banco de España (1874–1914): Un banco nacional," in *La Banca Española en la Restauración: Datos para una Historia económica*, ed. G. Tortella (Madrid: Servicio de Estudios del Banco de España, 1974); Rafael Anes Alvarez, "El Banco de España, la Deuda Pública y la política monetaria entre 1874 y 1914," in *La formación de los bancos centrales en España y América Latina (Siglos XIX y XX)*, ed. P. Marichal, and C. Tedde (Madrid: Servicio de Estudios del Banco de España, 1994); Pablo Martin Aceña, "La política monetaria durante la Restauración, 1874–1914," in *La España de la Restauración: Política, economía, legislación y cultura*, ed. José Luis García Delgado (Madrid: Siglo XXI, 1985); Pablo Martin Aceña, "Desarrollo y modernización del sistema financiero, 1844–1935," in *La modernización económica de España*, ed. N. Sánchez Albornoz (Madrid: Alianza, 1987); Comín

Comín, *Hacienda y economía en la España contemporánea (1800–1936)*; Francisco Comín Comín, "El arreglo de la deuda: la pieza clave de la política de nivelación de Villaverde," in *Hacienda Pública Española, nº extraordinario, 1999, pp.105-177*. For the stamp applied to sales, see J. M. Serrano Sanz, *Los Presupuestos de la Restauración (1875–1895)* (Madrid: IEF, 1987), 45. For the re-institution of the tax on products of consumption, see Miguel Artola Gallego, *Hacienda del siglo XIX: Progresistas y moderados* (Madrid: Alianza, 1986).
10. For more on this tax see, among others, G. García-Badell, *El catastro de riqueza rústica en España* (Madrid: Ministerio de Agricultura, 1944); J. A. García Martín and Fernández Muro, "Historia del régimen tributario de la agricultura en España," *Anales de Economía*, no. 12 (1971). Estapé Rodríguez, *La Reforma tributaria de 1845*; Francisco Comín Comín, "Las transformaciones tributarias en la España del siglo XIX y XX," *Hacienda Pública Española*, no. 108/109 (1987); Comín Comín, *Hacienda y economía en la España contemporánea (1800–1936)*; Pro Ruiz, "El poder de la tierra: una lectura social del fraude en la contribución de inmuebles, cultivo y ganadería (1845–1936)"; Pro Ruiz, "Las contribuciones de producto `antiguas´de 1845;" Rafael Vallejo Pousada, *Reforma tributaria y fiscalidad sobre la agricultura en la España liberal, 1845–1900* (Zaragoza: Prensas Universitarias de Zaragoza, 2001); Rafael Vallejo Pousada, "El Impuesto de Consumos y la resistencia antifiscal en la España de la segunda mitad del siglo XIX: un impuesto no exclusivamente urbano," *Revista de Historia Económica*, 14**,** (Spring–Summer 1996)**:** 339-370; Gabino Bugallal, in *DSC-CD*, November 8, 1915, no. 3, p. 34. For distribution and local political favors, see José Varela Ortega, *Los amigos políticos: Partidos, elecciones y caciquismo en la Restauración (1875–1900)* (Madrid: Alianza, 1977).
11. Regarding fraud, see Pro Ruiz, "El poder de la tierra: una lectura social del fraude en la contribución de inmuebles, cultivo y ganadería (1845–1936)"; Francisco Comín Comín, "Corrupción y fraude en la España contemporánea," in *Instituciones y corrupción en la historia*, ed. M. González Jiménez, H. Pietschmann, F. Comín, and J. Pérez (Valladolid: Instituto Universitario de Historia Simancas, 1998).
12. The appointments proceed of Saulo Quereizaeta, *Economía política y Legislación de Hacienda (Obra ajustada al programa de oposiciones a ingreso en el Cuerpo de Abogados del Estado de 31 de julio de 1924)* (Madrid: Reus, 1925), 237. Villaverde's appointment comes from L. V. Paret, *Modificaciones que en el actual sistema tributario exigen las condiciones de la vida social moderna* (Madrid, 1918), 83, 143. On the industrial contribution, see Paret, *Modificaciones que en el actual sistema tributario exigen las condiciones de la vida social moderna*, 71ff; Estapé Rodríguez, *La Reforma tributaria de 1845*, vol. 1; Corella Aznárez, "La tarifa tercera de la Contribución Industrial desde la reforma de Mon a la reforma de Villaverde," *Hacienda Pública Española*, no. 45 (1977); Fuentes Quintana, *Las reformas tributarias en España*; Comín Comín, *Hacienda y economía en la España contemporánea (1800–1936)*; Comín Comín, "La reforma fiscal de Mon-Santillán desde una perspectiva histórica"; and Pro Ruiz, "Las contribuciones de producto 'antiguas'de 1845."
13. For the tax on real property, see J. Marañón and F. Campuzano, *Legislación del Impuesto de derechos reales y transmisión de bienes* (Madrid, 1929); L. Beltrán, "Sobre la historia de los impuestos sucesorios en España," *Moneda*

y crédito, no. 10 (1944); F. Benítez de Lugo, "Evolución histórica de los impuestos sobre las sucesiones y sobre las transmisiones patrimoniales y actos jurídicos documentados," *Hacienda Pública Española* no. 2 (1970): 73–97; Fabián Estapé Rodríguez, *La Reforma tributaria de 1845,* and C. Sarmiento Uceda, "Impuesto General de Sucesiones: 1900–1976 sobre las herencias y su tributación," *Hacienda Pública Española,* no. 46 (1977). On the tax for personal registration cards, see Paret, *Modificaciones que en el actual sistema tributario exigen las condiciones de la vida social moderna.* For mining taxes, see Ignacio Villota Elejalde, *Vizcaya en la política minera española: Las asociaciones patronales, 1886–1914* (Bilbao: Servicio de Publicaciones de la Diputación Foral de Vizcaya, 1984) and Antonio Escudero, *Minería e industrialización de Vizcaya* (Barcelona: University of Alicante–Crítica, 1998).

14. The *encabezamiento* consisted of the cession of administration to local governments in exchange for a lump sum calculated on the basis of the number of inhabitants and mean consumption of each taxed item.

15. For information regarding collection of the tax, see Juan Pan-Montojo, "Lógica legal y lógica social de la Contribución de consumos y los derechos de puertas," in *Hacienda Pública Española, núm. Extraordinario,* 1994, pp. 217-229; and Vallejo Pousada, "El Impuesto de Consumos y la resistencia antifiscal en la España de la segunda mitad del siglo XIX: un impuesto no exclusivamente urbano," 343. For the tax on products of consumption, see also the following: *Comisión extraparlamentaria para la transformación del impuesto de Consumos: Dictamen de la ponencia* (Madrid: Imp. Sucesora M. Minuesa, 1906); J.R. Álvarez Rendueles, "Antonio Flores de Lemus y la Comisión extraparlamentaria para la transformación del Impuesto de Consumos," *Hacienda Pública Española,* no. 42–43 (1976); E. Domingo Solans, "La reforma de la Hacienda municipal de Flores de Lemus," *Hacienda Pública Española,* no. 42–43 (1976); Martin Niño, "1854: Una fecha en la historia del impuesto de consumos"; Joaquin del Moral Ruiz, *Hacienda central y haciendas locales en España: 1845–1905* (Madrid: Instituto de Estudios de Administración Local, 1984); and Miguel Martorell Linares, "La reforma pendiente: La Hacienda Municipal en la Crisis de la Restauración: El fracaso de la Ley de Supresión del Impuesto de Consumos," *Hacienda Pública Española,* no. 132 (1995).

16. For protests against the tax on products of consumption, see D. Castro Alfín, "Agitación y orden en la Restauración. ¿Fin del ciclo revolucionario?," *Historia Social,* no. 5 (1989): 37–43; Rafael Vallejo Pousada, "Pervivencia de las formas tradicionales de protesta: los motines de 1892," *Historia Social,* no. 8 (1990): 3–27; Vallejo Pousada, "El Impuesto de Consumos y la resistencia antifiscal en la España de la segunda mitad del siglo XIX: un impuesto no exclusivamente urbano." Regarding fraud, see Pan-Montojo, "Lógica legal y lógica social de la Contribución de consumos y los derechos de puertas"; and Rafael Vallejo Pousada, "Fiscalidad y fraude fiscal en Galicia en la segunda mitad del siglo XIX," in *Hacienda Pública Española, nº extraordinario, 1994, pp. 263-279.* For a discussion of the rescinding of the tax in 1855 and 1868, see Martin Niño, "1854: Una fecha en la historia del impuesto de consumos"; and Martorell Linares, "La reforma pendiente: La Hacienda Municipal en la Crisis de la Restauración: El fracaso de la Ley de Supresión del Impuesto de Consumos."

17. The quotes regarding the stamp tax are from Quereizaeta, *Economía*

política y Legislación de Hacienda, 542; and Paret, *Modificaciones que en el actual sistema tributario exigen las condiciones de la vida social moderna*, 145. See also F. Benítez De Lugo, "Evolución histórica de los impuestos sobre las sucesiones y sobre las transmisiones patrimoniales y actos jurídicos documentados," *Hacienda Pública Española*, no. 2 (1970). For the sugar and transport taxes, see Martin Rodriguez, "El impuesto sobre el azúcar de 1899 y su incidencia sobre la industria azucarera"; and Valdaliso Gago, "La reforma de los impuestos sobre el transporte."

18. For the participation of taxpayers in the process of dividing the primary taxes, see Pro Ruiz, "Las contribuciones de producto 'antiguas' de 1845," 131.

19. J. Piernas Hurtado, *Tratado de Hacienda pública y exámen de la española*, 5th ed., 2 vols. (Madrid: Victoriano Suarez, 1900–1901), vol. II, p. 264. For fiscal fraud, see *Hacienda Pública Española*, nº extraordinario, 1994; and Comín Comín, "Corrupción y fraude en la España contemporánea," 82. For political favors and involvement in unjust division of fiscal burden, see Javier Moreno Luzon, "'El poder público hecho cisco': Clientes e instituciones políticas en la España de la Restauración," in *Política en penumbra. Patronazgo y clientelismo políticos en la España contemporánea*, ed. Antonio Robles Egea (Madrid: Siglo XXI, 1996), 169 ff. For repercussions regarding the monetization of the deficit, see Fuentes Quintana, *Las reformas tributarias en España*, 40 ff.; and Comín Comín, "El arreglo de la deuda: la pieza clave de la política de nivelación de Villaverde."

20. López Puigcerver quote in E. Vincenti, *Proyectos de Hacienda. Estudio relativo al proyecto del Sr. ministro de Hacienda sobre la Contribución rústica y pecuaria, cédulas personales y cupos de consumo* (Madrid, 1888), 9. Vallejo Pousada, "El Impuesto de Consumos y la resistencia antifiscal en la España de la segunda mitad del siglo XIX," 366. See also Comín Comín, *Hacienda y economía en la España contemporánea (1800–1936).*

21. Alonso Olea, *El Concierto Económico (1878–1937)*, 424.

22. J. M. Serrano Sanz, *El viraje proteccionista en la Restauración; La política comercial española, 1875–1895* (Madrid: Siglo XXI, 1987), 40. For the Navarre accord, see Intervención General de la Administración del Estado, *Estadística de los Presupuestos Generales del Estado y e los resultados que ha ofrecido su iquidación. Años 1890–91 a 1907* 506 ff.; Joseba De La Torre, "Hacienda foral y crecimiento edonómico en Navarra durante el siglo XIX," in *Navarra siglo XIX: Cien años de Historia* (Pamplona: Caja Laboral, 1994), 149 ff.; and Joseba de la Torre and Mario Garcia-Zuñiga, "Hacienda foral y crecimiento económico en Navarra durante el siglo XIX," in *Hacienda y crecimiento económico: La Reforma de Mon, 150 años después*, ed. Joseba de la Torre and Mario Garcia-Zuñiga (Madrid: Gobierno de Navarra-Marcial Pons, 1998). For Germán Gamazo's role, see Angel Garcia-Sanz Marcotegui, "La insurrección fuerista de 1893: Foralismo oficial versus foralismo popular durante la Gamazada," *Príncipe de Viana*, no. 185 (1988).

Bibliography

Alonso Olea, E. J. *El Concierto Económico (1878–1937): Orígenes y formación de un derecho histórico*. Oñati, IVAP, 1995.

———. "La reforma de Fernández Villaverde y las haciendas concertadas." In *Hacienda pública Española*, nº extraordinario, 1999, 203–20.

Álvarez Rendueles, J. R. "Antonio Flores de Lemus y la Comisión extraparlamentaria para la transformación del Impuesto de Consumos." *Hacienda Pública Española*, no. 42–43 (1976): 213–28.

Anes Álvarez, R. "El Banco de España (1874–1914): Un banco nacional." In *La Banca Española en la Restauración: Datos para una Historia económica*, volume 1, directed by G. Tortella, 107–217. Madrid: Servicio de Estudios del Banco de España 1974.

———. "El Banco de España, la Deuda Pública y la política monetaria entre 1874 y 1914." In *La formación de los bancos centrales en España y América Latina (Siglos XIX y XX)*. Edited by P. Tedde and C. Marichal, 109–121. Madrid: Servicio de Estudios del Banco de España, 1994.

Artola, M. *La Hacienda del siglo XIX: Progresistas y moderados*. Madrid: Alianza, 1986.

Beltrán, L. "Sobre la historia de los impuestos sucesorios en España." *Moneda y Crédito* no. 10 (1944): 47–62.

Benítez de Lugo, F. "Evolución histórica de los impuestos sobre las sucesiones y sobre las transmisiones patrimoniales y actos jurídicos documentados." *Hacienda Pública Española* no. 2 (1970): 73–97.

Bernis, F. *La Hacienda española: Los impuestos; Como son en España; Como son en otras haciendas; Como deben ser en la nuestra*. Barcelona: n.d.

Castro Alfín, D. "Agitación y orden en la Restauración: ¿Fin del ciclo revolucionario?" *Historia Social*, no. 5 (Fall, 1989): 37–51.

Comín, F. *Hacienda y Economía en la España contemporánea*. Madrid: Instítuto de Estudios Fiscales, 1988.

———. *Historia de la Hacienda Pública, I: Europa*. Barcelona, Crítica, 1996.

———. "Corrupción y fraude en la España contemporánea." In *Instituciones y corrupción en la historia*, edited by M. González Jiménez, H. Pietschmann, F. Comín, and J. Pérez, 53–111. Valladolid: Instituto Universitario de Historia Simancas, 1998.

———. "El arreglo de la deuda: La pieza clave de la política de nivelación de Villaverde." In *Hacienda pública Española, nº extraordinario, 1999*, 105–17.

Comín, F., and R. Vallejo, eds. *La reforma de Mon-Santillán, 150 años después, Hacienda Pública Española*, nº extraordinario, 1996.

Comín, F., and J. Zafra, eds. *El fraude fiscal en la Historia de España: Hacienda Pública Española*, nº extraordinario, 1994.

Comisión Extraparlamentaria de Consumos. *Actas y trabajos*, Madrid, n.d.

Costas Comesaña, A. *Apogeo del liberalismo en "La Gloriosa": La reforma económica del Sexenio liberal*, Madrid, Siglo XXI, 1988.

———. "Las reformas impositivas de la Revolución Liberal de 1868: ¿Cambio o continuidad respecto al sistema de 1845?" In *Hacienda pública Española*, nº extraordinario, 1996, 227–38.

Corella Aznárez, I. "La tarifa tercera de la Contribución Industrial desde la re- forma de Mon a la reforma de Villaverde", *Hacienda Pública Española*, no. 45 (1977): 59–82.

Dobado González, R. "Algunas consideraciones acerca del Estado y la minería en España", *Hacienda pública Española,* nº extraordinario, 1994, 177–88.

Domingo Solans, E. "La reforma de la Hacienda municipal de Flores de Lemus." *Hacienda Pública Española*, no. 42–43 (1976): 229–65.

Escudero Gutiérrez, A. "El fraude fiscal en la minería española (1876–1935)." In *Hacienda pública Española,* nº extraordinario, 1994, 321–41.

———. *Minería e industrialización en Vizcaya*. Barcelona: Crítica, 1998.

Estapé Rodríguez, F. *La reforma tributaria de 1845*. Madrid: Instituto de Estudios Fiscales, 1971.

Fontana, J. *La Hacienda en la Historia de España, 1700–1931*. Madrid: Instítuto de Estudios Fiscales, 1980.

Fuentes Quintana, E. *Las reformas tributarias en España*, edited by F. Comín. Barcelona: Crítica 1990.

García-Badell, G. *El catastro de riqueza rústica en España*. Madrid: Ministerio de Agricultura, 1944.

García Martín, J. A., and M. J. Fernández Muro. "Historia del régimen tributario de la agricultura en España." *Anales de Economía* no. 12 (1971): 101–190.

García-Sanz Marcotegui, A. "La insurrección fuerista de 1893: Foralismo oficial versus foralismo popular durante la Gamazada." *Príncipe de Viana* 185 (1988): 659–708.

Intervención General de la Administración del Estado. *Estadística de los Presupuestos Generales del Estado y de los resultados que ha ofrecido su liquidación: Años 1890–91 a 1907*. Madrid, Imprenta de la sucesora de M. Minuesa de los Ríos, 1909.

Marañón, J., and F. Campuzano. *Legislación del Impuesto de derechos reales y transmisión de bienes*. Madrid, Reus, 1929.

Martín Aceña, P. "La política monetaria durante la Restauración, 1874–1914." In *La España de la Restauración. Política, economía, legislación y cultura*, edited by J. L. García Delgado, 171–89. Madrid: Siglo XXI, 1985.

———. "Desarrollo y modernización del sistema financiero, 1844–1935." In *La modernización económica de España*, compiled by N. Sánchez Albornoz, 121–47. Madrid: Alianza, 1987.

Martín Niño, J. *La Hacienda Española y la Revolución de 1868*. Madrid: IEF, 1972.

Martín Rodríguez, M. "Del trapiche a la fábrica de azúcar, 1779–1904." In *La cara oculta de la industrialización en España*, edited by J. Nadal and J. Catalán. Madrid: Alianza Editorial, 1994.

———. "El impuesto sobre el azúcar de 1899 y su incidencia sobre la industria azucarera." In *Hacienda pública Española, nº extraordinario, 1999*, 153–64.

———. *Análisis económico y revolución liberal en España: Economistas académicos en las Cortes liberales, 1834–1874*. Pamplona: Civitas-Thomson Reuters, 2009.

Martorell Linares, M. A. "La reforma pendiente: La Hacienda Municipal en la Crisis de la Restauración; El fracaso de la Ley de Supresión del Impuesto de Consumos." *Hacienda Pública Española*, no. 132 (1995): 143–53.

———. *El santo temor al déficit*. Madrid: Alianza Editorial, 2000.

Moral Ruiz, J. del. *Hacienda central y haciendas locales*. Madrid: Instituto de la Administración Local, 1984.

Moreno Luzón, J. "El poder público hecho cisco: Clientelismo e instituciones políticas en la España de la Restauración." In *Política en penumbra: Patronazgo y clientelismo políticos en la España Contemporánea*, edited by A. Robles Egea, 169–91. Madrid: Siglo XXI, 1996.

Pan-Montojo, J. L. "Lógica legal y lógica social de la Contribución de consumos y los derechos de puertas." In *Hacienda pública Española,* nº extraordinario, 1994, 217–29

———. "La imposición indirecta en el sistema tributario de Mon-Santillán." In *Hacienda pública Española,* nº extraordinario, 1996, 101–18.

Paret, L. V. *Modificaciones que en el actual sistema tributario exigen las condiciones de la vida social moderna*. Madrid: 1918.

Piernas Hurtado, J. *Tratado de Hacienda Pública y examen de la española*. 2 volumes, Madrid: 1901.

Pro Ruiz, J. "El poder de la tierra: Una lectura social del fraude en la contribución de inmuebles, cultivo y ganadería (1845–1936 In *Hacienda pública Española,* nº extraordinario, 1994, pp. 189–201.

———. "Las contribuciones de producto antiguas de 1845." In *Hacienda pública Española*, nº extraordinario, 1996, pp. 119-134.

Quereizaeta, S. *Economía Política y Legislación de Hacienda*. Madrid: Reus, 1925.

Santillán, R. *Memorias (1815–1856)*. Pamplona, Studium Generale, 1960.

Sarmiento Uceda, C. "Impuesto General de Sucesiones: 1900–1976 sobre las herencias y su tributación." *Hacienda Pública Española*, no. 46 (1977): 141–68.

Serrano Sanz, J. M. *Los Presupuestos de la Restauración (1875–1895)*. Madrid: IEF, 1987.

———. *El viraje proteccionista en la Restauración: La política comercial española. 1875–1895*. Madrid: Siglo XXI, 1987.

Torre, J. de la. "Hacienda foral y sistema financiero." In Joseba de la Torre (ed): *Navarra: Siglo XIX; Cien años de historia*, Pamplona, Instituto Gerónimo de Ustariz, 1994, p. 135–55.

Torre, J. de la, and M. García-Zúñiga. "Hacienda foral y reforma tributaria: Navarra, 1841–1876." In *Hacienda pública Española,* nº extraordinario, 1996, 151–165.

Tortella Casares, G. *El desarrollo de la España contemporánea*. Madrid: Alianza, 1994.

Valdaliso, J. M. "La reforma de los impuestos sobre el transporte." In *Hacienda pública Española,* nº extraordinario, 1999, pp. 137–152.

Vallejo Pousada, R. "Pervivencia de las formas tradicionales de protesta: los motines de 1892." *Historia Social* no. 8 (Fall 1990): 3–29.

———. "Fiscalidad y fraude fiscal en Galicia en la segunda mitad del siglo XIX." In *Hacienda pública Española,* nº extraordinario, 1994, pp. 263–79.

———. "El Impuesto de Consumos y la resistencia antifiscal en la España de la segunda mitad del siglo XIX: Un impuesto no exclusivamente urbano." *Revista de Historia Económica* no. 2 (Spring/Summer 1996): 339–70.

Villota Elejalde, J. I. *Vizcaya en la política minera española: Las asociaciones patronales, 1886–1914.* Bilbao: Diputación Foral de Vizcaya, 1984.

Vincenti, E. *Proyectos de Hacienda: Estudio relativo al proyecto del sr. ministro de Hacienda sobre la Contribución rústica y pecuaria, cédulas personales y cupos de consumo.* Madrid, Tip. de Manuel G. Hernández, 1888.

Zafra, J. "Inercias fiscales en la reforma de 1845." In Hacienda pública Española, nº extraordinario, 1996, pp. 7–20.

———. "La Hacienda del Estado liberal y la economía española (1808–1868)." Address at the Seminario de Historia Económica, Estado, Hacienda y economía en la historia de España: del absolutismo a la democracia actual (siglos XVI–XX). Fundación Duques de Soria, Soria, 23 de Julio de 1999.

3

Abolition of the Economic Agreement and Franco's Purge of the Tax Authority Staff of the Deputation of Bizkaia, 1937–1940

Aritz Ipiña Bidaurrazaga

With the city of Bilbao liberated by the National Army after great suffering, the authorities are to now proceed expeditiously in carrying out a purge of the staff of the various public services.
— *Communication from Franco to Bizkaia's Civil Governor, June 25, 1937*

Although a great deal has been written about the repression imposed by Francisco Franco's regime, and the physical violence employed by rebellious elements against the defenders of legally constituted order in February 1936, the current state of research does not provide the data needed to allow an accurate estimate as regards the administrative purges carried out throughout all of Spain, let alone Bizkaia.[1]

The present study does not claim to be an exhaustive analysis of the purges to which the Tax Authority of Bizkaia was subjected, since such an undertaking would require an examination of the files of individual workers and could not possibly be limited to just a few pages. Instead, our intention here is to carry out a study on the purging of staff members on the basis of the sanctions and reinstatements that were decreed, and citing examples of certain functionaries who were purged.

A number of studies have been written since the 1990s regarding the purging of functionaries, with most of these having been authored during the past five years.[2] One of these was authored by Josefina Cuesta and grew out of a conference held in Salamanca in April 2009. Cuesta's book is an indispensable reference, since it includes detailed studies of the functionaries of various state bodies, and also addresses the regulatory and legal bases for the purges that were carried out.[3]

The purges to which teachers were subjected at all levels, from primary education to university, are the best known aspect of this history, due to the many publications regarding the subject throughout Spain.[4]

However, there is a dearth of studies regarding the disciplinary measures that Franco's authorities imposed on employees of the

Basque Deputations, and there are no exhaustive studies regarding this subject. Edward J. Alons, an expert in Basque governmental administration and the Economic Agreement, has written a number of important works dealing with purges of the Cuerpo de Miñones of Bizkaia.[5] For events in Gipuzkoa, we have the work of Pedro Barruso, who among other matters has written about the violence suffered by those working in the Deputation of that province.[6] As for Araba, Santiago de Pablo has authored a comprehensive study of the repression exercised in that province that includes a list of functionaries of its Deputation, the sanction imposed on each worker, and the results of any appeals that were made.[7] Finally, and to round out the modest body of work regarding the subject, we have the presentation of Javier Gómez Calvo to the Congress of Contemporary History in Santander in 2010, which represents the results of a study he carried out as part of his doctoral thesis.[8]

The New Provincial Deputation, the Abolition of the Economic Agreement, and the Beginning of Purges of Tax Authority Staff

On June 21, 1937, two days after the last troops of the Basque Army Corps withdrew from Bilbao to Turtzioz, and the members of the Navarre Brigades entered the city, a new Provincial Deputation of Bizkaia was constituted. This body was presided over by Luis de Llaguno, with Lorenzo Hurtado de Saracho serving as Vice President, and with its deputies appointed by the military authority Ildefonso de Arrola, Miguel Vega y Haro, and Isidoro Delclaux.[9]

The first decisions of the Deputation, on the day that it was constituted, involved transferring the Virgin of Begoña to the Sacred Heart of Jesus and carving the following words on an accompanying plaque:

> I will reign in Spain, to avenge the Patron Saint of Bizkaia for the outrages, sacrilege, and crimes committed by the anarcho-syndicalist hordes, and as an expression of gratitude for the liberation of Bilbao from the red tyranny, and also to hold funerals for the victims murdered by the red hordes in ships, jails, and prisons, as well as for the soul of General Mola.[10]

However, just as in a fine meal, the best was left for last. The final decision that was made on the day of the constitution of the new Deputation was the dismissal of all of the body's employees, while at the same time, the latter were obliged to remain in their positions, and were given four days to request by letter that they be rehired by the Deputation. It was also decided to disseminate the news of this purge as widely as possible through the press and radio of Bilbao, Donostia, and Gasteiz.[11] All of the workers were presumably guilty of having collaborated with Republican authorities and the government of Euskadi. Therefore, from the point of view of the new authorities, it was easier to fire the entire staff, leaving those who believed that they were untainted to request their reincorporation by supplying references of good conduct, instead of opening files on each and every employee and supplying evidence of supposed misconduct. Those who did not request that they be rehired within the four days provided were permanently dismissed for having abandoned their jobs and fleeing to the zone still controlled by the Republic.

This was the beginning of the repression imposed upon individuals by the new Deputation. Then, on June 23, 1937, the territories of Bizkaia and Gipuzkoa were collectively punished when Franco decreed the abolition of the Economic Agreement.[12]

Andrés de Amado Reygonbaud de Villavardet, a state attorney and close collaborator and personal friend of José Calvo Sotelo, and a man who had participated in the renovation of the Agreement in 1926, became the first man to serve as Director of the Treasury of the National Defense Council. With the formation of Franco's first government on January 31, 1938, Villavardet was named minister of finance, a position he held until August 9, 1939, at the time of the formation of Franco's second government. Villavardet had organized the entire complex system of civil war financing on the rebel side.[13] The new authorities thus had firsthand knowledge of the Basque financial system. Therefore, when they decreed its abolition, they were well aware of the adverse effects this action would have on Bizkaia and Gipuzkoa.

The abolition of the Agreement had two different justifications, one political and the other economic. The political justification was based on the accusation that the provinces of Bizkaia and Gipuzkoa had engaged in rebellion. In the language of the decree's preamble, "Gipuzkoa and Bizkaia rose up in arms against the Movimiento Nacional." This was an isolated case of collective punishment of two provinces for supposed political attitudes—this despite the fact that it was well known that not all the inhabitants of Gipuzkoa and Bizkaia had opposed Franco.[14] At the same time, the revocation of the agreement emphasized the affront implicit in a reduced degree of fiscal pressure on the taxpayers of Bizkaia and Gipuzkoa and on the fraud committed against the nation's Treasury.[15]

Araba and Navarre, which had stood together in solidarity with "the true Spaniards" and had contributed a considerable number of soldiers to "the National Cause,"[16] did not have their Economic Agreements revoked. It seems that fiscal fraud was measured in each province on the basis of the color of the berets warn by their combatants.

As a consequence of the revocation of the Agreement, the Deputation lost the ability to collect taxes (a function which was taken over by the state) as well as other services, such as the aforementioned

Cuerpo de Miñones, its provincial school system, and half of its railway network.

The Budget of the Deputation of Bizkaia was dramatically slashed as a consequence of the abolition of the Agreement. The budget of 1935 (the last complete year prior to the outbreak of the Civil War) when the expense budget was 27 million pesetas, and the total allocation exceeded 55 million. In 1940, the first complete year following the end of the war, the total budget, including provisions for special expenses, was only 18 million.[17]

Absolute revenues suffered qualitatively because of the loss of autonomous tax-collection capacity and instead became based, as of the 1950s, on provincial taxes applied to alcoholic beverages and minerals.[18]

On June 25, 1937, Franco ordered Miguel de Ganuza, Civil Governor of Bizkaia, to begin the purge of different provincial institutions.[19] The purge of employees was to take place in accordance with Decree 108 of the National Defense Council,[20] and employees that had left their jobs without being reincorporated within the time allotted by the authorities would be summarily dismissed.

The repressive work against the staff of the tax authority of Bizkaia did not occur immediately. Instead, the first step taken by the newly constituted organization, on June 23, 1937, was that of rehiring six former workers who had previously been fired by the Republican overseers. Among these six individuals was Daniel Olartua Arana, who was named interim director of the authority until the employee with the most seniority (and therefore entitled to assume that post) was reincorporated to the staff.[21] A staff member reincorporated posthumously was Leto Andechaga, who had been killed on January 4, 1937, during an attack on the Los Ángeles Custodios prison, conducted in revenge for the indiscriminate bombing of Bilbao carried out by Nationalist rebels. The raid, on both Los Ángeles Custodios and other city prisons, where hundreds of right-wing inmates were interned, caused more than 200 fatalities.[22]

The month of July began with the dismissal of the man who had been the head of the tax authority during Republican rule, Jesús Zareza. Between June 23 and July 1, an order was issued that he be purged by the provincial corporation. This same order also stipulated that Zareza lose any rights that he had previously acquired as a result of his employment by the province.[23]

The personnel files for purged employees were, until the creation of the Office for Purged Employees, initiated by functionaries with ties to the new regime. Some of these individuals were readmitted to the service of the Deputation (after having been fired by the Republicans) in order to undertake *legal* actions against their former co-workers.

On July 23, 1937, the Deputation nominated Daniel Olartua Arana interim director of the tax authority. He and another employee who had also been fired by the Deputation during Republican rule, Olegario Velasco, were on that same day placed in charge of creating files for personnel to be purged.[24]

These two investigators lost no time and, on that same day, presented their first report about one of their co-workers. The cases that could most easily be presented of hostility to the new authorities and sympathy with Republican ideas concerned those individuals who had not yet shown up in the Deputation and who had also not requested reincorporation into the body. These were employees of the tax authority who were dismissed on July 23, 1937, for noncompliance with rule number two of the decree of June 25[25] because they had abandoned their jobs and had not shown up afterward at the Deputation. Another nine workers were somewhat more fortunate, because their positions with the authority were based in territory still under Republican control. For this reason, the dismissal of these individuals were put on hold until four days after the "liberation" of all of Bizkaia.[26]

The Purging Process: 1937–38

The purging process to which the workers of the tax authority were subjected varied among individual workers, and consisted of various phases, beginning with these workers sending letters to the Deputation requesting their rehiring.

These requests for reinstatement fell into two different categories. Those workers who stayed in their villages when Bilbao fell and sent their letters before the established deadlines, under the assumption that they would be readily accepted back, wrote letters that were short and direct. In these cases, the former employees identified themselves by first and last name and former job positions, and concluded with a simple request to return to work.[27] The second category comprised those employees who had been fired after they had been found not to have shown up to work. These individuals sent requests for readmission following the stipulated deadline and, in addition to providing the basic information supplied by the first group, included an explanation of why they had not previously shown up to work.[28]

Once the reincorporation requests were sent, the second phase began. This involved the Deputation naming an investigator[29] to open a purge file on the individual presumed guilty. This person was then scheduled for an interview with the investigator at a provincial office, where he was required to complete a questionnaire.

This questionnaire, which was titled *Provincial Tax Authorities of*

Bizkaia,[30] was similar to others that had to be answered by other employees of the Deputation31 and consisted of five questions.

The first question asked if the worker had collaborated with the Defense Council of Bizkaia or the Government of Valencia32 and against the Movimiento Nacional. As one might expect, all of the files that have thus far been consulted contained negative answers to this question.

The second question is a follow-up of the first, asking if the accused had engaged in anti-patriotic activities against the Movimiento Nacional. Logically, these questions were also answered in the negative.

The third question inquired as to whether the accused had any political or union affiliation prior to July 19, 1936. The responses to this question were more varied than the previous two, with some respondents denying any affiliation at all and others acknowledging that they had belonged to unions and political parties (as was the case for the fired tax collectors Enrique Zorrozua Ilardia, who was affiliated with, and who had voted for, the EAJ-PNV; and Juan Pages Rico, who had been affiliated with Izquierda Republicana[33]).

The fourth question, which was similar to the third, asked if there were any political or union affiliation after the date of July 19, 1936. In addition to responses denying any political or union affiliation, we also find a number of acknowledgements, such as that of Pedro Contreras, of continued payment of membership dues to the EAJ-PNV.[34] This was not the only means of inquiring into the histories of members of the Tax Authority. In addition, when Franco's troops entered Bilbao, a good deal of documentary material was confiscated which made the purging work easier. This was the case for Francisco Álvarez Seisdedos, whom documents revealed to have not attended to his job duties since July 25, 1936, because he was after that time under the orders of the "Frente Popular" and the Municipal Council of the Izquierda Repúblicana of Bilbao.[35]

The fifth and final item was an open-ended invitation to the respondent to add anything that he deemed appropriate (presumably in his defense).

After the declaration had been made to the investigator, the third phase of the purging process began. This consisted of each side, accused and accuser, presenting the necessary witnesses supporting either defense or sanction of the individual being investigated.

These witnesses had a variety of different affiliations, from public institutions, the sole official political party (i.e., the *Falange*), persons with some kind of religious affiliation, or simply private individuals who made themselves available to either support or refute the claim of the accused.

Those witnesses affiliated with public institutions were sent to present evidence from the towns where the accused had been born or where they had worked. They presented the ties of the worker in question with the witness and provided reports regarding his conduct. These reports sometimes merely dealt with the accused's behavior during the period of Republican rule. At other times, such information was supplemented with data regarding his political and moral conduct. The interim mayor of Bermeo, Ciriaco Gervasio Barturen, collaborated in the purging process for Pedro Contreras, sending the required "sociopolitical report" in which he accused him of being a Republican sympathizer and of being affiliated with the leftist UGT union. In Contreras's defense, however, Gervasio noted that he had not been involved in any activity either before or after July 18.[36]

Those reports of witnesses who were members of the *Falange* also made reference to the behavior and political ideology of the accused prior to the war. One example is seen in those reports sent by the Research and Information Office of the *Falange* of Guecho regarding Ildefonso Ormaechea, which provided proof that the accused distanced himself from any political attitude favoring individuals affiliated with right-wing forces who were subject to persecution by the Popular Front and indicated that he also refrained from providing economic assistance to the prisoners of Larrinaga.[37]

The information for purging the personnel of the tax authority, as well as the rest of the functionaries of the Deputation, was not only based on communications from governmental bodies. In addition, data provided by civilian sources (e.g., neighbors, friends, co-workers) was of fundamental importance in determining the fate of the accused. Denunciations from citizens and co-workers (as in the case of the *Miñones de Bizkaia*) were provided in the majority of cases involving purged employees. Such denunciations were not only not questioned by the authorities, but were ipso facto accepted as true, even if the information supplied was on the face of it banal and not particularly incriminating, as we will now see.

Julio García and Ángel Torquemada, both residents of Las Arenas, appeared separately before Olegario Velasco, inspector for the case of Ildefonso Ormaechea, on August 20–21, 1937. The two witnesses indicated that, on various occasions, they had heard the man shouting outrageous language against the National Army, that they had seen Ormaechea in the company of separatists, and that they had seen the accused, as well as his wife and children, ostentatiously waving the flag of the separatists and even demonstrating against Spain and its army.[38] Torquemada reported that he had heard the accused shouting against the National Army in the provincial savings bank and that the accused had declared that the soldiers of this army were murderers who had bombed Guernica, that the Nationalists had sold us out to foreigners, and the Nationalists would only be able to rule over his dead body.[39] Accusations of this kind, which allowed no possibility of determining the guilt of the accused, were common in the purging process that was carried out by the new authorities of Franco's regime, given that the accused did not benefit from the presumption of innocence, but were instead burdened with the presumption of guilt.

Those individuals who were purged were forced to take advantage of loopholes in the law that allowed them to produce their own corroborating witnesses. For this reason, when it was possible for them to find someone willing to fill such a role (since, of course, not everyone had the courage to stand up in defense of someone presumed guilty in the middle of a massive purge), this person would present favorable reports of the accused's political, moral, and work conduct. Because this was not a common occurrence, I'd like to emphasize the sixty-four signatures of residents of Las Arenas belonging to the Movimiento Nacional who vouched not only for Ildefonso Ormaechea's unimpeachable conduct and impeccably correct behavior in the performance of his duties, but also to his having provided assistance without shirking his duties, something that won him sympathy among those in the Movimiento NacionalMovimiento Nacional.[40]

Once the information-gathering process was completed by the investigator of the case of the individual to be purged, the investigator had to propose to the Deputation the punishment that he deemed fit. The provincial deputies were responsible for ratifying any punishment imposed, although in some cases these deputies increased or decreased the punishment recommended by the investigator, or sent the case back to him to collect more evidence, as occurred with Santiago Beascoechea y Goiri on April 13, 1938.[41]

The Office for Purging Staff was created on October 21, 1937, in the middle of the purging process of employees of the Deputation, and was intended as a temporary measure until such time as its work was completed.[42] Its function included initiating, processing, and reporting on the cases of staff to be purged, and which the Deputation assigned it (and also of bringing to a conclusion those cases that had already been initiated prior to the creation of the office. Thus, as of the date of the office's creation, it was assigned the purging of employees of the tax authority. Fernando de Echegaray was named director of the office, and he was paid a monthly salary of 625 pesetas.

Sanctions and Reinstatements

The documentary evidence that has been examined thus far[43] indicates that when the new provincial authorities decreed the dismissals of all of their employees on June 21, 1937, the Tax Authority had a total of ninety-nine active staff members (plus one who had been murdered in prison on January 4 of that same year). All of these employees were men.[44]

The sanctions and reinstatements of the employees did not all take place on the same day, but instead occurred as purge files were processed and decided upon by investigators or the Office for Purging Staff. Condemnations or acquittals for all ninety-nine active employees had concluded by June 30, 1938, nearly one year after the process had begun.

Yet this date did not signal the definitive end of the process of purging the tax authority, since some of the persons who had been fired embarked upon a long process of appeals, or struggles to gain recognition of their retirement benefits—a process that ended up being decided by the Ministry of the Interior.[45] Thus, the final cases were not definitively ruled upon until either the 1940s[46] or the 1950s.[47]

The resolution of cases of purging is summarized in table 3.1,

Table 3.1. First Resolution on Members Dismissed and Reinstated between June 23, 1937 and June 30, 1938

	Number affected
Members dismissed with loss of all rights due to provincial employees	62
Members reinstated with a warning or financial and/or labor penalty	13
Members reinstated without any penalty	36
Total	111

Source: Data from acts and purges files. A. F. B. Sección Adm. AJ-00808/001, AJ-00809/001, and boxAJ-02550.

which provides a quick and simple method of categorization.

The first resolutions that were issued by investigators of cases, and by the Office of Employee Purges, and then subsequently approved by the Deputation, revealed that 55.8 percent of staff had been purged. This was, without doubt, a high percentage. But these were not the only employees who were sanctioned, given that some kind of economic or work sanction was imposed on 11.7 percent of staff. These sanctions included the loss of five-year salary increases, rights to promotion and associated benefits; in addition to receiving warnings and reprimands. If we sum these percentages, then it is revealed that 67.5 percent of staff suffered some kind of sanction in the first resolution of their cases.

There were two different reasons used to justify dismissing those employees who were fired. Twenty-five individuals were thus punished for not showing up to work on the date stipulated by the new authorities, while the remaining thirty-three were terminated as a result of rulings issued for their particular cases (specifically, for being considered hostile to the Movimiento Nacional because they belonged to particular political parties or unions, because they had voted for parties of the Popular Front or the EAJ-PNV, proffered insults against the army, or had provided economic assistance to cultural organizations holding a Basque nationalist ideology).[48]

Some of the terminated employees who were accused of not showing up to work on the stipulated date requested reinstatement to their positions. Of this group, five were reinstated upon appeal between May 31 and June 10, 1938, because their absences were found to be justified.[49]

Newly Hired Employees of the Tax Authority: 1937–39

With the abolition of the Economic Agreement, the collection capacity of the Deputation came to an end, and this function devolved to some extent on the provincial Staff of the Tax Consumptions (i.e., the Cuerpo de Arbitrios). Thus, the firing of twenty-five collectors and the effective disappearance of another nine (who were in Republican-controlled territory) reduced the collection capacity of this latter body.

The Deputation was similarly affected, and for this reason announced the hiring on July 23, 1937, on a strictly temporary basis, of twenty-five additional employees to cover the positions that had been left vacant as a result of the mass firings of that same day. The intention of the Deputation was to reserve these positions for individuals who had actively supported the Movimiento Nacional, or who had "suffered for the nation." Those new employees who were selected earned annual salaries of 3,000 pesetas and were required to first pass a skills test that was devised by the Deputation.[50]

Many of the employees of the abolished provincial militia (Cuerpo de Miñones[51]) of Bizkaia were reinstated between 1937 and 1939 as part of the purging process. One of the many duties of the provincial militia had been collections and the prosecution of fraudulent tax claims. Thus, this body, and especially its most senior members, were well familiar with this kind of work.[52]

On October 21, 1937, five individuals were newly hired by the Staff of the Tax Consumptions of Bizkaia.[53] Later, on December 17 of that same year, another seventeen former members of the Cuerpo de Miñones were named officials of said authority on a temporary basis *for the purpose of assuming responsibility for taxes on spirits.*[54] And the hiring of new employees did not stop there, for on August 17, 1939, another four former members of the Cuerpo de Miñones were hired to carry out the same duties.[55]

Those who previously served in that militia were not the only individuals to be hired, for on March 23, 1938, the former forest ranger Gregorio Salegui Recagorri was also named an official of the tax authority.[56]

Once the Civil War was over, the tax authority became a popular destination for disabled veterans (*caballeros mutilados*[57]) because these men could be assigned jobs working in an office. To cite just a few examples, on May 25, 1939, Norberto Láriz, a disabled veteran, was hired as an inspector. Subsequently, Julio Apellaniz Corres and Eulogio Serna Rodríguez were hired as officials by the tax authority on July 27 and August 17 of that same year. Then, on August 17, 1939, Ángel Portero Díez was also hired as an official by the authority.[58]

As previously indicated, the tax authority continued to hire new employees during the first years following the conquest of Bilbao. The purge carried out by the new authorities had such an important impact that it severely reduced the number of the authority's employees, thus requiring it to be "resupplied" with new hires who could carry out the task of collecting taxes.

Conclusions

The first and most important conclusion that we should draw from the data presented here is that a significant number of employees were fired during the first year following Franco's triumph (i.e., 1937–1938). The dismissal of 55.8 percent of the staff of the authority, and the sanctioning of 67.5 percent, must surely have served as a warning, not only for the employees of the Deputation, but for all of Bizkaian society.

The firings were carried out for two different reasons: for abandoning one's position and as a consequence of the purging of employees who had been accused of activities detrimental to the Movimiento Nacional. The fact that the expulsions occurred for political reasons, and not because of the poor economic situation of the provincial Deputation following the abolition of the Economic Agreements, is shown by the fact that the Cuerpo de Arbitrios continued to hire new employees to collect taxes following the dismissal of former employees.

One should not lose sight of the fact that these dismissals were published in the *Boletín Oficial de Vizcaya*. Thus, these reprisals became public knowledge within a society that had just emerged from a civil war, that had witnessed executions by firing squad by the new authorities, and that, as the losers of the conflict, were being subject to important restrictions on their civil liberties. The newly constituted Deputation wanted to make clear from the outset who was in control under the new order, and the lengths to which they were willing to go to maintain this control.

Another important point that needs to be made in this connection is the role of part of the civil society, which compiled and sent out a large quantity of reports, most of which were negative, regarding persons who were subject to the purging process. Personal animosities, the need to save one's own skin by accusing others, or the ambition to ascend within the new order created following Franco's victory were all conducive to the manifestation of the basest of human instincts.

One proof of the importance of denunciations that took place in towns, and of the climate that prevailed during those times, is the following article, which was published on July 11, 1937, in *La Gaceta del Norte*:

> Complaints about subordinates who are "lying in wait"
> Numerous complaints have been received from towns where there are communist and separatist subordinates who are lying in wait to reclaim their previous positions.
> The Provincial Deputation advises citizens to remain patient, because a purging process has already begun that will leave no stone unturned in carrying out its mission.
> The Central Administration has agreed to reinstate staff of community schools who had previously been terminated, and has also carried out a number of new terminations that will, along with the new hires, be publically announced in due course.

Endnotes

1. Julio Prada Rodríguez. *La España masacrada: La represión franquista de guerra y postguerra* (Madrid: Alianza Editorial, 2010), 297. The communication that forms the epigraph of this chapter can be found in the personnel files of a number of purged staff members (e.g., that of Pedro Contreras). Foral Archives of Bizkaia. Administrative Section. AJ-02550/014. Henceforth, FAB-AS.
2. F. Hernández Olgado, "Carceleras encarceladas: La depuración franquista de las funcionarias de prisiones de la Segunda República," *Cuadernos de Historia Contemporánea,* 27 (2005): 271–90. J.C. Bordes Muñoz, *El servicio de Correos durante el régimen franquista (1936–1975): Depuración de funcionarios y reorganización de los servicios postales* (Madrid:Ediciones Cinca, 2009); Archivo Histórico Ferroviario, *Depuración del personal ferroviario durante la Guerra Civil y el Franquismo (1936–1975): Datos de un proyecto en marcha*, Fifth Congress of Railroad History, Palma, October 14–16, 2009.
3. Josefina Cuesta Bustillo, ed., *La depuración de funcionarios bajo la dictadura franquista (1936–1975)* Madrid: Fundación Largo Caballero, 2009.
4. For the CAV, see M. Ostolaza Esnal, *El garrote de la depuración. Maestros vascos en la guerra civil y el primer franquismo (1936–1945)* (Donostia: Ibaceta Pedagogía, 1996).
5. The *Cuerpo de Miñones* was a provincial police force in Bizkaia. See E.J. Alonso Olea, "Los forales, miñones y miqueletes," in *Los Ejércitos*, ed. Carmen Gómez (Vitoria-Gasteiz: Fundación Sancho El Sabio, 1994); *Continuidades y discontinuidades de la Administración Provincial en el País Vasco, 1839–1978: Una esencia de los derechos históricos* (Bilbao: IVAP, 1999); "Concierto Económi-

co y Haciendas Forales, 1937–2002," in *Dictadura, democracia y autogobierno: La nueva sociedad vasca, 1937–2004* (Donostia: LUR, 2004).
6. Pedro Barruso Barés, *Violencia política y represión durante la Guerra Civil y el primer franquismo (1936–1945)* (Gipuzkoa: Hiria, 2004).
7. Santiago De Pablo Contreras, "Represión y cambio político en Álava," in *Los nuevos Historiadores ante la Guerra Civil Española*, ed. Miguel Carlos Gómez Oliver and Octavio Ruiz-Manjón (Granada: Diputación Provincial de Granada, 1990), 376–88.
8. Javier Gómez Calvo, *La Depuración de funcionarios y empleados públicos en Álava (1936–1939)*, PhD thesis (supervised by Antonio Rivera).
9. Minutes of the constitution of the Provincial Deputation of Bizkaia of June 21, 1937. Foral Archive of Bizkaia, Administrative Section AJ-00808/001. For information on Hurtado de Saracho, see J. Agirreazkuenaga and M. Urquijo, *Bilbao desde sus alcaldes: Diccionario biográfico de los alcaldes de Bilbao y gestión municipal en la Dictadura,* Vol. III: 1937–1979 (Bilbao: Ayuntamiento de Bilbao, 2008). For information on Isidoro Delclaux, see Eduardo J. Alonso Olea, "Isidoro Delclaux Aróstegui," in *Los 100 empresarios vascos*, ed. Torres Villanueva (Madrid: LID, 2000), 344–49.
10. Provisions adopted by the Provincial Deputation of Bizkaia on June 21, 1937. FAB-AS AJ-00808/001.
11. Provisions adopted by the Provincial Deputation of Bizkaia on June 21, 1937. FAB-AS AJ-00808/001.
12. Decree-Law published in the *Boletín Oficial del Estado*, Burgos, June 24, 1937, nº 247.
13. Eduardo J. Alonso Olea, *El Concierto económico (1878–1937): Origenes y formación de un Derecho Histórico* Oñati: IVAP, 1995), 302.
14. José Luis de la Granja and Santiago de Pablo, eds., *Historia del País Vasco y Navarra en el siglo XX*, 2nd ed. (Barcelona: Biblioteca Nueva, 2009).
15. Eduardo J. Alonso Olea, Continuidades y discontinuidades de la Administración Provincial en el País Vasco, 1839–1978: Una esencia de los derechos históricos Bilbao: IVAP, 1999), 51.
16. Julio Arostegui Sánchez, "El Voluntario de Navarra en el Ejército de Franco, 1936–1939," Revista de Ciencias Sociales, 47 (1982): 77–100.
17. Eduardo J. Alonso Olea, "Concierto Económico y Haciendas Forales, 1937–2002," in *Dictadura, democracia y autogobierno: La nueva sociedad Vasca, 1937–2004* (Donostia: LUR, 2004), 2.
18. Ibid., 3.
19. Communication sent by Governor General of the State (i.e., Franco) to the Civil Governor of Bizkaia on June 25, 1937. A copy of this correspondence was placed in the majority of the files of tax authority employees to be purged (e.g., FAB-AS AJ-02550/013, AJ-02667/018, and AJ-02552/006).
20. *Boletín Oficial de la Junta de Defensa Nacional de España*, 22. Burgos, September 16, 1936.
21. Resolution adopted by the provincial corporation and formalized in its minutes of June 23, 1937, FAB-AS AJ-00808/001.
22. See Carmelo Landa Montenegro, "Bilbao, 4 de enero de 1937: Memoria de una matanza en la Euskadi Autónoma durante la guerra civil española," *Bidebarrieta: Revista de humanidades y ciencias sociales de Bilbao,* 18 (2007):

79–115.
23. Resolution adopted by the provincial corporation and formalized in its minutes of July 1, 1937, FAB-AS AJ-00808/001.
24. Ibid.
25. Rule no. 2 of the decree of June 25, 1937: "On the other hand, all those functionaries who have abandoned their jobs and not returned, in those instances in which the area where they worked had been liberated, will be summarily dismissed from those corporations where they had been employed, in accordance with the provisions of decree 93 of December 3, 1936." Published in the *Boletín Oficial del Estado*, 51, December 9, 1936.
26. Resolution adopted by the provincial corporation and recorded in its minutes of July 1, 1937. FAB-AS, AJ-00808/001.
27. Personnel file of purged employee Ildefonso Ormaechea. Letter requesting reincorporation, dated June 22, 1937, FAB-AS AJ-02550/015.
28. Personnel file of purged employee Ildefonso Ormaechea. Letter requesting reincorporation, dated June 22, 1937, FAB-AS AJ-02550/014.
29. The investigators of these files were Daniel Olartua Arana and Olegario Velasco.
30. This questionnaire is included in the personnel file for the purging of Pedro Contreras Ortega, FAB-AS AJ-02550/014.
31. See the questionnaire completed for the employees of *Draga Euzkalerria* (i.e., for the employees of that dredger), FAB-AS AJ-02667/018 and FAB-AS AJ-02552/005.
32. On November 7, 1936, the Republican government moved from Madrid to Valencia in the face of the apparent imminent conquest of the former city by the Nationalist rebels. However, Madrid managed to hold out, and remained in Republican hands. See Gabriel Cardona, *Historia militar de una Guerra Civil: Estrategia y tácticas de la Guerra de España* Barcelona: Flor del Viento, 2006).
33. Request for review of files of functionaries who had been fired as part of a purge. Provincial Deputation of Bizkaia, 1948, FAB-AS AJ-2550/017.
34. Answer of Pedro Contreras to the fourth question of the purge form. Personnel file for the purge of Pedro Contreras Ortega, FAB-AS AJ-02550/014.
35. Certification of the Popular Front of Bizkaia, sent to the Provincial Deputation of Bizkaia on July 25, 1936. Personnel file for the purge of Francisco Álvarez Seisdeos, FAB-AS AJ-02550/013.
36. Sociopolitical report sent by the Provincial Deputation of Bizkaia on October 13, 1937, and signed by the mayor of that city, Ciriaco Gervasio Barturen. Purge file of Pedro Contreras Ortega. FAB-AS AJ-02550/014.
37. Report sent by the Research and Information Office of the *Falange* of Guecho to the Provincial Deputation of Bizkaia on July 21, 1937, and signed by Fernando de la Puerta and José Luis Poncho. Purge file of Ildefonso Ormaechea Urizarbarrena. FAB-AS AJ-02550/015.
38. Appearance of Julio García before the inspector of the cases of staff of the Tax Authorities of the first and second zones on August 20, 1937. Staff purging of Ildefonso Ormaechea Urizarbarrena. FAB-AS AJ-02550/015.
39. Appearance of Ángel Torquemada before the inspector of the cases of staff of the Tax Authorities of the first and second zones on August 21, 1937.

Purge file of Ildefonso Ormaechea Urizarbarrena. FAB-AS AJ-02550/015.

40. Letter with favorable reports on Ildefonso Ormaechea, signed by sixty-four people, headed by Aurelio Pérez Hernando and with the final signature of Gabriel Rubias, then sent to the Provincial Deputation of Bizkaia on September 30, 1937. Purge file of Ildefonso Ormaechea Urizarbarrena. FAB-AS AJ-02550/015.

41. Resolution adopted by the provincial corporation and recorded in its minutes of April 13, 1938. FAB-AS AJ-00809/001.

42. Agreement of the Provincial Deputation of Bizkaia at the sesión of October 5, 1937. FAB-AS AJ-02718/004.

43. Minutes of the Deputation of Bizkaia, minutes of the Official Records of the Ministry of the Interior, and personnel files of purged employees of the Tax Authority.

44. We don't necessarily consider this number to be definitive, since additional information may eventually reveal the existence of additional employees of the Tax Authority during the period examined.

45. Hipólito Narvaiza Axpe, Dimas Santibañez, Eduardo Fernández Soto, and Enrique Zorrozua are examples of employees who, during the period May 17–31, filed appeals for reinstatement with the Minister of the Interior via the Deputation. Resolution adopted by the Provincial Corporation and recorded in the minutes of May 17, 19, and 31, 1938. FAB-AS AJ-00809/001.

46. Eduardo Charte Irezabal received a negative ruling regarding the recognition of his retirement benefits from the Provincial Deputation of Bizkaia in an oficial memorándum of October 21, 1940. Purge file of Eduardo Charte Irezabal. FAB-AS AJ-2552/016.

47. The Provincial Deputation of Bizkaia definitively rejected any possibility of review of the case of Francisco Álvarez Seisdedos on July 10, 1952. Purge file of Francisco Álvarez Seisdedos. FAB-AS AJ-2552/013.

48. Carlos Bustinza, chief inspector of the tax authority, was fired on September 15, 1937, for "having provided economic assistance to the Basque School of Galdácano." Report regarding purged employees from 1948. FAB-AS AJ-02550/017.

49. Resolution adopted by the Provincial Corporation and recorded in its minutes between May 31 and June 10, 1938, FAB-AS AJ-00809/001.

50. Resolution adopted by the Provincial Corporation and recorded in its minutes between May 31 and June 10, 1938, FAB-AS AJ-00809/001.

51. The Cuerpo de Miñones, along with the Cuerpo de Miqueletes, was abolished on August 19, 1937, in accordance with the order of the General-in-Chief of the Northern Army, Fidel Dávila. *Boletín Oficial del Estado*. Secretariat of War. Orders. Organization. Published in Burgos on August 25, 1937, p. 3032.

52. For more detailed information regarding the Cuerpo de Miñones de Bizkaia and its role in the collection of taxes, see E.J. Alonso Olea, E. J. "Los forales, miñones y miqueletes," in *Los Ejércitos*, ed. Carmen Gómez (Vitoria-Gasteiz: Fundación Sancho El Sabio, 1994).

53. Agreement of the Provincial Deputation of Bizkaia reached during the sesión of October 19, 1937, FAB-AS AJ02562/004.

54. Resolution adopted by the Provincial Corporation and recorded in its minutes of December 17, 1937, FAB-AS AJ-00808/001.

55. Agreement of the Provincial Deputation of Bizkaia reached during the session of August 17, 1939, FAB-AS AJ-02562/004.
56. Resolution adopted by the Provincial Corporation and recorded in its minutes of March 23, 1938, FAB-AS AJ-00809/001.
57. Those in Franco's army who were disabled in combat were known as *caballeros mutilados*.
58. Resolution adopted by the Committee of the Ministry of the Interior and recorded in its minutes of May 25, 1939, and August 17, 1939, FAB-AS AJ-01009/002.

Bibliography

Agirreazkuenaga, J., and M. Urquijo. *Bilbao desde sus alcaldes: Diccionario biográfico de los alcaldes de Bilbao y gestión municipal en la Dictadura.* Vol. III: 1937–1979. Bilbao: Ayuntamiento de Bilbao, 2008.

Alonso Olea, E.J. "Los forales, miñones y miqueletes." In *Los Ejércitos*, edited by Carmen Gómez. Vitoria-Gasteiz: Fundación Sancho El Sabio, 1994.

———. *El Concierto económico (1878–1937): Origenes y formación de un Derecho Histórico*. Oñati: IVAP, 1995.

———. *Continuidades y discontinuidades de la Administración Provincial en el País Vasco: 1839-1978; Una esencia de los derechos históricos*. Bilbao: IVAP, 1999.

———. "Isidoro Delclaux Aróstegui." In *Los 100 empresarios vascos*, edited by Torres Villanueva. Madrid: LID, 2000.

———. "Concierto Económico y Haciendas Forales: 1937–2002." In *Dictadura, democracia y autogobierno: La nueva sociedad vasca, 1937–2004*. Donostia: LUR, 2004.

Barruso Barés, Pedro. *Violencia política y represión durante la Guerra Civil y el primer franquismo (1936–1945)*. Gipuzkoa: Hiria, 2004.

Cuesta Bustillo, Josefina, ed. *La depuración de funcionarios bajo la dictadura franquista (1936–1975)*. Madrid: Fundación Largo Caballero, 2009.

Prada Rodríguez, Julio. *La España masacrada: La represión franquista de guerra y postguerra*. Madrid: Alianza Editorial, 2010.

4
The Economic Agreement of 1981

Pedro Luis Uriarte

The purpose of this chapter is to refresh memories of events that took place thirty years ago and to provide a personal analysis regarding our first "statutory" Economic Agreement (I think that it is the eighth such agreement all time).[1] I will be touching upon the most significant moments that have lodged in my memory regarding that intense period of my life in which I worked as the Economy and Finance Sailburu (Minister) for the first Basque government, during the four-year term of the first Legislature of the Basque Parliament.

During that time, I had the important responsibility and honor of being the president of the Negotiating Committee that recovered the Economic Agreement for Bizkaia and Gipuzkoa, and that substantially improved that of Araba.

I was a politician under "temporary contract," like so many of my generation that were willing to sacrifice themselves and take a stand in order to remedy the effects of a cruel and mediocre dictatorship and to develop the capacity for self-government provided by the Statute of Gernika.[2]

Nature of the 1981 Agreement: An Agreement and an Act of Faith

Article 41 of the Autonomy Statute of the Basque Country establishes that "Relations involving taxes between the State and the Basque Country will be regulated through the traditional foral system of Economic Agreement or Conventions."

Taking this indispensable statutory reference as a starting point, I would like to clarify one important matter at the outset: The Economic Agreement is not a simple "fiscal" law. Instead, it is something much more important.

It is an institution of transcendent value. The reason this is so is because it defines and clarifies in specific terms the tax (and financial) capacities of the Basque Country.

Over and apart from this formal aspect, the Agreement can be seen as a pact between the State and the Basque Country, and also as a "statement of faith" in the future of Euskadi.

The "pact" "referred to in the first Agreement, following the Autonomy Statute of Gernika, became reality in the following drawn-out process.[3] (1) The first steps of the process were initiated in 1979 by the Basque General Council, although no text was formally agreed upon.[4] (2) The Agreement was subsequently negotiated and forged during the year 1980 by the Negotiating Committee, which was composed of representatives of the new Basque Government, and the Foral Deputations, on the Basque side, and of representatives of the state administration, on the Spanish side. (3) The negotiations concluded, and the last of the articles agreed upon was signed, on December 29, 1980, at 10:30 p.m.[5] by the two co-presidents of the Negotiating Committee (i.e., the Minister of Finance, for Spain, and myself, as the Economic and Finance Sailburu, representing Basque institutions). (4) The signed agreement was ratified in a solemn public ceremony on January 9, 1981,[6] during which all of the members of the Negotiating Committee signed the agreement. (5) Part of the essential, as opposed to the formal, element of the document is the idea of an agreement between the Spanish state and the Basque Country. To this end, following the signing of the Economic Agreement, we two co-presidents embarked upon a new and complex negotiation process that dealt with the delicate and sensitive political and legal question of the Spanish Parliament's taking up of an agreement of this nature for consideration.[7]

I staunchly defended the position that the agreement approved by the Negotiating Committee not be subject to amendments on the part of the General Courts (i.e., the Congress of Deputies and Senate) as part of its deliberation in those bodies, demanding instead that it be accepted or rejected in its entirety.

After another round of tough negotiating, this point (which, as I will later explain, was critical for us) was finally approved. (6) The Agreement was signed into law and became effective as of June 1, 1981.[8]

In addition to having the character of a pact, the Economic Agreement was also an "act of faith" (reflecting the statement in the catechism that "Faith is belief in things unseen"). This agreement was concluded during a dark period in the history of Euskadi, owing to the dramatic events occurring at the time when the newly agreed form of self-government took shape.

During that year of 1980, the Basque Country (the Autonomous Community that today claims the highest per capita GDP, the highest income, and the lowest unemployment rate) suffered an alarming drop in GDP (i.e., −10 percent), entire sectors were mired in a grave crisis, large private companies were dropping like flies, and the rate of unemployment rose to over 20 percent. We lived in a prerevolutionary situation, and the various branches of ETA were competing with one another in terms of both activity and cruelty.

For this reason, the Agreement was a statement of faith in our future—evidence of our complete confidence in the ability of the Euskadi of that time to emerge from crisis.

As we can see today (and this magnificent Euskalduna Jauregia stands as evidence of it) we were entirely justified in our confidence, in our faith, and in taking our stand on behalf of the Economic Agreement.

Importance of the Economic Agreement

There is no question that the Economic Agreement is the cornerstone of autonomy in the Basque Country and that it is the element that most clearly distinguishes our Autonomous Community (along with that of Navarre, which has a similar system) from all others.

The Economic Agreement is something that is cherished by every Basque, and yet one that is not very well known (even in Euskadi), not widely understood, sometimes reviled, and of course envied by other Autonomous Communities (as can be seen in the recent Catalan elections). This envy is in fact testimony to its success.

Without the Economic Agreement that was negotiated in 1980 (not *any* agreement, but *this* particular Agreement) Basque Autonomy would be qualitatively different from what it is today. In addition, it would presumably have a vastly more limited scope than that which it has attained.

The recovered Agreement allowed residents of Euskadi, independently of their political preferences, to clearly appreciate that "Autonomy" is more than just a pretty little word with a certain political meaning.

Without the Agreement, the ability of the different administrative components of Basque government to offer public goods and services (e.g., in education, health, infrastructure, social services) would not have achieved what it has in terms of both quality and scope.

It is of course correct that the "statutory bandwagon" has always had its ups and downs, its slowdowns, and its stalls, and has had to negotiate quite a few tricky curves. And yet it must also be acknowledged that, during long stretches of time, it has rolled smoothly along. Such is the history of magnificent Statute of Gernika, something which I won't go into here, because it is not the subject of this paper.

At the same time, I'd like to make it clear that it would be childish and unfair to assess the Economic Agreement strictly in terms of its monetary value. Its importance is infinitely greater. This is a key point because, even though financial resources are important for any public activity, there are more important factors.

For example, there is the fact that the agreement was a completely novel concept that distinguished it from all previous agreements.

An Economic Agreement with a Completely Different Basis

The reality is that the Economic Agreement constituted an approach that I would not hesitate to call revolutionary, because it rested upon two theoretical pillars that had no precedent in any previous legislation. First, there was an extensive regulatory text that encompassed the entirety of the state tax system, which was "harmonized" with the Autonomous Community of the Basque Country in order to enable the development of a tax policy in the latter.

On the basis of the Statute of Gernika (Article 41.2.a) and article 2 of the Agreement of 1981, "[t]he competent Institutions of the Historic Territories may maintain, establish and regulate, within their own territory, [their own] tax system."[9]

The Economic Agreement contains points of reference to each and every type of exaction, for the purpose of sharing taxes collected within the Autonomous Community between the two tax collection jurisdictions recognized in the document: the authorities of the historical territories of the Basque Country (Araba, Bizkaia, and Gipuzkoa) and the so-called "common territory."

Thus, this model implied that the competent institutions of the historical territories could, on the basis of the Economic Agreement, begin to exercise authority over the entirety of the tax system.

The 1981 Agreement[10] established one exception: that of taxes "included in the Customs Revenue and those currently collected by means of Tax Monopolies," as well as "those imposed upon alcoholic beverages, over which the state will have jurisdiction." This limitation disappeared in 2001.

This was something completely novel in terms of models of fiscal federalism, because the fact that there was a de facto substitution of the state tax collection system in Basque territory distinguished the Economic Agreement from models of fiscal federalism, which

- distribute taxes collected within a territory on a percentage basis (something close to the current Spanish system);
- create a system of superimposed taxes (as in the case of the U.S. federal model); and
- distribute the different collected taxes (as is the case in Germany).

Second, there was the establishment of a totally novel system of tax payments (the so-called "tax quota") on the general expenses assumed by the state which are not assumed by the Autonomous Community (in other words, charges for those competences not transferred to the Autonomous Community).

This model of tax payments links the Economic Agreement with the competence system agreed in the Statute. This is because, to the extent that payments are made by the Basque Country to the state for competences that are exercised here (given that we are not an independent nation) there is a certain conversion of the institutions of the Autonomous Community (although this does not occur formally) into "state tenants" of said services.

These are the two pillars of the innovative model of the Agreement that we were equipped to negotiate, and that neither time nor new tax categories have altered in the least. It is a personal source of pride and satisfaction that a fundamental aspect of the novel contributions of the Agreement was due to the work of the Basque Negotiating Committee. I can vouch for the fact that it was also a source of satisfaction for the other two persons of that committee that are still alive and are present here today: the former Senator Juan Mari Ollora and the former Congressional Deputy Josu Elorriaga.

Thanks to this new conception that we were able to negotiate and have set down in a legal document, the Agreement was, is, and will ever be the cornerstone of our autonomy.[11]

For this reason, any attack on it, or anything that diminishes it, is not only a matter of supreme political importance, but also a personal affront to every Basque. This is because any such action adversely affects our institutions, businesses, unions, universities, nongovernmental organizations (NGOs), social entities, and even ourselves as individual citizens.

For this reason, it is the duty of each and every one of us to defend "our" Agreement. This is a fundamental fact that has not been sufficiently internalized in the Basque Country. This is a matter which requires our vigilance, because the past thirty years have witnessed numerous attacks against the Agreement on different fronts (e.g., from institutions and courts, in political venues, in the media, etc.). Basque society has not reacted with sufficient vigor to these attacks. This is a grave error that must be avoided in the future.

Creation of the 1981 Economic Agreement

It took a lot of hard work to reach that first 1981 Agreement.

First, we had to get past the phase of recognition and definition of its content and the scope of the Statute itself. Those whom I've spoken to who were involved in that intense negotiation process of 1979 have indicated that this was by no means easy. (According to what I've been told, the contribution of Carlos Garaikoetxea—his vision, his firm convictions, and his indefatigable negotiating capacity—were decisive, along with the efforts of the rest of the committee members who negotiated the Statute of Gernika, such as Juan Ollora and the politicians who represented in the state, led by then President Adolfo Suárez.)

Later, the concise statutory formula had to be developed within the broad text articulated in the Agreement. In terms of the implementation of our autonomy, this was the hardest and most meaningful negotiation for both the state and the Basque Country.[12]

As I previously pointed out, the preliminary negotiation began on October 19, 1979, by the Basque General Council, presided over by Carlos Garaikoetxea. The conversations came to a halt on March 3, 1980, with no agreement having been achieved, due to the elections for the formation of the first Basque Parliament. However a considerable text had by that time been drafted. This text was later thoroughly modified in order to infuse it with a broader, deeper, and much more substantive vision.

Following the formation of the first Basque Government on April 24, 1980, I was named Economy and Finance "Sailburu" or Counsel (equivalent to "Minister of that regional Government), as well as President of the Negotiating Committee of the Basque Country. A few days later, our government, at the behest of Lehendakari Garaikoetexea, decided to recommence negotiations, and the Spanish president agreed to do so as well. It was important to finalize the Economic Agreement.

With such a mandate, and full of hope and conviction, I alone began the new negotiation phase on May 6, 1980, with a meeting with Finance Minister Jamie García Añoveros, who belonged to the Spanish ruling party at the time, the Union of the Democratic Center (UCD).

At the time, I was thirty-seven years old, with no political experience. I also had no idea about anything to do with "Finance" and "Economy." And to top things off, the all-powerful Department of Economy and Finance of the recently formed Basque Government did not have a staff, a budget, or any money at all. And its headquarters were in a rented tiny office on Henao Street in Bilbao that just contained a large table and a number of empty chairs that were gradually filled in the coming weeks.

Among the first persons who joined Economy and Finance were the distinguished professor of tax law of the University of Deusto, José Ramón López Larrinaga, who accepted my offer of the position of Vice Counsel (equivalent to Vice-Minister of the Basque Government of Tax Administration, which he assumed on May 19, 1980.

On May 20,[13] the twelve members of the Negotiating Committee were named (6 each on the Basque and Spanish sides) and, after working over the course of many months and enduring numerous ups and downs, the entire negotiation process was completed at 10:30 p.m. on December 29, 1980, as I indicated above.

The conversations regarding agreement on the text therefore lasted seven months (or fifteen, if we add the conversations that had previously taken place within the Basque General Council). These conversations were, at times, especially difficult and demanding.[14]

The final phase of those very long negotiations, when we were essentially living, eating, and breathing the negotiating process, lasted twenty-one days during which we practically had no rest (December 4–29). The sessions during these days lasted between sixteen and eighteen hours (and we were limited by the Finance Minister to a strict diet of water, *serrano* ham and *manchego* cheese; this was because the public deficit at that time allowed nothing more).

This final negotiating phase required 346 hours of highly intensive negotiation in order to reach agreement—word by word, line by line, and article by article—on the text of the Economic Agreement.[15]

When the negotiation regarding one of the articles was concluded, the agreed text was transcribed, and the document signed by the co-presidents of the Negotiating Committee, the Finance Minister, and myself, as the Economy and Finance Council (Minister) of the Basque Government.

When, on the night of December 29, 1980, we signed the last of the articles, we had by then both signed a total of fifty-six articles, five additional provisions, seven temporary provisions, one repeal provision, three final provisions, and two agreements:

- The first agreement approved the text of the Economic Agreement between the State and the Basque Country and was incorporated into the minutes, with the operative detail that was previously cited.
- The second enjoined delivery of the negotiated text to be processed by "competent institutions." (The definition as to what these "competent institutions" were was subject to later negotiation, as I pointed out above.)

Those of us on the Basque negotiating team felt that the political situation was growing tenser by the day. For this reason, it was essential that we conclude the negotiation by December 31. We wanted to be able to take advantage of a once-in-a-lifetime political moment. And thus began a new era for the Basque Country.

The Basque Government and the Spanish Council of Ministers approved the agreed text on the following day, December 30, 1980 (although the actual bill was formally approved on January 23, 1981).

Approval by the Juntas Generales (Provincial Parliaments) of Bizkaia, Araba, and Gipuzkoa (in that order) followed during the first days of 1981.

Negotiators of the 1981 Economic Agreement

I want to make it clear that the success of those conversations would not have been possible without the exemplary efforts of the Basque Negotiating Committee, especially certain individual members of that body.

In accordance with Article 42.2.e for the negotiation of the quota, a Joint Committee comprising six members was created, over which I presided. It included three members of the Committee represented the Basque Government:

- José Ramón López Larrínaga, Vice-Counsel of Tax Administration
- The excellent economist and deputy Josu Elorriaga.
- I served as president and Economy and Finance Sailburu of the Basque Government.
- And one member for each of the historical territories:
- Deputy General of Bizkaia (President of that Provincial Government) José María Makua, who possessed an extensive knowledge of the foral system.
- Assistant Advisor for the Local Administration, Víctor Menchacatorre (for Gipuzkoa).
- Senator Juan María Ollora (for Araba), a man who knew a great deal about the Agreement, since he had participated in the negotiations initiated by the Basque General Council.

The Basque Negotiating Committee received ongoing support from the Deputies General of Gipuzkoa (the unforgetable Xabier Aizarna) and Araba (Emilio Guevara), as well as from a rather small, but exceptional, support staff. (At the time, the Basque Administration was, to put it generously, in a very early stage of development. Some of the members of the support staff were Juan Luis Lascurain, Xabier Galárraga, Juan Antonio Lasalle, and Alfonso Basagoiti.

Although we needed to resolve a good number of instances of internal tension, we were able to create a negotiating team that worked very well together, especially after Christmas Day 1980. This was a source of great strength to us in the final days of those very difficult negotiations. The work of José Ramón López Larrínaga and Juan Mari Ollora was extraordinary. Others on the committee whose work merits special mention include Josu Elorriaga and José María Makua.

The state appointed a very powerful committee, led by Finance Minister Jaime García Añoveros, who enjoyed the support of the brilliant Minister of Territorial Administration, Rodolfo Martín Villa, and of a team of high-ranking and eminently qualified officials of the Central Administration. The following members of this group are worthy of special mention: Miguel Martín, Assistant Secretary of Finance (and currently president of the AEB [Spanish Banking Association]); Alfonso Gota and Vicente Querol, Managing Directors; and Jaime Trebolle, Assistant Managing Director. This group was supported by a very able and powerful support staff of the state administration. It is interesting that one of the members of the support team was a mustachioed inspector of the Ministry of Finance named José María Aznar.

Course of the Negotiation within the Basque Committee

The difficult negotiations that allowed us to reach the Economic Agreement of 1981 were taken up at two levels: (1) internal, that is, among those representing the Basque side, for the purpose of defining what we wanted to propose and negotiate with the state. This task was by no means easy, and was one to which we needed to devote many hours in Room 348bis of Hotel Palace, in Madrid; and (2) formal, that is, between our Negotiating Committee and the state Administration.

Although it might seem incredible now, the internal debate was highly problematic. First, because there was a draft of the Agreement created by the Basque General Council in which various political parties had participated and that was clearly insufficient, because it accepted the limits of the Araba Economic Agreement that was in effect at that time.

Second, because it was necessary to achieve two different objectives vis-è-vis our two historical territories: Recovery of the agreement for Gipuzkoa and Bizkaia and needed adjustments to that of Araba. This was necessary because the agreement for that province, which had been approved in 1976, was slated to remain in effect until 2001.

In addition, in the Eighth Temporary Provision of the Statute,[16] it was indicated that the text to be signed "take its inspiration from the material contents of the Economic Agreement in the province of Araba currently in force, without prejudice of any kind to that province..."

Some held the opinion that members of our Committee never managed to understand the new model of the tax quota, the reference to the Araba agreement constituted the limit, or roof which was not to be exceeded. For me, as President of the Basque Negotiating Committee, the Araba Economic Agreement was instead the floor or foundation upon which we needed to find a way to construct a new model of the Agreement that went beyond it in every respect.

Therefore, the first temptation to be overcome was that of being content with what already existed. Instead, we needed to define a consensus proposal that exceeded the Araba Agreement in both quality and profundity. For this purpose, it was necessary to define a different and better schema. An intelligent interpretation of the Statute allowed us to do this.

It was very difficult indeed to identify this schema, mainly because it was necessary to define the new model of the quota that it made reference to. Above all, it was difficult to get all of the members of our Committee to recognize that this new schema was much more politically appropriate and much more advanced financially than the Araba agreement. In this respect, the decisive role of Araba Senator Juan María Ollar (who became deputy general of Araba in 1983) deserves special mention.

Yet, even in the face of a serious lack of understanding and moments of high tension, it was possible to reach this necessary internal agreement, and to proceed to negotiate the Agreement with the state.

The Course of Negotiation with the State

Negotiations with the representatives of the state comprised a number of different lines of work. The first of these lines involved conceptual negotiations between the two principal negotiators—the Minister of Treasury Jaime García Añoveros and me, as Economy and Finance *Sailburu* (or minister) of the Basque Government.[17] As was to be expected, these conversations, which aimed at reaching agreement regarding the broad outlines of the document, were very intense and extensive because they were something to which both governments paid a great deal of political attention and about which they were both constantly informed regarding advances, disagreements, and conversations.

Second, it was necessary to create a climate of personal confidence between the two commission heads (something indispensable in a negotiation of such complexity, importance, and scope). This is something that could only be achieved through dialogue, dialogue, and more dialogue—and hours and hours of debate.

Thanks to this formula, we slowly made progress, often just us two co-presidents in the ministry office, where we jointly resolved many points of conflict and identified others whose resolution proved decisive.

It is therefore only fair to point out that, without a minister of the professional stature, political vision, statesmanship, and positive attitude of Jaime García Añoveros (and of some of his colleagues on the Spanish government and the state Negotiating Committee, especially Rodolfo Martín Villa), it would have proved far more difficult to reach a satisfactory agreement.

Third, negotiations at the level of the co-presidents overlapped with the plenary sessions that involved drafting each of the points of the Agreement. All of the committee members participated in these negotiations, as did the Deputies General of both Araba and Gipuzkoa. Those plenary sessions included up to eighteen people, all of whom were involved in defining the text of the Economic Agreement, line by line, and concept by concept.

I still remember the epic debates between Subsecretary of Finance Miguel Martín and the Basque Vice-Counsel of the Economy and Finance Department of the Basque Country, José Ramón López Larrínaga, who, in the absence of any experience, but with a wealth of intellectual and professional resources, showed himself to be an able and tireless negotiator.

In addition, and in order to address important issues that arose, as the conversations advanced on these two levels (i.e., the personal and the plenary) other debates dealing with purely technical matters were held, in which experts of the two committees participated.

Finally, at the higher, institutional level, and away from the negotiating table, the astute political vision, the demands, and the constant encouragement Lehendakari Garaikoechea was also a decisive factor. He followed the course of the negotiations on a daily basis and, as part of his efforts to overcome any final political reservations and resistence, he was in contact with the Spanish President Adolfo Suárez and other high-level officials.

As an aside, after the Minister of Finance told me that he discussed the most sensitive of matters with the Spanish President from a special secured telephone for fear that his telephone was being wiretapped, I called the *lehendakari* from a public telephone near the Hotel Palace. Being a rather inept spy, it didn't occur to me that it might have been the phone in the Ajuria-Enea Palace, where the *lehendakari* office was being tapped.

After the Negotiation of the Agreement

After the formal signing of the Agreement, the members of the committee were profoundly satisfied, as well as honored, to see our work recognized in a ceremony held in Gernika's *Casa de Juntas* (historical Basque Parliament) on January 11, 1981, with *Lehendakari* Carlos Garaikoetxea presiding and the entire Basque Government also in attendance, along with the three Deputies General and other political dignitaries, including former *Lehendakari* Jesús Leizaola, who had served as a Finance Minister in the Basque government of 1936.

The ceremony was followed by a festive celebration at Gernika Fronton, attended by more than 1,500 persons, featuring a solidarity banquet where we on the Negotiating Committee were presented an exquisite silver platter that included the following personal dedication:

> Pedro Luis Uriarteri
> Ondasun Ituna Berreskuratzeko
> Bere Lan Neketsuagaitik.
> Esker Onez.
> Gernikan, 1981ko Urtarrilaren 11an
>
> To Pedro Luis Uriarte
> For his tiring work
> In regaining the Economy Agreement.
> With gratitude.
> Gernika, February 11, 1981

After the celebration, the work of the two co-presidents of the Negotiating Committee continued. At that point, we had to deal with an entirely new and unprecedented situation: the entire legislative process of bringing the Agreement into being, until its definitive approval by the Spanish Parliament.[18] This was a matter of critical importance because, until that time, all of the agreements, over the course of more than one hundred years between the state and the foral institutions, had been approved by a simple decree of the Spanish government.

The 1981 Agreement therefore had a higher regulatory status. This fact endowed it with a far greater legal force than previous agreements.

This legislative process was accompanied by a series of facts of great historical importance that were not uniformly positive in terms of securing approval of the Agreement as law:

- The announcement, on January 29, 1981, of the resignation of the Spanish President Adolfo Suárez;[19]
- The first visit of the Spanish Monarchs to the Basque Country, on February 3.[20]
- The attempted coup d'etat on February 23 that brought the nascent Spanish democracy to its knees and, if it had succeeded, would have put Basque institutions and—it goes without saying—the negotiators of the Economic Agreement, in a very difficult personal situation. A successful coup would also have blocked approval of the agreement, since what motivated that unfortunate action was the so-called "excesses of autonomy;"

- The formation of a new Spanish government on February 25, led by the former Vice President Leopoldo Calvo Sotelo,[21] who had not previously participated in the Economic Agreement negotiations;
- The initiation of activity aimed at approving the Organic Law Bill for Harmonizing the Autonomy Process (Ley Orgánica de Armonización del Proceso Autonómico, or LOAPA). This bill was agreed upon by gentleman's agreement several months following the Economic Agreement by the Spanish Parliament, with the support of the government party of Calvo Sotelo and the Spanish Socialist Workers' Party (PSOE); and
- The actual process of the legislative debate in the Spanish Parliament, where the Agreement was subject to opposition and harsh criticism.

During this legislative process, in both the Congress and Senate, two members of the Negotiating Committee of the Economic Agreement had especially prominent roles: Deputy Josu Elorriaga and Senator Juan Mari Ollora. In this complex and tense political scenario, the consideration of the Economic Agreement in the Spanish Parliament lasted seventy-six days.[22] This process can be summarized as follows:

- On February 25, 1981, two days following the failed coup d'etat, the bill, which had been approved on January 23 of that same year by the Council of Ministers, was presented in the Congress of Deputies, for priority discussion and deliberation.
- On March 4, 1981, the Board of the Congress studied the text delivered by the Spanish government, which was incorporated in the minutes signed by the Negotiating Committee and later passed on to the Finance Committee on March 17.
- On April 8, nearly one year following the formation of the Basque government, the Finance Committee of the Congress of Deputies certified the text.
- On the afternoon of that same day, the President of the Negotiating Committee of the State (and serving Minister of Finance) Jaime García Añoveros[23] had to explain in detail to representatives of the centrist UCD, which was at that time the ruling party in Spain, the purpose, legal foundations, and contents of the negotiation of the Economic Agreement, given the reservations and resistance that he encountered within that party.
- On April 9, the certified text was approved by the Congress of Deputies at a plenary session.[24]

It was both striking and revealing that there were a large number of deputies who did not attend the plenary session at which the Agreement was approved (a total of ninety-seven, of which sixty belonged to the UCD). This was evidence of the obstacles that had to be overcome to finally secure approval of the agreement.[25]

Of the total of 253 deputies that were present, 231 (91.3 percent) voted in favor, 6 against, and 15 abstained, and there was one null vote. The Agreement was approved by the Senate, by voice vote, on April 28, 1981.[26] Finally, Law 12/1981 of May 13 was published in the Official State Bulletin on May 28, and entered into effect on June 1, 1981.[27]

The Key to Negotiating Successfully

Those negotiations, I can now say without blushing, were carried out impeccably on the part of the Basque representatives, from both a strategic and tactical standpoint, because we always kept the following at the forefront of our minds:

- What we were trying to achieve (namely, a new Agreement that represented an improvement over the Araba Agreement);
- The means to achieving it (i.e., not abandoning negotiations until the deal was made, whatever the effort necessary); and
- The deadline for concluding conversations: December 31, 1980.

Therefore, a sense of anticipation prevailed—an enormous willpower—as well as a strong conviction regarding the position we were defending.

There was also a high degree of conceptual and technical knowledge of the issues being negotiated, whether they had to do with tax, tax payment, and local issues on the one hand or (and most importantly) with the tax quota that, as I've pointed out, we had to conceive as something entirely new.

In addition, if there had not been an overpowering emotional motivation—an awareness of the fact that what we were negotiating was critical for the future of Euskadi, it would not have been possible to physically or mentally endure such a difficult negotiation process. Above all, it would have been unthinkable to get as far as we in fact did.

The Support We Received

In that long and complicated negotiation process, the Negotiating Committee felt completely supported. We were never alone.

The Basque government and its *lehendakari* (who, during meetings with the Cabinet of the Basque government, which were held on Mondays) asked me to keep him apprised as to how things were going, offered me his ongoing support and encouragement, because he knew that the future was at stake.

I also received the generous support of the staff of my Department of Economy and Finance (and especially from Vice-Counsels Antón Galdiz, Gotzon Olarte, and José Ramón Urrutia), as well as from individuals in other departments of the Basque government. The following individual Counsels (Sailburu) merit special mention: Mario Fernández, Javier García Egocheaga, Xabier Caño, Pedro Miguel Etxenike, and Ramón Labayen.

At the political level, the unwavering support of the Basque government and the Basque Nationalist Party (EAJ-PNV) also deserve mention. The EAJ-PNV was able to not only create awareness among its members (who were mobilized when necessary) but also among other political parties and Basque public opinion generally, as regards the decisive importance of the Economic Agreement.

The positive support of all other Basque political parties within the "democratic bloc" also should be mentioned (i.e., UCD, PSE-PSOE, and EE). These parties did an exemplary job of closely and consistently following the negotiation process in the Basque Parliament without interfering or causing difficulties. In the end, these parties also supported the Agreement that was reached without (as far as I can remember) a single dissident vote. (In this respect, I should mention my former political opponents—and current friends—Juan Manuel Eguiagaray, of the PSE-PSOE party, and Javier Olaverri, of the Euskadiko Ezkerra party.)

In sum, as president of the Basque Negotiating Committee, I always felt strongly supported by my team and respected by those on the other side of the table. I owe all of these people my gratitude and respect. The Basque Economic Agreement of 1981 was *the work of all of these people*, and should be remembered and celebrated as such.

The Most Difficult Obstacles

As I recall, the most important problems that we had to overcome in order to reach agreement on a text had mainly to do with four very sensitive areas: politics, financial and tax matters, the contribution of the state, and legislative issues. Within these four areas, there were a total of thirteen very difficult matters to resolve.[28]

Three Political Obstacles

First, it was important that everyone understand that the Agreement was not a privilege. This was easily accomplished at the formal level by the inclusion of the reference to the "traditional foral system of the Economic Agreement or Conventions" in Article 41 of the Statute of Gernika. But it was necessary to give expression to this idea in a long and highly complex and integrated text, overcome reservations, and make it operational.

Unfortunately, this specter of "privilege" has continued to haunt the Agreement, and we see it frequently rearing its head, sometimes subtly, and other times more explicitly. This has been the case despite the fact that a famous conservative politician José Calvo Sotelo himself (a man who could hardly be classified as an ardent Basque nationalist) stated in the Spanish Parliament on December 5, 1935, that "not on account of privilege, but rather for historical reasons rooted in our oldest institutions, you Basques will enjoy the benefits of the system of Economic Agreements." Our Agreement is *unique*, rooted in a historical tradition "protected and respected" by the Spanish constitution. It has never been a privilege. This needs to be said loud and clear.

Second, addressing a petition of a state political party (i.e., the PSOE) which was not at that time part of the government, regarding the requirement that we Basques display solidarity with the rest of the state.

For this reason, we accept , without any resistance whatsoever, that the Basque Autonomous Community be required to contribute to the Interterritorial Compensation Fund, because this was only just. We accepted this requirement despite the fact that, at the time, the Basque Country was not a prosperous territory, but instead was enduring a severe economic and social crisis that resulted in a high degree of poverty.

Third, even while we defended the fact that the effective term of the Agreement was indefinite, the Basques representatives accepted, for the sake of consistency with the content of the Eighth Temporary Provision of the Statute of Gernika, that the effective term of the Agreement would be identical to that of the Araba Agreement (i.e., that it would last until 2001).[29]

Five Financial and Fiscal Obstacles

The first challenge was to convince those negotiators representing the state (especially, as regards me personally, as the Minister of Finance), as well as certain state departments, that we had no intention of using the Agreement in order to create a "tax haven" in Euskadi. This expression, which was a reflection of the high degree of mistrust with which many outside Euskadi viewed the agreement, is something that hounded us right up until the debate in the Spanish Parliament in mid-1981.

For this reason, we guaranteed that, in the Basque Autonomous Community, "effective global fiscal pressure" (a definition that I personally negotiated with the Minister of Finance) would always be, at minimum, the average of that of the state.

Today, this is clearly the case. Two examples should suffice to illustrate the truth of this assertion. If, during the past year, I had lived in Madrid, Barcelona, or Castro Urdiales (about twenty miles from here), I would have paid two points less on the marginal rate on my income (i.e., 43 percent rather than 45 percent). In previous years, the difference was three points. Now, in 2011, the marginal rate of 45 percent for the income tax starts in the Basque Country at 62,440 euros of taxable income. In order to reach this 45 percent in the state, taxable income needs to be 175,000 euros.

On January 7, 2011, the newspaper *Expansión* ran a five-column front-page story under the following headline: "Fortunes flee the Basque Country after tax hikes. 95% of SICAV Sociedades de Inversión de Capital Variable [open-ended mutual fund] has gone to Madrid or Barcelona to avoid paying 28% Corporate Tax."[30]

As a reference, it is important to note that 2,716 SICAVs (86.8 percent of the total) are located in Madrid, another 305 (9.75 percent) in Catalonia, and 15 in Navarre. Meanwhile, in the Basque Country, which is the eleventh ranked Autonomous Community in this regard, there are only 5.

Where, then, is the so-called Basque "tax haven"?

Second, within the context of this "effective global fiscal pressure," we managed to gain acceptance of the notion that the historical territories of Araba, Bizkaia, and Gipuzkoa would have the highest degree of regulatory autonomy possible vis-à-vis its collected taxes. Following arduous negotiations, a balanced agreement was reached that went much further than the provisions of the Araba accord then in effect.

As regards those taxes that might have an effect on prices (e.g., the IGTE, the predecessor of the current VAT) no substantial autonomy of any kind was recognized, given that such a measure could generate price differences with the rest of Spain. However, the historical territories were granted full regulatory autonomy over corporate income tax (when the taxed corporations were considered as "Basque corporations").

Over and above any technical considerations, which I am not qualified to discuss, I would like to point out that the series of judicial rulings regarding the rate of the corporate income tax established by the Juntas Generales (Provincial Parliaments) of the historical territories were incomprehensible to those of us who were involved in securing the Agreement.

With all due respect to the Spanish Courts, the rulings issued show no respect for the regulatory capacity that was an inherent part of that first Economic Agreement, and therefore means that a state authority (specifically, the Judiciary) has nullified an agreement, a pact, reached by the Executive, and which was later legally ratified by means of the Spanish Parliament.

The third challenge was the matter of very carefully identifying the meaning of those concepts that, because of their vagueness, might end up diminishing the scope of the Agreement and that could also be used by certain politicians and media outlets as a weapon to attack and vitiate its contents. (Among other issues, this fear applied to the concepts of "coordination with the state," "fiscal harmonization," and, above all, to "market unity" a notion frequently used nowadays to attack the autonomy model.)

Fourth, there was the issue of how to distribute among the state and foral tax system the taxes that were applied and collected in the foral and common territories.

For these purposes, a complex series of connection points were established, along with a relative percentage of business done in each Territory model. I'm not going to delve into this here in order to avoid dealing with technical issues. However, these connection points allowed us to divide the taxes collected from legal tax-paying entities that operated in both the common and foral territories between the state administration and the foral tax system.

The fifth challenge was the matter of agreeing upon an inheritance and donation tax. This was a relatively minor issue from the point of view of collections. However, it was a politically sensitive matter, given that the representatives of the state closed ranks around it in denying any capacity whatsoever to the historical territories, except for management alone. This was because they did not want the Basque Country to become a graveyard of elephants. I negotiated this sensitive matter personally with the Minister of Finance, who in the end accepted full regulatory capacity for residents of the Basque Country for more than ten years. Thus, the "graveyard of elephants" did not come to pass, and the suppression of this tax was extended in later decades to other Autonomous Communities.

Four Obstacles vis-à-vis the Contribution of the Basque Autonomous Community to the State

First, the definition of a quota system that was totally original, based on the following decisive principle established in article 41.2.d of the Statute of Gernika, to which I will later refer in some detail:

> The Basque Country's transfer to the State shall consist of an overall

> quota, made up of the individual Quotas of each of its Territories, as a contribution towards all State burdens that are not directly taken up by the Autonomous Community.

Second was the matter of assuring that the methodology of the quota system was incorporated into the Agreement itself. The representatives of the State were very resistant to this idea, because they felt that the text of the Economic Agreement ought to contain no more than regulations strictly related to tax collection.

From both the practical and economic point of view, this was decisive. Also decisive was the fact that, in personal negotiations with the Spanish Minister of Finance, I was able to introduce the Fifth Temporary Provision,[31] which recognized the automatic renewal of the annual quota, which would take effect in the case of failure to reach agreement with the state, at the end of the five-year quota currently in force.

This constituted a guarantee that Basque autonomy, once the collection of taxes in Basque territory had been carried out, would not be paralyzed in the future due to a lack of resources, in the event of failure to reach agreement with the state in negotiations regarding a new five-year period for the quota.

Third, it was necessary to specify the percentage of contribution of the Autonomous Community to the sustenance of the general expenses of the state that the former did not assume (i.e., the cost of the ministerial competences that the state would no longer be paying to the Autonomous Community once they had been transferred).

After months of technical negotiations, the Minister of Finance and I personally reached agreement regarding this matter during the final days of discussions. The agreed percentage of contribution, which remains in effect today, is 6.24 percent. This figure was established by dividing the Basque GDP by the total GDP of the state (with the crisis then taking place in Euskadi, which had resulted in a steep drop in its GDP, also taken into consideration).

Therefore we Basques, who today represent 4.67 percent of the total population of the state, contribute 6.24 percent to all of the state competences that have not been assumed by the Autonomous Community (which is equivalent to 33 percent more than that justified in terms of the population alone). (An additional interesting datum in this regard is the fact that, on December 31, 2009, the Basque GDP was equivalent to 6.23 percent of the state total, according to the INE, Spanish Institute for Statistics (Instituto Nacional de Estadística).)

The fourth difficulty had to do with the fact that I proposed (and the state representatives accepted) the Fourth Additional Provision[32] regarding joint financing of investments to be made in the Basque Country. The provision referred to investments that "because of their total amount, strategic value, general interest, and impact on various territories of the Basque Autonomous Community, or because of other special circumstances, were particularly conducive to this kind of financing."

This Additional Provision has remained very important for Euskadi, decades after having been established, because it has allowed the current financing of the construction of the "Basque Y" (i.e., the high speed train system), which, within the next few years, will unite the three Basque capitals and them with Madrid and the main Spanish cities and, in the future, with France.

A Legislative Obstacle

Finally, we were able to make progress regarding a key political issue, both with respect to the first Economic Agreement and also vis-à-vis the future.

Under the assumption that the Agreement was a "pact," I proposed (and it was accepted, once again in bilateral negotiations with the Minister of Finance following the public signing of the Agreement) that, once the Agreement were signed in the Negotiating Committee by the Basque and the state members, the final text be incorporated verbatim and without any modification, as an appendix to a single-article bill which would then be presented in the Spanish Parliament, without any possibility of its being amended.[33]

Law 12/1981 of May 13, which approved the Economic Agreement of the Autonomous Community of the Basque Country, has perhaps the shortest text of any known Spanish law. It reads as follows: "The Economic Agreement with the Autonomous Community of the Basque Country, as referred to in article 41 of Organic Law 3/1979 of December 18th, of the Autonomy Statute of the Basque Country, is hereby approved."

It would be difficult to achieve more with fewer words.

The Decisive Importance of the Quota

Overcoming these stumbling blocks, and securing the incorporation of the quota methodology proposed by the Basque Negotiating Commission into the text of the Economic Agreement, something that was historically unprecedented, was the most critical and important point of the entire excruciatingly difficult negotiation process.

This was because of the conceptual importance—and not merely the economic importance—of the new quota system for Euskadi. The agreed methodology indirectly guaranteed (i.e., as a result of no longer paying the state 6.24 percent of all of the competences that would be transferred to Basque territories) a level of financing for each competence exactly equivalent to the ratio of the Basque GDP to the state GDP (i.e., the agreed 6.24 percent).

Because of the historic dedication of resources of the Spanish General Budget to the Basque Country in a way that grossly underrepresented the relative weight of the population and GDP of that region in relation to the state total (something that we see today in the case of Catalonia, a fact that constitutes one of the bones of contention between the Autonomous Community of Catalonia and the Spanish government) the fact that the 6.24 percent of the Spanish budget would no longer have to be paid, once the competence was transferred to the Autonomous Community, in reality implied a greater financial capacity in the Basque Country, owing to the difference between, on the one hand, what had previously been spent and/or invested by the Spain in Basque territory and, on the other, the quota that became effective as part of the transference of competences.

This is therefore the equivalent of providing greater resources to the various public services provided by the Basque Autonomous Community in comparison with the previous situation, in which said resources had been provided by the state administration.

One example illustrates this important point. Before transferring the roadways that it had managed to the Basque Country, the expenses and investments in the Spanish Budget for the roads network of Euskadi represented (this was the approximate figure at that time) less than 2 percent of the Spanish Budget, while the Autonomous Community of the Basque Country was paying 6.24 percent of total expenses and investments for the whole Spanish territory, included in the Spanish Budget.

Obviously, at the time that this 6.24 percent ceased to be paid, following the transference of the authority over roadways to Basque institutions (in this case, to foral institutions), the expenditure capacity of the Basque Country automatically increased threefold. Of course, in those competences in which the Spain Administration dedicated more than 6.24 percent of its Budget to Euskadi, the financial effect was just the opposite: that is, there was a decrease in Basque expenditure capacity. But there were very few cases of that kind.

Moreover, this methodology was based on the assumption that, because the foral tax system was assuming the risk of collection of all taxes in its territory (a risk that can clearly be appreciated during the present global crisis), and because the Autonomous Community could not affect the Spanish Budget (and therefore could also not determine the amount of the quota), the financial capacity of Basque institutions increased as long as the pace of collection was greater than before. When this was not the case, then financial capacity decreased.

In addition to this greater potential financial capacity for the provision of public goods and services in Euskadi following the transfer, there was another advantage, which had to do with the fact (which had also been recognized in the Economic Agreement) that the Autonomous Community and the competent institutions in the historical territories had complete management freedom with respect to expenditures. This allowed it to determine how to distribute its most important resources among the different competences that were now being assumed by the Autonomous Communities. This represented a decisive recognition of autonomy, which was forged, and which also gained momentum, as a result of expenditures rather than through revenues.

In other words, and following the previous reference to investment in roads, the most important resources at the disposal of the Autonomous Community, after it no longer had to pay the 6.24 percent of the amount earmarked in the Spain General Budget for roads, did not necessarily have to be used in the construction of roads, but could instead be invested in any of the competences recognized by the Statute of Autonomy.

Third, and also very important, is the fact that, because the Agreement recognized the full expenditure capacity of Basque institutions, the resources obtained could be used for competences that had not been transferred, thus complementing the resources of the state budget.

This is what occurred, for example, for decades as regards competences related to research and development, or R&D ("scientific and technical research," in the language of the Basque Statute).

Despite the fact that these competences were not transferred until 2009, the Basque government, with the support of the Foral Deputations (provincial governments), invested in R&D through its own resources. These resources were diverted from less strategically important matters. Doing this allowed the Autonomous Community of the Basque Country (which in 1980 had invested a measly 0.16 percent of its GDP in R&D) to improve investment in science, technology, and innovation, eventually reaching an R&D investment in relation to GDP of 2.06 percent in 2009 (this represents a figure two and a half times that of the Spain, and 23 percent more than that reported for 2009 in Catalonia).

A Summary of Thirty Years of the Economic Agreement

I can say today, with pride, that the Agreement of 1981 was a watershed event.[34]

This is because, in that negotiation, the idea was not only to recover the previous Economic Agreement (and to renew that of Araba), but to achieve something completely new: that is, this particular Economic Agreement, one which, as previously noted, far exceeded the Araba agreement.

But it was not enough to just negotiate and recover this Economic Agreement for Bizkaia and Gipuzkoa, and to bolster that of Araba. It was then necessary to use the powerful leverage provided by the Agreement to the maximum advantage of Euskadi.

And this was of course achieved, because the men and women of the Basque Country now have at their disposal public institutions that have been able to manage our Economic Agreement, the Foral Deputations (provincial governments) of the three historical territories, and their respective tax systems and tax and finance departments in a highly satisfactory manner.

Therefore, it can be said that the Agreement has been well applied, and that the work accomplished during the course of these thirty years in the three tax systems of Araba, Bizkaia, and Gipuzkoa has been admirable (and this notwithstanding certain isolated events, such as the matter currently before the Courts).

Thus, on the basis of a complex idea that received expression in an extensive legal text, there have evolved three tax systems that function very well, in addition to the general tax system of the Basque Country.

Taking into account all the previous information, I'd like to propose the following threefold conclusion: (1) the Agreement has been a political, fiscal, and economic success; (2) the Basque governmental authorities have complied with the letter and spirit of the Agreement; and (3) we have witnessed a notable capacity to administer the tax collection system. This is evident in the marked reduction of tax fraud, one of the problems that we had back in 1980.

Everything I've just indicated, which should be a motive for rejoicing, should be perfectly compatible with another idea: we need to continue to improve the Economic Agreement. This is because there are still problems that need to be resolved and a lack of coordination that must be remedied. And above all, we need to improve because the world and the economic environment are changing at a rapid pace.

For this reason, our Basque tax system, both the foral and the general will—I firmly believe—be even better when we celebrate the golden anniversary of our agreement in 2030.

Recommendations for Optimization and Future Defense of the Economic Agreement

To conclude, and speaking now as an ordinary citizen, and yet with the memory still fresh of my previous responsibilities as President of the Basque Negotiating Committee of the Economic Agreement of 1981, I would like to venture a series of recommendations with a view to preserving and optimizing this institutional cornerstone of Basque autonomy.[35]

Here are my ten recommendations:

1. A concerted effort to "socialize" the Agreement that includes an intensive diffusion and explanation of the document within our Autonomous Community. The lack of knowledge within Basque Society regarding a matter of such importance is simply unacceptable.

According to the last poll of *Sociómetro Vasco*, published last December, only 9 percent of Basques indicate that they know the Agreement "well." Another 42 percent reported that "they have heard of it" and no less than 45 percent (equivalent to one million of the residents of Euskadi) have never even heard of it.

The Basque education system and communications media should take an active role in this effort to disseminate the Agreement.

2. Along the same lines, a significant effort should be made to "sell" the Agreement outside of the Autonomous Community of the Basque Country, pursuing a friendly policy of information and influence in political, academic, and public opinion venues of other Autonomous Communities and, especially, in Madrid.

In this task, Basque parties with a statewide presence, especially the PSE-PSOE and PP, should take an active role.

3. It will be important to take action to "calm the waters" on the Catalan front.[36] This is because Catalonia is very sensitive (and with good reason) regarding the problem of its financing, and uses the Basque Economic Agreement as a point of reference (the underlying idea being that it too should have an Economic Agreement similar to the one in place in the Basque Country).

Evidence that this is the case was seen in the last election campaign, during which that Autonomous Community focused on this very issue. This was particularly the case of both CiU (Convergencia I Unió), the political party that now controls the Generalitat de Catalunya (Government of Catalonia), as well as the majority of the other parties currently in the opposition.

This is further confirmed by the fact that, just two days ago, the President of the Generalitat (a formidable and able politician whom I admire a great deal) brought the issue before King Juan Carlos in his first audience after taking office, declaring that, by 2012, a new financing model should be in place in Catalonia.[37]

This is a matter that should be important to all of us, and should be closely followed in the Basque Country because, although Catalonia has every right to have a satisfactory financing model, attacking the Basque Agreement in order to attain it is unacceptable.

Thus, it is not permissible that an important Catalan politician, one who currently holds high-level positions within the *Generalitat*, as well as in the CiU, publically employ the expressions he used last November 30,[38] such as the following: "The Basque Economic Agreement, if someone wants to refer to it one of these days, is something that Spain does not benefit from. Moreover, a large proportion of the services provided by the State to the Basque Country are not paid for, and therefore that Community enjoys revenues that are disproportionate to its fiscal contribution." This aggressive and unfair accusation was capped off by the allegation that the solidarity shown by the Basque Country "is virtually nil."

I personally know full well that it was possible for Catalonia to attain an Economic Agreement thirty years ago, and that it rejected this alternative for reasons that those in political power at the time considered entirely logical.

And now it affirms its right to have a suitable financial system that makes good those obvious deficiencies of the present system. However, it seems neither logical nor conducive to Catalan interests to defend its right to an Economic Agreement while at the same time declaring that such an accord is actually a privilege.

It is therefore important to undertake the important political task, both within the Basque Government and the EAJ-PNV (given the latter's special political relationship with CiU) and also within other Basque political parties, to at least moderate these kinds of sentiments, since they not only damage the Basque Economic Agreement but do not benefit Catalonia.

4. It is also necessary to disseminate and explain the model of the Economic Agreement on the international level, and especially within European institutions. The unfortunate experiences of previous years, which placed the Agreement in the center of political debate, and which also witnessed the Agreement being the focus of attention in European Union institutions, make such a course of action advisable.

Fortunately, this situation became normalized following the historic ruling of the Luxemburg Court regarding the regulatory capacity of the foral tax system. But we should not let our guard down.

For this reason, it is fundamentally necessary to reinforce the capacities of the lobby of the competent institutions of the historical territories and of the Autonomous Community within the complex institutional web of Brussels.

It is also necessary to emphasize within European Community institutions that the methodology of the quota may be entirely valid for the purposes of establishing, in the future, a coherent model of contribution from the tax systems of the member states of the European Union (which collect taxes within their respective territories) to the general tax system of the European Union as a contribution to the sustenance of the "general European competences and responsibilities" that are not assumed by member states. In other words, the Basque model for defining the Quota may be used, as a valid reference, to develop a federal tax model in the European Union.

5. With a view to the future, it will also be necessary to know how to

energetically defend our Economic Agreement with effective ideas, concepts, and arguments. This is especially the case during the times in which we live when, interestingly, a climate prevails that is highly critical of the Spanish autonomy model, and some are defending a process of recentralization of the State, something that is beginning to smell like the model reflected in the Organic Law Bill for Harmonizing the Autonomy Process (Ley Orgánica de Armonización del Proceso Autonómico(LOAPA) of 1981.[39]

This will require a strengthening of the technical teams of the foral institutions, and of the general tax system of the Basque Country, with specialists in fiscal federalism that will help to renovate and consolidate the arguments and solid constitutional, legislative, and historical reasons that support the survival of the Economic Agreement as currently constituted.

Along the lines suggested by Carmelo Garitaonandia this morning, I will venture to recommend the creation of chairs in the three universities that comprise the Basque university system, and in certain European and American universities.

In addition, courses and specialized master's degree programs should be created, as should scholarships for supporting doctoral theses for studies of the Agreement, financed by the three foral tax systems.

6. As an immediate priority, it is necessary to undertake a satisfactory negotiation of a new quota, given that the one currently in effect is set to expire this year.

This is an extremely important matter, given the fact that the action capacity of Basque institutions (i.e., the Basque and local governments, and the foral territorial governments) will be determined by the amount of the Quota, and this at a particularly sensitive time for the two negotiating parties, both of which are in need of resources as a result of the impact of the economic crisis on the ability of the Tax and Finance Departments of the foral territorial governments to collect revenues, and also as a consequence of the need to reduce the Spain Budget deficit by all means possible.

7. It is also necessary to work on the revision of the Economic Agreement for the purpose of incorporating greater regulatory capacities vis-à-vis indirect taxes and all of the new tax categories that might be proposed by state or European authorities (e.g., the "green tax," which could be studied for particular kinds of financial transactions).

This is a historical claim of Basque institutions that has been systematically rejected by the state. However, given the current parliamentary arithmetic in the Congress of Deputies (Spanish Parliament), it might be plausible to propose it at this time.

8. The current level of the regulatory capacity (or whatever level might be achieved in the future) makes the more decisive utilization of said capacity advisable. In addition, the management capacity that the Economic Agreement grants the competent institutions of the historical territories should be reinforced, without fear of defending the conceptually justified differentiation.

9. It is important to continue to pursue the struggle against fraud and tax evasion at a time that is critically important both socially and

politically, and within a current economic context of strong growth of the "black Economy" (the Spanish Ministry of Labor indicated it represents 20 percent of GDP). This should be done for reasons of solidarity and equity, and also for the purpose of reinforcing the resources of the foral tax systems in this manner.

To this end, the three foral tax and finance departments should reinforce their capacities—both those traditional capacities of inspection as well as others that would make technological development possible.

In this regard, the agreement between the Tax and Foral Finance Department of Bizkaia with a specialized international firm for the purpose of "reinforcing systems to prevent tax evasion and improving fraud control" is a positive development.

10. Finally, it is necessary to avoid lack of coordination of the kind that has been seen in the past among the tax and finance departments of the three foral territorial governments, and between each of them and the tax system of the Basque Country.

For this purpose, it is essential that the Basque Parliament approve the Law (established in Article 41.2.a of the Statute of Gernika)40 making reference to theregulations dictated by the Basque Parliament "for coordination, fiscal harmonization, and collaboration" between the three historical territories and the Autonomous Community.

In my personal opinion, Law 3/1989 of May 3041 is a regulation bereft of content, and one in need of a thoroughgoing revision.

The superficial level at which this issue was approached could possibly be explained by the fact that it was approved in 1989. In other words, it was approved just six years following the high tensions that arose as a result of the approval of the Law of the historical territories42 of which I was not only a witness, but a direct victim of the definition of the provisions related to the Basque Public Treasury.

In addition to being notably inadequate for its supposed purpose, this law has an additional provision that should not be forgotten, for it would seem to point the way to a possible transactional agreement between the two parties presumed to be in conflict with respect to the definition of Law 3/1989 (i.e., the Basque government and the foral territorial governments). This provision reads as follows: "The Basque Government will continue to present proposed laws to the Basque Government characterized by fiscal harmonization of the various taxes. For this purpose, within a time frame of no more than one year, the Basque Government will present proposed laws reflecting the harmonization guidelines in articles 3, 4 d.), e.), f.), and g.)."

It is obvious that, twenty-two years later, the Basque government has not sent any Law proposal to the Basque Parliament. And today it is necessary, even more than it was then.

Conclusion

The Economic Agreement was a unique document that had deep roots in Basque history. It should be respected, preserved, and optimized, since it is part and parcel of our autonomy, and is indeed its key element.

The great success that has been achieved by the Economic Agreement in the past thirty years and that the present Congress seeks to fully acknowledge and acclaim, has been the fruit of not only the good work of those who negotiated the document, but also of the profound conviction that we had, when we were conducting negotiations in 1980, that we in the Basque Country had at our disposal the sufficient ideas, strength, and capacity to overcome the consequences of the very severe economic, social, and political crisis in which the Basque Country was submerged at that time.

It is very encouraging to see that these same convictions, strength, and capacities remain very much alive today, some thirty years later.

I would like to offer my most heartfelt congratulations to the Foral Deputations; the governments of Bizkaia, Araba, and Gipuzkoa, for their wisdom in sponsoring this commemorative Congress; and also to the Center for the Documentation of the Economic Agreement and the Foral Tax Systems, led by Eduardo Alonso Olea, for organizing this Congress.

In addition, I would like to offer my profound gratitude for the opportunity to participate in this event, both in my own name and in the name of those who, on that unforgettable night of December 29, 1980, had the honor of drawing to a close the negotiations of what has become one of the cornerstones of our autonomy: the Economic Agreement.

This has been one of the greatest pleasures of my life—a life that has been extremely fortunate in so many ways.

Endnotes

1. See Nicolás de Vicario y Peña, *Fiat Lux: Monografía sobre tributación comparada de Vasconia y de otras provincias españolas* (Bilbao: Bizkaiko Foru Aldundia/Euskal Herriko Zuzenbide Historikorako Institutua, 2000 [1923]); Eduardo J. Alonso Olea, *El Concierto Económico desde la abolición foral hasta su recuperación (1839–1981).* (Bilbao: Bizkaiko Foru Aldundia, 2010).
2. Organic Law 3/1979, of December 18, of the Autonomy Statute for the Basque Country. State Administration Office (BOE no. 306, December 22, 1979).
3. Law 12/1981, of May 13th, which approved the Economic Agreement with the Autonomous Community of the Basque Country. State Administration Office (*BOE* no. 127, May 28, 1981).
4. *Actualidad Economica*, "Por fin," January 24, 1981.

5. *ABC*, "Se ha llegado a un acuerdo sobre los Conciertos Económicos," December 30, 1980.
6. *Deia*, "Firmados los conciertos," January 10, 1980.
7. Ministry of Economy and Finance, *El Concierto Económico entre el Estado yel País Vasco: El debate en las Cortes Generales* (Madrid: Secretaría General Técnica, 1983).
8. Law 12/1981, of May 13, which approved the Economic Agreement with the Autonomous Community of the Basque Country. State Administration Office (*BOE* no. 127, May 28, 1981).
9. Organic Law 3/1979, of December 18, of the Autonomy Statute for the Basque Country. State Administration Office (BOE no. 306, December 22, 1979); Law 12/1981, of May 13, which approved the Economic Agreement with the Autonomous Community of the Basque Country. State Administration Office (*BOE* no. 127, May 28, 1981).
10. Law 12/1981, of May 13, which approved the Economic Agreement with the Autonomous Community of the Basque Country. State Administration Office (*BOE* no. 127, May 28, 1981).
11. Juan Porres Azkona, *Política y derecho: Los derechos históricos vascos* (Oñati: IVAP, 1992).
12. *La Gaceta del Norte*, "Entrevista a Pedro Luis Uriarte," November 11, 1980
13. José Ramón Lopez-Larrinaga, "La experiencia de un negociador del Concierto Económico," *Azpilcueta* 18 (2002) 367–80.
14. *Deia*, *"Hoy, entrevista Uriarte—García Añoveros sobre Conciertos Económicos,"* November 20, 1980.
15. *Deia*, "Conciertos Económicos y Policía autónoma en el sprint final;" December 7, 1980; "Las negociaciones de los Conciertos Económicos continúan el lunes," December 12, 1980; "Conciertos: El cupo provisional podría acordarse el lunes o martes próximos," December 13, 1980; "Conciertos Económicos: ayer continuó el debate del cupo provisional," December 15, 1980.
16. Organic Law 3/1979, of December 18, of the Autonomy Statute for the Basque Country. State Administration Office (BOE no. 306, December 22, 1979).
17. *Deia*, *"Hoy, entrevista Uriarte—García Añoveros sobre Conciertos Económicos,"* November 20, 1980.
18. Ministry of Economy and Finance, *El Concierto Económico entre el Estado yel País Vasco: El debate en las Cortes Generales* (Madrid: Secretaría General Técnica, 1983).
19. *ABC*, "Cincuenta y cinco meses," January 30, 1981.
20. *El Pais*, "El Gobierno de Euskadi da la bienvenida a los Reyes de España en Vitoria," February 3, 1981.
21. *ABC*, "Calvo Sotelo Presidente por 186 votos," February 25, 1981.
22. Ministry of Economy and Finance, *El Concierto Económico entre el Estado yel País Vasco: El debate en las Cortes Generales* (Madrid: Secretaría General Técnica, 1983).
23. *ABC*, "Garcia Añoveros ante el grupo parlamentario socialista," April 9, 1981.
24. *La Vanguardia*, "Aprobados los conciertos económicos con el País Vasco," April 10, 1981.

25. *ABC*, "En el Pleno del Senado, aprobado el Concierto Económico con la Comunidad Autónoma del País Vasco," April 29, 1981.
26. Minutes of the Congress of Deputies, Plenary Session 159, held April 9, 1981, and Plenary Session 101, held April 28, 1981.
27. Law 12/1981, of May 13, which approved the Economic Agreement with the Autonomous Community of the Basque Country. State Administration Office (*BOE* no. 127, May 28, 1981).
28. Pedro Luis Uriarte Santamarina, "Un pacto para construir un País," address at the Twenty-fifth Anniversary Congress of the Economic Agreement, 2005.
29. Organic Law 3/1979, of December 18, of the Autonomy Statute for the Basque Country. State Administration Office (BOE no. 306, December 22, 1979).
30. *Expansión*, "Las fortunas huyen del País Vasco," January 7, 2011.
31. Law 12/1981, of May 13, which approved the Economic Agreement with the Autonomous Community of the Basque Country. State Administration Office (*BOE* no. 127, May 28, 1981).
32. Ibid.
33. Ministry of Economy and Finance, *El Concierto Económico entre el Estado y el País Vasco: El debate en las Cortes Generales* (Madrid: Secretaría General Técnica, 1983).
34. Pedro Luis Uriarte Santamarina, "El concierto económico de 1980: Gestión, balance y perspectivas," Address for the occasion of the awarding of the first diploma for Administration of Public Finances, 2004.
35. Pedro Luis Uriarte Santamarina, "El concierto económico de 1981, un pacto y un acto de fe," *Deia*, April 19, 2011; "El concierto económico de 1981 superó escollos muy difíciles," *Deia*, April 20, 2011; and "El concierto económico debe ser potenciado y defendido," *Deia*. April 26, 2011.
36. *La Vanguardia*, "La mayoría quiere el Concierto Económico," November 23, 2010.
37. *ABC*, "Artur Mas expone ante el Rey su propuesta soberanista," February 1, 2011.
38. *ABC*, "Felip Puig ve inviable aplicar el concierto económico vasco en toda España," November 30, 2010.
39. *La Vanguardia*, "En vez de sacar los tanques," January 19, 2011.
40. Organic Law 3/1979, of December 18, of the Autonomy Statute for the Basque Country. State Administration Office (BOE no. 306, December 22, 1979).
41. Law 3/1989, of May 30, for Fiscal Harmonization, Coordination, and Collaboration. Published in the *BOPV*, June 9, 1989.
42. Law 27/1983, of November 25 regarding Relations between the Common Institutions of the Autonomous Community and the Foral Bodies of the Historical Territories. Published in the *BOPV*, December 10, 1983.

Bibliography

Alonso Olea, Eduardo J. *El Concierto Económico desde la abolición foral hasta su recuperación (1839–1981)*. Bilbao: Bizkaiko Foru Aldundia, 2010.

Lopez-Larrinaga, José Ramón. "La experiencia de un negociador del

Concierto Económico," 2002. *Azpilcueta* 18 (2002): 367–380.

Ministry of Economy and Finance. *El Concierto Económico entre el Estado yel País Vasco: El debate en las Cortes Generales*. Madrid: Secretaría General Técnica, 1983.

Porres Azkona, Juan. *Política y derecho: Los derechos históricos vascos.* Oñati: IVAP, 1992.

Vicario y Peña, Nicolás de. *Fiat Lux: Monografía sobre tributación comparada de Vasconia y de otras provincias españolas*. Bilbao: Bizkaiko Foru Aldundia/Euskal Herriko Zuzenbide Historikorako Institua, 2000 [1923]. Available online at www.ehu.es/ituna/pdf/FiatLux.pdf.

Part 2
Public Finances, Public Opinion

5
The Economic Agreement as a Tool

Mario Fernández

After a brief introduction, I will discuss the financial crisis and the current situation and outlook with respect to Spain and the Autonomous Community of the Basque Country. I am personally more interested in the future than in past history. In this respect, the future of the Economic Agreement, and of our country in general, will be determined by the consequences of the financial and economic crisis. As I will explain later, nothing will be the same once this crisis has ended—and until the next one strikes.

Therefore, once the present financial crisis is over, and until the next one comes along, I think it very important that we use the Economic Agreement as a tool to confront the challenges that our small country will be facing, in order to best prepare for the future.

As I've said, it makes sense to reflect on the situation we now face with the current financial crisis—a crisis which has led, as could be expected, to a general economic crisis, because it will have a determining effect on all aspects of our lives.

I'm sure that the forecast that I'm providing here will have to be revised in another two weeks. However, it will help give us some idea of both the current situation, and of the prospects for recovery.

Table 5.1 presents the rather alarming case of Germany. It appears that this country will end the year with a significant growth of 3.6 percent. Notice how the forecast of the International Monetary Fund for the coming years point to important declines—the figure for 2012 falling to almost 1.6 percent. I would argue that Germany is a part of the Basque Country. A large number of companies that make an important contribution to the GDP of Euskadi—and thus, ipso facto, that also make an important contribution in terms of employment—are extremely dependent on the health of the German economy. Perhaps the most striking example of this—although my no means the only one—can be found in the automobile industry. In the Basque Country, there is an important cluster of businesses tied to various automobile components. Therefore, it is obvious that the better the functioning of German factories that produce motor vehicles, the more work this will generate in Durango, Azkoitia, Derio, and other towns. It is therefore a matter of concern that forecasts predict a decrease in growth in Germany from 3.6 to 2 percent. In Spain, the decrease will be to between –0.2 and –0.3 percent. Thus, we are looking at a situation that will essentially be stable: no growth, but also no worsening of the most serious consequences.

Table 5.1 Changes in Estimated GDP (in Percentages)

	2009	**2010**	**2011**	**2012**
World average	–0.6	5.0	4.4	4.5
Advanced economies	–3.4	3.0	2.5	2.5
United States	–2.6	2.8	3.0	2.7
Eurozone	–4.1	1.8	1.5	1.7
Germany	–4.7	3.6	2.2	2.0
France	–2.5	1.6	1.6	1.8
Italy	–5.0	1.0	1.0	1.3
Spain	–3.7	–0.2	0.6	1.5
Basque Country	–3.8	0.3	1.5	—
Emerging market economies	2.6	7.1	6.5	6.5

Source:Instituto Nacional de Estadística (INE)

In the Basque Country, it seems that the year will end at about +0.3 percent: in other words, with a slightly positive growth. It also appears that growth of GDP will double next year as compared to the rest of Spain.

It is important to address—and I will clarify later exactly what this means—the subject of the appearance of emerging economies. Emerging economies have experienced a very important growth, and it appears that this will continue. But let's not forget one thing: the emerging nations comprise some million people, a large number of whom live in poverty. Therefore, anyone who thinks that that consumption will immediately be displaced from the first world to the emerging countries is gravely mistaken. Instead, fewer cars and washing machines will be sold, because the vast majority of those living in emerging countries live in poverty, and a number of years will be needed for these people to achieve a spending capacity that com-

Table 5.2. Current Ten-Year Bond Spread (Yields Are Based on Bid Prices, Standard Settlement, and Are Conventional)

	Den.	Fran.	Neth.	Fin.	Bel.	NEED	Spain	Ger.	Italy	Ire.	Port.
Port.	385.8	348.7	367.2	367.7	282.1	334.9	134.5	–550.8	214.6	–242.8	—
Ire.	628.5	591.4	610.0	610.4	524.9	577.7	377.2	–308.0	457.4	—	242.8
Italy	171.1	134.1	152.6	153.0	67.5	120.3	–80.2	–765.4	—	–457.4	–241.6
Ger.	936.5	899.5	918.0	918.5	832.9	885.7	685.2	—	765.4	308.0	550.8
Spain	251.3	214.2	232.8	233.2	147.7	200.5	—	–685.2	80.2	–377.2	–134.5
NEED	50.8	13.8	32.3	32.8	–52..8	—	–200.5	–885.7	–120.3	–577.7	–334.9
Bel.	103.6	66.6	85.1	85.5	—	52.8	–147.7	–832.9	–67.5	–524.9	–282.1
Fin.	18.1	–19.0	–4	—	–85.5	–32.8	–233.2	–918.5	–153.0	–610.4	367.7
Neth.	18.5	–18.6	—	.4	–85.1	–32.3	–232.8	–918.0	–152.6	–610.0	–367.2
Fran.	37.1	—	18.6	19.0	–66.6	–13.8	–21.2	–899.5	–134.1	–591.4	–348.7
Den.	—	–37.1	–18.5	–18.1	–103.6	–50.8	–251.3	–936.5	–171.1	–628.5	–385.8
YIELD	2.98	3.35	3.17	3.16	4.02	3.49	5.50	12.35	4.69	9.27	6.84
TIME	8:00	8:00	9:28	8:00	9:28	9:28	7:51	12/23	9:43	7:40	12/23
PCS	CBBT	CBBT	CBBT	CBBT	CBBT	CBBT	CBBT	CBBT	CBBT	CBBT	CBBT

pensates for the decreased spending capacity of what we call the "First World."

So what exactly is going on in Spain? A few basic facts will help explain the situation. First, look at the differential with respect to the German bond in table 5.2. France displays the least differential, and Belgium a somewhat greater differential. This trend continues with Spain, Greece, Italy, Portugal, and Ireland. Spain shows a differential superior only to Greece, Ireland, and Portugal. The first two of these countries were rescued by European Union action, and the third appears to be headed in the same direction. In the rest of the cases, the Spanish bond markedly suffers in comparison with the German bond. Later in this essay, I will discuss what is happening, for example, in the relationship among Spain, Italy, and the United Kingdom. What this relationship clearly shows is that there is a lack of confidence in the markets with respect to the Spanish economy, given that we are talking about differential rates that are really noteworthy. I'd like to draw your attention to the column in table 5.2 in which Finland appears. Finland, because of its size, seems to offer a number of points of comparison with the Autonomous Community of the Basque Country. We might therefore benefit from examining its evolution. Some fifteen years ago, Finland was in a worse situation than Spain finds itself in now. Today, as we can see in table 5.2, it enjoys a strong position.

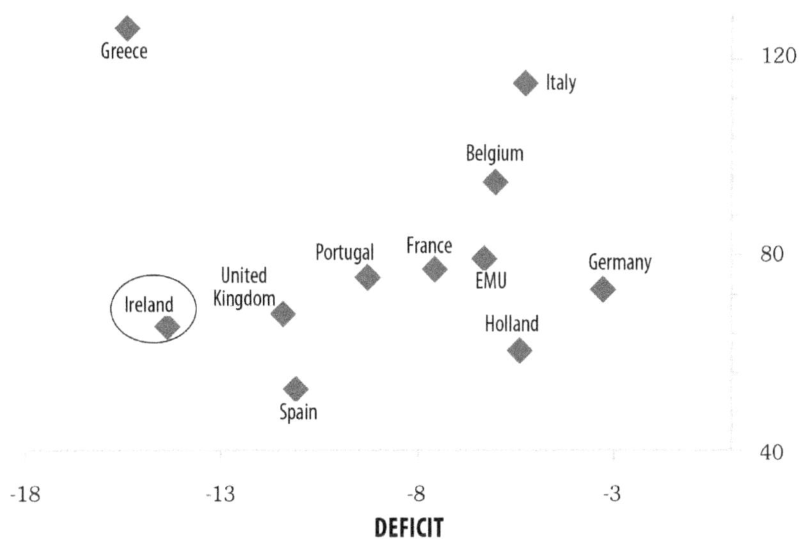

Figure 5.1. Deficit and debt of the principal EMU countries (2009 percentage of GDP). Source: Eurostat, November 10, 2009.

As far as the Spanish economy is concerned, it seems that people don't pay attention to the numbers. In the table, we can see debt in the upper portion and "deficit in relation to GDP" in the lower portion. Thus, for Spain, debt in relation to GDP is about 64 percent. This ratio for other countries is as follows: Italy, 106 percent; Belgium, 95 percent; Germany, 73.4 percent; France, 71.8 percent; and the United Kingdom, 68 percent. For the European Union as a whole, the figure is 79.2 percent. These numbers show that there is another critically important factor in the markets: *credibility*. Relatively speaking, Italy doubles Spain in terms of debt in relation to GDP; nevertheless, we see in figure 5.1 that even though Italy also has to pay an increased premium, this premium is markedly different from that which Spain is obliged to pay. Another example of this lack of confidence is the fact that, three weeks ago, BBVA turned to the markets, and had to pay a differential of 2.25 percent, while ING had to pay a differential of 0.60 percent and BNP Paribas had to pay 0.65 percent. All together, these data offer a picture of the solvency of Spain, rather than of BBVA.

Therefore, one could say that the Spanish "brand" has negatively affected BBVA in its access to markets. We thus face a very critical situation as a consequence of a lack of credibility. Finally, as one last example of this absence of credibility, we let's have a look at the closing figures for December 31, 2010, of the IBEX-35 and the EUROSTOXX 50 (a very important reference), and of other stock exchanges (table 5.3). The IBEX-35 finished with a loss of 17.43 percent and the EUROSTOXX 50 with a loss of 5.81 percent. In almost all of the other cases, there were varying levels of growth. Most surprising of all are the final two lines: BBVA finished with a loss of –38.19 percent compared to the previous year; and Santander with a loss of –31.36 percent. Anyone attempting to analyze the solvency and capacity of BBVA and Santander in comparison to the rest of the European banks from a financial point of view would have a hard time establishing that either of these two banks are less solvent and have worse future prospects

Table 5.3 Behavior of the Spanish Stock Market

Indexes	**2010 compared to 2009**
IBEX 35	–17.43%
EUROSTOXX 50	–5.81%
CAC / PARIS	–3.34%
DAX / FRANKFURT	16.06%
FTSE / LONDON	9.00%
DOW JONES	11.02%
NASDAQ	16.91%
NIKKEI / TOKYO	–3.01%
STOCKS	
BBVA	–38.19%
BANCO SANTANDER	–31.36%

than other European banks. Nevertheless, we are talking about a very important reduction in market capitalization. Therefore, what we see occurring here is an impact on the real economy, and especially on financial entities, as a result of the aforementioned lack of credibility of the Spanish government vis-à-vis the markets.

In the case of the Autonomous Community of the Basque Country, the situation is rather different. First, the rest of Spain is the economic structure of Euskadi. In this respect, important data include the role of industry, which is 10 percentage points higher in the Basque Country than in the Spanish economy. Second, a large proportion of services involve adding value to industrial products. Yet this economic structure did not arise by accident and is not artificial. As we have previously seen, from the point of view of GDP growth, the Autonomous Community of the Basque Country has a track record better than that of the Spanish economy. In absolute terms, growth is modest. But the difference is especially great in terms of unemployment, where the rate here is half that of Spain, and is roughly equivalent to the average of the European Union, or even the United States. In addition, according to recently published data, on December 31, 2009, the per capita GDP of Euskadi is 30,383 euros. The figures for Spain and Europe are 22,946 and 29,000, respectively. Once again, this is no accident, but rather the result of two important factors: (1) the activity of institutions over the course of many years, an activity specifically based on the financial opportunities provided by the Economic Agreement; and (2) the fact that the entrepreneurs and workers of Euskadi have made important efforts in terms of internationalization, modernization, and innovation. However, in my opinion, these efforts have been insufficient, and we need to experience a second stage in order to be where we need to be within the community of nations. Today, every company understands that the best way to assure the strength of companies and maximize the available number of job positions in the Basque Country is to invest abroad. For example, we can once again point to the case of the automobile industry, given that the companies within this sector are located all over the world. Automobile manufacturers are located in Europe, Brazil (where all of the U.S. and European companies have operations), and Mexico (where all of the U.S. companies have operations). We should therefore not think of internationalization as something adverse, either in terms of employment or in terms of the strengthening of Basque companies; in fact, it is just the opposite. Failure to internationalize implies creating walls around one's national borders, and this can only mean certain death.

The benefits of the Economic Agreement can be readily seen in this snapshot of the economic situation of the Autonomous Community of the Basque Country, even if we recognize that the situation

Table 5.4. Economic Structure of the Autonomous Community of the Basque Country Compared to Spain

2009 GDP	Basque Country	Spain
Services	58.5%	66.2%
Primary services	0.9%	2.5%
Industry	24.6%	14.4%
Taxes	7.1%	7.0%
Construction	8.8%	10.0%
Employment by sector, 2010		
Services	67.6	72.4
Agriculture	0.9	4.2
Industry	23.8	14.2
Construction	7.7	9.3

Source: INE, Eustat.

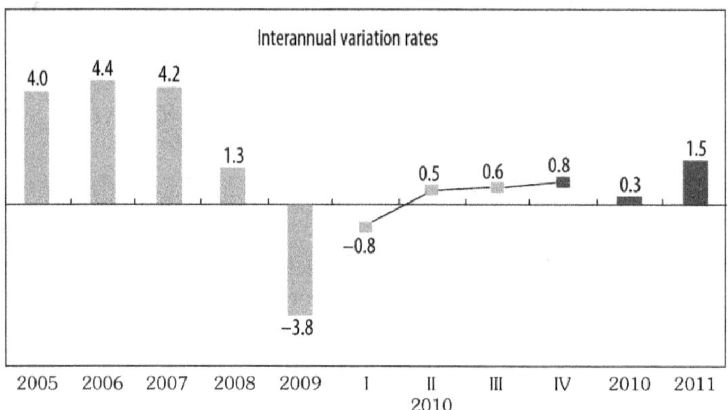

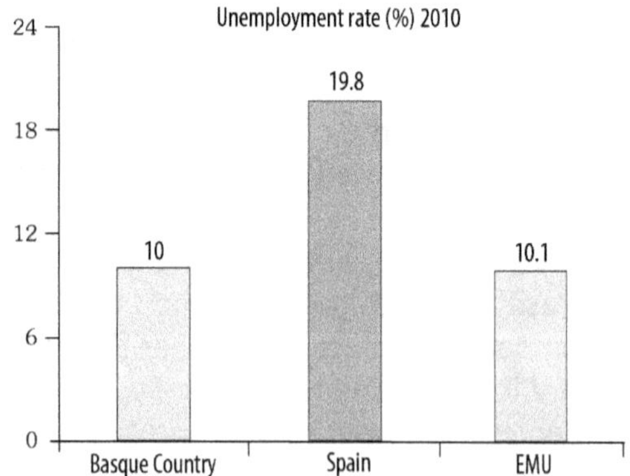

Figure 5.2. Evolution of GDP in the Basque Country.
GDP/Resident: 30.683 euros (First-ranking Autonomous Community)
Spanish mean: 22.946 euros
Source: Eustat and the Office of Economy and Planning

here gives cause for concern, since we are talking about very small growth indices, as well as an unemployment rate of 10 percent. All in all, Euskadi compares favorably with the rest of the Spanish state. Intelligent policies fostering the creation of companies and bolstering their strength have been implemented. Also relevant in this respect are the misleadingly named "tax holidays." It is important to note that this is not the only European territory where such aid is offered, and that no one would think tax holidays a problem if this were France. In the European Union, the operating premise is that all members are equal, but that some are more equal than others.

Although the Economic Agreement constitutes an essential component of self-government and has been a decisive element in this relatively positive situation, it has endured various ups and downs over the years. In fact, the Agreement has been continually called into question as a result of its being seen by some as a privilege. At the time that it was negotiated, back in 1981, highly distinguished politicians warned us that, if we signed the Economic Agreement, we would be assuming responsibility for the future of Euskadi. We need to place this sentiment in the context of the 1980s, a time of serious crisis—a crisis different from the one that we face today, since it was not financial in origin, with unemployment rates of 25 percent. And yet shipyards were closing, the steel industry was being abandoned, the chemical sector was closing, and small and medium businesses were facing an absolutely unacceptable situation. It is often willfully ignored that the Economic Agreement involves serious risk—namely, the risk involved in collecting taxes. It is also often willfully ignored that the Basque Country income tax rates are higher.

It should be recalled that, even though the Economic Agreement is grounded in the constitution, it also predates the current constitution. It is generally known that, during the period of Francisco Franco's rule, something along the lines of the present Economic Agreement was instituted in one of the three historical territories. The Agreement can therefore be characterized as one that is "preconstitutional" and grounded in the present constitution and legal statutes.

On the other hand, this constant questioning has at times been voiced by bordering Autonomous Communities. We are all aware of the important aid that exists in certain bordering Autonomous Communities that file various kinds of motions against the Foral Regulations of the Economic Agreement. We have also heard it said on any number of occasions that, as a result of the Autonomy Statute, there is no other region in Europe with more self-government than Euskadi. However, at the time of the famous ruling of the "Azores Doctrine,"[1] which introduced the equally famous issue of institutional, procedural, and economic autonomy, many agreed that it did not apply to the Autonomous Community of the Basque Country. Thus, in the eyes of many, the European Court of Justice did not so much issue a ruling as create a doctrine that belonged within the realm of science fiction, since it established conditions that no one in Europe complies with. And so, after the Azores ruling, doubts arose regarding whether the Autonomous Community of the Basque Country in general, and the Economic Agreement in particular (based upon the Foral Deputations), was or was not in compliance with these conditions. Finally, in November 2008, the ruling was issued by the Supreme European Court of Justice, applying the assumption to Euskadi, but at the same time leaving the door open for the possibility of some kind of legal challenge.

We thus come to the final phase, in which we witness a truly paradoxical situation: the pretense of applying the principle of equality is once again referred to in terms of privilege, and thus this principle has come to function as a kind of legal immunity—but not in the accustomed favorable sense in which this characterization has typically been used vis-à-vis the Autonomous Community of the Basque Country. Once it was clear that the Foral Regulation has, from the material point of view, the force and scope of law, attempts were made to show that any impugning of the Foral Regulations could only occur within the context of judicial actions that could be applied to any other law. The reasonable call for nondiscrimination was characterized as an attempt to encase the Economic Agreement in a kind of protective armor. As has always been the case, this was done for spurious motives and as a consequence of changing political winds. There is no doubt that Organic Law 1/2010 at the very least began to direct the discussion toward the future.

In my opinion, the Agreement has played a crucial role in preserving a relatively stable economic situation in the Basque Country during the present difficult times. The Economic Agreement has been used wisely and efficiently by the Foral Deputations and in a way that has promoted investment, innovation, and knowledge. It seems to me that it has been absolutely essential in creating the current situation in our Autonomous Community.

Having made this point, let me return to what I said at the beginning: what we need to analyze at this point is the future of the Economic Agreement. Up until now, I believe that it is possible to make only an unreservedly positive assessment of the role of the Agreement. However, in order to be able to consider its future, we need to analyze what is going on now and how the world will look once the current economic crisis is over.

As we can already see, there will be a reconfiguration of the international economic structure. As evidence of this, we can see, first of all, the declining relevance of Europe. However much it is asserted to the contrary, Europe is by no means a political project whose future is assured. From the political and economic point of view, it has less and less influence in the world. We can see this in terms of what is now going on in the Arab world, a situation regarding which the European Union has expressed its views in only the most timid fashion and has shown absolutely no initiative. The European Union clearly has a serious problem, however much it may be denied, "national interests" continue to be important. But the real underlying problem is that Europe as a project has not been undertaken for the benefit of Europeans or of individual states. It is a political model that has not been realized, that has not come together. And it also has no economic model. As a consequence of the current crisis—it would not have occurred otherwise—some kind of fiscal coordination has been initiated. Does this mean that Europe, and those of us who are part of it, are doomed? Is the proper European economic policy what receives Germany's blessing? Inflation has recently spiked: in Spain, it is at 3 percent, which, given the crisis, isn't all that bad. If inflation increases a bit more, we will see an increase in the interest rates of the Central European Bank in response to Germany's requirements, and this rate increase will place the Spanish economy in a very difficult situation. We all know that Germans seem incapable of living with inflation and deficit.

A second reason is the shift of the center of gravity to the Pacific and Southeast Asia. At present, the countries in that region not only have the workforce to manufacture Nike berets at low cost, but also some important high-tech companies that have been involved in very significant innovation efforts and that can compete with "First World" companies. The appearance of these emerging nations, as previously mentioned, is something of a mixed blessing. These countries, with approximately six billion persons, could benefit economically and socially from the expansion of international trade, and therefore possibly generate the capacity for an improved distribution of goods and services. But this is only a prospect in the distant future, because presently more than a third of these residents are living in conditions of extreme poverty. Therefore, the possibility that these persons could replace the purchasing power of those of us in the "First World" who are now buying or consuming goods and services is something that needs to be thought about in highly pragmatic terms. China is the primary creditor of the United States, the primary locus of public debt and also has an increasing stake in various European and Latin American companies. As a consequence, China, a new player in the market, with great economic power, is gaining force. The fact that China's currency is tied to the dollar and is also highly competitive with the euro, further bolsters its power.

I would like to conclude with some comments about the future, from the standpoint of both the Economic Agreement and the Basque Country.

We need to appreciate the fact that our country is small. If the Autonomous Community of the Basque Country were a city, it would, according to Google, be ranked the 182nd largest in the world. Given this reality, and in the face of the situation that may well prevail following the present crisis and before the emergence of the next one, it seems essential to seriously consider the need for a reappraisal and a more thoroughgoing internationalization of the Basque economy in every sector. But we have an additional problem, and that is the fact that the locus of decision-making makes it difficult to reach agreements. We need to assure that we exercise our influence so that, in the power-sharing process, we redirect the enterprise in which we participate to the real interests of Euskadi. This is difficult, but it can be done. What we cannot do is remain silent.

The Basque Country needs to evaluate its situation and possible strategies based on the premise that we are powerless to change the circumstances that we are currently faced with and that we might be faced with in the future. What we need to do now is define the strategy that, accepting these circumstances as givens, allows us to assure a prosperous future for our nation. As I said earlier, the Basque economy was markedly successful in weathering the crisis of the 1980s and 1990s. It also emerged relatively unscathed from the lesser "dot-com" crisis of 1999–2000. We are currently in an excellent position to successfully deal with the present crisis. We also need to see our location straddling the borders of two different states as a strategic focal point within Europe. We have 2,200,000 residents. In addition, we also have a "hinterland" of six million residents over which we can exercise influence. It is essential that we redefine ourselves within an international map in which functioning as part of a network is essential, and in which the formation of alliances is indispensable. And we most definitely need to do our best to intelligently advance our interests within the context of a reality that we are powerless to change.

At the beginning of this essay, I mentioned Finland, a country that has somewhat more than double the number of residents of the Autonomous Community of the Basque Country. The year 1993 ended with Finland reporting an unemployment rate of 19 percent, –12 percent GDP, and a 14 percent deficit. And today, as we saw earlier, that nation is in excellent financial health and trails Germany by only 18 percentage points. Therefore, it is not necessary to start from square one; instead, it is important to analyze successful models in nations of our size that have managed to find a place among the highest-ranking nations of the world.

Regarding companies, I am absolutely convinced that a redefinition of scope is absolutely necessary. It is also essential that we heed the famous adage of not placing all our eggs in one basket. For this reason, the process of internationalization that Basque companies have carried out is a step in the right direction. In the case of banks, for example, only 18 percent of the EBITDA (earnings before interest, taxes, depreciation, and amortization) of Banco Santander is in the Spanish market. This is a clear example of the internationalization that I am referring to.

This is the challenge of the Economic Agreement: making use of it as a tool in order to confront—in terms of our companies and of our nation as a whole—the situation that awaits us following the present crisis. Because when this one is over, we will need to be in the best position to deal with the next crisis that comes along.

It is beyond doubt that the Economic Agreement is an essential tool for the creation of wealth and the economic development of the Basque nation. This is a practical truth, and not simply a matter of theory. At the same time, we must resituate ourselves within the new scenario, and we should begin doing so sooner rather than later. We haven't a moment to lose.

Endnotes

1. This is how it is known in the European Court of Justice in relation to an assistance program in the Azores.

6
An Assessment of the Economic Agreement: Myths and Realities

Ignacio Zubiri

The system of the Economic Agreement is a mechanism to regulate the financial and fiscal relationships between the Basque provinces and the state dating back to 1878. This first Economic Agreement was the only element left of much more extensive foral rights abolished in 1876, after the defeat of the Carlists in the Third Carlist War. The Economic Agreement model lasted until 1936 when, after the victory of the Nationalists, Francisco Franco abolished it in Bizkaia and Gipuzkoa.[1] Franco's death and the approval of the Constitution of 1978 saw the re-establishment of the Agreement in all three Basque Provinces. In 1981, the first Economic Agreement Law of the new Spanish democracy was approved. It lasted twenty years before being replaced in 2002 by a second Agreement that was essentially identical to its predecessor, but of unlimited duration.[2]

Since its approval, the implementation Economic Agreement has raised many problems. Most of them had to do with two issues: First the size of the quota.[3] The quota, or to be more precise, the resources the Basque Autonomous Community (BAC) has after paying the quota[4] are considered discriminatory by many *common system*[5] Autonomous Communities (AC), significantly by Catalonia.

The second important problem is with the use of the tax power in tax the BAC has in the corporation tax. The corporate taxes approved by the BAC have led to numerous conflicts with neighboring AC, with the state,[6] and even with the European Commission. At one time or another all those institutions have expressed the opinion that the corporate tax of the BAC[7] was distortionary and, therefore, contrary to free competition. Since both the Economic Agreement and European regulations prohibit distortionary taxes, the result has been frequent lawsuits in Spanish and European courts.

The aim of this paper is to make a balanced assessment of the results of the Economic Agreement thirty years after its approval. Special attention will be paid to the most controversial issues of the Agreement: (1) The revenue the BAC obtains from the Agreement (in comparison to what common regime AC obtain), (2) the taxes in the Basque Country compared to those of the rest of Spain (total tax burden in general and, in particular, in corporate taxation), and (3) whether the Foral Deputations[8] have properly used their tax powers (conflicts with the state and the European Union). The starting point will be to describe what a Foral system is. The next part of this essay analyzes the fiscal autonomy of the BAC. It firsts describes the fiscal autonomy the BAC. After that, it analyzes the conflicts with the central government and the European Commission due to the tax autonomy. The third part of this essay compares tax collection in the BAC and in the rest of Spain, while the fourth part studies the transfers between the central government and the BAC (quota and fiscal adjustments). The fifth part measures the financial capacity of the BAC and compares it with that of the common system AC, while the sixth part analyzes the economic effects of the Economic Agreement. Finally, the last part summarizes of the main conclusions of the paper.

The Economic Agreement: Basic Characteristics

The Economic Agreement is a pact that regulates the financial and fiscal relations between the BAC and the Spanish State. The pact is based on two basic principles:

> (1) *Fiscal Autonomy of the BAC.* The management, collection and (subject to some harmonization restrictions) design of the main taxes belong to the BAC. The taxes assigned the BAC are called *agreed taxes.*
>
> (2) *Payment of the quota.* Given that the state continues to make expenditures for the benefit of the BAC, the latter makes a payment to the state called the quota as compensation for those expenses.

The model of fiscal and financial relations regulated by (1) and (2) is called the *foral financing system* to distinguish it from the *common system* (which is the financing model for all the other AC except Navarre[9]).

In line with previous historical tradition, *fiscal autonomy* has not been transferred to the BAC (to the Basque government) but to the governments of the three provinces (the so-called historical territories or HTs) of that make up the BAC[10] (the Foral Deputations). The HTs design and collect all the agreed taxes which, among others, include the personal income tax (PIT), VAT, and corporate taxes. In theory, the three HT can have very different taxes. In practice, however, taxes have been very similar. In 1989 the Basque Parliament approved the Law of Harmonization among the fiscal systems of the HTs.[11] This law establishes a number of general harmonization principles.[12] However, the usefulness of the law is limited because it does not clearly define what exactly needs to be harmonized or what happens if one of the HTs does not harmonize.[13] The law led to the creation of the Tax Coordination Bureau of Euskadi (TCB). This body, which comprises representatives of the Deputations and the Basque government,[14] is responsible for ensuring the harmonization (though not for imposing strict equality) of the tax systems of the HTs. The harmonization has been attained via consensus[15] rather than applying the vague Harmonization Law (which, in fact, has never been applied).

The harmonization within the TCB and the rules for distributing tax collection among the government levels of the BAC[16] partly explain why taxes in the HT a relatively low in the BAC:[17] because any HT that tries to increase taxes unilaterally (because it either needs or wants more resources) will face the opposition of the other HTs within the TCB. In addition, even if the HT seeking an increase ignores such opposition and goes ahead, because of the way that the Law of the Historical Territories[18] is formulated, it will end up with only a small fraction of the additional taxes collected. For example, Bizkaia would end with about 0.65 euros of each additional euro collected, Gipuzkoa with about 0.75 euros, and Araba with about 0.90. Furthermore, the Foral Deputations (which are the ones who decide if taxes increase) will have to give to the municipalities half of what is left. By this mechanism, for instance, the Foral Deputation of Bizkaia only keeps 0.33 cents of each euro of taxes it collects. And this is not certainly an incentive to raise taxes.

The second component of the Foral model is the quota. Historically, the quota was a renting fee for the agreed taxes. The quota was, therefore, equal to the estimated tax collection of the agreed taxes[19] (less the estimated expenditure needs of the HT). In its current design, the quota is a payment for what the state spends for the benefit of the residents in the Basque Country and, therefore, it is independent of the collection of agreed taxes. While taxes are agreed with each HT, the quota is set globally for the BAC. The resulting amount is paid by the Deputations in the percentages agreed upon in the Law of Contributions.[20]

Tax Powers: Delimitation and Use

The first pillar of the Economic Agreement is fiscal autonomy. The exercise of fiscal autonomy on the part of the BAC (strictly speaking, of the HTs) has been plagued by conflict, especially as regards the corporation tax. The BAC has frequently been accused of exceeding its powers and of reducing taxes on business beyond what is permitted by the Economic Agreement and by the of the EU regulations.

In this section, I will review the tax powers of the HTs before examining how they have used those powers. I will finally analyze the cause of the conflicts with the state and the European Union.

Tax Powers of the Historical Territories

To characterize the tax powers of the HTs it is necessary to determine which taxes are under their control (are agreed) and what they can do with those taxes. Table 6.1 analyzes the first question and details the fiscal revenues that have not been agreed with the HTs of the BAC. Obviously, the taxes not listed have been transferred to the HTs. As this table shows, all taxes have been agreed with only three exceptions. First, withholding taxes on the wages of state (central government) employees (civil servants or other). Second, withholding taxes on the interest of assets issued by the state or any AC or Municipality of Common Territory or Navarre. Third, Custom Duties, which as in the rest of the EU countries, are a resource of the European Union.

Table 6.1. Non Agreed Fiscal Revenues (2011)[1]

a) Taxes
Custom Duties
Withholding tax on wages of State employees
Withholding tax on interests of the Debt (or any other interest-bearing asset) issued by the State, or any AC or municipality in common territory or Navarre.
b) User Fees and Public Prices
User Fees, Public Prices, and other revenue linked to expenditures made by the State (expenditure responsibilities not assumed by the BCAC)
c) Social Security Contributions

1. The situation is the same since 1997 when excises duties were agreed upon

As for withholding taxes collected by the state, it should be first pointed out that everybody living in the Basque Country[21] (including all central government employees) has to file taxes in one of the HTs of the BAC and report all his income in the personal income tax (including the income from assets issued by the state or the AC and municipalities of common regime and Navarre). Therefore, even though the state collects the withheld taxes on certain incomes, that income is also reported to the Basque tax authorities. To compensate the HTs for the revenue loss,[22] an estimation of the taxes withheld by the state in the Basque Country is subtracted from the quota.

The second group on non-agreed fiscal revenues includes user fees and public prices. That is, what the state charges for services provided in the Basque Country. Again, these resources obtained by the state in the BAC are subtracted from the quota.

Finally, the state (strictly speaking the Social Security) collects social security contributions in the Basque Country. This is natural because in Spain social security contributions are used exclusively to finance pensions and unemployment benefits. Since the state provides in the BAC both, pensions and unemployment benefits, it also collects the necessary social security contributions. Obviously, the BAC would only collect the social security contributions if it assumed the responsibility to provide pensions and unemployment benefits—that is, if the Basque Country had a social security separated from that of the rest of Spain.

In conclusion, the central government almost does not collect taxes in the BAC. All the general taxes (PIT, corporation income tax, VAT, excise duties, and so on) are collected by the HTs of the BAC. This implies that, in a basic sense, the BAC is the region in the world with highest fiscal autonomy. Simply, the BAC is the only region in the world (including the most autonomous regions such as the Swiss Cantons, the states of the United States, and the province of Quebec in Canada) in which its central government does not collect any tax.

The fiscal autonomy of the HTs is subject to two types of constraints. First, there is a set of general restrictions that apply to the fiscal system as a whole. Second, there are specific restrictions on each tax.

General Limitations

The general principles of harmonization that the fiscal systems of the HTs have to satisfy are summarized in table 6.2. As the table shows, the fiscal systems of the HTs are subject to, basically, three constraints: (1) they must submit to the International Agreements or Treaties signed by Spain; (2) they should not distort the competence among firms or the free movement among regions (*principle of no distortion*); and (3) the fiscal pressure (tax to GDP ratio) in the *BAC*[23] has to be *equivalent* to that existing in the rest of Spain.

Obviously, some of these principles are, to say the least, ambiguous. For instance, it is not clear what *equivalent fiscal pressure* means. Does it mean that fiscal pressure in the *BAC* cannot differ more than 10 percent (above or below) from fiscal pressure in the rest of Spain? Or is the relevant figure 5 percent? More importantly, the main cause of the conflicts between the state and the *BAC* is the principle of no distortion. The principle has, however, a high degree of subjectivity. The reason is simple. Distortion is a matter of degree and any tax difference between the *BAC* and the rest of Spain, no matter how small it

Table 2: Harmonization Principles between the Tax Systems of the *BCAC* and the State (2012)

A. General Principles
1. Respect for the principle of solidarity in the terms laid down in the Constitution and in the Statute of Autonomy
2. Regard for the general taxation structure of the State.
3. Coordination, fiscal harmonization and cooperation with the State, in accordance with the rules laid down in the Economic Agreement.
4. Coordination, fiscal harmonization and mutual cooperation between the Institutions of the Historical Territories pursuant to the regulations enacted by the Basque Parliament for these purposes.
5. Submission to the International Agreements or Treaties signed by Spain.
B. Fiscal Harmonization
1. Respect the General Tax Law in matters of terminology and concepts
2. Use the same system for classifying livestock, mining, industrial, commercial, service, professional and artistic activities as is used in the so-called common territory
3. Respect and guarantee freedom of movement and establishment of persons and the free movement of goods, capital and services throughout the territory of Spain, without giving rise to discrimination or a lessening of the possibilities of commercial competition or to distortion in the allocation of resources.
4. Maintain an overall effective fiscal pressure *equivalent* to that in force in the rest of the State

Source: Economic Agreement

is, will cause *some* distortion. Simply, any tax difference will introduce *some* discrimination, reduce *somewhat* free competition and, and as long as productive factors are mobile, give rise to *some* changes in the allocation of resources. The fact that distortion is a matter of grade introduces a high degree of subjectivity in the decision about whether or not a tax measure is distortionary.

The problem is further complicated because there is not a clear method to measure the level of distortion created by a tax difference. Simply, there is not a clear rule to determine how distortionary is, say, a two point reduction in the corporation income tax rate or if this reduction is more distortionary (or less) than, for instance, an investment incentive.

Specific Limitations

After establishing the restrictions to the fiscal system as a whole, the Economic Agreement goes on to establish a series of restrictions for each specific tax, indicating what the HTs can and cannot modify in each tax. Figure 6.1 summarizes the regulatory capacity for each tax given to HTs in the Economic Agreement. As shown in the figure, basically, the HTs have *full autonomy in all direct taxes.* The only restriction is that they have to adopt the same withholding tax rates on capital income (interests, dividends, etc.) and capital gains that the state establishes in common territory. Beyond that, the Economic Agreement says that the HTs can design direct taxes as they want. In particular, the HTs can freely design the corporation income tax (for firms subject to Basque tax rules) and the non-residents income tax (for non-residents).

It should be pointed out that the regulations of the HTs are not applied to everyone who engages in an economic activity in the BAC. Simply, there are economic agents in the BAC paying taxes according to the tax rules of the HTs and others operating also in the BAC but paying the taxes established by the central government. In the case of the corporation tax, the tax rules of the Foral Deputations only apply to businesses with registered office in the BAC that are either small or large making more than 25 percent of their sales in the BAC. Large businesses registered in the BAC making at least 75 percent of their sales in the rest of Spain pay taxes in the BAC apply central government tax rules. Firms with registered office in common territory[24] always pay according to central government tax rules (unless 100 percent of its sales are in the BAC).[25] In 2007, for example, some 3 percent of firms that filed taxes in the BAC made used the tax rules of the central government (i.e., common territory tax rules). These firms represented somewhat more than 20 percent of the tax base and nearly 30 percent of the corporate taxes collected.[26] The non-residents apply the tax rules of the HT only when they operate through a permanent

Figure 6.1. Regulatory capacity of the historical territories

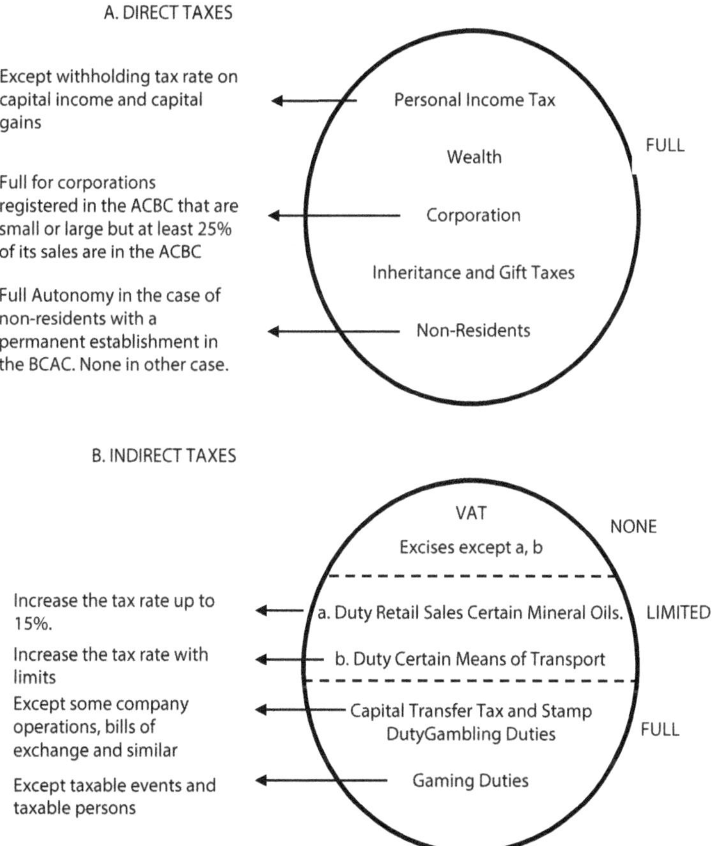

establishment.

Figure 6.1 also shows that the HTs *do not have any autonomy in the most important indirect taxes*. All the components (tax rates, tax bases, deductions, and so on) of the main indirect taxes (VAT and Manufacturing Excises) are determined by the state and HTs only have some autonomy in minor indirect taxes.[27] Basically the HTs do not have any autonomy in about 90 percent of the indirect taxes the collect. The autonomy in the indirect taxes is so limited because the European Commission does not allow regional differences in the main indirect taxes.

Conflicts with the State

The tax regulations of the HTs are subject to a series of general principles of harmonization. Specifically, they cannot distort competition among firms and must result in a fiscal pressure equivalent to that which exists in the common territory. At the same time, the Economic Agreement gives nearly complete autonomy to the HTs in many taxes (specific principles of harmonization), significantly in the direct taxes. The attempt to reconcile the autonomy conceded by the Agreement with the harmonization that it demands is, to say the least, surprising. If, for example, the HTs reduce the effective tax rate[28] on corporations, are they using the tax autonomy given to them by the Economic Agreement or giving economic privileges that will distort the economy and are contrary to the Economic Agreement? The answer is that, with a strict interpretation of the non-distortion concept, probably both. Because, as already mentioned, with that kind of interpretation, any corporation income tax difference is distorting.

In the end, the problem is that there is an obvious conflict between a strict interpretation of the general principles of harmonization established in Economic Agreement, and the tax autonomy that, at the same time, it grants to the HT. This contradiction is at the heart of almost all the disagreements between the state and the Basque Territories about the lawfulness of many tax regulations of the HTs. Nearly every conflict between the BAC and the state has referred to the corporate tax and has arisen as a result of the conflict between autonomy and harmonization. When the BAC has lowered the corporate tax (in comparison to the tax in common territory) the Spanish state (or another interested party[29]) has appealed the legitimacy of these regulations on the grounds that they were distorting and thus violated the general principles of the Agreement. For their part, the HTs have always argued that the regulations were consistent with the regulatory autonomy in the corporate tax conceded by the specific principles of the Agreement. This has resulted in frequent litigation in the courts, which have not proven able to establish a well-defined balance between autonomy (specific principles) and harmonization (general principles), perhaps because there lack objective references (to define a measure distortion) and have done no more than apply not well defined subjective criteria[30] that sometimes were different, other contradictory and, in some occasions, very difficult to justify.[31] In fact, one might have the feeling that some decisions express an a priori position either in favor or against the Agreement, rather than a search for a viable balance. In any case, recourse to the courts has not resulted in even an approximate delimitation of the real tax autonomy the Agreement gives to the HTs.

The lack of consistency shown in the court rulings is most glaringly evident in the fact that that Supreme Court has often overturned the many rulings of the Superior Court of Justice of the Basque Country. Figure 6.2 presents a summary of the results of appeals presented before the Supreme Court. As the figure shows, the Supreme Court has revoked 42.5 percent of lower court rulings. This suggests that those rulings were not based on solidly established legal criteria. It should not be thought that the criteria of the Supreme Court are particularly solid either simply because the question of how distorting is a tax measure and what is the degree of distortion compatible with the general criteria of harmonization established by the Agreement are far from being well answered.

All of the litigiousness (which has mainly involved the corporate taxes approved by the HTs), along with the delays in resolving the disputes, have had undesirable consequences for the BAC and its fis-

Figure 6.2. Appeals before the Supreme Court regarding the BAC tax measures

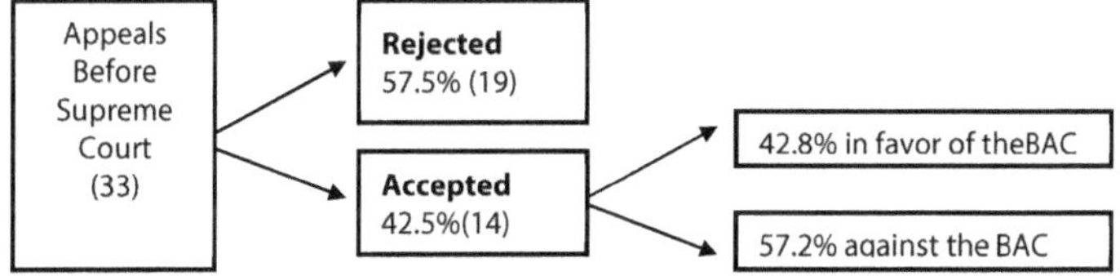

cal autonomy. First, it has led to a permanent tension between the state and the BAC regarding the scope of the Agreement that has prevented the foral model from functioning normally. Second, it has led to considerable legal insecurity for firms because the regulations in effect may end up being revoked after a process that might well last more than ten years. Third, this situation has led to absurd situations, such as the repeal of tax regulations that have been in effect for many years or the repeal of tax regulations that had already been revoked and nobody applies. Conversely, it is possible that a regulation repealed by the Supreme Court of Justice of the Basque Country (SCJBC) may be recognized as legitimate by the Supreme Court some years later.

A large part of this litigation has not been initiated by the state. Until 2010, the fiscal regulations of the HTs of the BAC did not have the status of law[32] and could be appealed to the SCJBC. The competence of the SCJBC regarding this matter meant, among other things, that the regulations could be appealed not only by the state, but by many other parties who felt that they were affected. This happened quite often and the tax regulations of the HTs were appealed, among others, by unions, federations of businessmen, and bordering ACs.

The ease of appealing the Basque fiscal regulations presented two problems. First, it multiplied the number of possible appeals (and therefore contributed to an insecurity surrounding the foral regulations). Second, it was discriminatory vis-à-vis the situation in the ACs of the common system and Navarre. The fiscal laws of both the ACs and Navarre are approved by regional parliaments. For this reason, in contrast with the tax regulations of the BAC, those of the other ACs and Navarre could only be appealed before the Constitutional Court.

In order to resolve these problems, the BAC for a long time advocated that its tax regulations (like those for the ACs of the common system and Navarre) only be subject to appeal before the Constitutional Court. This petition came to be termed—rather inappropriately— the *shielding* of the Agreement.[33] Finally, in 2010, the Spanish Parliament approved the legal modifications necessary to ensure that, from that time on, the Basque foral regulations could only be appealed before the Constitutional Court by the same agents allowed to appeal the regulations of the other ACs.

In any event, even though the "shielding" reduced the number of appeals, the ideal solution would be to minimize the conflicts between the state and the BAC. For this, it would be necessary to adopt a number of different measures. First, the meaning and scope of the general principles should be clearly delimited to reduce the subjectivity in their application. Second, bodies and mechanisms[34] should be established to analyze and even solve possible conflicts involving the interpretation of principles of harmonization before reaching the courts. In fact, both the Economic Agreement for Navarre and the Basque Economic Agreement are conducive to these kinds of arrangements to resolve conflicts because, given the ambiguity and contradiction of some of their principles, resorting to the courts will often result in unsatisfactory resolution as well as lend excessive weight to the subjective views of those who issue rulings.

Conflicts with the European Union (EU)

The European Union (EU) has never questioned the legitimacy of the

Agreement. However, in the past, concerns have been raised about whether the regulatory autonomy given by the Agreement in the corporate tax was compatible with the EU treaty. The basic question that raised concerns was whether a region of a country that enjoys fiscal autonomy recognized in the constitution (such as the Basque Country) can have an effective[35] corporate tax rate lower that that applied in the rest of the country (Spain) or if the lower tax rate constitute regional aid, and is therefore incompatible with EU regulations.

This issue, which has never been definitively resolved, was brought before the European Community Court of Justice (ECCJ) in 1997 because SCJBC had requested a preliminary ruling from the European Court regarding whether tax incentives introduced by the HTs of the BAC in 1993[36] were in conflict with EU regulations. The SCJBC asked the ECJC whether these incentives, given that they were only applied to Basque companies (1) were measures contrary to the freedom of establishment (article 52 of the EU Treaty) or (2) whether they could be considered regional State aid (article 92.1 of the EU Treaty).

In July 1999, the General Advocate[37] responsible for the Case, Antonio Saggio, issued his opinion, which held that the incentives conflicted with freedom of establishment because they were only applicable to Basque companies and that they constituted regional state aid because they were only applied in one region of a member state. Saggio's opinion went even further, declaring that any regional difference in corporate taxes, whatever their underlying cause, constitute regional state aid.

The first element of the opinion (that the incentives infringed upon the freedom of establishment) was not especially serious and had to do with the design of the points of connection.[38] This problem was resolved by allowing non-resident companies to receive fiscal benefits from the BAC under the same conditions as companies located in other areas of Spain. The question of regional state aid was more serious because it implied that any difference in taxes between the BAC and the state constituted state regional aid and that, basically, the HTs did not have any capacity to regulate their corporate taxes, which (according to Saggio's opinion) had to be equal to those of the state.

In response to this opinion, the BAC decided to sign the so-called "tax peace" with the state in 2000. This agreement called for the elimination of nearly all tax incentives in exchange for the state withdrawing its complaint before the SCJBC. Upon the withdrawal of the complaint, the pre-trial matter before the ECCJ was rendered null and void, and the European Court never had to render a definitive judgment regarding Saggio's opinion. However, from that moment forward, the idea that the fiscal incentives of the HTs were in conflict with

EU norms hung like the sword of Damocles over the tax arrangements in the Basque Country (and, more specifically, over the corporate tax).

The compatibility of the tax regulations powers of the BAC with the regulations of the European Union remained ambiguous for a number of years. The issue hung in the balance, under the threat of an opinion (not presented before the European Court) that considered the fiscal differences regional State aid and under the disproving eye of a European Commission that did not like regional fiscal differences. Matters changed significantly in 2006. In the ruling of a case against Portugal involving the reduction of direct taxes (i.e., personal income and corporate taxes) in the Azores that were held to constitute state aid,[39] the Luxembourg Court carefully defined the concept of "regional selectivity of fiscal measures."[40] The Court allowed that the fiscal regulations established by the regional government could be general, as long as the regional government was sufficiently independent of the central government. According to the ruling, "sufficient autonomy" requires compliance with the following principles:

- *Institutional Autonomy*. From the constitutional standpoint, the regional or local authority has a political and administrative status separate from that of the central government.
- *Procedural Autonomy*. Tax regulations must be adopted without the central government being able to directly intervene with respect to their content.
- *Financial Autonomy*. The financial consequences of any tax reduction (i.e., in relation to the taxes currently effect in the country) must be borne by the region and will not be compensated by transfers from the central government or other regions.

The above conditions guarantee that the regional governments are independent entities, freely regulate their taxes, and bear the burden of the financial consequences of any tax reduction. According to European regulations, it is the courts of the country of the region that enjoys such fiscal autonomy that must decide if the above criteria are being complied with.

In sum, now it is at clear that the regulatory autonomy of the HTs with respect to the corporate tax is compatible with EU regulations, even when this results in taxes that are lower than those in the rest of Spain. This is important for at least two reasons: (1) because it eliminates the fear of any fiscal regulation being revoked as a result of an appeal lodged in a European court, and (2) because it avoids the past situation of foral regulations of the BAC being appealed on the grounds that they contradict EU regulations.

In any case, it is important to point out that none of this means that the Deputations can establish any taxes they want because, just as in the case of the fiscal authorities of any EU nation, the Deputations are subject to the general European regulations (i.e., not to give selective state aid, not to adopt harmful taxes, and so on). In other words, the Deputations will be subject to the restrictions derived from European regulations under the same conditions as the fiscal authorities of France, Germany, or any other EU country.

The Regulatory Capacity of the Historical Territories: The State of the Question

The HTs of the BAC, while enjoying a broad regulatory capacity, are subject to two different kinds of restrictions. On the one hand are restrictions derived from EU regulations. On the other hand are those restrictions derived from the Economic Agreement.

Figure 6.3 provides a summary of the regulatory capacity of the HTs of the BAC within the design of its fiscal system. As it shows, the HTs essentially have full regulatory autonomy as regards direct taxes.[41] The most important restrictions involve the corporate tax, where

Figure 6.3. A summary of the regulatory capacity of the HTs

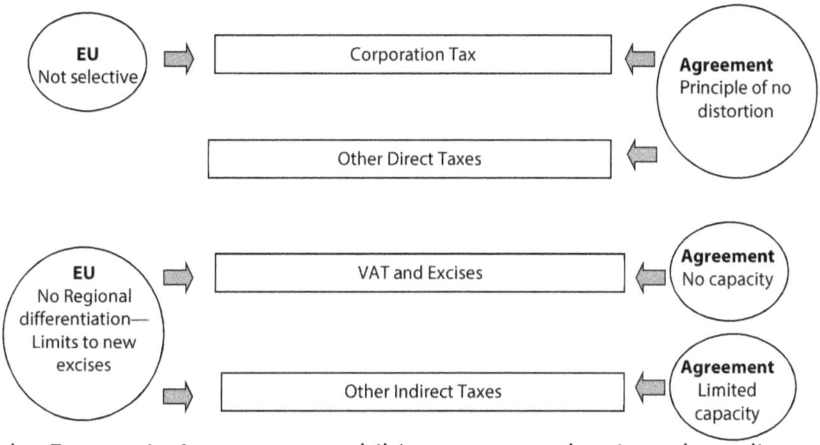

the Economic Agreement prohibits measures that introduce distortion and also where EU regulations prevent measures that are either selective or harmful for competition.

In the case of indirect taxes, the Agreement concedes hardly any autonomy at all. There is only some autonomy in minor indirect taxes that produce very little collection. In fact, with the regulations currently in effect, the state could not concede regulatory autonomy in the indirect taxes to the HTs even if it wanted to because EU regulations prohibit regions within a country having different indirect tax rates (in VAT and excise duties).

Level of taxes in the BAC

The question of whether the BAC has lower taxes than the state has frequently been debated. Table 6.3 explores this question and provides a detailed comparative analysis of adjusted fiscal pressure (ratio taxes to GDP) in the BAC, Navarre, and the common territory in the year 2008.

The Personal Income Tax (PIT)

Since the PIT is progressive and the BAC is substantially richer than the common territory (30% richer in 2008, as shown in table 6.3), if the BAC had the same tax rates and deductions as common territory (CT), it would collect much more. However, as the table shows, in 2008 the BAC collected 0.4 points less of GDP than the CT. The fact PIT collected less in the BAC than in the CT is not due to one factor (e.g., a much lower rates scale). It is due to the fact that in the Basque Country nearly all of the elements of the tax are somewhat more favorable to the taxpayer. Simply put, many elements like business income, pension plans, expenditure on buying or renting homes, and certain capital gains have a more favorable tax treatment. The only exception is that the top marginal rate is somewhat higher in the Basque Country than in the common territory (45 percent versus 43 percent).

As figure 6.4 shows, this difference was not specific of the year 2008. Between 1986 and 2004, the PIT to GDP ratio was very similar in the BAC and the CT. Given the fact that the BAC has always been significantly richer than the CT, this suggests that the PIT of the BAC has always been somewhat lower than that of the CT. Since 2004 until the drastic drop in collection in 2008, the gap between the BAC and the CT increased to a high of 0.7 GDP points. However, this was not the result of the BAC lowering the PIT more than the CT. In reality, both areas lowered PIT to a similar extent. What in fact happened was that the CT created a lot of jobs within a short period of time, and this translated into a substantial increase in PIT collection. The general tendency has therefore been that *the BAC has traditionally had a PIT that is somewhat lower than that of the CT*. This has probably resulted from the fact that the Deputations have transferred to citizens, via lower PIT, some of the economic benefits generated by the Economic Agreement.[42] Finally it is worth noting that the other foral community, Navarre, has traditionally had an IRPF (personal income tax) substantially lower than that of both the BAC and the CT.

In any event, it should be pointed that, despite the fact that PIT fiscal pressure is somewhat lower than in the CT, the greater wealth of the BAC implies that per capita collected taxes are much higher. For example, as evident in table 6.3, the BAC's per capita PIT collection in

Table 6.3. Taxes Compared in the BAC, the CT, and Navarre 2008 (ratio taxes to GDP)

	Common Territory[1]	Navare	BAC	BAC-CT	Tax Differences and Comments
Personal Income Tax	7.1	6.2	6.7	−0.4	More favorable treatment of housing and retirement plans, higher deductions (exempt minimum, deduction for labor income), better treatment to business income and to some capital income. Tax rates somewhat more progressive although top marginal income applied at higher income levels.
Corporation Tax	2.7	2.3	2.2	−0.5	Lower tax rates (28vs30). Higher tax incentives (investment, hiring workers, etc.)
Non Residents Income	0.2	0.1	0.3	+0.1	Lower tax rates for firms with a permanent establishment.
Wealth	0.2	0.4	0.3	+0.1	Eliminated in 2008, Restored in 2010.
Inheritance and Gift	0.3	0.3	0.1	−0.2	More favorable treatment, especially in gifts.
Other Direct	−0.0	na	0.5	0.5	Equal to the adjustment for Agreed Direct Taxes (see Table 6.6)
TOTAL DIRECT	10.5	9.2	10.2	-0.3	
VAT	4.8	4.8	6.3	+1.5	The ratio consumption/GDP is 0.62 in the ACBC and 0.61 in Navarre. In CT is almost 0.69.
Collected by the BAC	4.9	3.7	4.6	−0.3	
VAT adjustment	−0.1	1.1	1.6	+1.7	See VAT section below
Capital Transfer Tax	0.9	0.5	0.4	−0.5	Some tax rates are lower. In capital transfers one point lower (6 vs. 7) and in Stamp 0.5 lower (0.5 vs 1).

2008 (with a fiscal pressure of 5.6 percent less than that of the CT) was 31.5 percent higher.[43]

Corporate Tax

In the case of the corporate tax, the fiscal pressure within the BAC is nearly 20 percent (or 0.5 points of GDP) less than that of the CT. There are two main reasons for this:

(1) The distribution of corporate tax bases between the BAC

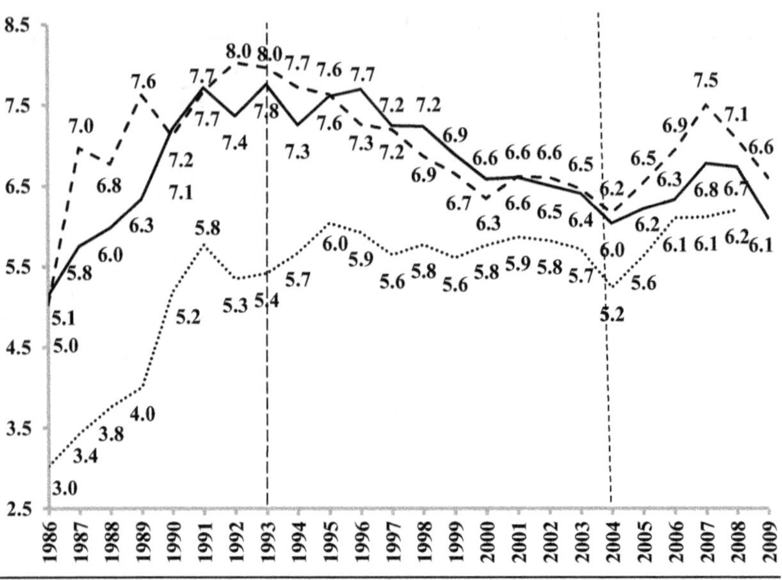

Figure 6.4. PIT (as % of GDP), BAC, Common Territory, and Navarre (1986–2009).

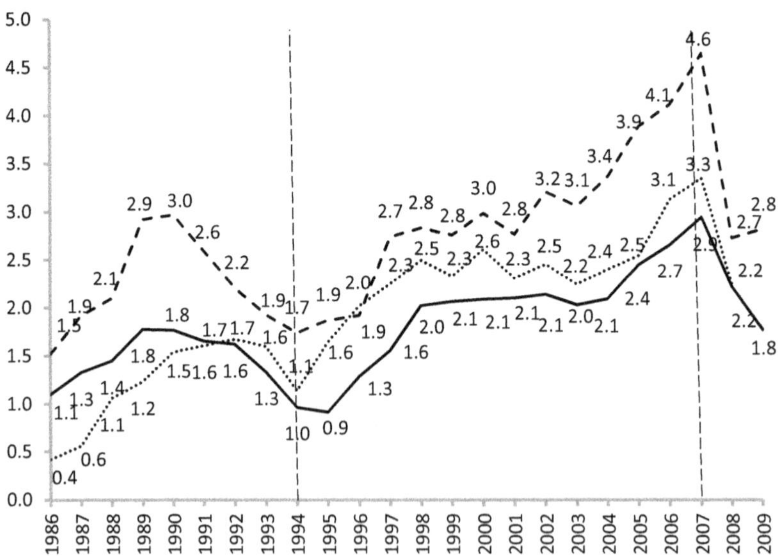

Figure 6.5. Corporate Tax (as % of GDP), BAC, Common Territory, and Navarre (1986–2009)

and CT has attempted to achieve simplicity not replication of the

GDP distribution. Simply, the profits subject to taxation in the BAC are not equal to the share of the gross added value generated in the BAC. For this reason, the ratio tax collection to GDP of the BAC and the CT would not coincide, even if taxes were identical.

2. Much more important is the fact that the corporate tax of the BAC is substantially lower than that of the CT. For example, in the year 2008, the tax rate was lower, incentives were higher, and many of the tax provisions were more generous.

As figure 6.5 shows, the fact that the corporate tax of the BAC is lower has been a historical constant. In fact, the difference in fiscal pressure between the BAC and the state in 2008 was the lowest ever. During most years, the BAC has had taxes between one and one and a half GDP points less than those of the CT. This is the equivalent to corporate taxes between 30 percent and 40 percent lower.

The reason that the corporate tax of the BAC is lower goes back to the economic crises of the 1980s and 1990s. The Basque Country has traditionally been one of the most industrialized areas of Spain, and thus these crises had an especially devastating impact on the Basque economy. In 1985, for example, the unemployment rate in the BAC reached 23 percent (the average for Spain as a whole at that time being 21.5 percent). In 1995, it reached 24.4 percent (and 24.1 percent in Spain as a whole). Although its effectiveness is probably limited,[44] the Deputations believed that the best way to stimulate job creation was to provide tax breaks to companies. This was no different from what was being done by the central government of Spain or the governments of other nations. However, the idea that it would be good for the corporate tax of the BAC to be lower than that of the rest of Spain took hold, and this tax strategy has been maintained even during periods of economic boom.

Other Direct Taxes

The inheritance and gifts tax collects lower revenues in the BAC than in the state. To a large extent, this is due to the fact that this tax is more generous in the BAC than in the rest of Spain. Thus, in the BAC, the inheritances and gifts of first-degree relatives are exempt from taxes. In other ACs,[45] allowances are not as generous. For example, within the common territory, only Castile and León, Castile La Mancha, Madrid, the Canary Islands, and La Rioja permit allowances that can reduce inheritance taxes to zero without any limits or conditions. As regards gifts, seven ACs provide allowances when these involve close relatives, but only the Canary Islands and Madrid provide a near total exemption without any conditions. Finally, table 6.3 includes the estimated collection of non-agreed reed of taxes valued as in the quota.[46]

Indirect Taxes

The regulatory capacity of the HTs with respect to indirect taxes is very limited. Yet, as table 6.3 shows, they have used what limited freedom they have to lower (or at least not increase) indirect taxes. For example, in 2008, the capital transfer tax and stamp duty collected only half of what was collected in the rest of Spain because the tax rates in the BAC were lower than in the CT.

The collection of VAT deserves special mention. The VAT collection is the sum of two elements: first what the Foral Deputations collect themselves, and second, the so-called VAT adjustments, which are VATs paid by residents of the Basque Country but collected by the Spanish state Treasury.[47] When these two elements are added, the VAT collected in the BAC (in terms of percentage of GDP) is 30 percent higher than that of the state. This is not a difference limited to the year 2008. In fact, since the Economic Agreement has been in effect, VAT revenue in the BAC has been substantially higher than in the CT. From an economic standpoint, this is a surprising result. The economic analysis suggests that the rich spend on consumption a lower percentage of their income than the poor. This property of individuals translates to countries (and regions) and as shown by the national (regional) accounts richer countries (regions) consume a lower percentage of GDP than poorer countries (regions). This suggests that, with the same tax rates, the collection of VAT as a percentage of GDP should decrease as income increases. In fact, one of the reasons why the European Union has been reducing the importance of the VAT resource in financing its expenses is precisely its regressive nature.

As shown in table 6.3, according to the Spanish regional accounts, the percentage of GDP dedicated in the BAC to consumption is smaller than in Spain. It is therefore highly unlikely that the BAC, even if it did a better job than the CT collecting the VAT, would be able to obtain as (percent of GDP) a 30 percent more than the CT. This suggests that the VAT adjustment is overestimated in favor of the BAC.[48]

Fiscal Pressure Resulting from Agreed Taxes

Table 6.3 clearly shows that, in 2008, the fiscal pressure resulting from agreed taxes was 0.5 points higher than in the CT, and 2.2 points higher than in Navarre.[49] This may seem surprising because, as previously said, many taxes (PIT, corporate taxes, capital transfer tax, and stamp duty) are lower in the BAC than in the CT. However, the (very generous) adjustments for both VAT and agreed direct taxes more than compensate for these differences and result in greater fiscal pressure.

Figure 6.6 depicts the evolution of fiscal pressure over time. There is not a well-defined tendency and the evolution over time of the fiscal pressure has basically been determined by the economic conjecture. Between 1997 and 2004, there was no identifiable trend at all, and fiscal pressure varied from one year to the next. During the economic boom of 2004–2007, increasing employment in the CT resulted in collections increasing more rapidly there than in the BAC. Conversely, the dramatic drop in collections in 2008–2009 affected the CT more than the BAC, resulting in a leveling of fiscal pressure in the two areas. In any case, it should be remembered that the fiscal pressure in the BAC includes both a VAT adjustment and an adjustment for agreed direct taxes.

All things considered, it seems clear that fiscal pressure (including adjustments) is similar in the two areas, and that what determines the yearly differences are the prevailing circumstances. Yet it should still be remembered that, since the BAC is richer, it should (given equal rates) have a higher fiscal pressure.

The greater wealth of the BAC is evident when one takes into account the amount collected per capita. As shown in table 6.3, with

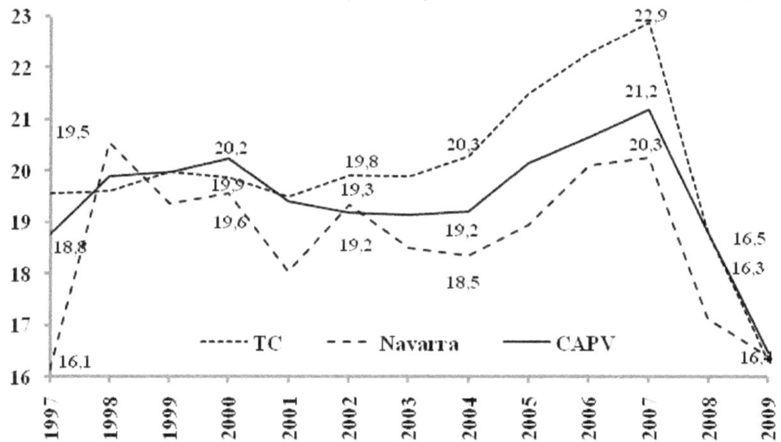

Figure 6.6. Agreed Taxes (as % of GDP) in the BAC, Common Territory, and Navarre (1997–2009). BAC and Navarre do not include the agreed direct taxes adjustment.

taxes similar to those in the CT, the BAC collected 41 percent more taxes per capita than the CT. Navarre, with a fiscal pressure nearly 10 percent lower than that of the CT, collected nearly 20 percent more per capita.

Some Concluding Thoughts

The fiscal system of the BAC has a PIT that is about 8 percent lower than that of the CT, and a corporate tax that is substantially lower (by about 30 percent). The PIT, although more progressive, generally offers more generous deductions. As for the corporate tax, the rate is lower and the fiscal incentives are considerably higher. On the one hand, the inheritance and gifts tax and, on the other, the capital transfer tax and stamp duty, are also lower. In the first case, the tax is lower for inheritances involving relatives who are not close, as well as for gifts,[50] In the second case, the rates are lower for capital transfers and, especially, for official legal documents. Generally considered, the gaming tax of the BAC is not lower than that applied in other Autonomous Communities.

Tax reductions in the BAC have not, however, translated into fewer services per capita than in other Autonomous Communities, for three reasons: (1) the BAC is richer (and therefore collects more money per capita, even though it has lower taxes), (2) the VAT adjustment is, probably, larger than it should, and (3) the quota is, probably, lower than it should.

Comparison with Other Countries

Table 6.4 compares the taxes (as percent of the GDP) in the BAC, Spain, and the EU countries. The tax data of the BAC include the agreed taxes, the estimated value (in the quota) of the adjustment for agreed direct taxes and, as in the other countries, the municipal taxes.

As can be seen in the table, taxes (as percent of the GDP) in the BAC are six points lower than the average of the EU27. This is not surprising because the BAC follows a tax pattern very similar to that of the rest of Spain. Simply, the BAC forms an integral part of the Spanish economy and, consequently, its taxes cannot be very different from those of Spain. Since taxes in Spain are low compared to the EU average, it is, then, natural that the same holds true for the BAC.

Financial Flows

The foral model gives rise to two different kinds of financial flows (transfers) between the BAC and the Spanish state.

1. *Compensatory transfers*. These are transfers that have the purpose of compensating the other party for an expenditure. In the past, there were a number of transfers of this nature (e.g., those made by the social security system that allowed the BAC to finance some social services). Currently, the only compensatory transfer that exits is the quota.

The quota is the basic transfer provided for in the foral system because it is the payment made by the BAC to the state for the agreement of taxes. In fact, the quota historically originated as a rental fee for the agreed taxes. Its value was determined as the potential collection of the agreed taxes, minus the expenses in the competences as-

Table 6.4. Taxes (as % of GDP) in the BAC, Spain, and the EU (without social security contributions), 2008

Belgium	29.2	Bulgaria	24.6
Denmark	46.8	Czech Republic	19.0
Germany	23.8	Estonia	20.0
Ireland	23.7	Cyprus	31.3
Greece	19.8	Latvia	20.5
Spain	20.7	Lithuania	20.9
France	26.3	Hungary	26.2
Italy	29.1	Malta	27.6
Luxembourg	25.2	Poland	22.8
Netherlands	23.7	Rumania	18.4
Austria	28.2	Slovenia	23.1
Portugal	24.5	Slovakia	16.8
Finland	30.5	EU27	26.2
Sweden	38.3	Iceland	33.8
United Kingdom	28.7	Norway	33.7
EU15	26.5	Switzerland	22.4
BAC[1]		**20.6**	

1. With municipal taxes and adjustments
Source: Eurostat and own calculations for BAC

sumed by the Deputations[51] (then, as now, basically public works and social assistance). Now the quota is linked to the expenditure side and is essentially a payment for expenditures that the state continues to make for the benefit of the residents of the BAC.

2. Transfers to refine the allocation of tax collection resulting from the design of the points of connection.

Fiscal autonomy implies that the BAC has to collect all the taxes paid by its residents. For this, it is essential to determine which taxpayers have to pay to each tax administration (foral or state) and in what proportions. Thus, for instance, it is necessary to determine which firms have to pay taxes to the BAC, which have to pay to the state, and which are obliged to make tax payments to both. In the case of firms having to pay to both, it is necessary to determine the percentage of the tax base that belong to each tax administration and which tax law applies. The criteria to determine who has to pay to which administration, how to divide tax bases between administrations, and which tax law applies are called *points of connection.*

For direct taxes, the points of connection replicate the criteria for dividing income used between countries, which generally combine the principles of concepts of territoriality and residence. In the BAC, for example, both the income generated in the BAC (territoriality) and the income obtained (anywhere) by the residents in the BAC (residence) are taxed.[52]

In the case of indirect taxes, the division criteria have to do with the taxable firms. In the end, however the indirect taxes are paid by the individuals no by the firms and, as a result, it is necessary to make adjustments to compensate the differences between what is collected in the BAC (what the firms pay there) and what the individuals in the ACBS pay (what the consumers of the BAC pay). The two most important compensating transfers are the adjustments for VAT and excise duties. There is another transfer, called *financial compensation,* that was established when the excise duties were agreed in 1997.[53]

Table 6.5 presents a summary of the transfers between the BAC and the state that derive from the Agreement, and specifies the direction of transfer in each case. As can be seen (and as is explained in greater detail below) the overall balance of transfers is favorable to the state, but only by a slight degree.

The Quota

The quota is the payment made by the BAC to the state as a compensation for its expenditures on behalf of the residents of the BAC.[54] It also includes a contribution to the solidarity with other regions of Spain. In what follows, I will analyze how the quota is defined and how much it costs to the BAC. After that, I determine which part of the quota is redistributive and which part is payment for state services (expenditures). Finally, I will discuss if the payment is sufficient to cover the expenditures of the state.

Table 6.5. Transfers between the BAC (BAC) and the State (S)

Flow	Direction		
Quota	BAC	⇨	S
VAT adjustment	S	⇨	BAC
Excise Duties adjustment	BAC	⇨	S
Financial Compensations	S	⇨	BAC
Other	S	⇨	BAC
TOTAL	BAC	⇨	S

Calculation of the Quota

The quota could have been calculated directly. It would have been sufficient to determine how much the state actually spends in the BAC[55] and to agree to a contribution to the solidarity with other regions. The sum of those two quantities would be the quota to pay. Instead of this, however, an indirect system of imputation was adopted. Within this system, a determination is made about how much the state spends in all Spain in competences not assumed by the BAC (including the solidarity) and, after that, a percentage of the total is imputed to the BAC.[56] This percentage is called the *imputation index,* and since the implementation of the Economic Agreement in 1981, it has been fixed at 6.24 percent.

The quota is regulated by five-year acts. For the first year of the five-year period,[57] a detailed calculation of the quota is made. The quota in the subsequent years of the five-year period is obtained simply by updating the initial quota (referred to as the *baseline quota*).

Calculation of Baseline Quota

To determine the quota the starting point is what the state spends in the BAC (E^{BC}). From this amount, it is subtracted the revenue the state obtains in the BAC (R^{BC}) and the deficit58 (R^{BC}). Thus, the base quota, Q_b, is given by:

$$Q_b = E^{BC} - R^{BC} - D^{BC}$$

As already mentioned, the expenditures, revenues, and deficit of the state in the BAC are not measured directly, but rather by using an imputation method. One measures how much the state spends (collects) in all Spain in competences (from revenue sources) not transferred to the BAC, and the 6.24 percent of the totals obtained is imputed to the BAC. Thus, the baseline quota becomes:

$$Q_b = 0.0624(E^S - R^S - D)$$

In this formula, E^S, R^S, and D are the national totals for, respectively, expenses not transferred to the BAC, revenues not transferred to the BAC, and the state deficit.

To obtain the final quota (called the *liquid quota* or LQ), a number of adjustments are made for competences assumed by the BAC that require special treatment (e.g., expansion of the Basque Police force) or for new competences. If we call the resulting amount AAC (adjustment for assumed competences) then liquid quota in the base year (LQ_b) will be:

$$LQ_b = 0.00624\ (E^S - R^S - D) - AAC = Q_b - AAC$$

Calculation of Quota in Subsequent Years

For the subsequent years of each five-year period, the quota is obtained by simply updating the baseline quota according to the growth of the collection in Spain of taxes that have been agreed with the BAC[59] and deducting from the resulting amount the compensations of year t (ACC_t). The liquid quota in year t, LQ_t, will be then:

$$LQ_t = Q_b (1 + \alpha_t) - AAC_t$$

Where, α_t represents the percentage increase (between the baseline year and year "t") in what the state collects (in all Spain) for taxes agreed upon with the BAC.[60]

Properties of the quota

The model of the quota is conceptually correct. The BAC pays for what the state spends on behalf of the BAC (adding a contribution to solidarity) net of the revenue obtained by the state in the BAC, and only pays with taxes the expenses that the state finances with taxes. Obviously, the coherence of the model requires including the amortization of debt and the interest payments among the competences not assumed by the BAC (and for which it pays with the quota). This is how it works in practice, and therefore the model is coherent from a conceptual point of view.

The problems with the quota therefore have to do less with the calculation mechanism per se than with how the variables that determine the quota (allocation index, competences not assumed, etc.) are measured in practice.

Before analyzing this issue, it is important to recall a number of characteristics of the quota:

- The quota does not pay for all state expenses, only for those financed with taxes.
- Each five-year period is strongly linked to the baseline year. Thus, for example, if there is a high deficit or surplus in the baseline year, then this same deficit or surplus is maintained throughout the five-year period and affects the quota, even if economic conditions subsequently change.
- What is paid depends on state expenses on behalf of residents in the BAC (which determines the base quota), and what is collected by the state in all of Spain for taxes that, in the Basque Country, are collected by the BAC (which determines index to update the base quota). The quota in no way depends on what the BAC collects from agreed taxes.

The fact that the quota does not depend on what has is collected in the BAC implies a unilateral risk borne by the BAC. This *unilateral risk* simply means that the BAC keeps every additional euro it collects (and loses every euro it does not collect). As a result, if the BAC increases its tax collection faster than the state (either because of better economic conditions or because taxes are administered more efficiently), it keeps all the extra revenue. Conversely, if its collection increases more slowly, the BAC stands all the cost. Obviously, the principle of unilateral risk induces efficiency in tax administration.

Assessment of Assumed Expenditures and Redistributive Impact

Table 6.6 provides a summary of the calculation of the quota for 2007, which was the baseline year for the current quota law (2007–2011).[61]

According to the data in table 6.6, in the calculation of the quota it is supposed that the BAC has assumed 54.5 percent[62] of the activities that the state carries out in other ACs. In order to determine

Table 6.6. Provisional Quota for the Autonomous Community of the Basque Country for Base Year 2007 (thousands of euros)

	State Budget	Imputation Index	Imputed to the Basque Country
Expenditure			
1. Total expenditure of the State	188,417,352.98		
2. Charges assumed by the Autonomous Community	102,664,732.79		
3. Total non-assumed charges (E^{BC})= 2-1	**85,752,620.19**	**0.0624**	**5,350,963.50**
Revenue			
4.For taxes not covered by the Economic Agreement	3,942,605.41	0.0624	246,018.58
5. For other non-tax income	7,589,293.77	0.0624	473,571.93
6. For direct taxes covered by the Economic Agreement			432,774.68
7. Total Revenue (R^{BC}) = 4+5+6+			**1,152,365.19**
Deficit			
8. For Budget Deficit (*D*)	**40,872,263.17**		**2,550,429.22**
9. Compensation and adjustments to be deducted = 7+8			3,702,794.41
10. Quota (Q = E^{BC} - $R^{BC\,E}$-*D*) = 3-7-8			**1,648,169.09**
Additional Compensations			
11. Compensations article 6 (Two), Quota Act[1]			82,088.07
12. Sole transitional provision, Quota Act[2]			(-)2,980.31
13. Alava Compensations[3]			3,823.80
14. Total Additional Compensations (AAC) = 11+12+13			**82,931.56**
15. Liquid Quota (LQ = Q – AAC) = 10-14			**1,565,237.53**

1. Compensation for the social security contribution used to finance Health before 2002. 2. This was a compensation in favour of the State for some savings in the cost of the Autonomous Police Force. This compensation was only for the year 2007. 3. Compensation for expenditure competencies only assumed by Alava.

Source : Five-year Quota Act, 2007–2011

if this is too much or too little, it would be necessary to have the list of (supposedly assumed) competences included in the line 2 of table 6.3. Unfortunately, this information is not available, and the only thing known is the total amount of what is considered to have been assumed.

Looking at the competences of the BAC and other ACs, it is observed that the main competences assumed by the BAC, but not by the other ACs,[63] are police, financing of municipalities, tax administration, housing, social services, and the maintenance of nearly all of the national roads. These unique competences (as well as some other less far-reaching competences) do not seem sufficient to justify that the BAC provides for itself of 54.5 percent of the state budget.[64]

Yet it is important to point out that the redistributive component in the imputation index may compensate for the overestimation of the value of the assumed competences. The reason is that, as explained below, the index is equal to relative income instead of to relative population, and this entails a significant degree of redistribution.

In any case, something that can be quantified is the part of the quota base (line 3 in table 6.3) that is a solidarity contribution to other ACs. The only non-assumed expenditure that can be considered as solidarity contribution and that is included in line 3 is the Inter-territorial Compensation Fund,[65] which represents 1.4 percent of the non-assumed expenditures. Therefore, the solidarity contribution in the quota base (non-assumed expenditures) is 1.4 percent of the total. To this it must be added the redistribution that occurs via the imputation index. The following section explores this question.

Imputation Index and Solidarity Contribution

The imputation index is the percentage of expenses of the central government that the BAC must pay. In principle, and from a redistributive viewpoint, the index can be determined in three different ways:

- *Neutral index.* The Foral Community would pay according to what it actually receives from the state. In this case, it would be calculated how much the BAC benefits from each expenditure of the state (not assumed competence) and the quota to be paid would be the sum of all the benefits. Obviously the percentage of each expenditure to be paid would be different. In some cases, the percentage would be the relative population (for instance, for defense). In others the relative income (for instance, for the contribution of Spain to the European Union) or some other indicator (for instance, for public works).
- *Progressive Index.* The Foral Community would pay for com-

petences not assumed in proportion to its relative income. To some extent, this would be like financing the competences not assumed with a proportional income tax.[66] This is redistributive insofar as the benefits the BAC receives from the non-assumed competences are proportional to its population. However, as just mentioned, in some cases it's not that way, and the benefits of the BAC are proportional to its income. The denomination "progressive" is, therefore, approximate.

- *Regressive Index.* The Foral Community would pay for competences not assumed in proportion to its population. This would be the equivalent of financing competences not assumed with a poll tax. Once again, to the extent that certain competences actually benefit the BAC in proportion to its population, the label "regressive" should be interpreted with caution.

The Economic Agreement requires that the imputation index should be equal to the relative income of the BAC. Given that the value of the index was fixed at 6.24 percent in 1981 and has not changed since then, it is obvious that its value is more a political agreement than the result of any economic estimate. However, perhaps due to some version of the invisible hand, the relative income of the BAC, which in 1981 represented 7.5 percent of the Spanish economy, converged to 6.24 percent over the course of the following ten years and since then has remained around that value. As a result the imputation index is now equal to the relative income of the BAC.

Figure 6.7 summarizes the evolution of the relative income and population of the BAC. At the beginning, in 1981, it seems clear that there was a compromise between a progressive and a regressive payment of the not assumed competences, because the imputation index agreed, the 6.24 percent, is just in the middle of relative income (progressive) and relative population (regressive). Since then, the relative income in the BAC has progressively decreased, until stabilizing at about 6.24 percent during the 1990s. For its part, relative population has steadily decreased.[67] In this way, the imputation index has gone from regressive to progressive.

Sometimes it is asserted that using relative income imputation index could well be considered a solidarity contribution on the part of the BAC. This is only partly true because, as has already been indicated, there are state expenditures that benefit the BAC in proportion to its income. In any case if, ignoring this latter fact, we were to interpret the difference between the 6.24 percent and the regressive index as a contribution to solidarity, we would find that, for 2008, nearly 25 percent of the quota was a solidarity contribution from the BAC to the financing of other ACs.

Amount of the Quota

Table 6.7 presents the amount paid as a quota in relation to a number of different indicators. This table shows that in normal times, the quota represents about 2.5 percent of the GDP of the BAC and 12 percent of the agreed taxes collected. At its maximum, in 2007, each resident of the BAC paid a quota of 750 euros.

The recent economic crisis has resulted in a substantial drop in the quota, which, during the past two years, has fallen nearly 50 percent. The basic reason for this reduction has been that the unilateral risk has functioned in favor of the BAC. Simply put, as agreed taxes

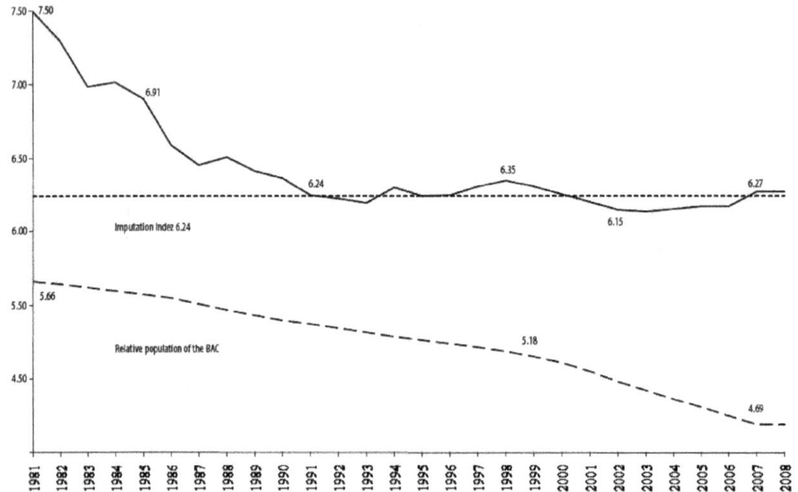

Figure 6.7. Relative Population and GDP of the BAC (as a % all of Spain), 1981–2008.
Source: Population and GDP, INE (www.ine.es)

collection in the BAC have fallen to a lesser extent than in the rest of Spain, the quota has decreased as a percentage of GDP (because collected taxes as a percentage of GDP have decreased) and of agreed taxes (because they have fallen less than in the rest of Spain).

In any case, the normal situation (and one that will likely return once the economy starts growing again) is that which was in place before to 2007. This means a quota representing about 2.5 percent of the GDP of the BAC and 12 percent of the agreed taxes.

Fiscal Adjustments

The model of the Agreement includes three fiscal adjustments in the form of transfers that have the purpose of refining the distribution of the tax collection that results from the design of the points of connection. The three adjustments, which are analyzed below, are the VAT adjustment, the excise duties adjustment, and the financial compensations.

Table 6.7: The Quota (1997–2009)

	Euros		As a %	
	Millons	Per capita	GDP	Agreed Taxes
1997	742.2	358	2.4	12.6
1998	753.3	364	2.2	11.1
1999	836.6	404	2.3	11.4
2000	932.0	449	2.3	11.6
2001	979.7	471	2.3	11.9
2002	1064.2	510	2.4	12.3
2003	1123.3	537	2.3	12.2
2004	1188.8	566	2.3	12.0
2005	1357.0	644	2.4	12.0
2006	1497.7	707	2.5	11.9
2007	1595.9	749	2.5	11.6
2008	1172.9	548	1.7	9.1
2009	721.8	339	1.1	6.7

1. Liquid Quota without the deduction for Alava.
Source: OCTE (several years) and *INE*

VAT Adjustment

The VAT is a tax on consumption that is collected through a tax on production (or, to be more precise, on the value added net of investment and exports). The VAT adjustment tries to compensate for differences between what is collected in the BAC (which depends of the tax base production less investment less exports in the BAC) and what residents of the BAC pay (which depends on final consumption). Given the fact that, as will later be seen, the tax base in the BAC is less than the consumption of its residents, in practice this adjustment seeks to return to the BAC the VATs paid by its residents, but collected by the state.

The VAT adjustment represents the sum total of two sub-adjustments. The first of these is for VAT paid on imported goods (i.e., from countries outside of the European Union). This VAT is paid by residents of the BAC (via output VAT[68]), although the state collects it at the border. The transfer of the state to the BAC for this category of sub-adjustment is called the *external market adjustment.*

The second sub-adjustment is for the consumption of goods produced within Spain (or imported from EU countries). The purpose of this adjustment is to compensate for differences between (relative) consumption of the BAC and the (relative) tax base within the BAC. In principle, this adjustment could result in favor of either the BAC or the state. If, for example, if the consumption of the residents of the BAC was larger than the tax base located in BAC (i.e., the BAC was a net importer of goods from the rest of Spain), then the state would be collecting VATs paid by the residents of the BAC and the state would have to transfer these revenues to the BAC. Conversely, if the consumption of the residents was smaller than the tax base, the BAC would be collecting VATs paid by residents in the CT and would therefore be obliged to make a transfer. In practice, national accounting data suggest that consumption in the BAC exceeds the tax base located in the BAC, and therefore it is the BAC that has to make the transfer. The resulting transfer is called the *internal market adjustment.*

External Market Adjustment

VAT collection at customs offices is made by the state. Since part of the goods imported is actually consumed by residents of the BAC, the state makes a transfer to the BAC ($\tilde{R}^{BC}$) equal to:

$$\tilde{R}^{BC} = \frac{\tilde{C}^{BC}}{C} R^{customs} = \alpha R^{customs}$$

In the above equation, C stands for consumption in Spain as a whole, $\tilde{C}^{BC}$ for consumption in the Basque Country, $R^{customs}$ for VAT collection at customs, and $\alpha = \tilde{C}^{BC}/C$ is the relative consumption of the Basque Country. The value of the coefficient α was set at 0.06875 in 1986 and has not been changed since then. This means that, as is the case for the imputation index, this value represents more a political agreement than a parameter reflecting an economic variable.

Internal Market Adjustment

The Foral Deputations collect the VAT from firms that pay taxes in the BAC. If it is the effective tax rate of the VAT, what the BAC collects in VAT (R^{BC}) is equal to:

$$R^{BC} = tTB^{BC} = t(GDP^{BC} - I^{BC} - X^{BC})$$

Where TB stands for the VAT taxable base firms that pay taxes in the BAC, GDP^{BC} and I^{BC} are the GDP and gross capital formation (Gross investment) respectively of the Basque Country, and XBC represents exports from the BAC.

On the other hand, the VAT paid by the residents of the BAC ($\hat{R}^{BC}$) is :

$$\hat{R} = tC^{BC}$$

Where C^{BC} is the consumption (of non-imported products) of residents of the BAC. To the extent that taxable base in the BAC is less (greater) than the consumption of residents of the BAC, the state will make (receive) a compensatory transfer to (from) the BAC.

The compensation is made via the internal market adjustment. Essentially, this mechanism functions of the basis of differences between relative consumption and the relative taxable base of the BAC. The adjustment says that:

If $a = (C^{BC}/C) > (TB^{BC}/TB) = b \qquad T = (a\text{-}b)R$

If $a = (C^{BC}/C) < (TB^{BC}/TB) = b \qquad T = (b\text{-}a)R$

In the above equation, *a* and *b* respectively stand for the relative consumption and the relative taxable base of the BAC, *T* for the state transfer to the BAC,[69] and *R* for the sum of VAT revenues in the BAC and the state.[70]

What these equations say is that, when relative consumption in the BAC is greater (less) than relative taxable base, the state must make (receive) a transfer from (to) the BAC. From the beginning, the values for *a* and *b* have been 0.06875 and 0.05765 respectively. Thus, $a - b = 0.011$.

Table 6.8 presents the size of the VAT adjustment and total VAT in the Basque Country (the sum of the VAT adjustment and the VAT collected by the Foral Deputations). For the purposes of comparison, VAT collection in Spain as and various indicators of potential VAT collection, are also included.

As table 6.8 shows, VAT revenue (A + B) in the BAC is substantially greater than in the common territory.[71] For example, in 2006, the BAC collected 7.7 percent of GDP, while the common territory only collected 6.3 percent. This does not make much economic sense. Richer regions typically dedicate a lower percentage of GDP to consumption than poorer regions. Therefore, VAT collection (as a percentage of

Table 6.8. VAT in the BAC and the Common Territory (% of GDP)

	VAT Collection				Consumption		Effective Tax Rate[1]	
	Own Collection(A)	Adjustment (B)	BAC A+B	CT	CT	BAC	CT	BAC
2000	4.4	2.6	7.0	6.0	59.6	54.0	10.1	13.0
2001	4.4	2.3	6.7	5.8	59.0	53.5	9.8	12.6
2002	4.2	2.3	6.5	5.8	58.0	52.6	9.9	12.4
2003	4.3	2.4	6.8	5.9	57.4	52.0	10.3	13.0
2004	4.7	2.4	7.1	6.0	57.6	51.8	10.4	13.6
2005	5.3	2.2	7.5	6.2	57.5	51.2	10.8	14.6
2006	5.7	2.0	7.7	6.3	57.1	50.5	11.0	15.2

1.(Collection+Adjustment)/Consumption

Source: Based on OCTE (several years) and INE.

GDP) is typically lower in richer regions.

Table 6.8 confirms the fact that richer regions dedicate a lower percentage of their income to consumption than poorer regions, and shows that the BAC (which has a 30 percent greater per capita income than the rest of Spain) dedicates almost six points of GDP less to consumption than the common territory. The fact that the BAC collects relatively more, even though it consumes relatively less, suggests that the VAT adjustments may be using parameters that (at least now) overestimate the transfer the state should be making to the BAC.

The last columns of table 8 reaffirm the suspicion that the adjustment is overestimated. As can be seen in these columns, despite the fact that the nominal VAT tax rates of the BAC are the same as in the rest of Spain, the effective tax rate is between three and four points greater. Although part of this difference may be due to a more efficient administration of the VAT in the BAC, it seems clear that at least another important part is due to the generosity of the VAT adjustment.

In any case, what is quite surprising is the basic parameters of the adjustment (indices *a* and *b*, representing relative consumption and relative taxable base respectively) have not been modified (except for technical reasons) since they were introduced in 1986. It appears clear that they should be revised so that the VAT adjustment more closely reflects the real situation.

Adjustment for Excise Duties

The adjustment for special taxes has the same logic as the VAT adjustment. Some excises are not charged at the point of consumption, but rather at bonded warehouses or at the points of production or of import. In these cases, there are differences between what Foral Deputations collect (which depends on the point of production or distribution) and what residents of the BAC pay (which depends on the consumption that has occurred in the BAC). Adjustments are made for the excises on alcohol and beer, intermediate products (also a tax on alcohol), mineral oils, and manufactured tobacco. As table 6.9 shows, in 2007, all of these adjustments were favorable to the BAC except for mineral oils.[72] But since the mineral oils adjustment is much greater than the other three, the final adjustment balance results in a transfer from the BAC to the state.

Financial Compensations

Excise duties on manufactured products were agreed with the BAC in 1997. Before that year, the BAC received (through reduction of the quota) 6.24 percent of what was collected in all of Spain for excise duties. Some were afraid that the agreement of the excises would significantly increase the financial resources of the BAC. In order to avoid this, a financial compensation was established. This compensation is simply a transfer between the BAC and the state for the difference between what is collected in the BAC for the agreed excises and the 6.24 percent of the collection for excises in Spain. The purpose of the financial compensation was to ensure the financial neutrality of the agreement of the excises. Even though the compensation was established to prevent the BAC from increasing its resources with the agreement of excises, the perhaps surprising result was that the state ended up making transfers to the BAC.

Table 6.9: Adjustment for Excise Duties between the BAC and the state, 2007 (thousand euros)

Mineral Oils	–213,427
Manufactured Tobacco	46,266
Beer and Alcohol	45,503
Intermediate Products	14,713
TOTAL	–106,944

Source: OCTE.

The value of the compensation was calculated just once in 1997. Since then the value used has been the 1997 value updated with the same index used to update the quota.

Table 6.10 shows the financial compensations in 2007. As the table shows, the BAC loses with all the compensations except with that of manufactured tobacco. This compensation dominates the others and the final balance is in favor of the BAC. The financial compensation is about 70 percent of the VAT adjustment.

The Final Balance

Table 6.11 presents the balance of transfers between the BAC and the state. The two most important of these transfers have been the quota and the VAT adjustment. These are of similar magnitude, although flowing in opposite directions. On the other hand, the adjustment for special taxes and the other transfers are considerably less important and, similar to the case for the quota and VAT adjustment, tend to largely cancel each other out.

The final result is that the balance between the BAC and the state is small (between 0.03 and 0.66 of the GDP of the BAC), and its direction varies over the course of time. In 2003, 2004, and 2009, the balance was favorable to the BAC while, in the other years it was favorable to the state. The fact that the balance is small (or at times negative) should not be interpreted as meaning that the BAC does not finance the state (and even less that the state is subsidizing the BAC). It simply means that the state obtains revenues in the BAC that are

Table 6.10. Financial Compensations, 2007 (Thousand Euros)

Mineral Oils	–37,334
Manufactured Tobacco	121,710
Alcoholic Beverages	–9,408
Beer	–2,609
TOTAL	72,359

Fuente: OCTE (2009)

similar to its tax financed expenditures in the BAC.[73]

Comparative Financial Capacity

One of the most hotly debated questions regarding the Foral system has to do with the financial capacity granted the Foral Communities in comparison with the ACs of the CT. Table 6.12 explores this issue.

To table compares the resources that ACs have to finance similar competences. To do so, the revenue figures have been adjusted to compensate for differences in expenditures competencies.[74] It should be pointed out that 2007 was an economic boom year.[75] Therefore, collection levels were very high. This means that the resources of the Foral Communities (which have a territorial base) were much higher (in comparison with those of the CT) than in times of more moderate growth or stagnation.

Bearing in mind these caveats, table 6.12 shows that, in 2007, to finance the same competences, the BAC had almost 30 percent more

Table 6.11: Balance of the Transfers between the BAC and the state , 2003-2009 (millons of euros)

	2003	2004	2005	2006	2007	2008	2009
1. Quota	1123.3	1188.8	1357	1497.7	1595.9	1172.9	721.8
2. VAT Adjustment	1163.5	1241.3	1212.7	1208.9	1176.3	1092.2	768.9
3. Excises Adjustment	–88.9	–63	–53.2	–56	–106.9	–123.5	–114.5
4. Other[1]	62.2	66.9	72.6	75.5	98.3	82.3	99.1
5. Net Balance Paid= 1–2–3–4	**–13.5**	**–56.4**	**124.9**	**269.3**	**428.2**	**121.9**	**–31.7**
6. Per capita payment	–6.4	–26.8	58.8	127.2	201	57.0	–14.8
7. Payment as % of GDP	–0.03	–0.11	0.22	0.44	0.66	0.18	–0.04

1. It includes the financial compensations and some conditional transfers received form the State.

Source: Own calculations using OCTE and INE

of its GDP than average common system AC had more resources (in percentage of GDP) than the BAC. Extremadura, for example, had 30 percent more resources, and Castile La Mancha had 7 percent more. At the other extreme, there were huge differences between the BAC and the common system AC with similar levels of wealth. Madrid, for example, had 45 percent less resources than the BAC, and Catalonia had 35 percent less.

Since the BAC is (along with Madrid), the richest AC, the differences of per capita resources are much greater than the differences of GDP resources. Thus, in 2007, the per capita resources of the BAC were almost 70 percent higher than those of the average common system AC. As previously said, this figure is somewhat higher than that for other years, because tax collection in 2007 was exceptionally high. In other years, additional per capita resources of the BAC were in the range of 55 percent and 65 percent.

In any case, it is clear that the foral system gives rise to much more financial resources than the common system. This should come as no surprise, because the foral system is based on territoriality (the financial resources of the AC depend on its income) while the common system is based on need (the financial resources of the AC depend on its estimated needs[76]). The key question, then, about the foral system is not whether it gives rise to more resources than the common system,[77] but whether the transfers (quota, adjustments, etc.) are or are not well designed in relation to their objectives.

Economic Effects of the Agreement

The previous sections have analyzed the characteristics and implications of the Economic Agreement and some results of its application (tax level, financial resources for the BAC, etc.). Figure 6.8 summarizes the ways in which the Agreement has affected the income and well-being of the residents of the BAC. As this graphic shows, the Agreement has increased the well-being of the residents of the BAC because it has provided regulatory autonomy and more financial resources than the common system.

The regulatory capacity has allowed to adjust better the level and structure of taxes to the preferences of the residents of the BAC. That is, to collect what is needed to finance what Basque residents want to spend and using the taxes Basque residents want. Allowing, for instance, the deductions Basque residents want or reducing taxes contrary to the preferences of the majority of the population (as seems to be the case, for instance, with the tax on inheritances and gifts).

On the other hand, the regulatory autonomy has allowed to use general or selective corporate tax reductions as an instrument of industrial policy and the creation of jobs. The effectiveness of corporate tax reductions to stimulate economic activity and create employment is highly questionable. Yet there are those who think that tax incentives are effective instruments to grow and create more employment.

Finally, regulatory capacity increases the credibility of the BAC in financial markets because it allows control of the level of revenues. In particular, it allows easy access to financial markets and the securing

Table 6.12: Financial Resources in the Common and Foral Systems (2007)

	Income		Resources			
			As a % of GDP		Per Capita	
	Value	Index	Valor	Index	Value	Index
Extremadura	16153	69	19.8	165	3194	116
Castile-La Mancha	18187	78	16.2	135	2952	107
Canary Islands[3]	20703	88	16.1	134	3326	120
Andalusia	18122	77	15.4	128	2794	101
Galicia	19816	85	15.3	127	3023	109
Cantabria	23518	100	14.1	117	3316	120
Asturias	21635	92	13.6	113	2951	107
Castile And León	22629	96	13.4	111	3032	110
Murcia	19388	83	13.3	111	2582	93
La Rioja	24991	107	12.8	107	3207	116
Aragón	25524	109	11.6	96	2953	107
Valencia	21261	91	11.5	96	2447	89
Catalonia	27507	117	9.7	81	2673	97
Balearic Islands	25403	108	9.5	79	2407	87
Madrid	30541	130	8.2	68	2495	90
TOTAL COMMON[1]	23004	98	12.0	100	2765	100
Navarre	29505	126	14.1	117	4152	150
Basque Country	*30540*	*130*	*15.2*	*127*	*4652*	*168*
TOTAL FORAL[1]	30313	129	15.0	125	4542	164
TOTAL NATIONAL	23450	100	12.3	102	2873	104

1. It includes all the resources g(adjusted for differences in expenditure competences) given by the financing system and the funds form the interterritorial compensation fund (ICF). This is AC (ceded) taxes + shares in State taxes + Transfers + ICF.
2. Agreed taxes +Tax Adjustments- Cost of expenditures only Foral Communities have (Police, Financing of Municipalities, National Roads, tax administration, social services, etc).
3. Includes revenue form the Special Tax Regime of the Canary Islands.

of long-term commitments. One example of this is that an operation as complicated as the agreement with the Guggenheim Foundation was made easier because of the tax autonomy of the BAC.

On the other hand, the greater financial resources given by the Agreement have resulted in lower taxes and better services. This has had direct effects on the income and well-being of taxpayers, as well as indirect effects on income. The direct effects are evident because paying less taxes and receiving more subsidies has increased citizens' income. Similarly, receiving more public services (education and health, for example) increases citizens' well-being.

However, beyond these direct effects, there is an induced effect that tends to increase income. Due to the foral system more income remains in the BAC.[78] This extra income (that with a common system would have gone to other AC) increases aggregate demand in the BAC and through multiplier effect increases income considerably. If, as shown in table 6.12, the foral system gives the BAC 3 GDP more of financial resources,[79] and we assume that the multiplier is 1.5, then the extra financial resources provided by the Economic Agreement would produce a GDP increase of 4.5 points. This is to say that 4.5 percent of the GDP of the BAC is due to the Economic Agreement.

Figure 6.8. Effects of the Economic Agreement on the income and well-being of BAC residents

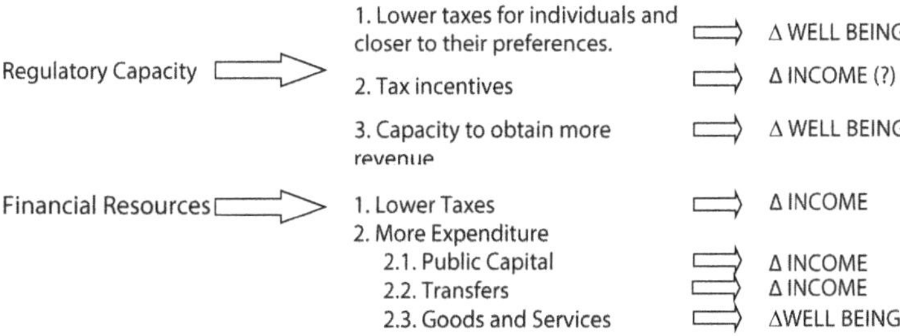

Per Capita Income of the BAC

The evolution of per capita income depends on many factors not related to the Economic Agreement. However, it is interesting to analyze the evolution of relative income of the BAC during the time the Agreement has been in force. This information is shown in figure 6.8, which shows the evolution of the income of the BAC in relation to the Spanish average and, beginning in 1995, the income of Spain's richest AC. Between 1995 and 2006, Madrid was the richest AC. In 2008, however, it was overtaken by the BAC.

As shown in figure 6.9, at the beginning of the 1980s the Basque Country was 36 percent richer than the average of Spain. At that time, the Basque Country was, in fact, the richest region in Spain. During the next ten years, the relative income of the Basque Country declined. The main reason was that the Basque Country was especially hurt by the recessions between 1975–1985. The crises seriously affected productive sectors that historically had been the base of the Basque Economy (iron, steel, ship building, home appliances, etc.). As a result the Basque Country had to rebuild and reshape its economy shifting from heavy industry to more technological activities.

After the decrease in the 1980s, for most of the 1990s the relative income of the Basque Country stabilized around 118 percent of the national average. The turning point was 1997. That year, the relative wealth of the Basque Country started to grow, and in ten years it returned to the situation of the early eighties. In 2009 the Basque Country has regained its traditional position as the richest region in Spain, with almost a 35 percent more (per capita) income than Spain.

It is difficult to quantify the role played by the Economic Agreement in the process of income recovery in the BAC. However, it seems fair that both the tax autonomy and the additional resources provided by the Agreement may have played a significant role.

Provision of Public Services

Table 6.14 provides, however, some indicators of the level and efficiency of some of the three most important expenditures made by the Basque public sector: health, education and public infrastructures.

In the Basque Country, the expenditure (per user) in primary and secondary education is 30 percent higher than the Spanish average. The resulting system of education is considered one of the best in Spain. For instance, a study reviewing 50 indicators of quality,[80] gave the education system of the Basque Country 9.4 points out of 10. This was, by far, the highest score attained by any AC. The expenditure on Health is 9.5 percent higher than the Spanish average. The analysis of seventeen indicators[81] rates the public health care system of the Basque Country among the best in Spain. The score of the Basque Country is 6.5 out of ten, while the average of all the AC is only 5.7. Finally, table 6.14 shows that the Basque Country has the highest density of roads and a stock of public capital[82] that is almost 30 percent above the average. Taken altogether, the data in table 6.14 suggest that the expenditure in the Basque Country is somewhat higher than in other ACs and the quality of the public services is substantially better.

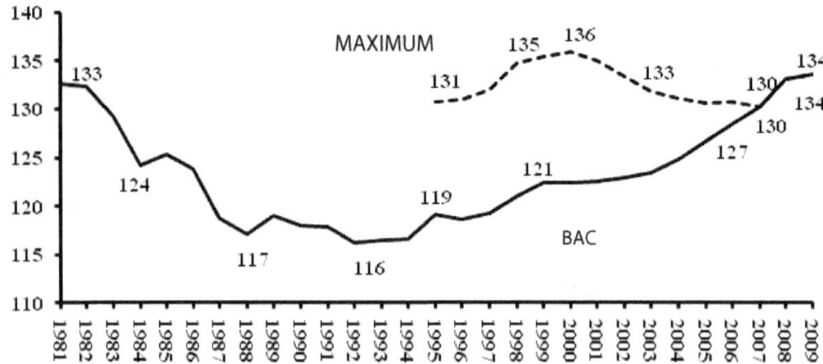

Figure 6.9: Evolution of per capita GDP of the BAC, 1981–2009 (average of Spain 100).
Source: Based on INE data.

Table 6.14: Some Indicators of the Quantity and Quality of Public Services in the BAC.

	Education Expenditure per Student[1]	Quality[2]	Health Expenditure per capita[3]	Quality[4]	Capital Roads Per sq. Km[5]	Public Capital Per Capita[6]
Andalusia	87.4	2.1	93.5	6.6	89.3	86.2
Aragon	99.6	6.3	110.8	5.9	47.8	152.5
Asturias	120.4	7.3	110.4	6.8	199.4	135.9
Balearic Islands	104.4	3.1	102.7	5.7	100.4	82.6
Canary Islands	102.6	2.4	105.1	4.3	244.4	95.5
Cantabria	113.3	6.1	122.0	5.4	210.7	131.5
Castile and Leon	109.3	6.5	107.9	6.3	56.2	139.5
Castile-La Mancha	103.8	2.5	106.0	6.2	43.0	117.8
Catalonia	98.5	5.5	97.0	6.3	207.4	83.0
Valencia	92.2	4.0	94.3	3.8	184.4	84.8
Extremadura	101.6	2.7	109.9	6.2	39.6	125.4
Galicia	113.4	5.7	102.8	5.0	144.6	107.5
Madrid	94.5	6.6	94.0	4.6	407.1	94.7
Murcia	86.2	2.5	102.1	4.6	84.8	78.6
Navarre	120.6	7.4	110.4	6.5	113.8	132.0
Basque Country	127.9	9.4	109.5	6.5	451.9	123.6
La Rioja	102.5	4.9	112.6	5.6	122.5	128.2
SPAIN	100	5.0	100	5.7	100	100

1. 2007, primary and secondary education. Index relative to the mean. 2. 2007, average of 50 indicators of quality (graduation rate, students per teacher, and so on) each valued from 0 to 10. For details see Profesionales por la Etica (2008). 3. 2005. 4. 2008, average of 17 indicators of quality (characteristics of the Health system and opinion of the users). For details see Federación de Asociaciones para la Defensa de la Sanidad Pública (2008). 5. 2005, money value of the roads per square km. Index relative to the mean. For more details see Fundación BBVA (2009). 6. It includes all public infrastructures and the value of capital in public services (health, education, and so on). Index relative to the mean. For more details see Fundación BBVA (2009).

Conclusions

The Foral model is based on two basic pillars: tax autonomy and payment to the state of a quota as compensation for expenses made by the latter on behalf of residents of the BAC.

The BAC has almost full autonomy in the direct taxes and none in the most important indirect taxes (VAT, mineral oils, and manufactured tobacco, etc.). It also has some autonomy (in most cases power to set tax rates) in some less important indirect taxes (gaming taxes, inheritance and gift taxes, capital transfer tax and stamp duty, etc.).

Conflicts with the state have almost always involved the corporate tax, and they arise because the Economic Agreement is contradictory when gives the Deputations full autonomy designing the corporation tax and, at the same time, requires that the corporation tax does not distort either competition or the allocation of resources. Courts have not succeeded in finding a balance between autonomy and no distortion that would resolve this contradiction. In addition, the number of appeals to the courts increased because, in contrast to the fiscal regulations of other ACs, the Basque regulations did not have the status of laws. This meant that they could be appealed to the SCJBC by anyone with the capacity to do so (including unions, business organizations, etc.). In order to avoid this (and to also avoid discrimination against other ACs), the Basque fiscal regulations were accorded the status of laws in 2010. Thus, from that time forward, they could only be appealed before the Constitutional Court. This change in legal status has been erroneously named as the "shielding of the Economic Agreement."

Tax autonomy in the corporate tax has also been challenged by the European Commission. In 2006, following a long period of ambiguity and uncertainty, the Constitutional Court of Justice of the European Union in Luxembourg clarified the requirements that needed to be met in order for a region to have a corporate tax different from that of the country of which it forms a part (namely, institutional, procedural, and financial autonomy). Spanish courts have recognized the fact that the BAC complies with these requirements, and thus it is no longer possible for a reduction in the corporate tax to be appealed on the basis of it constituting regional state aid.

In any event, the BAC does not enjoy full regulatory autonomy. The Deputations must respect not only the general principles of harmonization established in the Economic Agreement (non-distortion and equivalent fiscal pressure) but also the regulations of the European Union with respect to state fiscal aid (under the same terms any member nation of the European Union).

The application of fiscal autonomy has translated into taxes that in general are somewhat lower in the BAC than in the rest of Spain. The largest difference is in the corporate tax, which is about 30 percent lower in the BAC. Despite having lower taxes, a number of generous fiscal adjustments (for VAT and agreed direct taxes) have resulted in the fiscal pressure (tax to GDP ratio) in the BAC being similar to that of the CT. On the other hand, the higher per capita income of the BAC has meant that, with this similar fiscal pressure, the per capita collected taxes have been considerably higher (40 percent higher in 2008).

The foral system implies two types of transfers. On the one hand, there are compensatory transfers that have the purpose of paying for competences provided by the other party. Currently, the only such transfer that exits is the quota. On the other hand, there are fiscal adjustments that serve to compensate for taxes paid by taxpayers of one administration that are collected by the other. The most important adjustments are for VAT and excise duties. Financial compensations can also be included in this category.

The quota is the payment of the BAC to the state in compensation for expenses (financed by taxes) incurred by the latter on behalf of the residents of the BAC. The quota also includes a solidarity contribution. The quota is conceptually well defined. During normal times, the quota is equivalent to about 2.5 percent of GDP and 12 percent of agreed taxes. During the current recession the size of the quota has temporarily decreased. The share of the quota that can be considered a redistributive contribution ranges between 6 percent and 25 percent. On the other hand, a preliminary analysis suggests that there is certain underestimation of the value of central government expenditures (in favor of residents of the BAC) in the calculation of the quota.

The VAT adjustment is probably overestimated, while the adjustment for excise duties appears to be reasonable. Financial compensations, on the other hand, represent more of a political agreement than an economic adjustment. Although such was likely not the intention when financial compensations were introduced, they have benefited the BAC.

The foral system is territorially based (in other words, what the BAC retains depends on its income), while the common system is based on need (that is, what each AC receives is based on its estimated need). It is therefore no surprise that the foral system generates far more resources than the common system. In 2007, which was an exceptional year in terms of tax collection, the BAC had resources that were three GDP points higher than those of the common system, and that were five to six points higher than the richest Autonomous Communities of the common system. This gave rise to per capita resources that were 70 percent higher than in the CT. In years when collections have been lower, the additional resources of the BAC (as compared to the average of the common system) have ranged between 55 percent and 65 percent.

The Economic Agreement has had an impact on the income and well-being of the residents of the BAC in a number of different ways. The Agreement has allowed, among other things, the use of taxes as an industrial policy instrument, the generation of greater confidence in financial markets (i.e., to secure loans and facilitate multinational partnerships), and the adjustment of the fiscal structure to the preferences of the residents of the BAC. Among other advantages, the Agreement has also resulted in revenues being adjusted to desired expenditure levels, the reduction of taxes for many taxpayers, and the provision of more services.

Although it is difficult to precisely quantify the economic impact of these measures, a number of indicators suggest their importance. For example, the fact that the BAC has greater resources has a multiplying impact that is capable of generating up to 4.5 percent greater additional wealth. In addition, following the grave crisis of the 1980s, the BAC was able to reconvert its economy and has recovered its position as the Autonomous Community with the highest per capita GDP in Spain. Similarly, it spends more, and obtains better results in its health, education, and infrastructure services.

Endnotes

1. After the war Araba and Navarre maintained their Economic Agreements because, in contrast to Bizkaia and Gipuzkoa, they had supported the Nationalists from the beginning.
2. Obviously, the Economic Agreement Laws have been modified several times to accommodate it to major reforms of the Spanish tax system (e.g., the introduction of VAT in 1986 or the creation of new taxes) or to increase the fiscal autonomy of the Basque Country (e.g., in 1997, the collection of excises was transferred to the Basque Country).
3. This is the payment the Basque country makes the central government in return for the expenditures of government expenditures in the Basque Country.
4. This is simply the taxes collected minus the quota paid.
5. The Basque Country and Navarre have a foral system of financing. All the other AC follow the so-called "common system." The financing of AC under a foral regime follows a principle of territoriality (according to income) while under the common system the financing is according to (estimated) need.
6. The state means the central government.
7. Each Basque province establishes its own taxes. However, as explained later, the differences among the three fiscal systems are very small. They can therefore be treated as a single tax system.
8. The Foral Deputations are the governments of the provinces. All the tax powers belong to them.
9. Navarra has also a foral system that is basically identical to the system of the BAC. The Canary Islands although formally are under the common system in practice have a mix between the common and foral systems because they enjoy a higher degree of tax autonomy than other common regime AC.
10. The three HTs (provinces) are Bizkaia (Biscay), Gipuzkoa, and Araba. Bizkaia is about 50 percent of the BAC; Gipuzkoa, 35 percent; and Araba, 15 percent.
11. Law 3/1989 of May 30 of Fiscal Harmonization, Coordination, and Collaboration (*BOPV*, June 9), (modified in 1998).
12. The law basically allows for fiscal differences as long as fiscal pressure (taxes as percentage of the GDP) is the same in each of the HTs. It also enables the Basque Parliament to issue harmonization laws within the limits defined by the law.
13. For a discussion of these issues, see the papers in *Juntas Generales de Gipuzkoa* (2010).
14. It is composed of three representatives of the Basque government and one representative from each of the three Foral Deputations.
15. The consensus has led to harmonization when most of the institutions (the Basque government and the three Foral Deputations) were controlled by the same political party. When each institution was controlled by a different party, sometimes the consensus could not be reached and taxes in the HTs were somewhat different. The first scenario has been, though, much more usual.
16. The taxes collected by the Foral Deputations have to be shared with the Basque Government and the municipalities. The Basque government keeps

about 70 percent of total tax collection, while the Foral Deputations and the municipalities split the rest.

17. The other reason is that since the Economic Agreement gives more resources than the common system, the taxes needed to finance expenditures similar to those of other AC are lower.

18. This is the law regulating the division of taxes among levels of government. See Law 27/1983, of November 25, de Relaciones entre las Instituciones Comunes de la Comunidad Autónoma y los Órganos Forales de sus Territorios Históricos.

19. Usually the estimate was well below the real collection of the agreed taxes.

20. The percentage for each HT, known as the "contribution coefficient, is determined on the basis of two factors: the relative income of each HT (70 percent of the coefficient) and relative fiscal effort (30 percent). For example, in 2011, the coefficient was 50.22 percent for Bizkaia, 33.00 percent for Gipuzkoa, and 16.78 percent for Araba.

21. This means that in a given year the person lives in the *BAC* at least 183 days.

22. Since withheld taxes are credited against personal income tax liabilities, this means that the state collects the withholding taxes and the *BAC* gives them back to taxpayers in the form of a tax credit. Reciprocally the *BAC* withholds the wages of its employees working outside the *BAC* and the interests on any asset issued by the Basque Public Sector (even if paid to a non-resident in the BAC).

23. Notice that the requisite applies to the whole Basque Country, not to each territory.

24. This term refers to Spain less the foral regions (Basque Country and Navarre).

25. Whichever tax rules they apply, large business (more than seven million euros sales) that operate in both the BAC and common territory pay taxes in both jurisdictions in proportion to the sales in each area.

26. Firms using common territory tax rues represent higher percentages of the base than of collection because they are generally larger, and larger firms pay higher effective tax rates.

27. The autonomy in the gambling duties is full and limited in the capital transfer tax and the stamp duty. In the cases of the tax on certain means of transport and the retail sales tax on certain mineral oils, the HTs can change the tax rates within some limits established by the central government

28. This can be done in several ways: reducing the nominal tax rate, increasing tax incentives (for investment o employment), or depreciation allowances, and so on.

29. Due to the fact that, until the year 2010, the fiscal laws of the HTs of the BAC only had the status of regulations, they could (and were) appealed in the SCJBC by union and business organizations, governments of neighboring ACs, and so on.

30. Expressions such as "a measure disproportionate to its legitimate purposes" are an example of this. After all, why would a 20 percent tax reduction be considered disproportionate and not a reduction of 15 percent? What, in the

end, is the "legitimate purpose" of a measure?
31. As, for example, the ruling of the Supreme Court revoking the 1988 incentives.
32. They only had the status of regulations because they were approved by the Juntas Generales (provincial parliaments) of each HT, rather than by the regional parliament (the Basque Parliament).
33. This obviously had nothing to do with any "shielding" that prevented the verification of the legality of the Basque fiscal regulations, but instead involved avoiding the abuse of resources and with ensuring equivalence between the procedures of the Basque tax regulations and those of other ACs (including Navarre).
34. For example, the current Economic Agreement envisages the creation of an arbitration board and a coordinating committee between BAC and the state. However, these bodies have not yet played a significant role in the implementation of the Agreement.
35. The effective rate is the tax rate really paid (taxes paid/profits) after deductions, incentives, exemption, and so on. The effective rate in the Basque Country might therefore be less than that of the state for a number of reasons (lower nominal rate, higher incentives, more generous deductions, etc.).
36. These incentives consisted of a long list of corporate tax exemptions, deductions, and rebates that included (among other measures) a ten-year tax for new businesses that complied with certain conditions of investment and employment creation (the so-called tax holidays), and investment incentives for fixed assets (25 percent tax credit), R&D programs (30 percent credit), and foreign investments (25 percent). There were also other incentive measures (50 percent base deduction of amounts dedicated to the creation of a special reserve for productive investments, 15 percent tax credit for the creation of employment, 10 percent credit for professional training activities, and 25 percent deduction of capital increases of small businesses, etc.).
37. The General Advocate is charged with the task of supporting the court that hears a case by issuing an impartial report regarding the case (an opinion) that represents the interests of the European Community. Although these opinions do not form part of the deliberations, they carry weight in arriving at a final decision.
38. The points of connection are the criteria to determine which taxpayers pay taxes to which tax administration (state or Foral) and if, to both, in what proportion and according to which tax law.
39. See *Portuguese Republic v. Commission of the European Communities*, C 88/03, September 6, 2006.
40. A fiscal reduction in the region of a country was considered State aid because it was selective. This was because it was not applied to all the companies of a nation, but only to those that were located within a given region.
41. However, see also Figure 6.1 above.
42. See below about the benefits of the Economic Agreement in comparison with the CT.
43. As table 6.3 shows per capita income was 37 percent higher.
44. See, for example, Zubiri, "La justificación y los efectos económicos del Impuesto de Sociedades."

45. In Spain, the Inheritance and Gifts tax belongs to the ACs.
46. This is a raw (and probably generous) estimation of the tax collection of these taxes. See below.
47. See section below on the VAT adjustment for additional details.
48. This same idea can be found in Monasterio and De la Fuente.
49. The figure for Navarre does not include the adjustment for direct taxes.
50. In the most of the ACs, inheritances received by first-degree relatives are nearly exempt from taxes (although sometimes under certain conditions).
51. Collection potential was usually underestimated, which led to the quota being very low.
52. There is not double taxation because each administration gives a full fiscal for the taxes paid to the other administration.
53. For a more detailed analysis of the points of connection, see Zubiri, "Las transferencias en un sistema foral" and The Economic Agreement between the Basque Country and Spain.
54. Some of the expenditures are made in the BAC (airports, pensions for the poor, etc.) and other outside the BAC (defense, contribution to the European Union, etc.).
55. This would be similar to the so-called *effective cost method* used to finance the ACs of the CT of Spain during the beginning of the decentralization in the 1980s.
56. This way, for instance, the BAC dos not pay for what the state actually spends in the airports of the BAC. Instead the BAC pays a fixed percentage of what the state spends in all the airports of Spain.
57. Strictly speaking, the calculations are made for the latest year for which the necessary data are available. Occasionally this year has been prior to the first year of the five-year period of the act.
58. The deficit is subtracted because otherwise the BAC would be paying with taxes what the state pays with deficit. Should that be the case, the BAC would be suffering the consequences of debt financing (inflation, crowding out, etc.) without benefiting from its advantages (delaying the payment of expenditures). The interest and repayment of the debt will be included in later quotas (as a part of EBC).
59. This means that the growth of the quota depends on what the central government collects (of taxes agreed with the BAC) and not on what the BAC collects.
60. More precisely, this index is the ratio of revenues from agreed taxes (excluding taxes assigned in full to the Autonomous Communities for the fiscal year for the liquid quota) to revenues estimated by the state for the same tax categories in the baseline year of the five-year period. All calculations of the quota are initially made using the state budget. Later the quota is corrected once the budgets are settled.
61. See Quota Law, 2007–2011.
62. That is the ratio (line2)/(line 1) in table 6.6.
63. The competences of Navarre are, however, similar to those of the BAC.
64. For a detailed analysis of this issue, see C. Monasterio, "Federalismo fiscal y sistema Foral: ¿Un concierto desafinado?", and and A. De la Fuente "¿Está bien calculado el cupo?".

65. This is a fund created to finance investments in the less developed ACs.
66. Obviously "progressive" is used in relation to this index in a different way from the usual in reference to taxation (where it means growth of the average tax rate).
67. Clearly, with relative population falling and relative income remaining stable, per capita income has increased.
68. This is the VAT charged by sellers.
69. This is negative when it is the BAC that is obliged to pay.
70. In practice, an adjusted collection is used that rewards the administration that is more efficient collecting the VAT.
71. The revenue of Navarre is also higher than that of CT.
72. This is due to the fact that there is a petroleum refinery (Petronor) in Bizkaia.
73. Recall that part of the state expenditures are financed with debt.
74. For instance, the resources of the Basque Country have been reduced for the estimated cost ot its additional competences (police, national roads, etc.).
75. Of course, 2007 was the last good year before the crisis of 2008.
76. This continues to be true, even following the reform of the system in 2009. See, for example, Zubiri, "El nuevo sistema de financiación de las Comunidades Autónomas: La
financiación autonómica."
77. The answer is trivially yes.
78. If the BAC had the common system, the income of taxes paid by Basque residents that would have remained in the BAC would have been smaller.
79. Probably is more than this, because the resources of BAC have to be compared, not with the resources of the average AC of common regime, but with the resources of a rich AC of common regime.
80. See Profesionales por la Ética .
81. See Federación de Asociaciones para la Defensa de la Sanidad Pública.
82. It includes all public infrastructures and the value of capital in public services (health, education, and so on).

Bibliography

De la Fuente, A. "¿Está bien calculado el cupo?" *Moneda y Crédito* 231 (2011) 93–150.

Federación de Asociaciones para la Defensa de la Sanidad PÚBLICA. *Informe 2008 sobre los Servicios Sanitarios de las CC.AA* (Report no. 5) 2008. Available at www.fadsp.org/pdf/CCAA08.doc.

Five Year Quota Act, 2007–2011. Available at www.ogasun.ejgv.euskadi.net/r51-341/es/contenidos/informacion/concierto_quinquenal/es_4177/adjuntos/Kuporen_legea_es.pdf (last accessed October 1, 2013, available in Basque, Spanish, French, and English).

Juntas Generales de Gipuzkoa. *La Armonización Fiscal.* Law 3/1989, of May 30, de Armonización, Coordinación y Colaboración Fiscal (BOPV, June 9). 2009. Available at www.bizkaia.net/Ogasuna/Zerga_Arautegia/Indarreko_arautegia/pdf/ca_3_1989_Ley.pdf (last accesssed October 4, 2013).

Mas Ivars, Matilde, and Vicent Cucarella Tormo. *Series históricas de capital público en España y su distribución territorial (1900–2005).* Bilbao: Fundación BBVA, 2009. Available at: www.fbbva.es/TLFU/tlfu/esp/areas/econosoc/publicaciones/libros/fichalibro/index.jsp?codigo=454.

MINHAC (2010): *Recaudación y Estadísticas del Sistema Tributario Español* 1998–2008. Available at www.minhap.gob.es/Documentacion/Publico/Tributos/Estadisticas/Recaudacion/2008/Analisis_estadistico_recaudacion_2008.pdf (last accessed October 1, 2013).

Monasterio, C. "Federalismo fiscal y sistema Foral: ¿Un concierto desafinado?" *Hacienda pública española* no. 192 (2010): 59–104. Available at www.ief.es/documentos/recursos/publicaciones/revistas/hac_pub/192_Art_3.pdf (last accessed October 1, 2013).

OCTE. *Informe Anual Integrado de la Hacienda Vasca.* Various years. Available at www.ogasun.ejgv.euskadi.net/r51-19220/es/contenidos/informacion/estudios_publicaciones_dep/es_publica/informe_anual.html (last accessed October 1, 2013)..

Portuguese Republic vs. Commission of the European Communities, C 88/03, September 6, 2006. Available at http://curia.europa.eu/juris/liste.jsf?language=en&num=C-88/03 (last accessed October 1, 2013).

Profesionales por la Ética. *Las Políticas Educativas en España: Ranking de Excelencia Educativa.* 2007. Available at http://profesionaleseti-ca.org/descargas/downloads/downl_238_1.pdf.

Zubiri, I. "La justificación y los efectos económicos del Impuesto de Sociedades." *Ekonomiaz* 38 (1997): 122–45. Available at www1.euskadi.net/ekonomiaz/taula4_i.apl?REG=474 (last revised June 27, 2013).

———. *The Economic Agreement between the Basque Country and Spain.* Bilbao: Ad Concordiam, 2010.

———. "El nuevo sistema de financiación de las Comunidades Autónomas: La financiación autonómica." In *XVI Jornadas de la Asociación de Letrados Parlamentarios,* 275–309. Madrid: Ed Technos, 2010.

———. "Las transferencias en un sistema foral." *Jornadas de finaciación autonómica* (2010): 93–150.

7
Public Opinion of the Economic Agreement

Victor Urrutia Abaigar

An in-depth analysis of the law of the Economic Agreement naturally results in a series of perspectives. This is something that can be seen in the program of this congress. The issue that I have the task of addressing, which involves "public opinion," offers a number of different possibilities of interpretation. These should be clarified before going any further.

First, when we talk here about "public opinion," we are referring to opinions expressed by citizens, which are gathered by technical survey methods using the same scientifically validated sampling procedures that are employed by the majority of institutes of recognized standing.

This approach can be seen to stand in contrast with another approach to the idea of "public opinion"—one that is frequently confused with "published opinion," and that is utilized in the analysis of the content of communications media, especially in print media.[1]

Second, we should remember that public opinion is the reflection of social processes and habits that are in continual evolution, and which help shape the thinking of citizens. This thinking does not arise full born from nothingness by any means. On the contrary, it is a social product that acquires meaning within a specific context, and that requires a certain amount of time in order to "crystalize." The contents of the Economic Agreement involve the system and procedure of tax collection in the Basque Country. It is a law that has endured numerous political vicissitudes and that was finally amended and restored in 1981, a critical juncture of our democracy. Leaving aside the political uncertainties that led to fears of the continued existence of democracy under those circumstances, it should be remembered that that it represented the beginning of a new fiscal and tax collection culture in Spain. For the first time, following a dictatorship that promoted individualism, that eviscerated civil society, and that negated values such as freedom, justice, and solidarity, a new era was born in which citizens were asked to contribute, through their IRPF (personal income tax) tax payments, to the coffers of the state in order to enable the provision of public services in a dignified manner. What we witnessed, in other words, was a time of cultural sowing—a beginning of a long process of collective socialization that has made it possible to harmonize the Spanish fiscal system with those of the most advanced European countries, and to build the so-called "welfare state."

It is within this context that our autonomy system has gained the trust of Basque citizens and has made it possible for the Economic Agreement to be "naturalized" both institutionally and collectively. The Agreement has come to form a part of our social construct, without it being necessary to be overly concerned about either its details or its technical or legal formulations.

The analysis of the Economic Agreement from the perspective of public opinion has a long if not systematic history in the work of the Office of Sociological Research. In addition, this approach is represented in a publication that combines an historical analysis of the Agreement with two studies of opinion, one qualitative and the other quantitative. All of this has been accomplished since 1991, just twelve years ago. There is a wide gap between the years 2002 and 2008, a time during which this matter was not surveyed at all. The most recent study was conducted in November, 2010, when the most recent issue of *Sociómetro* (No. 44) (as of this writing) was published.

We should also be clear here about the difficulty of investigating public opinion about a matter—a law—as technical as the Economic Agreement. We all know about its economic and political importance in terms of the fiscal autonomy of the Basque Country. But it is difficult for citizens to know the details, even its most important details, because it is not a part of their daily lives (even though it does indirectly influence them).

We are not discussing here an institution that is administratively and physically recognizable and that has a face reflected in its representatives. We also are not referring to a fundamental law that defines the terms of our society along the lines of a magna carta (i.e., constitution or statute). We are instead talking about a law that, like other important laws, is frequently talked about and constantly referred to in communications media.

The law by virtue of which the Economic Agreement with the Autonomous Community of the Basque Country was approved (in brief, "The Basque Economic Agreement") is, in spite of its lengthy text, not very socially visible.

Having said this, I also want to stress its importance. In addition, want to make it very clear that ignorance of its more technical aspects does not in any way diminish its importance for our citizens. Therefore, asking questions in a way that aims at capturing the perception of its importance should be by reference to the most simple and broad content and effects of that law (in simplified form, as the

"Economic Agreement").

For this reason I have on this occasion resorted to other sources of information that have explored this question.

I have conducted an analysis of all those studies of both the Office of Sociological Research (i.e., *Sociómetro* as well as monograph studies conducted from 1999 until the present), such as the research of *Euskobarómetro*, carried out under the auspices of the UPV-EHU since 2002, the year it first began asking questions about the Agreement. Furthermore, I have organized the information obtained by consolidating the data in homogeneous series whenever the way in which questions were asked allowed me to do this. Finally, I have focused on the fundamental points of the law that are capable of shedding light in a way that will help us better understand its impact on the administrative structure of the Basque Country and, most importantly, give us an idea of how the Economic Agreement is represented in the collective imagination of our society.

Knowledge and Importance of the Economic Agreement

Continuity

As evident in table 7.1, since 1999 those within the population studies

Table 7.1. Have You Heard of the Economic Agreement? (Sociometros) (%)

	Surv., Oct. 99	Surv. Oct. 01	Tel. int. 02	Surv. Feb. 02	Tel. int. Mar. 02	Tel. int. Sep. 08	Surv. Nov. 10*
YES	49	46	55	68	55	61	51
NO	50	50	44	29	45	38	45
NS/NA	1	4	1	3	1	1	4
TOTAL	100	100	100	100	100	100	100

Source: GPS. Various issues of Sociometros and telephone surveys.
*The sum of the two options: "I know the Agreement well" and "I have heard of it, but I don't know it well."

who indicated that they had heard of the Agreement ranged from 46 percent (in October 2001) to 61 percent (in September 2008), with the exception of a spike of 68 percent in February 2002 (explainable in terms of the context of negotiation of the law that received extensive coverage in the communications media).

The most recent figure, for November 2010, is 51 percent. In this case, those surveyed responded to the following question: "Do you know the Economic Agreement well, have you heard of it but don't know it well, or have you never heard of it?"

The figure in the final column represents the sum of the first two options (i.e., know the Agreement well [9 percent] and have heard of it, but don't know it well [42 percent]). The outlying figure for February 2002 is explainable, as noted before, because it was during a critical juncture of the negotiations of the Agreement.

Age Matters

We can observe a positive correlation between age and knowledge of the agreement (62 percent within the 46–64 group and 54 percent in the 30–45 group). In the 18–29 group, 41 percent report knowledge of the agreement and, logically, the percentage reporting ignorance is the highest (at 55 percent).

Importance of the Economic Agreement

Once the negotiations ceased to be a prominent news item, the level of information reported by citizens dropped. Table 7.3 above clearly shows this. In contrast to the opinions that had previously been expressed in February 2002, just three months later, the level of reported information had fallen 14 points.

Level of knowledge is independent of the generic perception of the importance of the Agreement. A very significant minority (75 percent) in the 2008 study indicated that "the Economic Agreement" was very important or rather important to Basque autonomy. Yet it is the series of surveys, which have been conducted since 1991, which most strikingly reveal this opinion (which has fluctuated between 69 percent and 83 percent). (See table 7.5.)

The final survey, conducted in 2010, asked a different question in a different way, but with the same underlying substance (see table 7.4). In that study, we see that 55 percent of those persons consulted agree that the Economic Agreement is "very important" or "rather important" for the citizens of the Basque country.

This question was asked of those who indicated that they had

Table 7.2 Knowledge by Age Groups

		Totals	Age Groups 18–29	30–45	46–64	≥ 65
Let's talk now aout the basque economic agreement. Do you know the agreement well? Have you heard of it even though you don't know it? Or have you never heard of it?	Knows the agreement well	9	6	7	12	8
	Has heard of it but	42	35	47	50	34
	Has not heard of it	45	55	43	35	53
	Not specified/Not	4	4	3	3	5
	Vertical percentages	100	100	100	100	100
	n (unweighted	(2,198)	(451)	(671)	(621)	(455)

Source. GPS. *Sociometro* 44 (November 2010).

Table 7.3. In recent months, there has been a lot of discussion of the Economic Agreement. Would you say that you are minimally informed about what it means or involves for the Basque Country? (May 2002)

	%
YES	37
NO	45
NS	16
NA	2
TOTAL	100

Source: Euskobarometro

Heard the Agreement spoken of (55 percent) in the study on "Negotiations regarding the agreement and budgets for 2002." The trends over the last nine years regarding this question are clear. The perception regarding the importance of the Agreement having been affirmed between 75 percent and 83 percent of respondents between the years 2001 and 2008. However, when the question was asked in terms of whether the agreement was "helpful" or "harmful," 55 percent of respondents indicated it was "very helpful" or "rather helpful" (a decrease of 20 percent), while the number of persons who indicated that they did not know how to respond increased to 21 percent.

A majority of those who did offer an opinion indicated "economic autonomy" (24 percent) rather than "privilege" or "the achieving of progress or well-being" as the most important aspect of the Agreement.

Special Circumstances: Agreement Negotiations

As is well known, the parliamentary debates to approve the 2002 bud-

Table 7.4. Helpful or Harmful?

In general, do you have the impression that the Economic Agreement is very helpful, rather helpful, rather harmful, or very harmful for the citizens of the Basque Country?

	%
Very helpful	10
Somewhat helpful	45
Neither helpful nor harmful*	15
Rather harmful	7
Very harmful	1
Not specified/Not applicable	21
TOTAL	100

Asked only of those who indicated that they knew the Economic Agreement well or had heard of it (51 percent of the population).

* This option was not read to respondents.

Source: GPS. *Sociómetro* 44 (November 2010).

Table 7.5. The Economic Agreement establishes the capacity of Basque institutions to dictate fiscal regulations, collect taxes, and manage expenses. What, in your opinion, is the importance of the Economic Agreement for Basque autonomy? (in percent)

	SEPT. 99	OCT.01	JAN.02	SEPT.08
Very important	31	49	52	45
Rather important	38	34	30	30
Not very important	8	8	5	5
Not important at all	2	1	2	3
Not specified / not applicable	22	9	11	17
Total	100	100	100	100

Table 7.6. Most Important Aspects of the Economic Agreement

	%
Economic autonomy	24
More resources for progress and welfare	4
Privileges or few taxes	1
Other	7
Not specified / not applicable	46
No basis for an opinion*	19
Total	100

Source: *Eukobarometro*, May 2002.
*Persons who answered "NS/NA" to the previous question, and who indicated that they did not have even minimum information regarding the Agreement.

gets of the Autonomous Community led to a great deal of controversy that coincided with the time of the renewal of the Agreement. All of the parties were opposed to the budgets, albeit for different reasons. Thus, the Basque government lacked sufficient support to move negotiations forward.

In an attempt to avoid an extension of the previous budget (as had occurred in the previous fiscal year), the president of Parliament decided to change the procedure for approving the budget. This change involved voting for amendments separately rather than in a block. In addition to creating strains in the political climate, this process led to a stalemate that resulted in non-approval of budgets for fiscal year

Table 7.7. Interest in the Negotiations of the Economic Agreement

	%
High	5
Moderate	16
Low	21
None	54
Ns/na	4
Total	100

Source: Euskobarometro (May 2002).

2002. In any event, and in the absence of a budget law, on January 1, 2002, the extension of previous budgets automatically entered into effect. Finally, on January 23, in the session held for the purpose of approving the 2002 budgets, an event unprecedented in parliamentary practice occurred: the partial approval of some sections of the budget, but not of others.[2]

This turn of events created still greater political tension and, together with ETA terrorism, was hardly propitious to a healthy climate for negotiating the Economic Agreement.

All together, these circumstances contributed to lending a higher profile to negotiations regarding the agreement from the perspective of public opinion, which had acquired a heightened sensitivity regarding the issue. This explains the higher percentage of respondents who, in February 2002, claimed to have heard of the Economic Agreement (see table 7.1).

However, once the media coverage of the negotiations subsided, so did public interest in those negotiations (see table 7.7).

Comparison with Other Communities

The question asked of citizens in successive studies regarding the financing of Basque self-government through the Economic Agreement is shown in table 7.8.

A plurality (37 percent) indicated that Basques have benefited somewhat in comparison to other communities. A smaller percentage (20 percent) indicated that they believed the Basques had been treated equally. A significant 26 percent did not offer an opinion. The change in perspective evident over the course of three surveys conducted over the course of seven years (i.e., 2003–2010) may be due to the effects of the current economic crisis, given the relatively good

Table 7.8 Benefit/Harm vis-à-vis Other Communities (in Percent)

Taking into account the results of the financing of Basque self-government through the economic agreement, would you say that, in comparison with the other Autonomous Communities, Basques have benefited greatly or somewhat, treated equally, or somewhat or greatly harmed, given the current situation of the autonomous communities.

	2003	2005	2010*
Benefited greatly	2	5	6
Somewhat benefited	29	22	37
Treated equally	27	27	20
Somewhat harmed	30	33	8
Greatly harmed	4	5	2
NS/NA	8	7	26
TOTAL	100	100	100

* Question asked of respondents who indicated that they knew the Agreement well, or have heard of it (51 percent of total).
Source: *Euskobarometros* (May 2003 and May 2005) and GPS/*Sociometro* 44.

position of the Basque Country relative to that of other communities with respect to almost all economic indicators, especially levels of unemployment. In other words, the public may be crediting the Agreement with the higher capacity of our economy in comparison to others, during these difficult times.

Fiscal Competences or Powers

As regards public opinion as to which institutions are responsible for collecting taxes, we have data taken at two different collection points in recent history (i.e., 2008 and 2010). Both occurred at a time distant enough from approval of the Agreement to allow the assumption that those surveyed would have internalized information with respect to the institutions responsible for its implementation.

It is therefore surprising that the Deputations were not identified with greater frequency as the institutions responsible for collecting the most important taxes. Although a plurality of those surveyed (45 percent) attributed this function to the Deputations, one out of every four persons incorrectly identified either the central government (6 percent) or the Basque government (6 percent) as the bodies responsible for this function. Almost another fourth of respondents (23 percent) indicated that they did not know or did not venture an answer. (See table 7.9 and Figure 7.7)

But the results were considerably different when the question was limited to the perception regarding the ability and freedom to establish taxes. In this latter case, a majority of respondents (57 percent) indicated that "the autonomous communities of both the Basque Country and Navarre had a greater degree of fiscal independence than the other autonomous communities of Spain." However, the fact that 31 percent of those surveyed either indicated that they did not know, or did not state an opinion, is indicative of a widespread ignorance

Table 7.9 Institution Responsible for Collecting the Most Important Taxes (in Percent)

	2008	2010
Central government	12	6
Basque government	16	22
Deputations	46	45
City/town governments	--	4
Not specified/Not applicable	26	23
TOTAL	100	100

Source: GPS. Monograph, October 2008. Telephone survey, July 2010.

regarding this issue (table 7.10 and figure 7.8).

A question complementary to that of the function of collecting taxes was asked regarding responsibility with respect to establishing regulations for the most important taxes. In this case, the responses were more varied than in the companion question. Deputations were identified to a lesser degree (34 percent), while the perception of Basque government (27 percent) and central government (14 percent) as regulatory institutions was greater. One out of every four persons continued not to have a clear idea regarding the issues (table 7.11 and figure 7.9).

It appears that, with respect to our intricate web of institutions, the *regulatory function* is perceived as something that is provenance of higher-level institutions that carry more legal and legislative weight, whereas the *collective function* is seen as more properly belonging to the Deputations.

Table 7.10. Ability and Freedom to Establish the Most Important Taxes

	%
The autonomous communities of the Basque Country and Navarre have a higher degree of fiscal independence than the other autonomous communities	57
All autonomous communities have the same level of fiscal independence	12
Not specified/not applicable	31
TOTAL	100

Source: GPS. Monograph, October 2008

Table 7.11 Regulatory Responsibility for the Most Important Taxes

	%
Central government	14
Basque government	27
Deputations	34
City/town government	3
Not specified/not applicable	22
Total	100

Source: GPS. Telephone survey, July 2010.

Conclusions

The most salient conclusions of the studies reviewed here highlight the following points: (1) There is a relative knowledge of the Agreement on the part of the population (recorded at between 50 percent and 60 percent) that varies with age (with the age group 46–64 reporting greatest knowledge of the law). (2) A perception on the part of the majority was noted regarding the importance of benefits for citizens (55 percent). Most striking, the importance of the Agreement for Basque autonomy is widely appreciated (as reflected in the endorsement of some 80 percent of respondents). (3) The peak of knowledge of and citizen interest in the Agreement coincided with the time during which negotiations took place (i.e., during 2002) and this interest subsided once negotiations were concluded. (4) In comparison with the other autonomous communities, the most notable (although not majority) opinion expressed was that "Basques have benefited greatly or somewhat" from the financing of Basque self-government by means of the Economic Agreement (43 percent). However, when asked this question, one-fourth of the population either did not have a specific answer or did not respond. (5) As regards knowledge of the different fiscal competences, with respect to both regulatory and collection capacity, a certain confusion or disparity of opinions was noted. Thus, 45 percent of the population indicates that the Deputations are responsible for collection, a figure that drops to 34 percent when it comes to assigning responsibility to the selfsame Deputations. (6) There is greater clarity of opinion regarding the higher degree of fiscal autonomy enjoyed by the Autonomous Communities of the Basque Country and Navarre in comparison to other Autonomous Communities, with 57 percent of respondents stating their agreement with such an affirmation (according to data from 2008).

Endnotes

1. See Maider Ensunza, La opinión pública española sobre el Concierto Económico vasco 1952–2002, (Bilbao: Ad Concordiam, 2005). In this work, the concept of "public opinion" refers to articles in the press, with reference to both their form and substance.
2. For the context of the negotiations, see Cuadernos sociológicos 12: 55–56.

Bibliography

"El concierto económico vasco: Historia y renovación; Las valoraciones de la población de la capv al respecto." Soziologiazko Euskal Koadernoak/Cuadernos Sociólogicos Vascos 12 (2002): 51–98.

Euskobarometro, May 2002, May 2003, May 2005, February 2011. University of the Basque Country.

Office of Sociological Research (GPS). Basque Government Sociómetros, no. 11 (October 1999), no. 17 (October 2001), no. 18 (February 2002), no. 44 (November 2010).

Surveys

"Negociaciones Sobre el Concierto Economico y los Presupuestos" January 2002, Telephone Survey: (N) 1000.

"Acuerdo sobre el Concierto Económico" March 2002, Telephone Survey: (N) 1000.

"Conocimiento y Opiniones de la Ciudadanía Respecto al Concierto Economico Vasco."

October 2008. Telephone Survey: (N) 1000.

"Crisis Economica y Fiscalidad" November 2010. Telephone Survey: (N) 1000.

8
Ten Years of the Ad Concordiam Association

Jose Rubí Cassinello

The Birth of the Ad Concordiam Association: Justification

The Ad Concordiam Association for the Promotion and Dissemination of the Economic Agreement is a private non-profit organization created in accordance with Law 3/1988 (the "Associations Law") approved by the Basque Parliament. Ad Concordiam was legally constituted on November 16, 2000, with the following entities serving as its promotional partners: the Foral Deputation of Bizkaia, the University of the Basque Country (UPV-EHU), and the University of Deusto.[1]

The mission of the association is the study and dissemination of materials related to taxes and the public Treasury, with special reference to issues involved in the unique regulatory and institutional characteristics of the historical territory of Bizkaia. In order to carry out this mission, the association carries out a number of different activities: the dissemination of information for the general public as well as for subgroups with specific needs and concerns; the production (of its own accord or through subcontracting) of studies and monographs; the organization of courses, seminars, and presentations; and, in general, all manner of instructional and informational activities regarding the above-described materials and issues.

The constitution of the association was drafted in close collaboration with the Treasury and Finance Department of the Foral Deputation of Bizkaia, the director of said entity also serving as the president of our Association. This director (currently José María Iruarrizaga Artaraz) works directly with the UPV-EHU and the University of Deusto.

With the approaching end of the effective period of the Economic Agreement of 1981 (approved by Law 12/1981 of May 12, Basque institutions once again were faced with the need to negotiate new terms of the fiscal pact with representatives of the state—terms that it was hoped, based on recent history, would remain effective through much of the twenty-first century.

The need to make progress in the recovery of fiscal sovereignty in order to guarantee the continuation of autonomous fiscal and economic policy meant that the renegotiation of the Economic Agreement was a watershed event. Although it was obvious that the positions of the Basque representatives would aim at increasing the scope of regulatory and management autonomy, both with respect to tax collection as well as administrative and financial matters, the question remained as to what the position of the other side (i.e., the social and political climate determining the stance of the state representatives) as regards a possible agreement that would give more maneuvering room to the Foral Tax System.

No one should overlook the fact that the situation of our Economic Agreement was by no means ideal at that particular time. It was being questioned within the European Community, criticized by the rest of the Autonomous Communities in Spain (which see it more as an unjustified privilege than as an instrument of responsibility and self-government) and by state representatives who, by means of an ongoing appeal for judicial review, were continually calling into question each and every one of the measures exercised by the foral institutions pursuant to the competences granted by the Agreement. For all of these reasons, the resulting outlook did not seem to be especially propitious for engaging in a negotiation process aimed at the renewal of the Economic Agreement.

All of these obstacles, while difficult to overcome in and of themselves, would not have been quite so formidable if our representatives would have had the unanimous support of the society on whose behalf they were acting. But this was by no means the case. While previously, the mere mention of our unique foral system aroused passions of unconditional support, the institutions of Basque society were now viewed by the majority of citizens with a high degree of indifference. Added to this was a general ignorance with regard to the meaning, essence, and history of those institutions. In this light, the widespread lack of interest in the Agreement, and in the authority it grants, was certainly no surprise. Even the actions of political parties representing citizens are often governed by what is most politically expedient at a given moment, and thus the parties lose sight of the respect due to the Economic Agreement, over and above any legitimate disagreement regarding its implementation.

Opinion surveys have presented a rather depressing picture (as show in table 8.1): 50 percent of Basques have indicated that they have never heard of the Economic Agreement; 89 percent report that they know nothing of its origin; and, of the remaining 11 percent, only half (correctly) identified it as stemming from the Autonomy Statute. In response to the question as to when Basques began administering their own taxes, half of the population did not even dare offer a response.

Yet it can also accurately be stated that those who reported

Table 8.1. Degree of Knowledge and Importance Given to the Economic Agreement

Degree of Knowledge about the Economic Agreement	1999	2001	2002	2004	2010
Knows well					9
Heard of it, but does not know well	49	46	55	59	42
Has not heard of it	50	50	45	41	45
No knowlege / No answer	1	4	1		4
Total	100	100	100	100	100

Degree of Importance of the Economic Agreement	1999	2001	2002
Very important	31	49	
Fairly important	38	34	82
Of little importance	8	8	
No importance	2	1	7
No Knowledge / No answer	22	9	11
Total	100	100	100

ignorance of the Agreement did understand that it was a critically important instrument for self-government.

Another survey datum is also important in this connection: the identification on the part of a solid majority of the population (60.4 percent) of the defense of the Economic agreement with a single political party, the EAJ-PNV. All other political parties trailed far behind in public opinion, in this regard. This identification, while understandably a source of pride for the EAJ-PNV's leaders, also shows the distance perceived among citizens between the instruments of self-government and the various parliamentary representatives across the political spectrum.

The Department of Treasury and Finance of the Foral Deputation of Bizkaia attempted to address this state of affairs by including in the General Budget of the Historical Territory for the year 2000 a new program called the "Economic Agreement." This program will, under the supervision of the General Technical Secretariat of the Department, have the general goal of preparing the citizens and institutions of the historical territory of Bizkaia to effectively ensure a process of renewal of our unique instrument of self-government.

Successfully dealing with this situation at all levels has been, and today continues to be, the most critically important activity to be implemented within the framework of this program. The problem has been how to mount a successful attack on a problem of the scope that has been identified above.

Given that there is no way to change the past, the focus has instead been on neutralizing the situation and protecting the Agreement in the future by generating useful arguments. The defense of the Agreement requires a sober, thoughtful, and systematic approach.

These kinds of actions are of course to be expected of political and administrative entities. However, it is also clear that such actions must transcend these entities to include robust initiatives—and at times even a leadership role—on the part of civil society.

We feel that it continues to be a matter of urgency to renew a collective sentiment of support for the Economic Agreement and an appreciation of its importance for the Basque Country. But this goal will only be achieved if we can get the citizens of Euskadi to understand that the Economic Agreement is good for everyone. For this purpose, we need to use all of the means at our disposal to reach these citizens. This includes students of all ages, communications media, scientific institutions, and universities—without, of course, neglecting the governmental administration itself and its workers (who often suffer from the same ignorance for which they scold the citizens they serve). The next effort of this nature will take place in the two universities located in Bizkaia: UPV-EHU and the University of Deusto. These two institutions were highly receptive to the idea, and eagerly offered to collaborate with us, the first through its Department of Social Sciences and the second through the Institute of Basque Studies. This partnership continues today. As we will shortly see, it has yielded important results.

Yet, as we said, it was important that any action undertaken be coordinated and systematic in order to achieve the identified goals. For this purpose, it was necessary to act in a number of different sectors. We will attempt to describe this process below.

The obvious heterogeneity of the population that is the target of these efforts required a compartmentalization of our activities, which were grouped in homogenous clusters as a function of certain basic variables that frequently overlapped with one another:

- The goal to be achieved, whether informational, academic, or technical.
- The public that is targeted: citizens in general, schoolchildren, university students, businessmen, local entities, and government employees.
- The geographical scope of the activities to be implemented.

Given this starting point, the most important obstacle involved overcoming the previously discussed lack of knowledge regarding the primary institutions of self-government in order to foster a collective sentiment of identification with the Economic Agreement. In the case of activities outside of our territory, our goal was to transmit a clear and unambiguous image of the nature and meaning of the Economic Agreement and to combat as aggressively as possible the image of privilege or "tax haven" that has taken hold in the Spanish state over the course of many years.

Each one of these activities contained objectives and approaches that were very clearly defined and that aimed at the creation of an improved social and political image for the Economic Agreement. An additional objective in this regard, within the wider European context, was to refute the opinion, widespread among European leaders and especially among those working for the Commission, which sees that body as the perfect instrument for bringing about the de facto termination of the Economic Agreement.

Within the Basque Country itself, we defined three specific objectives:

- Knowledge: Providing critically important data regarding the Economic Agreement.
- Universalization: Getting citizens to see that the Agreement is a tool from which all Basques derive benefit.
- Raising awareness: Making them aware of the Agreement's strategic importance for the Basque Country.

Activities of the Ad Concordiam Association

Based upon the above objectives, we initially devised the following kinds of activities:

Informational and/or Educational Activities

These involved remedying the ignorance identified above as regards the primary institutions of self-government in order to foster a collective sentiment of identification with the Economic Agreement.

Consideration of the situation in which each group of citizens might be expected to approach the Agreement, and therefore each of their particular educational and informational needs, led us to identify four different subgroups within our target population:

The General Public

The three previously mentioned principles—knowledge, universalization, and raising awareness—were initially defined in a basic way through the exhibition "Historia eta Sentzazioak," the purpose of which was to foster a renewed appreciation of the basic importance of the Economic Agreement through activities aimed at fostering, on the one hand, a general awareness of the origin, history, and meaning of our historical rights, and their evolution until the present time and, on the other hand, a knowledge of those rights within a contemporary social and political context.

Using this exhibition as the primary tool, a number of complementary activities were developed (e.g., conferences, courses and seminars, distribution of didactic material, direct publicity campaigns, and media advertising). The aim of all these activities was to disseminate knowledge of the existence of a foral tax system which has as its purpose in the present-day the collection of taxes to fund public services in Bizkaia, but which also served functions which our citizens had granted over the course of centuries. This exhibition was installed in a pavilion constructed in the Bizkaia Plaza in Bilbao, and was open between March and July of 2001. During that time, it attracted almost 30,000 visitors. In addition to the exhibition itself, each attendee also received a packet that included an informational book and CD regarding the Foral Tax System, as well as a board game that tested players' knowledge of the history of the Economic Agreement. Within the space of the exhibition, other activities such as conferences and debates were also held that expanded the scope of its content. Renowned specialists in various knowledge areas, as well as distinguished protagonists of recent history were involved in these events. One notable participant was José Ramón López Larrinaga (one of the negotiators of the 1981 Agreement in his capacity as Assistant Advisor of the Ministry of Finance in the Basque Government, acting under the orders of Senior Advisor Pedro Luis Uriarte).

In order to provide information about the activities of the association, a website was created that, in addition to incorporating the contents of the exhibition Historia eta Sentzazioak, also explains the Agreement from varying points of view, as well as its history, its present, and the activities of the Foral Tax System.

The year 2003 marked the 125th anniversary of the Economic Agreement. Ad Concordiam marked the occasion with a number of celebrations aimed at the general public. These events included live presentations, animated presentations for children, and activity workshops. In March of that same year, conferences were held in four different locations within Bizkaia (i.e., Gernika, Durango, Balmaseda, and Bilbao) that explained the history and justification of the Agreement, as well as its contents and its current meaning.

On the occasion of the anniversary of the agreement, Ad Concordiam printed a commemorative newspaper containing articles written regarding four renewals of the agreement (i.e., 1878, 1906, 1981, and 2002).

Schoolchildren

This comprises a group of almost 200,000 persons aged six to eighteen, ranging from the first year of primary education to the final year of secondary education. This is unquestionably an important group to reach, considering its influence on the family environment. Because it comprises such a large range of ages, it makes sense to subdivide the group in order to identify appropriate activities and modes of communication:

- Required primary education students (through age twelve) who were provided very simple materials that were entertaining and easy to understand.
- Required secondary and optional secondary students (ages thirteen to eighteen), which also included students in unregulated educational institutes (i.e., private tuitions). This group received materials similar to those described above that were aimed at the general public.

Both groups were easily accessible through their educational institutions as well as through parent associations. This in turn facilitated the preparation of activities to be implemented with teachers who required instruction in the material so that they could then present it to their students. In addition, presentations and didactic materials were prepared that were directly aimed at students.

University Students

The efforts aimed at this group were limited to students pursuing degrees that bore some historical or technical relations to the instruments by which we are governed (e.g., law, economics, history, Basque philology), and which therefore require a more in-depth knowledge of said instruments than students pursuing other careers (for whom activities directed at the general public suffice).

As with primary and secondary students, this group offered the advantage of easy access, given the fact that the two universities of Bizkaia are partners in the present project. It thus was a very easy to offer the following kinds of activities at these institutions of higher learning:

- Introduction of the study of the Agreement in the syllabi of various courses.
- Introduction of the topic in summer school programs, and its inclusion in the master's program in taxation.
- The creation of a university chair at UPV-EHU in the Economic Program.

Public Employees

Within a section dedicated to educational activities, we cannot ignore a particularly important target group: public employees of the administrative entities of Euskadi. This is a group of special interest because of the desirability that they serve as role models in their service to the general public. Thus, special training programs were devised for this group in collaboration with the Instituto Vasco de Administración Pública (IVAP), and which were directed at all employees working in governmental entities in the Basque Country (i.e., the Basque Government, local governments, and Foral Deputations). With this extensive coverage, there was in the end no public employee who remained ignorant of the essential features of the governing institutions in which they served.

Scientific and Academic Activities

The work of disseminating information regarding the Economic Agreement that has thus far been carried out, and which has been directed at citizens in general, has been perfectly complemented by the promotion of research and publishing activity regarding its more scientific aspects. The encouragement of interest in and study of aspects of the Economic Agreement in environments which have as part of their very mission an understanding of its nature and potential is of course indispensable.

The Foral Deputation of Bizkaia, through its Department of Treasury and Finance, has for some time been conducting activities related to such scientific and academic endeavors by means of the publication, in collaboration with the UPV-EHU, of two collections: Classics of the Foral Tax System and Doctoral Theses of the Foral Tax System. The aim of these endeavors is to recover texts of interest in materials related to the Economic Agreement from the historical or academic point of view.

Specifically, in 2002, at the time of negotiations for the renewal of the Economic Agreement of 1981, a contest was announced calling for articles and monographs on topics related to the Economic Agreement. A similar contest, this time for monographs only, was announced in 2004. Two different prizes were awarded, the first for a study of the main issues that proved contentious during the negotiations and the second for a biography of one of the most distinguished negotiators of the Economic Agreement. Both monographs were later published by the association.[2]

In October 2003, a two-day seminar was held at the Palacio Euskalduna where the regulatory aspects of the Agreement, as well as the persons involved in negotiating it, were analyzed in detail. This event featured the participation of both academic and business experts. In October 2006, a one-day seminar was held at the UPV-EHU on the Agreement and communications media, which focused for the most part on documentations centers and the dissemination of knowledge regarding specific aspects of the Economic Agreement and the existence of peripheral tax collection systems. At the end of 2006, an International Congress was held at the University of Deusto for the purpose of analyzing issues of the Economic Agreement within the context of the European Community (EC)—especially as applied to EC restrictions on state aid. The Azores ruling, which had just recently been issued the previous September, opened up a wide range of possibilities, as was pointed out by a number of experts who attended the Congress. Other notable presenters at that event included EC experts who analyzed several different models or variants of decentralized tax systems in Portugal, Finland, Germany, and the United Kingdom.

Publishing Activity

Ever since its founding, Ad Concordiam has engaged in ongoing publishing activity. Its first publications were the materials distributed at the exhibition Five Hundred Years of the Foral Tax System[3] and continued with twelve volumes that dealt with the Economic Agreement from a variety of perspectives. Beginning in 2002, documentary materials were published that grew out of the renewal of the Agreement in that same year. In addition, works were published that provided different points of view of the document, as well as an analysis of public opinion regarding it,[4] including the prize winning monographs of 2003[5] and the research project sponsored by the association on the oral history of the negotiation of the 1981 Agreement.[6]

Ad Concordiam has had a special interest in legal matters, and has published compilations of regulations, as well as bibliographies and analyses on the legal system of the Agreement.[7] More recently, with a view to disseminating information regarding the Agreement beyond the borders of Spain, and to contrast its particular features with those of other models of fiscal federalism, the proceedings of the Congress discussed in the previous section were published.[8]

The most recent book, which was published only in English, attempts to explain the functioning and impact of the Economic Agreement. This work, by Ignacio Zubiri, has attempted to serve both to disseminate information about the Agreement within international academic circles and to generate a "vocabulary" of the Economic Agreement in English aimed at facilitating understanding of its aspects, concepts, and methodologies, none of which fit neatly within the historical, legal, or economic categories of other nations, something which constitutes an important obstacle for the proper dissemination of information regarding the Agreement outside of the Spanish-speaking world.

All of these volumes have been designed as part of a series of publications that is easily recognizable by its common design. They do not form a "collection" per se, but rather a series with a shared design (i.e., in terms of their covers, text formatting, and size) that makes them easy to identify.

As we've indicated, a number of these publications are the fruits of research that was financed by the association. This was the case of two works on public opinion, as well as another of oral history. All three of these projects were directed by Miren Alcedo. Yet there have been other important works that it has not yet been possible to publish. For example, a project of iconographic research conducted by Susana Serrano and Nuria Moret was subsidized in 2003 that involved the construction of an iconographic database that would make possible the identification of useful or interesting images that could illustrate other activities of the association.

Within these practical parameters, a number of other projects have been undertaken, such as one that is now in its final phase that constitutes an analysis of the contents of the Economic Agreement over the course of time. The aim of this study is to allow an examination of the evolution of the tax districts created by the Agreement. It is expected that this work will be completed this year, and that it will be published in 2012.

Redesign of the Association's Website

The most recent project of Ad Concordiam is the redesign of its website, and the recent Congress proved the ideal scenario for its unveiling. The old website was based on the exhibition Five Hundred Years of the Foral Tax System. As mentioned earlier, this exhibition was held in 2001 in the Plaza Bizkaia of Bilbao, on the occasion of the twentieth anniversary of the recovery of the Economic Agreement.

While the former version of the website met the needs of the times in which it was created, we believe that the time has come for a thorough redesign of its contents and the reflection of a new philosophy. Thus, we wanted our redesigned website to both serve as a complement to the Documentation Centre of the Economic Agreement and the Foral Treasuries (UPV-EHU) and to meet a need that the Center itself could not meet, given its focus on academic matters and its primary appeal to specialists, historians, researchers, and others who have a specific interest in the Agreement. For this reason, the website of Ad Concordiam has attempted to limit its purpose to disseminating general information regarding the Agreement to the public at-large.

In order to achieve this objective, we have devised a three-tiered website. The first level called "To make a long story short." This level targets those who have minimal or no acquaintance with the Economic Agreement and is thus dedicated to answering four basic questions about it (i.e., What is its origin? What are the main characteristics of the current Agreement? What is its purpose? What is a quota?).

The second level is called "In Depth" and is directed to site visitors who would like to obtain somewhat more detailed information, without investing massive amounts of time. Specifically, we have in mind students who need somewhat more detailed knowledge of the Economic Agreement, its meaning, and its contents. Thus, the aim of this second level is, through diagrams, summaries, and simple exposition, to explain the entire contents of the Economic Agreement.

Finally, there is the third level, called "Documentation," which is aimed at professionals who work with the Agreement, and who need specific information, and/or who need stay up to date regarding the most recent developments, even of the most detailed nature. For this level, we have been uploading all of our publications, as well as books and historical texts from our collection, Foral Tax Systems Classics, and theses published by Ad Concoriam. All of this information can be easily downloaded. Each of the texts can be requested in either digital or traditional format.

This specialist level is itself divided into three sublevels. The first sublevel includes the administrative foundations of the Economic Agreement, specifically information regarding the Tax Authority Council consultation with the Coordinating Committee regarding the Economic Agreement, court resolutions, and decisions of the European Commission. The second sublevel includes material related to jurisprudence, while the third contains the works of various authors. This last section has not yet been fully developed due to copyright issues, but we will be trying to provide an exhaustive inventory of all articles dealing with the Economic Agreement that have been published in specialized journals.

We will also have pages within the site dedicated to resources, questions, graphics, and the 2001 presentation. We will also be including a board game and trivia questions regarding the Economic Agreement.

Finally, we want to assure that anyone interested can stay informed regarding events concerning the Economic Agreement (via either RSS or e-mail alerts) that can be subscribed to. We hope that the website proves to be as useful as we've designed it to be, and we invite everyone to visit it. Its web address is www.conciertoeconomico.org. You can also contact us directly via e-mail at adconcordiam@ bizkaia.net.

Endnotes

1. The first Board of Directors comprised José Rubí (General Technical Secretary of the Foral Tax System of Bizkaia, who served as board president); Guillermo Onandía (also of the Foral Tax System, who served as treasurer), and Eduardo Alonso (of the UPV-EHU) who served as treasurer. Finally, Joseba Agirreazkuenaga (of the UPV-EHU) served as secretary and Santiago Larrazabal (of the University of Deusto) as spokesman. The same group continues to serve on the Board today, with the exception of Eduardo Alonso, who was replaced by Alberto Atxabal in 2003.
2. Miren Alcedo Moneo, *La identidad pactada: primer proceso estatutario y concierto económico, 1981* (Bilbao: Ad Concordiam, 2006).
3. Eduardo J. Alonso Olea, *500 años de Hacienda Foral. 500 Foru Ogasunaren urte* (Bilbao: Ad Concordiam, 2001).
4. Maider Ensunza Arrien and Luis de Guezala, eds. *La opinión pública española sobre el concierto económico vasco* (1952–2002) (Bilbao: Ad Concordiam, 2005); Sonia González García, Asun Merinero Sierra, Tatiana Urien Ortiz Tatiana, and Luis de Guezala, eds., *La opinión pública española sobre el concierto económico vasco (1878–1937)* (Bilbao: Ad Concordiam, 2003).
5. Gregorio Castaño San José, *Adolfo Gabriel de Urquijo e Ibarra (1866–1933): Un artifice del concierto económico* (Bilbao: Ad Concordiam, 2005); and Enrique Lucas Murillo de la Cueva, *Crisis y renovación del Concierto Económico* (Bilbao: Ad Concordiam, 2005).
6. Miren Alcedo Moneo, *La identidad pactada: primer proceso estatutario y concierto económico, 1981* (Bilbao: Ad Concordiam, 2006).
7. Alberto Atxabal Rada and Javier Muguruza Arrese, *Recopilación del Concierto Económico vasco. Legislación, jurisprudencia y bibliografía. 1981–2004* (Bilbao: Ad Concordiam, 2006) and Fernando de la Hucha Celador, *El régimen jurídico del Concierto Económico* (Bilbao: Ad Concordiam, 2006).
8. *Congreso Internacional Concierto Económico Vasco y Europa, Concierto Económico, Fiscalidad Regional y Ayudas de Estado = International Conference of the Basque Economic Agreement and Europe: Economic Agreement, Regional Tax Regulation, and State Aid: Bilbao, 12–14 de diciembre de 2006* (Bilbao: Ad Concordiam, 2007).

Bibliography

Alcedo Moneo, Miren. *La identidad pactada : Primer proceso estatutario y concierto económico, 1981*. Bilbao: Ad Concordiam, 2006.

Alonso Olea, Eduardo J. *500 años de Hacienda Foral: 500 Foru Ogasunaren urte*. Bilbao: Ad Concordiam, 2001.

Asociación para la Promoción y Difusión del Concierto Económico. "El Concierto Económico." Website www.conciertoeconomico.org/en.

Atxabal Rada, Alberto, and Javier Muguruza Arrese. *Recopilación del Concierto Económico vasco: Legislación, jurisprudencia y biblio-*

grafía. 1981–2004. Bilbao: Ad Concordiam, 2006.

Castaño San José, Gregorio. *Adolfo Gabriel de Urquijo e Ibarra (1866–1933): Un artífice del concierto económico*. Bilbao: Ad Concordiam, 2005.

El Concierto Económico Vasco: Historia y renovación; Las valoraciones de la población de la C.A.P.V al respecto. Cuadernos sociológicos vascos, número 12. Vitoria-Gazteiz: Servicio Central de Publicaciones del Gobierno Vasco, 2002.

El Concierto Económico y las empresas de Bizkaia. Barómetro Empresarial de Bizkaia. Departamento de Información Económica y Empresarial. Bilbao: Cámara de Comercio de Bilbao, 2000.

Congreso Internacional Concierto Económico Vasco y Europa, Concierto Económico, Fiscalidad Regional y Ayudas de Estado = International Conference Basque Economic Agreement and Europe, Economic Agreement, Regional Tax Regulation and State Aid: Bilbao, 12–14 de diciembre de 2006. Bilbao: Ad Concordiam, 2007.

De la Hucha Celador, Fernando. *El régimen jurídico del Concierto Económico*. Bilbao: Ad Concordiam, 2006.

Ensunza Arrien, Maider, and Luis de Guezala, eds. *La opinión pública española sobre el concierto económico vasco (1952–2002)*. Bilbao: Ad Concordiam, 2005.

Gonzalez García, Sonia, Asun Merinero Sierra, Tatiana Urien Ortiz, and Luis de Guezala, Luis de, eds. *La opinión pública española sobre el concierto económico vasco (1878–1937)*.Bilbao: Ad Concordiam, 2003.

Federalismo fiscal y Europa = Zerga federalismoa eta Europa. = Fiscal federalism and Europe: VIII Jornadas Internacionales celebradas en Donostia-San Sebastián los días 13, 14 y 15 de noviembre de 2007. Vitoria-Gazteiz: EuskoLegebiltzarra - Parlamento vasco, 2008.

Lucas Murillo de la Cueva, Enrique. *Crisis y renovación del Concierto Económico*. Bilbao: Ad Concordiam, 2005.

Zubiri Oria, Ignacio. *The Economic Agreement between the Basque Country and Spain*. Bilbao: Ad Concordiam, 2010.

9
Thirty Years of Economic Agreement

Eduardo J. Alonso Olea

This chapter presents a summary of the activity in recent years of the Center for Documentation of the Economic Agreement and the Foral Tax Systems.

Specifically, the present study will attempt to draw conclusions regarding this work, which has involved the gathering, storage, and distribution of knowledge regarding the Economic Agreement. We will explore both the topics that have most concerned us, as well as those that have been of most interest to the users of the Center over the past four years.

This paper presents certain results related to a different way of producing knowledge. We refer to knowledge in a context of its application. As Michael Gibbons argues in *The New Production of Knowledge,* the task of research is to produce useful knowledge. This does not automatically mean to say that one should solely produce for the market, but that the result of the research must include the aim of its diffusion through society.

We will begin with our monitoring of press activity and continue with our description of regulations. In addition, we will be drawing upon our bibliographical and biographical materials. As indicated previously, we will also be focusing on the information center utilized by those using our resources. The most striking element of this history has been the continual expansion of access to the information page that we included in Wikipedia, a resource that has recently multiplied the number of pertinent Internet searches.

Finally, we will address future prospects and the possible expansion of certain aspects of the Center's work, such as the blog and online library, which have recently witnessed increased demand on the part of the Center's users (at least in terms of online resources).

In sum, and in terms of the Center's work, we see how the general knowledge in Basque society regarding the agreed arrangements is limited—and even more limited outside the Basque Country. We can identify a number of examples where we can hope that our influence has been of assistance in explaining and illustrating aspects of the special (if not privileged) arrangements in our territory. In any event, the opinion that the Basque Country is a tax haven continues to be widespread.

The Center of Documentation of the Economic Agreement and Foral Tax Systems (2007)

The Center began its work in May 2007 on the basis of a partnership agreement between the University of the Basque Country (UPV-EHU) and the Foral Deputation of Bizkaia, which was signed that same month in order to serve as an instrument of scientific knowledge with respect to the Economic Agreement and the Foral Tax Systems. This knowledge had to be generated by gleaning sources of information regarding both the present and the past, and disseminating them through open channels that would make them available to researchers and others interested in the Agreement and related topics. Later, in November 2009 and March 2010, other agreements were reached with the foral Deputations of Araba and Gipuzkoa.

The relationship between the Department of Contemporary History and the Foral Deputation of Bizkaia dates from a much earlier period. Back in 1997, the former collaborated with the Department of the Foral Tax System in initiatives such as the publication of a series of classic works concerning the Foral Tax System, a series that at present totals nine volumes.[1] In addition, the Department of Contemporary History has, along with the University of Deusto, partnered with Ad Concordiam in the promotion and dissemination of the Economic Agreement.[2]

Since the time of the aforementioned 2007 accord, the work of the Center has always involved the collection of highly varied kinds of information, its conservation in a number of different media, and its dissemination, primarily through its website (www.ehu.es/ituna) by means of the publication of databases that group and systematize the data obtained.

Databases

From its very inception, one of the primary activities of the Center has been the creation and maintenance of various databases for the purpose of their later dissemination on the Internet.

The most extensive of these databases is the one which gathers news published in the press regarding the Economic Agreement, the activities of the Foral Tax Systems and, in the most general sense, any other matters that might affect the financing system of the Basque Country (i.e., contributions, budgets, debates on fiscal federalism, and a host of other topics). The Center currently boasts a collection of 6,000 press references dating from 1878 and continuing through the present. These references include data such as the headline, name of publication and author, a brief summary of the article's content, a graphic reference, and a number of other fields containing different kinds of descriptors (i.e., subject, geographical, and personal names).

The purpose of this database is to facilitate the identification, on the basis of any individual field, of news or references in a way that facilitates information related to the label of the field, either in clusters or in individual units. To the extent to which this work goes beyond the generation of press references based on the daily monitoring that is an ongoing part of our work, and includes "historical" press references, it allows us to have at our disposal a complete profile of the impact of the press on the Agreement. In addition, and to approach matters from a somewhat different angle, such references allow us to later analyze the various process involved in developments such as the negotiations to renew the Agreement.

The sources of our daily work spring not only from the daily press, but also from many other sources: weekly newspapers, economic magazines, blogs, and even institutional publications containing tax-related information, such as the journal of the European Commission's Committee for Taxation, Customs, Anti-Fraud, and Audit, and of the Foral Deputations (e.g., Bizkaimedia). Such publications contain news regarding, among other matters, the Foral Tax Systems. The economic press includes Abc.es, Cincodias.com, *El Correo*, Eldiarovasco.com, *The Economist*, elEconomista.es, *El Mundo*, *Europa Press*, Expansion.Com, *The Washington Post*, and *The Financial Times*. News Gathering services for economic news (Spain and international) include noticias24horas.com, *Estrategia Empresarial*, and Financierodigital.es. The general information press includes Berria.info, *Deia*, *Diario de Navarra*, *Diario de Noticias de Álava*, *Diario de Noticias Navarra*, Euskalherria.com – *Le journal du pays basque*, *Gara – Euskal Herriko egunkaria*, *Izaronews*, La Razón Digital – Economía, *Lavanguardia*, *El País*, *Público*, and *El Mundo*.

Another topic about which the Center has a great deal of archived material are regulatory matters. It should not be forgotten that both the Economic Agreement as well as the activity of the Foral Tax Systems are based on the application of regulations at different levels and from different bodies. The Center's objective is to collect all of these regulations, and to include them in the proper databases in a way that facilitates their subsequent retrieval.

Within this category, we have nearly 400 records containing all of the historical versions of the Agreement, from 1878 until the present day. In addition, our records include many of the regulatory measures involved in creating the Agreement. Naturally, our emphasis is on the most salient of the documents (e.g., we don't have a collection of completed tax forms). Included in our archives is a printed reference that can be consulted in the Center itself. In addition, there are legal databases that are much more exhaustive than those presented here but without the chronological breadth (1839–2011) or degree of specialization. These searches regarding regulations are Asociación Española de Asesores Fiscales (AEDAF), IBERLEX (for legislation), GAZETA (for history), *Boletín Oficial del País Vasco* (BOPV), *Boletín Oficial de Gipuzkoa* (main page), Foral Deputation of Araba – *Boletín Oficial del Territorio Histórico de Álava*, *Boletín Oficial de Bizkaia*, EUR-Lex, EUROPA – Taxation and Customs Union / Inventory of taxes in the EU, Web of Tax Inspectors, Expatax, International Bureau of Fiscal Documentation (IBFD), http://antonioesteban.com.blogspot.com (a blog discussing fiscal news), and the Fiscal Web Forum of Bizkaia (current tax information)

Other references at our disposal include publications about the Agreement and/or Foral Tax Systems. We have been especially ambitious in this regard, and our database includes, in addition to texts containing current or historical information regarding the Agreement, publications that deal with more general issues, such as fiscal federalism, new taxation trends, and the context of the European Union, as well as historical, biographical, legal, economic, political, and parliamentary aspects of the Agreement. In addition to preserving these references, the purpose of the center is to also try as much as possible to create a library where researchers have ready access to the works themselves. On many occasions, this is logically not possible, but we try to expand our collections with the acquisition of materials of interest, as well as the recovery of older texts.

Finally, by way of concluding this section regarding databases, we must also mention the smaller volume of collections that are by no means lacking in interest, such as those involving biographical information. Reflecting a broad view of history, such material not only makes reference to the legal aspects of the Agreement, but also to its protagonists and architects, at least to the extent to which a biographical angle is essential to indicating the lines of development of the Agreement.

The reality is that the Economic Agreement has been negotiated since—and even before—1878 and until the present day, and the personal element is of fundamental importance in understanding its evolution. For this reason, we have constructed a database about those who have negotiated the Agreement. This database currently ends with the Spanish Civil War. The purpose of this biographical aspect of our endeavor is to identify these negotiators and reconstruct their personal profiles and relations with others.

Data regarding those who have negotiated the Agreement are obtained through a twofold process: first, through a search for the negotiation of particular agreements and, second, by means of an examination of the personal database generated of the individual in question. This process most certainly involves introducing personal data that are related to the Agreement (but not solely related to the Agreement, since we have also included general biographical information, including data pertaining to political, professional, and administrative positions currently and previously held[3]).

Expanding the Reach of the Center: The Internet

The recent presentation of data on the Internet marks a true watershed in the academic world. In our case, access to the previously discussed databases can occur via Internet searches. Because of copyright issues, not everything is available on the Internet. However, at least some limited data are accessible that can allow a researcher (or any other individual who might be interested) to access basic information that can later, if needed, be expanded by visiting the Center, located in the Central Library of the UPV-EHU.

The purpose of these Internet databases is therefore to provide synthetic references that provide access to information regarding particular topics that can later be expanded, either via other resources or through exploring materials available at the Center itself. For this purpose, we have bibliographical and periodical databases that are updated on a weekly basis.

In addition, we have at our disposal another important element of information: a digital library. Specifically, we have 128 volumes that have been electronically formatted, with their corresponding search sections, that any interested party can consult in a pdf file (we will soon introduce epub files as well) directly via our website. Most of these are older books and pamphlets (once again, because of copyright issues) that are often difficult to find in libraries. In addition, in some instances, we have included recent editions of old titles, such as the series of classics of the Foral Tax Systems, which was the product of the previously mentioned collaboration between the UPV-EHU and the Department of Treasury and finance of the Deputation of Bizkaia. This digital collection will soon exceed 200 titles, and will include, in addition to more general works, various fiscal regulations of the three Deputations that are parties to the Economic Agreement.

This collection is of particular value to the Center's website. This is an effort that, in addition to digitization and uploading to the website, has also involved the important task of determining which titles to reproduce. We are confident that, during the next phase of the Center's growth, we will be able to continue to expand the richness and variety of the texts that we make available.

Most readers are aware that the Internet (which is not exactly an old technology in itself) has developed a new medium complementing its "traditional" use. This development is called "Web 2.0."

Web 2.0 can be defined as the realization of a vision of the Internet as a social space that has room for all kinds of social agents—a space capable of providing support and participating in a true information, communication, and/or knowledge society. This society has developed as the result of the interface of social action with a new technological design.[4]

In addition to this "static" access to the bibliographical production related to the Agreement and the Foral Tax Systems, we also include a blog on our website that we use for the purpose of informing those interested in the latest news regarding these entities. This involves not only gathering journalistic information but also providing notification of upcoming events, activities at the Center and elsewhere, rulings, obituaries, and other matters regarding the day-to-day activities of the Agreement and the Foral Tax Systems. This blog constitutes an immediate and direct channel to the most important current events related to the world of the Economic Agreement.

Another noteworthy aspect of the Center's activity, in addition to its projection to the general public through its website, has been its incursions into "the world of wiki." As is well known, the best example of this form of collaborative writing is Wikipedia, which is without doubt the most ambitious and fastest growing example in recent years. We have composed the Wikipedia entries related to the Economic Agreement in Spanish, Basque, and English.[5]

James Bridle has stated that he feels that Wikipedia is "Wikipedia is a useful subset of the entire internet, and as such a subset of all human culture. It's not only a resource for collating all human knowledge, but a framework for understanding how that knowledge came to be and to be understood; what was allowed to stand and what was not; what we agree on, and what we cannot."[6]

Examining the statistics with respect to the access of the Wikipedia page for the Economic Agreement, we can see that interest has varied in recent years, and this leads to a number of conclusions.

As can be seen in table 9.1, since last summer, interest in the Wikipedia content regarding the Agreement has only increased, reaching its peak in November (possibly because the debate on the Economic Agreement was a phenomenon that polarized electoral opinion in Catalonia, which held community-wide elections that same month. This is evidence of the need to disseminate the contents of the Agreement beyond the confines of the Basque Country. And this should not be done only in Spanish, but also in English, in which language we have recently observed an increase in visits. During the past three

Table 9.1 Monthly Visits to the English and Spanish Versions of the Economic Agreement Page of the Wikipedia (December 2009 through January 2011)[1]

Month	Spanish	English
December	681	49
January	762	44
February	935	53
March	799	80
April	712	151
May	867	200
June	742	103
July	611	86
August	800	124
September	1537	130
October	1403	135
November	4797	154
December	1712	154
January	1542	145
Average	**1,279**	**115**

1. As of time of publication, the Basque version did not compile usage statistics

months, there have been an average of 140 monthly visits.

Center Activities: Print and Electronic Publications

In addition to internet access, a new print newsletter has also been published,[7] and attained a maximum circulation of 1,100 in November 2010 to subscribers in academic, institutional, and professional settings. This newsletter includes recent data, as well as legislative, judicial, and hemerographic news.

More recently, in December 2010, we have begun to distribute in digital format a smaller but more frequent publication that places special emphasis on the latest news regarding the Agreement and the Foral Tax System.

In addition to these materials, which are more or less finished products, we also publish a report on legal texts that primarily emphasizes the texts of the Agreement itself, along with others that had not yet been distributed on the Internet (e.g., databases from the nineteenth through the twenty-first centuries related to budgets and quotas). These are tools that allow the researcher to access data that are more or less scattered, and that we have consolidated and distributed at the request of researchers. These databases have allowed us to publish a study on the use of the Economic Agreement as a long-term anti-cyclic tool during the period 1867–1980.[8]

These elements will be amplified in the coming months, to the extent that the Center's finances allow, to include other materials, such as multimedia, social networks, expansion of databases, and so on. The aim of this amplification will be to increase academic institutionalization within the university environment of the Economic Agreement. This activity is a clear reflection of the Center's commitment to public service.

There is no doubt that our activity has been consistently focused on the gathering and dissemination of knowledge of issues related to the Economic Agreement, but we have not limited ourselves to the legal document alone, and have in addition included many other of its facets: political, economic, fiscal, parliamentary, and so on. And the numbers keep growing: 6,000 press references, 9 bulletins with a circulation of between 400 and 1,100, 980 bibliographical references, 300 biographical entries, another 300 regulatory references, and so on.

We have retained an interest in the academic perspective, but have at the same time promoted public service as a reflection of our recognition that a new society like the current global society requires new ways of producing knowledge.

We advocate a scientific approach that is also accessible to the lay public, within a context of critical cross-sectionality. The research strategy is not limited to the academic and university setting, but instead needs to be extended to a broader pubic that has different demands for information. In the Basque case, this is especially important, given that the aging population of our community has led to an increasing interest on the part of older adults, who have displayed higher levels of cultural and vital interest and have demanded the opportunity to acquire more knowledge—a knowledge that includes both formal and informal education. Another element related to the system of the sources of the Agreement, and one rooted in the context of historical rights, is the important role of the past in the system. For this reason, the recovery and maintenance of its history and assuring "visibility" of the historical content is not reduced to mere academic interest in history, but is instead another argument for its very continuity. This explains the interest which, as we have shown, is evident on those occasions when public interest (one not necessarily or exclusively academic) is analyzed, as the high attendance at the present congress has clearly shown.

Endnotes

1. The first two titles published were José María Estecha Martínez, *Régimen político y administrativo de las Provincias Vasco-Navarras: Colección de leyes decretos, Reales Órdenes y resoluciones del Tribunal Contenciosos administrativo relativos al País Vasconavarro.* 2nd ed. and appendixes 1 and 2, ed. Joseba Agirreazkuenaga (Bilbao: Instituto de Derecho Histórico de Euskal Herria: Diputación Foral de Bizkaia, 1997) and Nicolas de Vicario y Peña, *Los Conciertos Económicos de las Provincias vascongadas (Apéndice),* ed. Eduardo J. Alonso Olea (Bilbao: Instituto de Derecho Histórico del País Vasco-Diputación Foral de Bizkaia, 1909 [1997]).

2. Iñaki Alonso Arce, ed., *El Concierto Económico vasco. La renovación de 2002. Fuentes documentales* (Bilbao: Ad Concordiam, 2003). This was the first volume that was published. The latest volume published is Ignacio Zubiri, *The Economic Agreement between the Basque Country and Spain.* (Bilbao: Ad Concordiam, 2010).
3. The contents of the databases were generated from previous work of the IT346-10 Research Group of the Basque University System, one of whose lines of research is precisely that which we are presenting here.
4. Antonio Fumero and Genís Roca, *Web 2.0* (Madrid: Fundación Orange, 2007), 10. As is generally known, the Web 3.0 project has also been worked on since 2001 (this being the so called "data web" that allows a new level of data integration and interoperational applications, thus making data as accessible linkable as web pages themselves. The "data web" is the first step toward a complete "semantic web").
5. See es.wikipedia.org/wiki/Concierto_económico, en.wikipedia.org/wiki/Basque_Economic_Agreement, and eu.wikipedia.org/wiki/Euskal_Autonomia_Erkidegoko_Ekonomia_Ituna.[AU: Please provide full references for these URLs.]
6. See booktwo.org/notebook/wikipedia-historiography/.[AU: Please provide full reference for this URL.]
7. In addition to being published in a print addition, it is also uploaded to the web page of the Center: www.ehu.es/ituna/letter_es.html.
8. Eduardo J. Alonso Olea, "El Concierto Económico como herramienta: Crisis económicas y políticas anticíclicas de las Diputaciones vascas, 1867–1936, "*Boletín de Estudios Económicos* LXV, no. 201 (2010): 517–62.

Bibliography

Alonso Arce, Iñaki, ed. *El Concierto Económico vasco: La renovación de 2002: Fuentes documentales*. Bilbao: Ad Concordiam, 2003.

Alonso Olea, Eduardo J. "El Concierto Económico como herramienta: Crisis económicas y políticas anticíclicas de las Diputaciones vascas: 1867–1936 " *Boletín de Estudios Económicos* LXV, no. 201 (2010): 517–62.

Estecha Martinez, José María. *Régimen político y administrativo de las Provincias Vasco-Navarras: Colección de leyes decretos, Reales Ordenes y resoluciones del Tribunal Contencioso administrativo relativos al País Vasconavarro.* 2nd edn and appendices I and II. Edited by Joseba Agirreazkuenaga. Bilbao: Instituto de Derecho Histórico de Euskal Herria. Diputación Foral de Bizkaia, 1997.

Fumero, Antonio and Genís Roca. *Web 2.0.* Madrid: Fundación Orange, 2007.

Gibbons, Michael et al. The New Production of Knowledge: The Dynamics of Science and Research in Contemporary Societies. London: Sage, 1994

Vicario y Peña, Nicolas de. *Los Conciertos Economicos de las Provincias vascongadas (Apendice)*. Edited by Eduardo J. Alonso Olea. Bilbao: Instituto de Derecho Histórico del País Vasco- Diputación Foral de

Bizkaia, 1909 (1997).
Zubiri, Ignacio. *The Economic Agreement between the Basque Country and Spain*. Bilbao: Ad Concordiam, 2010.

Part 3

The Legal Underpinning of the Agreement: Boundaries and Context

10
The Constitutionality of the New Control Procedures for the Foral Tax Regulations of the Basque Historical Territories

Santiago Larrazabal Basañez

Organic Law 1/2010 of February 19, 2010, which modifies the Organic Laws of the Constitutional Court,[1] changed the control procedures for the Fiscal foral regulations of the Basque historical territories of Araba, Gipuzkoa, and Bizkaia. This is because, after the new law became effective, only the Constitutional Court could hear cases involving disputes regarding said regulations. In this presentation, I will limit myself to studying this one issue, which is present in numbers one and two of the new Fifth Additional Provision, which was appended to the Organic Law of the Constitutional Court by Organic Law 1/2010. I will not be entering into a discussion of matters regarding the new process for resolving conflicts with respect to the foral autonomy of the Basque historical territories, as contemplated in paragraph three of the aforementioned Fifth Additional provision. Organic Law 1/2010 has been subject to three different claims that it is unconstitutional, which have been brought before the Constitutional Court, and which are still pending resolution. These claims have been brought forward by the Government Council and Parliament of La Rioja, and by the Council and Courts of Castile and Leon.

The first part of this chapter briefly explains why I believe that the contents of this Organic Law are in accordance with the Constitution, and why I therefore believe that the aforementioned claims against it should be denied.

The Problem

As is well known, the First Additional Provision of the Constitution of 1978 establishes that the Constitution protects and respects the historic rights of the foral territories, and that the renewal of the foral system will, if it occurs, take place within the framework of the constitution and the autonomy statutes. One of these undeniable historical rights is the Economic Agreement. The renewal of the Agreement occurred via the Basque Statute of Autonomy of 1979 and the subsequent Laws of the Economic Agreement (the regulation of which is now governed by Law 12/2002 of May 23, 2002). In reality, Article 41.1 of the Autonomy Statute of Gernika establishes that tax arrangements between the state and the Basque Country will be regulated via the transitional foral system of the Economic Agreement and Pacts. In addition, Article 41.2.a.) also stipulates that "the competent jurisdictions of the historical territories may maintain, establish, and regulate the tax systems within their territories in accordance with the general tax structure of the state, regulations for coordination, fiscal harmonization, and collaboration with the state, as specified in the Agreement and as dictated by the Basque Parliament for these selfsame purposes within the Autonomous Community. Any such Economic Agreement must be legally approved."

What this means is that the regulation of the tax system is something for which the Basque Autonomous Community is responsible—not the Common Institutions of that Community (i.e., the Basque Parliament or the Basque Government), but instead the bodies of the historical territories, which form the Basque Country, (i.e., the Juntas Generales and Foral Deputations of Bizkaia, Gipuzkoa, and Araba, each in its respective territory). This is a matter that the historical territories alone—and never the Basque Parliament or Government—can regulate, as established in Article 37 of the Statute of Gernika. This is because the matter falls within the category of what has come to be known as the "inviolate nucleus of the foral system" that is directly enshrined in the Constitution, as recognized by the Constitutional Court in its well-known Ruling 76/1988, issued April 26, 1988.

In each of the three Basque historical territories, it is the Juntas Generales—in other words, the Assemblies of each territory that are directly elected by the people—that are competent to establish and regulate each particular tax, in the same way that occurs in the Foral Community of Navarre (which also enjoys a system similar to that which exists in the Basque Country by virtue of historical rights which are also enshrined in the Constitution—referred to in their case as the "Economic Pact"). There, it is the Parliament of Navarre that dictates the regulatory procedure for taxes. In contrast, within the so-called "common territory" (i.e., all of Spain with the exception of the Basque Country and Navarre), it is the Spanish Parliament ("Cortes Generales") that hold jurisdiction for the purposes of legislating such matters. To illustrate by way of an example that will be readily understood, the Individual Income Tax is regulated in the common territory by the Law of the Spanish Parliament, in the Foral Territory of Navarre by the Foral Law of the Parliament of Navarre, and in the Basque Autonomous Territory by the foral regulations of Bizkaia, Gipuzkoa, and Araba, as administered by the Juntas Generales of each respective territory.

A problem arises in the case of the foral regulations of the historical territories because, in spite of the fact that they regulate the same matters as the Law of the Spanish Parliament and the Foral Law of Navarre, they are not formally recognized as *laws*. Article 25 of the Basque Autonomy Statute indicates that it is the Basque Parliament that exercises legislative authority, although it then adds "without prejudice to the competences of the institutions referred to in Article 37 of the present Statute" (i.e., those instutions forming part of the aforementioned "inviolate nucleus of the foral system" of the historical territories, and that includes matters—including taxes—in which the Basque Parliament has no role). I want to make sure that you understand what I'm saying here. What Article 25 of the Statute clearly says is that the Basque Parliament can dictate laws. What this Article does not state (although it must be acknowledged that the language used is ambiguous) is that the Juntas Generales are able to dictate laws. In any event, the matter seems to be clarified in Article 6.2 of Law 27/1983 of November 25, 1983 (the Law of Relations between Common Institutions of the Autonomous Community and the Foral Bodies of their historical territories, better known as the Law of the historical territories or LTH). The LTH affirms that, "in all instances, the authority to dictate regulations that have the status of Law belongs exclusively to Parliament" (i.e., the Basque Parliament).

This is really the heart of the matter: the historical territories alone, though their Juntas Generales (and *not* the Basque Parliament) are able to exercise the right to dictate tax regulations, as part of the kind of historic right represented by the Economic Agreement, through foral regulations. Yet, despite the fact that these regulations govern exactly the same matters as those regulated by analagous laws of the state or of the Foral Community of Navarre, given the fact that the Juntas Generales of the Historial Territories cannot dictate regulations that hold the formal status of *laws*, their foral regulations are considered provisions that hold a status inferior to that of laws and, therefore, until Organic Law 1/2010 entered into force, could not be challenged in the Constitutional Court (i.e., contrary to the analgous laws in the common territory and Navarre). Instead, the foral regulations of the historical territories could only be challenged in ordinary Administrative Law Courts. What this has led to is a steady stream of appeals lodged by public and private institutions, especially by some neighboring Autonomous Communities. These appeals in turn have led to persistent questioning about foral tax regulations—which are regulations that are general in nature—and have resulted in a legal uncertainty surrounding said regulations.

Possible Solutions to the Problem

We in the Basque Country were well aware that something had to be done to put a stop to the constant questioning of the legitimacy of the Basque foral tax regulations. This was something that also was endangering the continuing enforcement of the Economic Agreement, for the applications of each of this instrument's regulations was also being questioned. In order to attempt to resolve the problem of the absence of express legal authority of the foral tax regulations without reforming the Basque Autonomy Statute (a process that has been, and continues to be, very complicated, given the current political situation in the Basque Country) a number of different options were considered:

- Repeal of Article 6.2 of the Law of the historical territories. Yet this alone would not resolve the problem, because Article 25 of the Basque Autonomy Statute does not expressly recognize the legislative authority of the Juntas Generales to dictate foral tax regulations.
- Attempt to ensure that a law of the Basque Parliament validate the foral tax regulations by giving them formal legal status. In principle, this solution involved a fundamental problem: the lack of competence on the part of the Basque Parliament as regards the regulation of taxes (a matter for which the historical territories were responsible, in accordance with Articles 41.2a and 37.3 of the Basque Autonomy Statute. The only jurisdiction held by the Basque Parliament in this regard is that which it is granted by Article 41.2a as regards the coordination, collaboration, and fiscal harmonization of the regulations of the historical territories vis-à-vis taxation matters. Yet this jurisdiction does not allow the Basque Parliament to completely regulate the different taxes, something that would not only be contrary to the Statute but also unconstitutional (given that it would impinge upon the inviolate nucleus of the foral system, which is expressly protected by the First Additional Provision of the Constitution).
- Creating a regulatory schema based on a linkage between a law of the Basque Parliament and the foral regulations by exercising the powers of fiscal coordination, collaboration, and harmonization that I've referred to above. Yet this would not change the fundamental problem, given the fact that the Basque Parliament would have to encompass nearly all of the regulation of taxation matters in order to give them protected

formal legal status, and this would once again involve supplanting the exclusive competence of the historical territories regarding these matters. And, as I've just indicated, such an action would be both contrary to the Basque Autonomy Statute and unconstitutional.

Thus, the most direct solution would have been to modify the Basque Autonomy Statute (which would obviously need to include both repeal of Article 6.2 of the Law of historical territories) and express recognition of the authority of the Juntas Generales of the historical territories to dictate regulations that would have the status of law. However, as I've previously indicated there has never been, and there is not today, a political consensus among us regarding the propriety of reforming the Statute, either as regards this matter or many others.

Given this state of affairs, some action was clearly needed to resolve the problem, and it was felt that the best possible solution at this time and under these political circumstances was to modify the trial procedures for challenging the foral tax regulations by transferring the authority to hear said challenges from oridinary administrative law courts to the Constitutional Court. Doing this seemed to be far more in keeping with the material (rather than formal) nature of regulations that functioned de facto as laws, and had the virtue of avoiding constant challenges, given that the standards for recurring to the Constitutional Court are much more strict than those for resorting to ordinary courts, and also taking into account the fact that a judgment of the Constitutional Court is one of constitutionality rather than of legality.

Constitutional Justification of the Solution Adopted

So this was how, in the end, the problem was finally resolved: Organic Law 1/2010, which changed the trial system for challenging the foral tax regulations, a law whose constitutionality has been challenged in various different venues. In my opinion, even though the solution chosen may not have been the most technically pure choice, I am convinced that it was by no means unconstitutional. Of course, the last word on this matter rests with the Constitutional Court, which will have an opportunity to address the issue when it rules on constitutional challenges to this Organic Law.

This new Organic Law included the addition of a Fifth Additional Provision to the *Ley Orgánica del Tribunal Constitucional* (LOTC, Organic Law of the Constitutional Court). This provision establishes that the Constitutional Court will have the exclusive right to hear not only legal challenges against the Fiscal foral regulations of the territories of

Araba, Gipuzkoa, and Bizkaia, as well as questions posed at the pretrial stage by jurisdictional bodies regarding the Organic Law's validity.

With control of the regulations granted to the Constitutional Court, administrative courts of laws could no longer hear challenges to them. Organic Law 1/2010 has thus modified Article 9.4 of Organic Law 6/1985 of July 1 [1985)] of the Judiciary (henceforth OLJ). In this same regard, it has added a section (letter "d") to Article 3 to Law 29/1998 of July 13, which regulates the jurisdiction of the Administrative Law Courts (henceforth JALC). This regulatory change is popularly referred to as the "legal immunity of the Basque Economic Agreement." This expression, which has quickly caught on because of its particularly evocative nature, should not lead to misunderstandings. The reality is that the Basque foral regulations have not been solidly grounded in the law in a way that makes them immune from challenge, or exempt from some kind of control. Such immunity would in fact be entirely unconstitutional. Instead, the trial procedures involving challenges to the regulations have been modified in such a way that their legal jurisdiction has been passed from Ordinary Administrative Law Courts to the Constitutional Court.

The reason for this regulatory change, which was carried out via Organic Law 1/2020, has to do with adjusting the system for challenges and control in a manner befitting the material being regulated. In other words, the matters should be regulated in a manner similar to the way the selfsame matters are regulated by the Parliament of Navarre and the Spanish Parliament—namely, via a Constitutional Court and not ordinary administrative law courts. Thus, challenges in the case of regulations here should be handled in the same way they are handled in Navarre and the common territory. In this connection, it is important to point out that the Autonomous Communities only have recourse to the Constitutional Court regarding laws, provisions, or other enactments with the force of law of the state, but not those of other Autonomous Communities. This is in accordance with Article 32.2 of the Organic Law of the Constitutional Court. The contral exercise over such matters should be—as it is in the case of state and Navarran laws—a constitutional and not a legal control. In the case of laws of the state and of the Foral Community of Navarre, since these derive directly from the Constitution and do not depend on or serve as the basis for other laws, they are not submitted to legal controls (i.e., the kind of controls exercised by ordinary courts) but rather to constitutional controls, which is the exclusive province of the Constitutional Court.

Similarly, foral tax regulations are not subject to any law of either the state or the Basque Parliament, given that neither the laws of the Basque Parliament or the state are capable of regulating these matters. It therefore does not seem logical that they be subject to legal rather than constitutional control, like analagous laws of the state and the Foral Community of Navarre, and that they be challenged before the Constitutional Court, as is the case in those jurisdictions. As regards the argument that the foral regulations are subject to the Law of the Economic Agreement, rather than directly to the Constitution, the same can be said of the Foral Laws of Navarre that deal with taxation, which are also subject to the law that approved the Economic Agreement in that Autonomous Community. When, in these cases, it is alleged that the regulations are not subject to the law but derive directly from the Constitution, this means that no tax law is issued by either the Basque Parliament or the Spanish Parliament. Instead, on the basis of a constitutional mandate, jurisdiction is accorded regarding a matter that belongs squarely within the realm of the inviolate nucleus of the foral system, and that is directly protected by the Constitution. This nucleus is, I feel bound to repeat yet again, is something which must remain inviolate with respect to any law, whether of the Basque Parliament or the Spanish Parliament.

The underlying logic of this argument seems clear, and yet it comes up against an apparent formal obstacle, which derives from the Spanish doctrine of the sources of law. Namely, if the foral regulations do not have the formal status of law then, even though they may serve the same material regulatory purpose as laws, and if the Constitutional Court in principle only governs laws, enactments, and regulatory provisions with the force of law, then the following fundamental question arises: Is Organic Law 1/2010 rendered unconstitutional as a result of its attributing to the Constitutional Court exclusive capacity to hear challenges against regulations that do not have the formal status of law? This is the main objection of those who hold that this Organic Law is unconstitutional.

All of this forces us to enter into the question of the legal nature of the roral regulations, since these do not fit neatly into the dogmatic categories of law and regulation of the Spanish system of law sources. Furthermore, we are all well aware that, as the Japanese proverb has it, "it is the nail that sticks out that gets hammered down." The foral regulations reside somewhere in the borderlands between law and regulations. The Supreme Court itself has offered an explanation of how they fit into our system of sources: In Court Consideration number 3 of its ruling of May 3, 2001 (Third Court, Second Section), it declared that the Law of historical territories recognizes that the regulations hold "an entirely new category of authority . . . that is different from mere regulatory authority," and, in referring to the foral regulations, further indicated that the latter reside at "the highest internal ranking of the internal hierarchy of each foral system. Even though

. . . they are regulatory in nature (given that the laws of the Basque Autonomous Community arise from its parliament alone) their position within the general legal system is unique, since they arise directly from the Statute of 1979 and the Constitution, without the mediation of any law whatsoever, either of the state or the Autonomous Communities (within the limits of respect for the system resulting from agreement with the state). In this declaration, the Supreme Court qualified the foral regulations as "autonomous regulations that are unique in nature." Thus, through these foral regulations, the Juntas Generales enjoy "the full capacity to implement the equivalent of a state taxation law." The Constitutional Court therefore concluded that the "this regulatory capacity of the historical territories is comparable, within its jurisdiction, to that of the State legislative authority."

What this all means is that the foral tax regulations are not regulations with the status of law, but rather that they regulate matters that the Constitution views as falling under the principle of taxation law (Articles 31 and 133). In the face of this paradox, and by way of explaining both how it is possible for some regulations that do not have the status of formal law to regulate matters that in theory ought only to be subject to law and why nobody (at least from an orthodox standpoint with respect to sources) has not cried foul over this state of affairs, I would venture to say that the Supreme Court really had no choice other than to appeal to the unique nature of the Basque system, which is derived from the First Additional Provision of the Constitution of 1978. Thus, in its ruling of September 9, 2004 (Third Court, Second Section), this court rejected the notion that the foral regulations are autonomous regulations (an assertion that contradicted the Ruling of 2001), declaring in its Court Consideration number 3 that "the regulatory capacity of those territories is exercised within the framework of the Constitution and the law, although the limits defined by the law may on occasion be extremely broad and in practice imply a lack of legal authority as regards matters of taxation, something which the aforementioned First Additional Provision of the Fundamental Regulation has rendered possible." Court Consideration number 9 then affirmed that

> the principle of according the status of law and legality regarding taxation matters, which in itself is relative in its scope, becomes still more relative and narrowly applied with respect to the Historical Terrritories. What this means is that the demand for the subordination and the complementarity of the Regulations vis-à-vis the law are not required with respect to the regulatory norms dictated by the *Juntas Generales* under the same general terms established by said class of norms within the area of taxation. It is beyond question that the principle of according legal status, as established in article 31.3 of the Spanish Constitution is necessarily qualified for the Foral Territories

> by the principles recognized in article 8.1. of the LHT with respect to matters that are the exclusive jurisdiction of the *sui generis* regulatory authority that said principles address.

To muddy the waters still further, the Constitutional Court, in Ruling 255/2004 of December 23, 2004 (Court Consideration no. 2), and Ruling 295/2006 of October 11, 2006 (Court Consideration no. 3), commenting upon the jurisprudence of the Supreme Court, indicated that the foral tax regulations "involve regulatory provisions that, although they cannot rightly be called mere regulations for carrying out State law, at the same time lack the status of law and, as such, as the State Attorney so rightly points out, cannot be subject to any claim of lack of constitutionality." As Enrique Lucas Murillo de la Cueva[2] has indicated, this response was logically plausible given that, at that juncture, the possibility of presenting these kinds of appeals (specifically, an appeal or challenge based on lack of constitutionality, or on similar grounds, against the foral regulations, presented before the Constitutional Court) was not something envisaged in the Organic Law of the Constitutional Court. But if, on the contrary, it had been foreseen in the Organic Law of the Constitutional Court (as is now the case), would the Constitutional Court have made the same declaration?

In view of what has been described above, it seemed clear that the only viable solution to the problem at the political juncture in which we found ourselves was to change the trial system for presenting challenges with respect to the foral tax regulations. And Basque institutions were ready to offer assistance in enacting this reform. Two different initiatives for instituting such a change in the Juntas Generales of Bizkaia and Araba. The first was a proposed law approved by the Juntas Generales of Bizkaia on May 1, 2005, and later presented for approval to, first, the Basque Parliament, and then the Spanish Parliament. This initiative proposed the modification of Article 27.2 of the LOTC that, among other things, redefined the jurisdiction of the Constitutional Court in order to allow it to hear appeals presented vis-à-vis the foral regulations in matters involving the agreed taxes, the introduction of testimony defending foral autonomy, and the reform of Article 9.4 of the OLJ, which clarified that, with the institution of that reform, the administrative law courts would relinquish their right to hear appeals presented vis-à-vis the foral regulations.

The second initiative was a Proposed Law approved by the Juntas Generales of Araba on October 17, 2005, and then presented to the Basque Parliament (which, had it approved the measure, would have sent it on to the Spanish Parliament). The Araba initiative requested that Article 6.2 of the LTH be repealed; that Article 27.2 of the LOTC be modified in a way that provided the Constitutional Courts jurisdiction to review all of the foral regulations that that enabled exclusive jurisdiction in the historical territories (not limited to matters involving taxation); the modification of Article 9.4 of the LOPJ in a way that would allow Administrative Law Courts to be exempt from the review of those regulations, and the introduction of an action in defense of foral autonomy.

The proposal of the Juntas Generales of Araba was not approved by the Basque Parliament which instead admitted the aforementioned Bizkaia proposal and on June 29, 2007, unanimously approved a Proposed Law for modifying the LOTC and the OLJ, sending the law on to the Spanish Parliament for its approval. The Proposed Law of the Basque Parliament constituted a revision of the proposal of the Juntas Generales of Bizkaia but retained its spirit, including modifications of Articles 27–32, 35, 37, 39, 40, and 75 of the LOTC in such a way as to include the foral regulations regarding agreed taxes among the competences of the Constitutional Court (and, concommitantly, depriving the Administrative Law Courts of said competence, which also involved the modification of Article 9.4 of the OLJ, including the action in defense of foral autonomy).

As regards the subject of this presentation (and leaving aside the subject of the defense of foral autonomy, which I will not be discussing here), the proposal of the Basque Parliament essentially revolved around the modification of Article 27.2 of the LOTC, including the foral regulations among the regulatory provisions with the force of law, and whose control was the exclusive competence of the Constitutional Court.

Enrique Lucas Murillo de la Cueva[3] has brilliantly defended the constitutionality of that measure, pointing out that Article 27.2 places not only laws under the control of the Constitution, but also other regulations that are not formally laws, such as parliamentary regulations, law decrees, legislative decrees, and acts of both the state and the Autonomous Communities that have the force of law such as, for example, the Statute of Personnel of the Spanish Parliament. Thus, he has defended that the constitutionality of the measure under discussion, taking as my point of departure the doctrine formulated by the Constitutional Court in its Ruling 139/1988 of July 8, 1988, which confirms the constitutionality of the control by the Constitutional Court of the Statute of Personnel of the Spanish Parliament despite the fact that said statute does not have the status of law. The Constitutional Court justified this decision on the basis of Article 72.1 of the Constitution, which materially and formally establishes a privilege for the Statute of Personnel of the Spanish Parliament, based on the fact that said Statute has the character of a regulation that is directly connected to the Constitution. In other words, it is a primary regulation, which means that the regulatory activities that define it are beyond the reach of any other legal regulation, which in turn signifies that it enjoys the de facto force of law, at least in the passive sense. Because of this, no other regulation within the legal system can replace it for the purpose of the regulatory activities over which it enjoys the exclusive rights.

This same ruling also affirms that the Statute of Personnel in question has a position in the current system of sources of law that cannot be explained in terms of the traditional principle of the regulatory hierarchy, and that it is instead necessary to resort to other criteria, among which *competence* is a defining factor. Thus, that Statute cannot be compared in any way to the regulatory norms because, in contrast to these latter, the Statute is not subordinate to the law, but instead constitutes an integral component that is inextricably linked to the Constitution. For all of these reasons, the Constitutional Court recognized that the Statute of Personnel of the Spanish Parliament is one of those acts with the force of law that are referred to in Article 27.2 of the LOTC, the control of which is to be exercised exclusively by the Constitutional Court and not by ordinary courts.

Enrique Lucas Murillo de la Cueva has defended the applicability of this same doctrine to the foral regulations, since these latter meet the requirements that the Constitutional Court defined for recognizing the constitutionality of the provision that established that regulations that do not have the status of law ought to be reviewed exclusively by the Constitutional Court, such regulations deriving directly from the Basque Statute and the Constitution (i.e., from the "bloc of constitutionality") without being mediated by any law whatsoever (as expressed by the Supreme Court Ruling of May 3, 2001). In addition, said regulations have a formal passive force that is equivalent to that of laws, given that any law of the Spanish Parliament or of the Basque Parliament that attempts to either modify or repeal a Basque foral regulation is to be deemed unconstitutional on the grounds of impinging upon the exclusive competence regarding such matters of the historical territories and, therefore, of the so-called "inviolate nucleus" of the foral system (i.e., Articles 37.3 and 41.2.a of the Basque Statute, and the First Additional Provision of the Constitution). The conclusion, then, is obvious: if the Basque foral regulations meet these requirements, then they too can be included within the purview of Article 27.2 of the LOTC, and so can those acts and regulatory provisions with the force of law of the state and of the Autonomous Communities, by means of the timely reform of the LOTC, without being unconstitutional. And this was the path followed by the Proposed Law that was approved by the Basque Parliament, and then sent by this body to the Congress of Deputies.

Juan José Solozábal Echavarría,[4] with whom I had the pleasure and honor of debating, and a man whom I dared contradict when we spoke of this matter at a roundtable in Valladolid in which we both participated a little over a year ago, has himself rejected the notion expressed above because, in his opinion, even conceding the premises with respect to control of constitutionality contemplated in Article 27 of the LOTC, said premises do not only refer to laws and regulatory provisions with the status and force of law, but also to other kinds of regulations. According to his understanding, those instruments, which fall under the control of the Constitutional Court as regards appeals and challenges involving constitutionality (and he has specifically in mind here International Treaties and Parliamentary Regulations) cannot be equated to foral tax regulations. Therefore, in his view, the application by extension to said regulatory provisions of the same control is not justified. Solozábal instead believes that both sources, which are regulations that are subject to constitutional review according to Article 27 of the LOTC have, in comparison to the fiscal regulations, the clear force of law.

For his part, Luis María Díez-Picazo Giménez[5] has indicated that such a possibility is defensible. In other words, it is his view that the modification of Article 27.2 of the LOTC for the purposes of including the foral regulations in its purview is legitimate. Although he also makes it clear that he would reject such a notion if Article 27.2 is interpreted as indicating the existence of a *numerus clausus* of kinds of regulations with the status of law. He has even gone so far as to acknowledge that there are good arguments for recognizing that the foral regulations have, as a result of their very nature, the status of law. Furthermore, Díez Picazo has said that a case could have been made for the foral regulations to be directly subject to appeal or challenge on the grounds of constitutionality, without the need to modify the LOTC. This last suggestion, however, seems difficult to accept, given the literal meaning of Ruling 255/2004 of December 23, 2004, of Ruling 295/2006 of October 11, 2006, of the Constitutional Court, and of the Rulings of the Supreme Court, which I will refer to shortly.[6]

The modification of Article 27.2 of the LOTC seemed an interesting possibility, but in the end this option was eschewed by Organic Law 1/2010. In reality, the Proposed Law approved by the Basque Parliament was sent to the Congress of Deputies of Spanish Parliament in July 2007 and, after the Spanish Parliament was dissolved, the initiative was sent to the newly constituted Ninth Legislature of this Parliament. It was the subject of deliberation by the Plenum of Congress on October 19, 2009, at which time the Partido Nacionalista Vasco or EAJ-PNV (Basque Nationalist Party) and the Partido Socialista Obrero Español or PSOE (Spanish Socialist Party), within the framework of budget negotiations, presented four joint amendments which thoroughly revised the text of the proposed law that had been sent by the Basque Parliament.

The revised version did not modify all of the Articles of the LOTC that were included in the original Proposed Law of the Basque Parliament. Instead, a more common and traditional approach in cases involving the creation of ad hoc regulations within general state laws, one that took account of the unique aspects of the Basque context: the inclusion of a new Fifth Additional Provision in the text of the LOTC which attributed to the Constitutional Court the exclusive right to hear challenges to the foral tax regulations (reference being specifically made to foral tax regulations and not to foral regulations involving the agreed upon taxes, as had been the case in the proposed law of the Basque Parliament. In addition, an action to protect the foral autonomy was provided for. Furthermore, Article 9.4 of the OLJ was modified to establish that direct or indirect appeals against the foral tax regulations decreed by the Juntas Generales of Bizkaia, Gipuzkoa, and Araba would no longer be heard by the administrative law courts, and would henceforth be heard only by the Constitutional Court. In order to leave no room for doubt regarding this change (and this was an innovation that had not been part of the Proposed Law of the Basque Parliament) a letter "d" was added to Article 3 of the JALC that denied administrative law courts jurisdiction over direct and indirect appeals against the foral tax regulations.

As regards the system for challenging foral tax regulation becoming the exclusive province of the Constitutional Court, the justification for this change was not the modification of Article 27.2 of the LOTC, which had been the basis of the initiative of the Basque Parliament. Instead, the basis for said change was Article 161.1.d of the Constitution (although this was not explicitly acknowledged). Thus, a specific process was included in the LOTC that provided for control by the Constitutional Court of the foral tax regulations. This had been done on previous occasions (and on the basis of the same constitutional article). Three notable examples involved the prior constitutional control of organic laws and the autonomy statutes, conflict between constitutional bodies, or the defense of local autonomy.

Why was the legal justification of the new competence of the Constitutional Court changed in Organic Law 1/2010? In my opinion, the change occurred as a result of an attempt to avoid the complex legal debate that any attempt to modify Article 27.2 of the LOTC would have entailed. Such a debate, which would have been emotional and yet also substantive, would have revolved around the force of law of the foral tax regulations, and the question of whether the modification of Article 27.2 of the LOTC was or was not comparable as regards its procedures for controlling the foral tax regulations with the provisions and acts having the status and force of law that were subject to constitutional control. Rather than embarking upon this legal debate, it was decided to take a much more direct route: the inclusion of new material directly defined as falling under the jurisdiction of the Constitutional Tribunal, in accordance with the provisions of Article 161.1.d of the Constitution.

In my view, the road taken by Organic Law 1/2010 was less technically pure than the one I mentioned previously, although it was also completely constitutional. Of course, the problem had to do with the fact that the foral tax regulations could not be controlled by the Constitutional Court because such jurisdiction was not expressly provided for in the LOTC. This had specifically been indicated by the Supreme Court in two well-known Rulings. The Ruling of December 9, 2004, that was previously mentioned held in its Third Court Consideration, letter "a" that "in any event, as long as there is no reform of the LOTC that allows the presentation before this Court challenging the foral regulations, any product of the Juntas Generales that has regulation as its purpose must be submitted to the constitutional and legal controls of the administrative law courts, in compliance with the demands of judicial protection (Article 24.1 of the Spanish Constitution) and of the submission to the Law of public authorities." The Supreme Court Ruling of December 9, 2009 (Third Court, Second Section), also said, in its Third Court Consideration that "the taxation powers of the authorities of the Basque historical territories being recognized, the nature of the foral regulations has aroused a great deal of controversy, resulting in the regulatory product of the Juntas Generales being submitted—because of a lack of an express provision in the LOTC that would allow the hearing of challenges to the foral regulations by this Court—to the control of the administrative law courts, in compliance with the demands of judicial production in Article 24.1 of the Spanish Constitution, and of the submission of the Law to public authorities."

Thus, as can clearly be seen, the Supreme Court did not reject the possibility that the foral tax regulations could be controlled by the Constitutional Court if the LOTC were reformed. Instead, the Supreme Court simply said that, before any such reform were instituted, some body had to be charged with the competence to review said regulations and that, in such circumstances, administrative law courts would necessarily bear the responsibility for reviewing any challenges. The purpose here was to guarantee effective legal protection in accordance with the demands of Article 24 of the Constitution, and with the submission to the Law of public authorities, as established in Article 9.1 of the Constitution. But it seems that it can be deduced from such reasoning that, if such a reform were to be instituted, the new system of challenges of the foral regulations would not be prejudicial to either the effective legal protections guaranteed in Article 24 of the Constitution, or the submission to the Law of Public Authorities that is established in Article 9.1 of the selfsame document.

And this is precisely what those crafting the new legislation did: They modified the LOTC in that regard, not by reforming Article 27.2 of that law (i.e., because they did not want to get into a debate about the force or status of the Foral Regulation, and they did not expressly equate the foral regulations with the law), but instead by granting the Constitutional Court a new competence in accordance with Article 161.1.d of the Constitution, which states that "the Constitutional Court has jurisdiction in the entire territory of Spain, and it has the competence to hear: . . .) other matters attributed to it by the Constitution or Organic Laws." This is precisely what Organic Law 1/2010 has done, but without expressly quoting the previously cited Article of the Constitution.

As I have previously noted, the legislative body had taken the same road on other occasions. The last instance in which it did so involved the granting of a competence to the Constitutional Court vis-à-vis the resolution of conflicts in defense of local autonomy. Thus, it was held that this new competence, which was not implicit in either Article 161.1 or Article 163, was nonetheless within the constitutional purview. The obvious question that arises, then, concerns whether this same path can be utilized as a kind of "back door" for the purposes of attributing new and unlimited constitutional processes to the Constitutional Court. In this regard, the Constitutional Court has not clearly defined limits, and has indeed admitted that this new constitutional process, which is protected by the clause of Article 161.1.d of the Constitution, "which empowers the organic legislative body to attribute jurisdiction to the Constitutional Court for the purpose of hearing other matters not contemplated in constitutional precepts, as long as such attribution does not run counter to the Constitution" (Constitutional Court Ruling 240/2006 of July 20, 2006). How does one interpret such a general and obvious limit? The Constitutional Court has not yet clarified this matter.

In the case of the new procedures for challenging the foral tax regulations, I think that their justification in terms of Article 161.1.d is constitutional, because these are in fact new procedures that involve a specific means of enabling an adequate defense of the foral tax regulations, whose system of challenges within the administrative law courts is not entirely consistent with its unique character within the system of sources of Spanish law. I offer the following reasons for this assertion:

- They are regulations of taxes, just as is the case with the tax laws of the Parliament of Navarre and of the Spanish Parliament;
- They regulate matters that are the exclusive provenance of the foral regulations, and that not even the Basque Parliament can legally interfere with, given that they form part of "the inviolate nucleus of the foral system" that is directly protected by the First Additional Provision of the Constitution;
- They are directly derived from the Constitution, given that they are not subordinate to any law, and are not derived from any law. Instead, they are unique with respect to their form and scope (Constitutional Court Ruling 252/2005 of October 11, 2005) and do not have the character of mere regulations for executing state law (Constitutional Court Ruling 255/2004 of December 23, 2004, and 295/2006 of October 11, 2004);
- They are regulations that have been drafted by the Juntas Generales, which are representative bodies of a parliamentary nature that have been directly elected by the people, and have been created in accordance with parliamentary procedure. The Juntas Generales thus does not function as a public administration authority when exercising its regulatory authority with respect to the taxation system, as has been expressly recognized by the Supreme Court in Court Consideration number 3 of its Ruling of December 9, 2009: "As regards the regulations reviewed here, it can clearly be seen that the Juntas Generales only function as a Public Administration authority with respect to acts and provisions regarding personnel and resource management, but not when exercising regulatory authority vis-à-vis taxes." This is so undeniably true that the Court has even characterized the Juntas Generales as a "foral legislative body."

There can be no question that, in the words of Susana García Couso, "... it would thus seem that the foral tax regulations are sufficiently unique in character as to be regarded as arising from the creation of a new process for controlling the constitutionality of regulations lacking the force of law, and that this makes them different from all other regulatory norms."[7]

The Main Objections to the Constitutionality of the Solution Adopted

As regards the constitutional objections that have typically been made to the legal solution that has been adopted, I agree with Enrique Lucas Murillo de la Cueva[8] that this regulation does not contradict either (1) Article 106 of the Constitution (which stipulates that Courts control regulatory authority and the legality of actions of administrative entitites) because rights accorded to the Judiciary which are implied by this attribution are, in Articles 97 and 153c of the Constitution, accorded to the government and the administration of the Autonomous Communities; or (2) Article 38.3 of the Basque Autonomy Statute (which provides that acts, agreements, and regulatory norms issued by the executive and administrative organs of the Basque Country can be appealed to administrative law courts) because regulations drafted by representative bodies of a parliamentary character are not subject to this consideration, and we have already seen how the Supreme Court itself has ruled that the Juntas Generales, which it has gone so far as to characterize as a foral legislative body, are not a public administration entity when they exercise their regulatory authority with respect to taxes.

Susana García Couso and Enrique Álvarez Conde[9] have answered another of the common objections to this Organic Law, pointing out that there is no question that the Constitution provides for the control on the part of the Constitutional Court of provisions that hold a status inferior to that of laws. This is something that has occurred with respect to appeals for legal protection based upon the violation of fundamental rights resulting from the application of regulatory norms. Regarding such appeals, the Constitutional Court itself has acknowledged the possibility of its exercising its control, and even of declaring such provisions invalid. The same thing has occurred with respect to conflicts of jurisdication, and challenges regarding provisions that have the force of law.

In my view, there has also been no violation of the legal protections provided in Article 24 of the Constitution as a result of individual parties or the Autonomous Communities not being able to directly challenge the regulations before the Constitutional Court (a limitation that also, incidentally, applies to the taxation laws of both the Parliament of Navarre and the Spanish Parliament). It is also not the case that the foral tax regulations are exempt from any kind of control—something that would clearly be unconstitutional. What *is* the case is that, instead of being controlled by Ordinary Courts, from now on they will be controlled by the Constitutional Court under the same conditions as laws that regulate the same matters as the Basque foral regulations. In addition, through the concrete application of such laws, ordinary courts can always raise preliminary questions regarding constitutionality before the Constitutional Court. I therefore see no violation of Article 24 of the Constitution.

As regards any possible violation of Article 161.1 of the Spanish Constitution, I am in agreement with García Couso,who has written that

> the Fifth Additional Provision of the Law itself seeks to distinguish appeals, which it does not characterize in any way, on the one hand, from the issues it characterizes as "preliminary" for any appeal, along with the issue of constitutionality—both of which are regulated by Title II of the LOTC—on the other. For this reason, and without seeing them as one and the same thing, she refers to them—as I have pointed out—solely in terms of the process of their regulation. Without a doubt, we have here an ingenious legal solution, because it skirts the problem of any possible lack of constitutionality as a result of violating Article 161.1 of the Constitution by leaving intact the limits to which the processes of the new creation are subject, neither expanding the purpose of the control of the appeal or the issue of lack of constitutionality, nor creating a process that has as its purpose regulations that are equated with regulations that have the status of law. Instead, a new appeal is identified for the purpose of norms that are regulatory in nature and which, because of their very nature and content, can justify (as we will see later) a judgment of constitutionality, and not a judgment solely of legality.[10]

In this same regard, Juan Carlos Duque Villanueva has written that "it is obvious that, as has been previously expressed, there is no shortage of similarities and common features in the regulation of constitutional processes created by Organic Law 1/2010 and the procedures for declaring lack of constitutionality of Title II of the LOTC, but it is doubtful as to whether these, as applied to the specific unique features of those processes, are of sufficient intensity as to allow the appreciation, given the scope of creative freedom of those crafting the legislation of the LOTC, of any evident and irreconciliable conflict between the latter and the text of the constitution."[11]

Conclusion

I will now conclude my presentation with a number of reflections that should not go unmentioned merely because they might seem obvious. First of all, one must always operate on the assumption of the constitutionality of the laws that are currently in existence. This is because, as is well known, the declaration of unconstitutionality should only occur in instances in which it is materially impossible to preserve the constitutionality of a regulation.[12] If an interpretation of a regulation that is in accordance with the Constitution fits, then that regulation should be accepted as constitutional. I accept the fact that there may be interpretations of Organic Law 1/2010 that are not constitutional. I naturally respect such interpretations, even though I myself do not share them. At the same time, it seems to me that there are interpretations of that selfsame law that are perfectly compatible with the Constitution. For this reason, if it indeed turns out that these latter interpretations are constitutionally viable, they should serve as grounds for rejecting appeals based on supposed unconstitutionality that have been lodged against Organic Law 1/2010.

As Juan Carlos Duque Villanueva has written,[13] the Constitutional Court has declared, as regards the scope of control of constitutionality that needs to be in place as part of any modification of the LOTC, that the oversight of such activity should exercise an extreme caution befitting any prosecution on the part of the legislative body in way that takes into consideration the link between the Court and the LOTC. And it is indeed the case that, in Ruling 49/2008 of April 9, 2008 (Court Consideration no. 4), the Court held that

> the control of the Organic Law of the Constitutional Court should be limited to instances in which there is an assumption of an obvious and irreconciliable conflict between said law and the constitutional text . . . because . . . otherwise (i.e., to exercise any stricter control) would not only mean weakening the presumption of constitutionality of any regulation approved by the democratic legislative body, but would also place the Court in a position not in keeping with the right, enshrined in Article 165 of the Spanish Constitution, of the legislative body, via the Organic Law of the Constitutional Court, to directly ensure implementation of and compliance with Title IX of the Spanish Constitution—the legal implementation of which this Court has an inherent interest.

Second, as regards the greater or lesser technical quality of Organic Law 1/2010, or the aptness of its legal foundation (e.g., whether it would have been better to reform the Statute of Basque Autonomy by giving express legal status to the foral regulations of the historical territories, etc.) it should be remembered that this is a matter that has nothing whatsoever to do with the issue of constitutionality. This is due to the fact that the Constitutional Court—as it itself has indicated—in no way functions as a judge of technical correctness, legal aptness, or the utility of laws. This is because the judgment of constitutionality has nothing to do with legislative technique.[14]

Finally, I would like to mention one last consideration: I cannot help think that the accusation of unconstitutionality against the new system for challenging the foral tax regulations is nothing more than what could be called a tangential issue. I think that what is really at the bottom of this entire matter is that there are people who have never accepted the Economic Agreement as a special financial and taxation system within the Basque Autonomous Community (just as in the case of the similar Economic Agreement in effect in the Foral Community of Navarre)—one that is not shared by the other Autonomous Communities—as an express right derived from the recognition and protection of its historic rights by the Spanish Constitution. Throughout the history of the Basque Economic Agreement, ever since its beginnings in 1878, this has consistently been the underlying issue. It is now the year 2011, and we continue to hear the same old tune sung to the same old lyrics: privilege and discrimination. At root, the assymetry that the Constitution itself enshrines is considered inequitable, and as constituting a detestable privilege. Thus, there are always those who take advantage of any opportunity to (paraphrasing the Japanese proverb I mentioned earlier) "give a good whack to the nail that sticks out." Yet some who deny the legitimacy of the Economic Agreement while at the same time zealously defending the Spanish Constitution, should really in fact be defending the entirety of this latter document, including its First Additional Provision. Though they might not like it, this provision is also an integral part of the Spanish Constitution, and it in fact serves as the basis for our undeniable historic right to the Basque Economic Agreement.

Endnotes

1. Published in the *Boletín Oficial del Estado* (no. 45) on February 20, 2010.
2. Enrique Lucas Murillo de la Cueva, Pablo, "La reserva al Tribunal Constitucional del control jurisdiccional de las Normas Fiscales Vascas y la creación del conflicto en defensa de la autonomía foral frente a las Leyes del Estado," in *El privilegio jurisdiccional de las normas forales fiscales vascas*, ed. Enrique Álvarez Conde (Madrid: Instituto de Derecho Público de la Universidad Rey Juan Carlos, 2010), 110–12.
3. Enrique Lucas Murillo de la Cueva, "La garantía jurisdiccional del Concierto Económico," *Jado. Boletín de la Academia Vasca de Derecho* 7, no. 17 (septiembre de September 2009): 139–45, and also in "La reserva al Tribunal Constitucional del control jurisdiccional de las Normas Fiscales Vascas...," 105.
4. Juan José Solozábal Echavarría, "El blindaje foral en su hora: Comentario a la Ley Orgánica 1/2010," *Revista Española de Derecho Constitucional* 90 (2010): 22–23.
5. Luis María Díez-Picazo Giménez, "Notas sobre el blindaje de las Normas Forales Fiscales," in, *El privilegio jurisdiccional de las normas forales fiscales vascas*, ed. Enrique Álvarez Conde (Madrid: Instituto de Derecho Público de la Universidad Rey Juan Carlos, 2010), 77–80.
6. The Supreme Court's Rulings of December 9, 2004, and December 9, 2009.
7. Susana García Couso, "La Ley Orgánica 1/2010, de 19 de febrero: el control constitucional de las Normas Forales Fiscales vascas," in *El privilegio jurisdiccional de las normas forales fiscales vascas*, ed. Enrique Álvarez Conde (Madrid: Instituto de Derecho Público de la Universidad Rey Juan Carlos, 2010), 174.
8. Murillo de la Cueva, "La reserva al Tribunal Constitucional del control jurisdiccional de las Normas Fiscales Vascas...," 133.
9. García Couso, "La Ley Orgánica 1/2010, de 19 de febrero: el control constitucional de las Normas," 175–76.
10. García Couso, "La Ley Orgánica 1/2010, de 19 de febrero: El control constitucional de las Normas," 165.
11. Juan Carlos Duque Villanueva, "Los procesos constitutionales de control

de las Normas Forales Fiscales Vascas," *Revista Española de Derecho Constitutional*, 90 (2010): 70.
12. Constitutional Court Ruling 11/1981 of March 8th, 1981 (Court Consideration no. 4).
13. Duque Villanueva, "Los procesos constitucionales de control de las Normas Forales Fiscales Vascas," 69.
14. Sentencia del Tribunal Constitucional 109/1987, June 29, 1987, Fundamento Jurídico 3rd.

Bibliography

Álvarez Conde, Enrique. "Comentarios preliminares a la Ley Orgánica 1/2010, de 19 de febrero, de modificación de las Leyes Orgánicas del Tribunal Constitucional y del Poder Judicial." In *El privilegio jurisdiccional de las normas forales fiscales vascas*, edited by Enrique Álvarez Conde, 17–64. Madrid: Instituto de Derecho Público de la Universidad Rey Juan Carlos, 2010.

Criado Gámez, Juan Manuel. "Motivos de inconstitucionalidad de la Ley Orgánica 1/2010, de 19 de febrero, de modificación de las Leyes Orgánicas del Tribunal Constitucional y del Poder Judicial." In *El privilegio jurisdiccional de las normas forales fiscales vascas*, edited by Enrique Álvarez Conde, 185–219 (Madrid: Instituto de Derecho Público de la Universidad Rey Juan Carlos, 2010).

Criado Gámez, Juan Manuel, ed. *El blindaje de las normas forales fiscales*, Madrid: Iustel, 2011.

Díez-Picazo Giménez, Luis María. "Notas sobre el blindaje de las Normas Forales Fiscales." In *El privilegio jurisdiccional de las normas forales fiscales vascas*, edited by Enrique Álvarez Conde, 65–80. Madrid: Instituto de Derecho Público de la Universidad Rey Juan Carlos, 2010.

Duque Villanueva, Juan Carlos. "Los procesos constitucionales de control de las Normas Forales Fiscales Vascas." *Revista Española de Derecho Constitucional*. 90 (2010): 29–71.

García Couso, Susana. "La Ley Orgánica 1/2010, de 19 de febrero: El control constitucional de las Normas Forales Fiscales vascas." In *El privilegio jurisdiccional de las normas forales fiscales vascas*, edited by Enrique Álvarez Conde, 157–84. Madrid: Instituto de Derecho Público de la Universidad Rey Juan Carlos, 2010.

González Hernández, Esther. "El apartado 3º del artículo primero de la Ley Orgánica 1/2010, de 19 de febrero, de modificación de la Ley Orgánica del Tribunal Constitucional y la Disposición Adicional Primera de la Constitución española de 1978. ¿Punto de llegada o punto de partida?" In *El privilegio jurisdiccional de las normas forales fiscales vascas*, edited by Enrique Álvarez Conde, 221–59. Madrid: Instituto de Derecho Público de la Universidad Rey Juan Carlos, 2010.

Larrazabal Basañez, Santiago. Review of Enrique Álvarez Conde, Enrique (dir.) and Alic López De Los Mozos Díaz-Madroñero, Alicia (coord.), *El privilegio jurisdiccional de las normas forales fiscales vascas*, Instituto de Derecho Público, Universidad Rey Juan Carlos, Madrid, 2010. *Revista Vasca de Administración Pública*, 91 (2011): 327–46.

Merino Merchán, José Fernando. "Cuestiones que plantea la Ley Orgánica1/2010." In *El privilegio jurisdiccional de las normas forales fiscales vascas*, edited by Enrique Álvarez Conde, 81–92. Madrid: Instituto de Derecho Público de la Universidad Rey Juan Carlos, 2010.

Lucas Murillo de la Cueva, Pablo."La reserva al Tribunal Constitucional del control jurisdiccional de las Normas Fiscales Vascas y la creación del conflicto en defensa de la autonomía foral frente a las Leyes del Estado." In *El privilegio jurisdiccional de las normas forales fiscales vascas*, edited by Enrique Álvarez Conde, 93–155. Madrid: Instituto de Derecho Público de la Universidad Rey Juan Carlos, 2010.

Solozábal Echavarría, Juan José. "El blindaje foral en su hora: Comentario a la Ley Orgánica 1/2010." *Revista Española de Derecho Constitucional* 90 (2010): 11–28.

11
Making the Economic Agreement "Ironclad"

Aitor Esteban

Why Was Parliamentary Action Necessary?

The problematic nature of the misleadingly termed "ironclad making" of the Economic Agreement has been with us ever since the restoration of the foral1 institutions, and in two distinct manifestations. On the one hand, there is the high level of court involvement to which the foral regulations dealing with taxes (comprising about 90 percent of the total number) were submitted from the very beginning. I can well remember, during the time I sat as Chairman on the *General Assembly*2 of Bizkaia, when one after another of the tax regulations were appealed, without exception. Even though the administrative law courts did not automatically impose suspension of a regulation when it was appealed, the atmosphere of fiscal uncertainty that resulted was not exactly conducive to generating the feeling of legal security that is so sorely needed by economic and social agents and that should be the objective of any regulatory system.

On the other hand, there is the helplessness of the foral institutions in the face of intrusions upon their competencies on the part of other institutions in circumstances in which they had no recourse to either the courts or to arbitration. Let's take up this last issue briefly. The approval of the Law of the Arbitration Committee of the Basque Country in 1994 represented the opening of a channel aimed at resolving differences surrounding overlapping competencies with the Basque Parliament. But the Constitutional Court made it clear, in response to the attempt of the Foral Deputation3 of Bizkaia (at that time led by the unforgettable General Deputy4 José María Makua) to appeal "the electoral law for the General Assemblies" that had been approved by the Basque Parliament in 1987 (i.e., prior to the creation of the Arbitration Committee) that the foral institutions lacked legal standing to bring matters before the Constitutional Court. This was not because the Spanish Constitution prevented such actions, but rather because the LOTC did not expressly mention such authority in the version of that law that was in force at that time.

As a consequence, until the recent reform resulting from Organic Law 1/2010, the foral institutions remained absolutely helpless in the face of infringements on their competencies, which no longer were the result of actions on the part of the Basque government and Parliament (a matter which had been resolved since 1984 through the Arbitration Committee) but rather from state institutions. The fact that this later activity could indeed constitute a violation of the competencies of the foral institutions can be appreciated when it is considered that constitutional jurisprudence has itself indicated that these latter enjoy a scope of competence with which state or Autonomous Community legislation has no right to interfere.

Such a state of affairs was unacceptable. And it was even less acceptable when, during this same time, access to the Constitutional Court had been given to local entities (as a result of a series of reforms) for the purposes of defending their autonomy. With their own distinct legal nature, foral institutions once again were relegated to a limbo where they remained excluded and ignored, marginalized as a category beyond the boundaries of what was known and accepted in the rest of the state, one which did not deserve either attention or guarantees.

But let's return to the first point, that of the high degree of court involvement in foral regulations.

The situation that resulted from the "normas forales"[5] being challenged in the courts on a more or less constant basis, was a progressive eroding on the foundations of the Economic Agreement. Sometimes one single unfortunate ruling can be enough to reduce or change irreversibly the powers assured in the Economic Agreement. This perception was notably enhanced following the ruling of the Supreme Court of December 9, 2004, when, in an unusual gesture, this body declared that the regulation being challenged violated European Union Competition Law.

When we began talking about making the Economic Agreement "ironclad," what we were mainly trying to do is start a discussion as to whether it was legally acceptable that a system of tax regulations applicable to all citizens, such as the income tax, the corporate tax, or the inheritance tax, can be subject to challenge on the part of any individual, union, or business association. I have no doubt that if what instead was under scrutiny was legislation of the state or the Autonomous Community, the response of any lawyer or judge would be that this would not be normal.

It cannot be normal according to either comparative Law or to the Constitution itself, which declares that regulations addressing tax matters must have the status of a law. Well, tax matters constitute 90 percent of the regulations passed by the General Assemblies, although semantically their regulations are called "normas forales / Foru Arauak" and not "laws," which is in the origin of the problem we are discussing. One might contend that this precarious status is typical of foral regulations. In fact, nothing could be further from the truth. One only need consider the fact that, in the case of the tax regulations of Navarre,6 appeals are made—as in the case of all other laws—before the Constitutional Court and are only initiated by subjects holding the legal status to do so (again, as in the case of any other law).

What the legislative change was therefore attempting to do was repair an unfair measure and generate the legal security needed by economic and social agents.

Attempts to Remedy the Situation

Many different attempts have been made to remedy this situation. A comprehensive historical review in this regard is beyond the scope of this article. Suffice it to say that, during the period 2004–2009, there were no fewer than four attempts at legislative reform.

While it is true that the call to make" ironclad" the Economic Agreement has been raised by all political forces within the Basque Country whenever the matter has been debated in either the Basque Parliament or the General Assemblies of the historical territories of Bizkaia, Gipuzkoa, and Araba, only the representatives of the Basque National Party (EAJ-PNV) in the Congress of Deputies has taken active steps in this direction, presenting legislative measures, amendments to laws under consideration or proposed by the government, as well as appeals, motions, and questions. No other group has taken these kinds of initiatives.

This has resulted in Basque politicians from other parties alleging that "the EAJ-PNV has been using the Agreement as an excuse to display aggression against other Communities," or that "the EAJ-PNV never presents a question at the right time," or even that "the EAJ-PNV wants to be the only player when it comes to defending the Economic Agreement."

When the chips are down, some political parties forget the important responsibilities that Basque self-government involves. In contrast, it is precisely at such times that the EAJ-PNV is there to answer the call, assume responsibility for its defense, and pay all the political and parliamentary costs involved in taking such actions.

Below, we will briefly review the last three initiatives that have been taken.

The LOTC Reform Project of 2006

In 2006, the Spanish Government decided to promote the reform of the Constitutional Court for the purpose of reducing the number of appeals related to Constitutional individual rights legal protection and in order to ensure the primacy of the Constitutional Court over the Supreme Court in the wake of recent controversies involving the two bodies. Once discussion opened regarding possible amendments, the EAJ-PNV presented amendments aimed at strengthening the Economic Agreement. In order to facilitate the removal of obstacles to the proposed reforms, the Parliamentary Group of the EAJ-PNV initiated a series of contacts to explain the rationale of the proposed amendments in Madrid. This was first done at the highest levels of the Constitutional Court itself, where no objections to amendments regarding making the Agreement ironclad were brought forth. Our arguments were clear: the matter had to do with an issue that fundamentally touched on the Constitution to the extent that it involved the First Additional Provision of said document, and it could not be foreseen that the matter would lead to litigation that would markedly increase the volume of work of the high tribunal. There is thus nothing that would seem to justify any radical opposition to our proposal. The president of the Court and other magistrates agreed and supported our idea.

The Parliamentary Group then explained the rationale for the amendments to the Socialist representatives of the government, making them aware of the unanimous support that they enjoyed (at least formally) on the part of Basque political forces, including the Partido Popular (PP) and the Partido Socialista Obrero Español (PSOE). The Socialists told us that Ignacio Astarloa was vehemently opposed to our amendments. But we also realized that Vicente Martínez Pujalte conducted a straw poll among the leaders of the Basque PP, in which the latter were shown to support the reform. Everything seemed to point to the fact that Astarloa was alone in his opposition, which he justified in terms of the narrow-minded ideas of the centralist wing of the PP.

We made progress in our negotiations with the government (negotiations in which Francisco Caamaño, who later would become Minister of Justice, assumed a key role) and, even though reservations were expressed, the various ministries began to approach a consensus position. This was evident in the fact that, at the meeting of the "ponencia"[7] at which a draft proposal of the measure was presented, the Socialist spokesman, Ramón Jauregui, publicly recognized that the registered amendments, with some small changes, would be approved at the next session of the committee. Unfortunately, a number of deliberate leaks resulted in statements by politicians from other

Autonomous Communities in the press opposing the measures. The government then got nervous and decided to break its promise and negotiate the text with the PP instead of with the rest of the political parties.

Until that time, the Basque Socialists thought that reaching an agreement with the EAJ-PNV regarding the immunization of the Economic Agreement was a great achievement. However, from the time that the Spanish government decided to reject our amendments, the discourse of the Basque Socialists changed and they contended that such an agreement was not a good solution. Here is what Jáuregui said:

> The law, and especially the Constitution, establish a very clear principle for us, and it is that, in article 161 of the Constitution, only laws can be appealed before the Court, and these are not laws. We cannot make them into laws for the sole purpose of making them subject to a procedure that we might call 'paraconstitutional.' This isn't a very easy matter because, among other reasons, such a modification would imply very complicated reforms in the laws pertaining to the European Union and with respect to the Organic Law of the Judiciary itself. In this connection, it should not be forgotten that we are taking from the higher courts a competence that, from the jurisdictional point of view, has been properly assigned to them. I think it true that there is a problem, but I also think that there is a very easy solution: these regulations of the General Assemblies can be made into laws in the Basque Parliament. It's thus very simple. The Foral Regulations can be made into laws via the single reading procedure, and thereby be automatically immunized vis-à-vis the Constitutional Court.

Jáuregui's contention that article 161 only allows appeals before the Constitutional Court with the formal status of law is simply not true. Section D of the first point of this constitutional provision contains an open clause according to which the high court is enabled to hear "other matters attributed to it by the Constitution or organic laws."

The bill that we were seeking to pass was organic in nature. Thus, nothing prevented appeals against the foral regulations of the Juntas Generales from being included within the scope of competence of the Constitutional Court, whatever status these regulations had.

It also is untrue to maintain, as Jáuregui did, that the proposed modification involved "very complicated" reforms of the laws pertaining to the European Union. In fact, our proposal involved no reform whatsoever of European laws. What's more, there was no way that it could have, because European laws can neither be created nor modified by the Spanish Parliament.

On the other hand, the alternative proposal that Jáuregui presented to the Committee was and is legally untenable. The idea of processing foral tax regulations as bills in the Basque Parliament through the special procedure of a single reading not only depreciates the Juntas Generales, reducing them to bodies of little or no institutional importance, something that surely should have been subject to debate. In addition, it ignores the fact that, according to provisions of Article 41.2 of the Statute of Gernika, the competence for maintaining and establishing the "tax system deemed appropriate" belongs to the competent institutions of the historical territories and not to the common institutions of the Autonomous Community.

The Basque Parliament is empowered by this article to establish coordination regulations. But the tax system that the Basque Parliament is able only to coordinate belongs to the historical territories, which are the only entities competent to formulate their respective tax systems, within the limits established by the state. How could this division of powers be reconciled with a practice in which the regulatory instrument that comes into force taxes was a law of the Basque Parliament?

The debate of the full Spanish Parliament, held on March 15, served as another occasion to present the same arguments. Josu Erkoreka, the head of the Basque Parliamentary Group (EAJ-PNV) asked Jose Luis Rodríguez Zapatero at question time about the measures the latter had planned in order to defend the Economic Agreement from the progressive deterioration to which it had been subjected. In a statement filled with empty phrases and clichés, Zapatero justified his refusal to support our amendments, declaring that "this was neither the time nor the place to deal with this issue."

A bizarre statement indeed: we had been negotiating the way to incorporate our proposal into the text of the LOTC and now, after they had unilaterally abandoned the negotiating process, they told us that "it was neither the time nor the place."

The speeches made in the full session of the Senate were really shocking. A simple reading of them leads to the conclusion that they were entirely clueless with respect to the subject they purported to discuss—that they were speaking on the basis of, at best, second-hand information. An example of this is the speech made by socialist senator Mansilla Hidalgo[8] which, in its rambling, empty, and incoherent confusion that was utterly bereft of any substantive content whatsoever, revealed her profound ignorance of the subject:

> We have tried from the first day until the last—this is why we have been negotiating with you—to find an effective and legally valid solution, because the competencies of the Committee[9] established by article 41 of the Autonomy Statute of the Basque Country may be resolvable in some other way. We are going to all study the possible resolutions because, even though the Juntas Generales do not

> have the power to appeal before the Administrative Law Courts vis-à-vis the basic development regulation, it is true that, in the end, the Juntas Generales should at least enact development regulations and therefore . . . there are many ways to bring forth appeals—either through a basic regulation or through regulatory provisions that are developed.
>
> I therefore ask whether we will be able to find a solution. Yes. But we have to say that the relevant autonomy here is not that of the Juntas Generales, which enjoy autonomy within the Basque Country, but instead of the Autonomous Community of the Basque Country. It is with this latter entity that we are negotiating, and attempting to find a solution—that may be the solution of an internal problem. To the extent that it may affect territories outside the Basque Country, we need to be able to discover a way forward . . . .
>
> I wonder how we can, through the Organic Law of the Constitutional Court, give the status of law to a "norma foral" of the Juntas Generales that, in theory, are the development of a regulation that already exists in the Basque Country. Everyone seems to share this confusion, including us.

He was really confused, that is true. It is clear that the person who uttered these words had no idea of what the Juntas Generales or foral regulations ("normas forales") are or even of what the purpose of the amendments was.

The declarations of PP spokesman Gutiérrez Gonzales was not better:

> . . . [it] is an issue of sources of Law if we appeal in one way or another but, in the end, if we grant the possibility of direct appeal to the Constitutional Court, what we are doing is proposing the assimilation of the foral regulation dictated by the Deputation to what might be a law of the Basque Parliament or the Spanish Parliament. In the end, we are proposing the assimilation of a body that has certain competencies but that bears no similarity to a legislative chamber, just as the councils of the Canary Islands or the Balearic Islands do not bear any such similarity. They are therefore different kinds of institutions.
>
> The appeal doesn't concern me so much. What concerns me is that through modifying the system of access to appeals in a way that is equivalent to the law, we could be modifying the distinct legal nature of an institution (i.e., the Foral Deputation) that is not a legislative chamber. For this reason, and as Mr. Molas has indicated, we are going to touch upon, on the one hand, the issue of sources of law and, on the other, the legal nature of the institution. I repeat that this concerns me, because this is something that affects the State, because these also exist in the Canary Islands and the Balearic Islands. This needs to be discussed and agreed upon, and a consensus needs to be reached.

How ridiculous! To contend that the system of appeals proposed for the "normas forales" changes—or can change—the legal nature of the Deputations shows an ignorance of what is at stake when the immunization of the Basque Economic Agreement is requested. This is something that any of his colleagues who sit on the Juntas Generales of the Basque Historical Territories could have explained to him.

I hate to say it, but from a parliamentary perspective, this is really quite typical. Everyone talks about the Agreement only in order to denigrate it and inveigh against it, but very few such people have any idea of what they are talking about. In fact, from a political and parliamentary perspective, the Economic Agreement has been wielded as a weapon by other Autonomous Communities in order to attack local political adversaries and win votes. We will see more of this later. This is all done without citing data or facts and without discussing the Agreement's mechanisms, but instead by tossing about words like "discriminatory," "privilege," "unconstitutional," and "relocating." Such language turns out to be very useful during an election campaign.

The Basque Parliament Initiative of 2007 and Its Fruits in 2009

In June 2007, the Basque Parliament approved a bill to be sent to the Spanish Parliament which called for a reform of the LOTC and the Organic Law 6/1985 of July 1 of the Judiciary

(OLJ). This bill, which was formulated in the Juntas Generales of Bizkaia, was slated for debate much later, more than one year later, in accordance with the scheduled sessions of Congress. Given that the Luxembourg ruling was still pending at that time, it made sense to expedite the debate of the bill. To this end, in May 2008, we asked the government to register two bills (one to change the LOTC, another the OLJ) with the same contents that had been approved in the Basque Parliament.

Both Arantxa Mendizabal, an elected Socialist deputy representing Bizkaia, as well as Ignacio Astarloa, a PP deputy from the same territory, accused us of illegitimately appropriating an initiative as our own when the fact was, because it had been brought forward by the Basque Parliament and enjoyed the unanimous support of its members, it belonged to all the parties that had supported it.

I do not agree with the allegation that any manipulation on the part of the EAJ-PNV was involved. Mendizabal and Astarloa seem to have simply used such an argument to justify their opposition—an opposition, it should be pointed out, that was already in evidence some months previously. In my opinion, an initiative to enhance Basque self-government always deserves support regardless of who proposed it, PP, PSOE or EAJ-PNV. What's more, it should be appreciated that the EAJ-PNV parliamentarians have been the only ones in the forefront of such initiatives—initiatives that would appear to be in the interest of all Basques.

The truth is that the legislative calendar, which we thought would constitute an obstacle, serendipitously coincided with the period of Spanish budget negotiations a year and a half later. We were not the ones who decided that the matter would be considered in October 2009. This happened purely by chance. And I would say that this was a fortunate circumstance indeed, because I have no doubt that we would not have reached an agreement to approve the initiative if it had not been for the EAJ-PNV representatives' vote in the matter of the 2010 state budget. The budget agreement clearly included more issues, but we made it clear to the government that this matter was an indispensable condition for beginning negotiations. I have to confess that, given the backdrop of events, I did not hold out much hope our proposals would be accepted. However, in spite of some initial reservations, the miracle happened, and we finally reached an agreement after more than ten years of futility.

After the initial debate in the plenary (one can easily deduce, on the basis of a reading of my speech in that very session of Parliament, that at that point agreement was not assured) a bilateral commission comprising EAJ-PNV and PSOE representatives was formed for the purpose of reaching agreement regarding the final text of the reform. The Socialists on this committee were Txiki Benegas, Elviro Aranda, and Juan Luis Rascón, while the Nationalists were Josu Erkoreka and I. I feel compelled to acknowledge at this point the spirit of collaboration that prevailed among the committee's members. And I think we made the correct decisions.

We did not want to get sidetracked by a debate regarding the nature and status of the foral regulations. For this reason, and as we've previously pointed out, the concrete proposal that was made was based on the open clause of Article 161.1 d of the Spanish Constitution, which allows expansion of the scope of competence of the Constitutional Court, broadening it to include the capacity to hear cases involving "other matters attributed it . . . by the organic laws." On the other hand, the constitutionality of the "normas forales" was analyzed in terms of its relationship with the Law of the Economic Agreement itself. The Constitution includes the First Additional Provision, which guarantees the existence of an agreed tax system for the Basque territories. The Law of the Economic Agreement comprises a number of harmonization principles which reflect similar principles within the Spanish Constitution as regards market unity. It is the violation of these rules of harmonization which is typically alleged when challenges are made to the foral tax regulations ("normas forales") before the administrative law courts. This would remain unchanged, but the Law of the Economic Agreement itself would be used to define the parameters of Constitutionality. In addition, and as I've previously pointed out, we made sure that there would be a remedy for foral institutions in the face of any possible state intrusion upon their competencies.

My only regret is that I personally would have preferred to include in that mechanism *all* of the foral regulations ("normas forales") and not just those pertaining to taxes. We in fact discussed this point within the Committee, where no one thought it was a wild idea from a legal perspective. The foral regulations function within the system as if they were laws, in the strictest sense they are not regulations, and they originate in a parliamentary chamber (i.e., the Juntas Generales) that is directly elected, and that forms part of a parliamentary system that includes an executive branch that it itself elects and controls.

The "normas forales" are not regulations that develop laws. They take the position of the law in the foral system. The category of "regulation," within the realm of the foral system, as something subordinated to, developing the law, comprises "Foral Orders." These "Foral Orders" are made by the executive branch (Foral Deputation) and are subordinated to the "normas forales" made by the legislative (Juntas Generales or General Assemblies). All of this has been discussed and established by other lecturers these days.

But by virtue of the mandate of the Basque Parliament, and so acting in the Bilateral Committee, we were able to secure agreement on limiting our amendments to tax regulations only. It should be noted that "tax regulations" is a term that in fact includes too regulations beyond those dealing strictly with taxes.

The situation became very uncomfortable indeed for the Basque PP deputies who saw how their party voted "no" on something that they had supported in Gasteiz.10 They were not present during the initial debate. But in the final vote, their party forced them to show up and cast negative votes. The night before the law was approved, the leader of the Basque PP, Antonio Basagoiti, indicated that, even though he had not been able to convince his party to vote in favor, he was sure he would be able to convince them not to appeal the vote. Once again, he was mistaken. As I mentioned at the plenary session of the Spanish Parliament, there would always be someone in one of the Autonomous Communities to make an appeal without fifty congressional deputies from the PP providing their signatures.

Parliamentary Objections to the Reform in Different Institutions

Arturo García-Tizón of the PP defended his "no" vote in Congress in the following terms:

> Because of the circumstances surrounding this bill, and because it affects the very structure of the Autonomous Community—the very

> structure of the foral framework, which is the essence of our autonomous state, I felt that it needed to be addressed within a national context by an agreement between the Socialist Party and the Popular Party.

Thus, a decision that had been unanimously adopted (except for one vote from the Unión Progreso y Democracia, UPyD) in the Basque Parliament was underestimated. Those times seemed very far away indeed when it had been argued that, in order for Basque initiatives to be processed in Madrid, they needed to first enjoy an ample consensus in the Basque Parliament!

García Tizón continued:

> there has been a factor that has completely distorted this situation and this vision, and which has kept our group from voting in favor during the initial debate of this bill. It is neither more nor less the fact that this bill—this "ironclad making", as it is called in the media—has been associated with the approval of the State Budgets...

Rajoy, the leader of the PP at the time, had said the same thing in the press. But if he really thought unacceptable that the EAJ-PNV was trying to introduce the "ironclad making" of the Economic Agreement into the budget negotiations, then he could have avoided it by announcing that his Parliamentary Group would behave in line with the position defended by the PP members of the Basque Parliament and by giving his full-throated support to the "ironclad making" in the Spanish Parliament. And if he had, in addition to doing this, also invited the PSOE to do the same thing, then it would not have been necessary for the EAJ-PNV to "mix" the two matters together. Thus, something that he found "unacceptable" could have been avoided.

UPyD representative Rosa Díez made the following argument:

> They are trying to arrange things so that the Autonomous Communities, unions, and associations, and parties that frequently lodge appeals—you are well aware of this—will be unable to appeal in the future. There is an intend to assure that they lose their capacity to appeal and defend general interests before the courts. And that is why I am telling you, my fellow deputies, that you need to be clear about what my vote means. It is precisely my intention to defend the principles of justice and equality—to defend the democratic State of all Spanish citizens. As regards you deputies of leftist parties, I say to you that our vote, my vote, would be opposed to this proposal. It will be so to defend the democratic state of all Spanish citizens, as well as justice and equality for all.

In other words, it seemed to her a good idea that anyone could appeal the Basque regulations, and that Basque citizens could lack legal security, but that Spanish regulations could only be appealed by a restricted category of parties. This seems a strange notion of "equality and justice for all."

In the Parliament of Castile and Leon, it was Jesús Jaime Encabo Terry of the PP who argued against reform of the LOTC, in the following terms that I enumerate henceforth:

> 1. "In the first place, because we feel that it goes against the so-called 'fundamentals of constitutionality,'[11] affecting not only Article 161.1 of the Spanish Constitution, but also the Organic Law of the Constitutional Court, because the Foral Tax Regulations do not fall within the category of those provisions in which appeals on the grounds of unconstitutionality are admissible."

This statement is incorrect. To begin with, the Economic Agreement does form a part of the "fundamentals of constitutionality". But, leaving this matter aside, OL 1/2010[12] does not formally include the foral regulations (normas forales) among those provisions that can be appealed on the grounds of unconstitutionality. Article 161.1 d of the Spanish Constitution contains an open clause that allows the scope of competence of the Constitutional Court to be expanded, making it applicable to the hearing of "other matters that may be attributed to it by the organic laws." This is the course that has been chosen. And, in this way, a controversy regarding the status and nature of the regulations is avoided.

> 2. "It constitutes an egregious violation of the Autonomy Statute of the Basque Country, given that the Statute establishes that it is the Parliament that has sole authority to decree laws."

The Autonomy Statute says nothing whatsoever regarding the regulatory status of anything approved by the Juntas Generales.

> 3. "The Statute itself provides that the Constitutional Court alone will judge laws of the Basque Parliament."

The Statute actually does not say this. What it does say is that the laws of the Basque Parliament can only be tried by the Constitutional Court. It does not say that other regulations cannot also be thus tried.

> 4. "The Law of the State can in no way modify the Autonomy Statute of an Autonomous Community without such a proposal for reform being formally made by the corresponding Autonomous Parliament."

But the LOTC is not reforming the Statute of Gernika in the least.

> 5. "It places its beneficiaries (i.e., businessmen) as regards the Corporate Tax, in a more favorable financial position than other taxpayers, and such a state of affairs has consistently been interpreted by the European Court of Justice as State aid."

In 2008, the European Court of Justice made it clear that, under certain conditions, some regions having tax systems different from those of the rest of the country is compatible with European regulations. If a region has institutional autonomy (i.e., its own political statute), procedural autonomy (i.e., freedom to make decisions regarding taxes), and economic autonomy (i.e., the absence of any requirement for a lowering of taxes to be compensated by the central government), then the fact that its taxes are lower cannot be considered state aid.

> 6. "Such an advantage, from the financial point of view, is attained at the expense of State resources."

Incorrect. There is no compensation from the state government to the foral treasury.

> 7. "This situation is conducive to businesses moving out of the bordering Autonomous Communities—especially Castile and León—and relocating to the three Basque provinces."

The economic data do not lie. Miranda13 is not doing bad at all. And it also doesn't seem to appear that the investment of the port of Bilbao in Pancorbo14 will harm Castile and Leon. The rest of the bordering territories have always been barren lands as far as industry is concerned.

But let's hear what Mr. Encabo's fellow party members have to say about this point. On April 17, 2002, PP member Aguilar Cañedo made the following statement in the Full Session of the Parliament of Castile and Leon:

> But let me say further: There has been no adverse impact or industrial decline, Mr. President. Have you reviewed the data about the number of new corporations in Burgos15 and Araba.16 Do you know what the capital gains were in either of these provinces?

Or we can review the response of the Economic Advisor Carrasco Lorenzo, at her appearance before the Economic Committee of the Parliament of Castile and Leon on April 14, 2000, to the specific question as to whether there are grounds for any grievance, or whether businesses have moved out of that Autonomous Community:

> Well . . . when it comes to Burgos . . . you are influenced by the newspapers, and you love to repeat what they read there. But let me tell you what the businessmen and unions in the region say: Such things really don't exist. One cannot properly speak of any relocation, and no one has any study showing that any relocation has resulted from the regulations of the Basque Country. I can tell you that the regions bordering this Autonomous Community—Burgos and Miranda—are the most developed of their Autonomous Community. . . . So what has been the effect? Someday, we will be able to debate the effects of relocation, perhaps as regards bordering areas other than the Basque Country, and which, incidentally, have the same tax system as ours.

She then continues:

> But there are objective data that . . . enable us to study what is going on from a macroeconomic standpoint. And from a macroeconomic standpoint—and here I have to repeat what I already said: in 1975, or rather 1985, which was more recent—Burgos was ranked 18th among

> Spanish provinces in terms of revenues and their distribution, while Araba was ranked second and Bizkaia seventh, and in 1995, Burgos was 11th and Bizkaia was 15th. And in terms of including a consideration of Gross Added Value in millions of pesetas, by 1996, the mean in the Basque Country has increased thirty-something percent—37 or 39—while in Burgos it has increased 49.29 percent. Therefore, there couldn't have been much of a negative effect of the tax havens on Burgos. In addition, while we continue to argue against this, we have to recognize that there hasn't been a real fiscal impact.

As regards La Rioja, let me simply refer to the economic data, number of businesses, and population growth. On February 1, 2011, President Pedro Sanz was interviewed by the newspaper *ABC*. According to him, Rioja's economic indices are above the European average. I am convinced that this is not simply election campaign propaganda. Things cannot be going all that bad for an Autonomous Community that keeps Highway A-68 tolls free for its citizens.

And speaking of unfair competition and the relocation of companies, the following question needs to be asked: What should we think of the policy of providing industrial land as "gifts" when it is a policy that the Government of La Rioja has been carrying out for many years in its territory?

Let's go back to Mr. Encabo and his enumerated reasons against making the Economic Agreement ironclad. He added:

> 8. "The matter could have been resolved by modifying the Autonomy Statute of the Basque Country. The Autonomy Statute of the Basque Country could easily have been modified at the request, of course, of the Basque Parliament in a way that established that authority over the tax system of the Basque Country remained in the hands of Parliament, to the detriment of the Juntas Generales."

Does this mean that it would be okay if it were approved by the Basque Parliament? That, in such a circumstance, there would no longer be unfair competition with Castile and Leon or La Rioja? What would be the difference in the impact on the supposed economic effect that they are complaining about?

On the other hand, if we follow the advice of Mr. Encabo, there would be a conflict with constitutional jurisprudence, which provides the so-called foral guarantee. Let's not forget also that the basis of the Economic Agreement is in the First Additional Provision which is about foral rights (surely Castile and Leon and La Rioja would argue against the legal acceptability of this novation of the subject deemed to hold legitimate authority for exercising competence).

Let's have a look at other proposals that have been made by various politicians. Suppose that we modify the Law of the Historical Territories17 in order to accord the status of law to the "normas forales" of the Juntas Generales. Does anyone really believe that the distinguished lawmakers of the PP and PSOE are so feckless as to accept a system of sources that could be modified by a regulation other than the Constitution or the Autonomy Statute—or, indeed, any regulation that does not form a part of the "fundamentals of the constitution"? An appeal would not be long in coming, and would have one additional supporting argument so increasing the legal insecurity of the Agreement.

The same thing can be said regarding the other alternative that José Antonio Pastor, spokesman of the PSE, suggested in various media outlets, calling for the ratification by the Basque Parliament of the foral regulations of the Juntas Generales. Every Basque politician surely knows that the competence to establish regulations regarding tax matters forms a part of the intangible core of the foral system that is protected by constitutional jurisprudence. Therefore, apart from the fact that it would constitute an affront to the foral institutions, it would also be contrary to the Autonomy Statute of Gernika. Thus, approval of such ratification would run the serious risk of turning the foral regulations into provisions lacking proper legal force. In other words, this would provide further grounds for appealing their legitimacy.

The venue where legislative reform needs to be addressed is without doubt the Spanish Parliament. This body is able to undertake such a task without violating the Constitution in any way. This is because the joint interpretation of Article 133 of the Spanish Constitution, and of the First Additional Provision of the Spanish Constitution upon which the Economic Agreement is based, offers a solid basis for the "normas forales" to receive a treatment comparable to that of laws, if this is indicated in the organic development laws.

The Arguments in Favor

In addition to those reasons which have been adduced in response to arguments opposing the reform, and by way of summary, we could indicate those arguments in favor of reform prepared by Basque parliamentarians for later presentation to the Congress.

Here are the words of Mr. Gatzagaetxebarria, a EAJ-PNV representative in the Basque Parliament:

> The authority to establish regulations or to regulate taxes resides, in the case of the Basque Country, in the foral organs of the Historical Territories. Specifically, the fundamental authority regarding tax matters resides in the Juntas Generales and is developed further by the deputations as well. Therefore, it is these foral bodies of the Historical Territories—the Juntas Generales of Bizkaia, Gipuzkoa, and Araba—which hold authority on the basis of the regulations previously set forth in order to establish, regulate, or dictate regarding tax matters in the case of the Basque Country. When this authority is exercised by

> the Juntas Generales of Araba, Bizkaia, and Gipuzkoa, what is understood—on the basis of a vast body of jurisprudence in the Supreme Court and the Constitutional Court—is that the regulation carried out by the Juntas Generales of the three Historical Territories is respectful of the principle of Legal Reservation reflected in article 31 and 101 of the Constitution. Thus, no one has questioned the fact that the regulation of the relationships between citizens and the Basque Foral Tax Systems , when these latter exercise disciplinary control over tax relations between citizens and public authorities do so via foral regulations, for such action is in compliance with the principle of "law rank reservation." In other words, implementation and compliance is not with any law of an Autonomous Community or the State but, instead, there is a substitution of a general law of a parliament of an Autonomous Community or of the Spanish Parliament.
>
> It has therefore been understood that, because of this vast body of constitutional and Supreme Court rulings, the principle of "law rank reservation"[18] is guaranteed and that therefore these regulations, with all guarantees, organize and discipline the relationships of citizens with the tax authority—in this case, the Historical Territories of the Basque Country—through the tax relations that they may have as taxpayers within each of the tax systems of the deputations of Araba, Bizkaia, and Gipuzkoa.

Mr. Damborenea, a representative of the Basque Parliament who belongs to the PP, defended the initiative in the following terms:

> Basques should enjoy the same equality for the purposes of legal fiscal security as all other Spanish citizens, because in our traditional foral system, it is the Juntas Generales that that have the capacity to approve taxes. And it is evident that, because the Juntas Generales are not autonomous parliaments, tax regulations don't have the status of laws. Yet it is also evident that, as our Constitution says, fiscal matters need to fulfill the principle of "law rank reservation." Therefore, legal matters are indeed being regulated in this regard. It also seems logical that Basque citizens and Basque businessmen can and must enjoy the same legal security as all other Spanish citizens, not only as regards the Corporate Tax, but also vis-à-vis the income tax or the inheritance tax.

It would be really important if the insertion of the system of the Economic Agreement into the legal and institutional structure of the state is finally being completed in the future in a coherent manner, one not limited to tax regulations but instead extended to all regulations of the Juntas Generales of the Historical Territories that, in effect, function as laws. But this would-be achievement by no means negates—and instead should reinforce—the obvious advance and achievement represented by the Basque Tax Regulations that, like all other such regulations, provide a system of appeals that assure that their enforcement will never be subject to the mere whim of any one citizen.

Endnotes

1. Anything related to the institutions and rights that the Basques had in the Ancient Régime, some of them still in force today.
2. Juntas Generales or Batzar Nagusiak: Each of the three provincial level parliaments in charge of passing tax regulations in the Basque Autonomous Community.
3. Each of the three provincial governments in the Basque Country.
4. The head or premier of the provincial governments.
5. The name of the regulations passed by the Juntas Generales (General Assemblies). All taxes come into force through them. They are not recognized "law rank" as they don't bear that name but in fact, as we will see, in practice function as laws.
6. A Foral Autonomous Community too.
7. The group within a parliamentary committee in charge of studying a proposed law before the committee as a whole meets.
8. From Castilla-La Mancha. He left his party three years later when accused of corruption for a sale of lands.
9. The "Comisión Mixta de Concierto." A bilateral committee made up of representatives of the Spanish government and those of the Basque Institutions in charge of discussing issues related to the Cupo (the amount of money from collected taxes that Basque institutions will pay to the Spanish government) or of preparing future changes in the text of the Economic Agreement.
10. Vitoria-Gasteiz—the name of the capital of the Basque Autonomous Community, where the seat of the Parliament is.
11. Or "Bloque de Constitucionalidad," the group of laws attached directly to the Constitution and which are used to interpret it.
12. The Organic Law containing the clauses to change LOTC in order to make the Economic Agreement ironclad.
13. Miranda de Ebro—a town in Castile very close to the border with the Basque Country.
14. Another small town in Castile, not far from the Basque Country.
15. A Castilian province.
16. A Basque, and consequently foral province, which shares border with Burgos.
17. The Basque law (passed by the Basque Parliament) that distributes powers among Basque government and the foral institutions.
18. *Principio de reserva de ley,* in Spanish. This principle orders that a specific matter must be regulated through a law.

Bibliography

Comisión Constitucional. Diario de Sesiones de las Cortes. Congreso. Nº 434. 3-12-2009.

Cortes de Castilla y León. Comisión de Economía y Hacienda Diario de Sesiones DS(C) n. 96/5 del 14-4-2000, p. 24 y ss

Cortes de Castilla y León. Diario de Sesiones Pleno de las Cortes. DS(P) n. 66/5 del 17 de abril de 2002, p.79. Proyecto de Ley Orgánica 6/2007, por la que se modifica la Ley Orgánica 2/1979, de 3 de octubre, del Tribunal Constitucional. BOCG. Congreso de los Diputados Núm. A-60-1 de 25/11/2005 Pág.: 1. Iniciativa

Diario de Sesiones de la Cortes. Congreso. 18/4/2008; _BOCG. Congreso de los Diputados, serie D, número 12, de 9 de mayo de 2008. (Número de expediente 162/000031.)

DS. Congreso de los Diputados Núm. 769 de 05/03/2007 Pág.: 2. Comisión Constitucional Designación o ratificación de la Ponencia y Dictamen

DS. Congreso de los Diputados Núm. 240 de 15/03/2007 Pág.: 12131. Pleno. Aprobación Proposición no de Ley del Grupo Parlamentario Vasco (EAJ-PNV), por la que se insta al Gobierno a presentar sendos proyectos de ley de reforma de la Ley Orgánica 2/1979, del Tribunal Constitucional, y de la Ley Orgánica 6/1985, del Poder Judicial.

Pleno. Diario de Sesiones de las Cortes. Congreso. n_ 133,. 17 de diciembre, 2009.

Proposición de Ley Orgánica de Modificación de las Leyes Orgánicas del Tribunal Constitucional y del Poder Judicial por parte del Parlamento Vasco; Boletín oficial de lasCortes Generales. Congreso de los Diputados. Serie B, n_ 11-8. 2 de diciembre de 2009;

Senado. Comisión Constitucional. Diario de Sesiones del Senado. 2 de febrero de 2010.

Senado. Pleno. Diario de Sesiones del Senado. 10 de febrero de 2010. , n_ 67, pp, 3460-3474. Cortes de Castilla y León. Diario de Sesiones Pleno de las Cortes. DS(P) n. 88/7 del 24-2-2010, p.3753 y ss (p. 35)

12
Jurisdictional Defense of the Economic Agreement

Susana Serrano-Gazteluurrutia

It is generally acknowledged that the Economic Agreement is the constitutional, statutory, and legal instrument that regulates tax and financial matters between the Autonomous Community of the Basque Country (Euskadi) and the Spanish state. It is also widely appreciated that the Agreement has deep historical roots and that it is a cornerstone of self-government in Euskadi.[1] The Economic Agreement was created and modified within both an internal and a state-level regulatory context. However, it is now evident that Spain's membership in the European Union has also had a legal effect on this instrument. Evidence of this can be seen in the conflicts recently generated regarding the issue of whether the content of the Agreement is legitimate from the point of view of EU Law. This is a conflict that has largely been played out in the courts. In the present paper, we will attempt to briefly analyze why and how such multinational European law has come to exercise such an important influence on the fate of the Economic Agreement. In particular, we will explore how this influence has directly impacted upon the jurisdictional application of European law on its dynamics and development.

European Competences of the National Judge vis-à-vis the Economic Agreement

Theoretical Perspective

It is important to remember that, since the time that Spain entered the European Union, the Spanish state has been subject to European laws as well as its own national laws. In other words, the legal bodies of Spain carry the burden of applying two sets of laws that complement one another (i.e., because any internal regulation of the member States that are contrary to European Law cannot be applied, and must be revoked).

For this reason, with respect to jurisdiction, national judges exercise a broad range of competences (which also could be considered obligations) that can be utilized by virtue of the fact that these judges also act as European Union judges. These competences include the following:

- Direct application of European law, and non-application (and, if applicable, revocation) of internal law that proves to be incompatible with European law;
- Appropriate interpretation and assuming responsibility on behalf of the State in instances involving noncompliance with EU laws;
- Application of measures involving preventive suspension; and
- Reference for a preliminary judgment (preliminary challenges with respect to interpretation/preliminary challenges with respect to validity).

This set of competences are used (and must be used) in accordance with the European principles of loyal cooperation, institutional autonomy, procedural autonomy, and the autonomy of the proceedings (i.e., as regards the judge, procedures, the course of the trial and so on continue to be determined in accordance with internal regulations) and also in accordance with the principle of judicial cooperation. Therefore, in attempting to resolve cases within their proper jurisdictions, national judges are duty bound to always ensure application with EU laws, thus ensuring that said laws are adhered to and that their sphere of competence is respected.

These are competences that the judge exercises within an internal context and reflect the fact that he or she functions as an arbiter of both state and EU law (i.e., in those instances in which cases require application of both legal standards). These competences are therefore also powers that the judge exercises (along with the obligations resulting therefrom) in cases in which EU law and its application appear to have a bearing upon—and perhaps even contradict—the system of the Economic Agreement and the foral fiscal autonomy of the historical territories in their fiscal regulations.

In order for national judges to also fulfill the function of applying EU law within the state (and to wield the accompanying "arsenal" of European competences) in matters regarding foral tax regulations, there needs to be an evident connection between said regulations and the laws of the European Union. In other words, national judges must be confronted with a situation in which EU laws and Basque foral tax norms converge in a manner that gives rise to some kind of conflict as regards the conformity of said regulations with European laws. This kind of confluence requires jurisdictional action that ensures full compliance with European law (e.g., cases involving non-application or insufficient application of European regulations that do not have a direct effect; non-application of proper regulatory or administrative measures; or other kinds of incompatibility of state action with the laws of the European Union).

Either the settings or points of connection and conflict can be rather diverse in nature. It is important to appreciate the fact that EU law holds jurisdiction as regards customs duties (i.e., it is the European Union, and not individual states, that enforces, via regulations, matters regarding customs duties) and that there are also a series of guidelines that harmonize a (specific) series of indirect taxes.[2] These guidelines must be complied with (even though it is the state that holds jurisdiction as regards their regulation, taxation, etc.). All other indirect taxes, and all direct taxes, are not subject to direct harmonization on the part of EU law, such matters falling within the jurisdiction retained by individual states (or, if applicable, by infra-state entities).

It is therefore clear that competence as regards the tax regulations of states—and, in the specific case that concerns us here, the competence within the historical territories arising from the Economic Agreement—may come into contact, and into conflict, with EU laws in two different ways.

First, whenever foral tax activities contradict existing European regulations regarding certain indirect taxes. In cases in which there is a contradiction or clash with any other European regulation, even if said regulation does not directly deal with taxes (e.g., with the European regulations governing the internal market of the European Union and defining the fundamental freedoms of the European Union that are characteristic of that market [free circulation of workers, merchandise, capital, and services, as well as freedom of establishment] or with European regulations regarding state aid).

The fact of the matter is that conflicts between the Economic Agreement and European laws (or, if one prefers, the legal regulation of the foral tax norms in a manner that takes into account the larger European context) have largely arisen as a result of the second cause identified above, and most especially as a result of a clash (or an apparent clash) between the content of the foral tax norms regarding the corporate tax and the European regulations governing state aid (for example, Articles 87 ff. of the Treaty of the European Community (TEC) and 107 ff. of the Treaty on the Functioning of the European Union (TFEU).[3]

The Corporate Tax

From the internal standpoint of the Spanish state, the common basic regulation of the corporate tax can be found in Royal Legislative Decree 4/2004 of March 5, and in Royal Decree 1777/2004 of July

30.[4] These fundamentally important regulations are accompanied by numerous complementary laws that regulate the fiscal aspects of particular entrepreneurial sectors (e.g., transportation, shipbuilding, venture capital, etc.), as well as by regulatory measures that address a number of different issues—most especially those promoting the knowledge and exchange of tax information by the administration—in addition to other regulations regarding fiscal benefits. Delving for the moment into specific issues, some corporations include important tax matters as part of their specific regulations.[5] And, to muddy the waters still further, there are regulations specific to the territories of the Canary Islands,[6] the Basque Country,[7] and Navarre[8] (i.e., Economic Agreements). Finally, we should not forget that this set of regulations is usually revised on an annual basis by means of the State Law of General Budgets, as well as (on occasion) by various regulations containing fiscal, administrative, and social measures. From the standpoint of the European Union, there are, parallel to all of the foregoing provisions, a set of regulations governing European production. These regulations become important to the extent that companies (especially larger companies) conduct part of their activities beyond the borders of the states in which they are based.

This tax can best be analyzed in terms of the fact that it is a direct, personal, and periodically assessed tax. It is a direct tax, in that it directly assesses a rate based on the taxpayer's income and is not legally transferrable. The tax is personal, in that the determination of the amount of income taxed uses as a basic point of reference (i.e., as the object of the tax) the corporate entity that obtains the income. Finally, it is a periodic tax, the taxable amount of which is determined on an annual basis in a manner adjusted to the fiscal year of the corporate entity.[9]

As regards the scope of its application, the corporate tax is assessed in all of the territories of the Spanish state[10] (i.e., the entire peninsula, the Balearic Islands, the Canary Islands, Ceuta, and Melilla, without prejudice to the foral systems of the Basque Country and Navarre, which follow their own regulations or the international treaties signed and ratified by the Spanish state). Within the common system, a series of "special systems" based on the particular good or service being taxed are in place, and which should not be confused with the foral systems, which are also sometimes called "special" because they are limited to particular territories.

We will not be entering into a detailed consideration of this tax here. Instead, we merely wish to make clear what we consider the fundamental point for our present purposes: that the different regulations in existence within the Spanish State with regard to the distinct elements comprising the tax has until now been the main reason for the friction between the common and foral legislation vis-à-vis the laws of the European Community. A distinctive element of this friction is the attitude of the European Commission, which has sought to find different solutions that would harmonize the corporate tax regulations of their member states in a manner consistent with the stated purposes of the European Union.

State Aid

We will pause here to present a couple of key ideas regarding the way in which the EU regulations regarding state aid is linked with the foral tax norms comprising the corporate tax, for it is this connection that has given rise to a large proportion of the national litigation concerning the Economic Agreement in terms of its relationship with EU law.

Without going into excessive detail, we will merely note by way of summary that the regulations referring to state aid (i.e., Article 87 ff. of the European Community Treaty and Article 107 ff. of the Treaty for the Functioning of the European Union) basically consist of[11] defining which kinds of aid are incompatible with the common market (Article 107.1), which kinds are always compatible, and which kinds might be defined as compatible, as determined by the Commission's interpretation of the circumstances of a particular case (Articles 107.2 and 107.3). In addition, these regulations have the purpose of setting forth the system of such aid in a way that assigns and authorizes the Commission a critically important role in controlling and applying the different kinds of aid that states are able to provide (Article 108).

As I. Alonso Arce points out by way of summary, these regulations might lead one to conclude that "the real fundamental issue when it comes to state aid has to do with whether a measure does or does not qualify as selective [i.e., in the sense of benefiting or not benefiting particular companies or particular kinds of production as compared to other companies or kinds of production]. This is because, in the first instance, the issue is subject to the system provided in articles 87 and 88 of the Treaty[12] and, therefore, would have to be communicated to the European Commission for the purpose of obtaining required authorization and a declaration of compatibility with the common market prior to entering into force. The second instance, however, involves a general measure that could be directly applied without any kind of authorization being required on the part of the European Commission." With respect to this, it should be borne in mind that, if a measure does constitute state aid and is carried out in the absence of communication to the European Commission, it constitutes an illegal act, and its revocation would be recovered.[13]

At this juncture of our exposition, it is important to note that the truly important point of connection and conflict as regards state aid and the corporate tax that is regulated by the historical territories by means of foral norms has specifically to do with the issue of whether said regulation "should be considered selective or general in terms of a criterion of regional or geographical selectivity or—what amounts to the same thing—if, for the purposes of the regulations regarding state aid, the valid term of comparison is the territory of a member or State or whether, in certain circumstances, a transnational entity enjoying autonomy in relation to the Corporate Tax might serve such a purpose."[14]

Moreover, the direct effect of the regulations on state aid should also be considered in terms of what it implies as regards the direct jurisdictional application on the part of national judges. As M. Sobrido Prieto[15] sums up the matter, the Luxembourg Court of Justice has established the direct effect—and has therefore ipso facto recognized the direct applicability—of Article 86.2 of the Treaty of the European Community (TEC) (concerning the special system of companies supplying services of a general economic interest and fiscal monopolies); of Article 88.3 of the European Community Treaty (prohibition on implementation of aid projects that have not definitively been ruled upon by the Commission); of the EU regulations of the Council that have been adopted on the basis of Article 89 of the TEC (e.g., Regulation 659/1999); and of the Decisions of the Commission adopted on the basis of Article 88.2 of the TEC (i.e., decisions involving declarations as regards the compatibility [or, if applicable, the modification or suspension] of any aid).

On the other hand, the above cited regulations do not recognize the direct effect of Article 87 of the TEC (currently Article 107 of the Treaty for the Functioning of the European Union), which establishes that, unless the treaty itself indicates otherwise, aid granted by states or via state funds by any means whatsoever and that distorts or threatens to distort competition and to favor particular kinds of companies or productions, will be incompatible with the common market. What this means is that it is not appropriate for private parties. This is due to the fact that the latter "cannot resort to national judges and oppose any national aid that they consider contrary to EU law solely on the basis of Article 87 of the TEC, because this provision must have been applied, either in general terms . . . or on an individual basis (i.e., via petition or a decision regarding a specific form of state aid)."

But what private parties are able to do is demand that such measures not be carried out until such time as the Commission has ruled upon them. Thus, if national judges believe that state aid is indeed involved, and therefore that the exception of Article 86.2 of the Spanish Constitution is not applicable, then they will proceed in accordance with Article 88.3 of the TEC: suspension, provision recovery, and reimbursement for damages."[16]

A Practical Perspective

It is generally evident from all of the foregoing that, on the basis of past experience, the package of competences and jurisdictional obligations offered by EU law to national judges for the purpose of enabling them to operate or act as judges who apply European Law is not something empty or something that applies exclusively within the realm of theory. Instead, this package also has a practical value that has proven to be effective.

Specifically, and in a peculiarly special way, this bundle of European powers and obligations provided to national judges have been applied with maximum force within the realm of the foral tax regulations, especially in relation to those that regulate the corporate tax of the various historical territories, and with particular reference to their "discrepancies" with EU regulations governing state aid.

A demonstration of both the theoretical and practical application of this package can be found in the Spanish Supreme Court Judgment of December 9, 2004,[17] an immediate precedent of the preliminary Judgment issued in 2006, which gave rise in turn to the September 2008 preliminary Judgment of the European Court of Justice.

In any case, and before beginning a discussion of how the aforementioned legal competences have been used—a question that is still highly controversial in many respects—we need to make it clear that the description that follows does not seek to be an assessment or judgment either in favor or against particular uses of those competences, but merely a description of the competences that exist and that have been applied. Thus, no attempt will be made to assess either the appropriateness of their existence or of the use to which they have been put. Instead, they will simply be described. For this selfsame reason, we will not be paying close attention to the details of the factual background of the cases examined, or to their legal bases or the aforementioned Spanish Supreme Court Judgment (or to either the latter's antecedents or subsequent related resolutions). We will instead be focusing closely on those issues that are noteworthy from the standpoint of legal powers).[18]

Revocation of a Provision of a Foral Tax Regulation on the Grounds of Its Being "Anti-European"

The first point worthy of mention here is the fact that the Spanish Supreme Court Judgment of December 9, 2004, has a precedent in the Judgment of the Spanish Supreme Court of Justice in the Basque

Country (SCJBC) of September 30, 1999 (especially the appeal for reversal filed by the Federation of Business Owners of La Rioja against said Ruling, in reference to the challenging of the foral norms regarding the Corporate Tax of 1996 presented by said Federation).[19]

The Spanish Supreme Court of Justice in the Basque Country (SCJBC) expressly declared that it saw no reason at all for affirming any direct contradiction between the foral norm and EU law (nor for referencing a preliminary Judgment for the benefit of the European Court of Justice). Still, it should be pointed out by way of summary that "in the revocation of article 26 of the foral norms regarding the Corporate Tax, there was one argument that weighed heavily: in having infringed upon the EU regulations regarding state aid because it constituted a selective measure on the basis of material criteria, there was also an ipso facto violation of the limits of harmonization contained in the Economic Agreement."[20]

Both parties to this process lodged appeals for reversal with the Supreme Court.[21] A Judgment issued January 21, 2002, rejected these challenges, filed by Confebask (the Basque Federation of Business Owners), the Foral Deputation of Araba, and the Juntas Generales of Araba. The briefs opposing said appeals were in turn filed before the Court considered the matter in question.[22]

With respect to this, it is interesting to note that the Federation of Business Owners of La Rioja argued that the aforementioned foral norm (i.e., all of the provisions thereof) constituted state aid in terms of the stipulations of what was previously Article 87 of the TEC (now Article 107 of the TFEU). For this reason—argued the Federation of La Rioja—there was an unmet obligation on the part of the state authorities holding jurisdiction to inform the European Commission regarding the bill now under challenge at the time when it was merely a proposed bill, and to await said Commission's approval prior to implementing the measure.

Be that as it may, the fact of the matter is that the Spanish Supreme Court Judgment of December 9, 2004 dismissed the appeals for reversal lodged by the Juntas Generales (foral legislative chambers) and the Foral Deputations (foral government) while partially admitting the appeal filed by the Federation of La Rioja which "revoked" the thirteen provisions of the foral norm of corporate taxes of the historical territories on the grounds of such provisions being contrary to EU law. The judgment did not clearly declare that the foral norm in question constituted state aid. Yet it did state that there were indications that such was the case, while stating at length that the duty to notify the Commission (Article 88.3 of the Treaty of the European Community) was also applicable to those provisions that, circumstantially speaking, constituted state aid. In reality, the notion of the provisions being in violation of EU law was not based (at least not directly) on said provisions constituting state aid, but instead on the argument that there had been a violation of EU law because the requirement for communication to the European Commission of regulations that could possibly be construed as state aid.[23]

To state the matter in somewhat more detailed terms, the judgment ordered the revocation of various provisions of Foral Norm 3/1996 of June 26 that governed the corporate tax of the historical territory of Bizkaia, and of the parallel norm or regulations in the other two historical territories, and included an exhaustive analysis of the Economic Agreement in light of EU regulations, makes it rule on the invalidity of single row radial part of the examined "makes it rule on the invalidity of single row radial part of the consideration to have omitted the necessary notification to the European Commission established in art. 93 ECT, (currently article 108 TFEU) for measures seems that may constitute 'state aid.'"

In this case, the Spanish Supreme Court cited consolidated jurisprudence of the European Court of Justice (jurisprudence that both Rubí Casinello and Advocate-General Geelhoed each independently concluded did not exist[24]) as the basis for concluding that the foral regulations, by virtue of being applicable only within the territorial boundaries of each of the historical territories, involved the element of territorial exclusiveness characteristic of state aid. These regulations were therefore sanctioned for containing terms that specially benefited the taxpayers of said territories in a way that the equivalent regulations in those territories governed under the Common System did not. In addition, the Spanish Supreme Court conducted a segmental analysis of each provision without taking into account (as precedents concerning this same matter previously had) of the general applicability of the corporate tax, or even of the foral Treasury system. Thus, in order to reach the conclusion that the foral tax measures constituted an advantage that could properly be defined as state aid, the court compared each measure with the regulation currently in effect in the territory governed by the Common System, appealing to a principle of regional or territorial selectivity that had never previously been utilized by European institutions in any of their administrative or jurisdictional decisions regarding those regulations comprising the tax system of either the state or the historical territories of the Basque Country or Navarre.

In its judgment, the Spanish Supreme Court expressly recognized that it was using the criteria for regional selectivity in order to judge the provisions of the foral norm governing the corporate tax that was being challenged when it established that, in order to constitute state aid, such provisions needed to be selective measures that accorded special treatment with respect to a general regulation, and that such measures had to include (according to the doctrine of the European Court of Justice) not only aid to a particular kind of company or specific production sectors, but also aid destined for companies established within a particular region. The Court further indicated that it was enough for the companies enjoying such special benefits to be identifiable as a result of meeting particular criteria, such as the establishment or implementation of their activities within a specifically defined territory. Furthermore, the Court also evoked the concept of regional selectivity in referring to the existence of fiscal measures whose scope of application was limited to a particular zone of the territory of the state, alongside a general system applicable to the rest of the territory of the state (i.e., the common territory), as a consequence of regulations involving the granting of competences regarding fiscal matters.

An argument expressed in such terms of territorial selectivity attacked the very essence of the Economic Agreement (i.e., regulatory capacity regarding direct taxation). This is because it led to the conclusion that there was no difference at all between state regulations and foral regulations, given that, if there were such a difference, any system operated in a way as to result in a special benefit would ipso facto have to be classified as selective. The judgment thus involved a circular kind of reasoning of requiring prior notification of its intended adoption to the European Commission (under the terms of 87.3 TEC/107.3 TFEU). Furthermore, it is possible to conclude that the Spanish Supreme Court refrained from specifying other requirements that define a fiscal measure as constituting state aid. This is because the concept of state aid requires that the following criteria be met: territorial selectivity, the presence of an advantage, responsibility on the part of the state or public authority for the measure in question (or financing via state funds), and the existence of a direct impact on exchange rates within the EU member states (Article 87 TEC/Article 107 TFEU).

In any event, and regardless of whether one accepts the arguments of the Supreme Court, it is clear that there are a series of regulations that the Spanish Supreme Court has revoked because it considered them illegal from the standpoint of the European Union. Any national judge who applies or provides guidance concerning the correct domestic application of EU law in litigation he or she rules upon can and must decline to apply any internal regulation that stands in contradiction to EU law. And if any such judge exercises the requisite competence, he or she should revoke any such measure in order to prevent its continued existence (even if it is not applied), since failure to take such action jeopardizes legal certainty.

Requests for a Preliminary Ruling

The Spanish Supreme Court Judgment of December 9, 2004, reveals the existence of a substantive and fundamental problem: the determination in the most objective manner possible (i.e., in European terms) as to when a particular measure does or does not constitute state aid, in accordance with the provision of EU law regarding such matters. What was needed, in other words, was a Judgment of the European Court of Justice (CJEU) regarding the point in question. And the best way to accomplish this was through the referencing of a preliminary Judgment that supplied an interpretation.

As had previously been stated,

> the later battle [i.e., following the Spanish Supreme Court Judgment of 2004] would inevitably have to be fought within the context of the EU. It would therefore be critically important to clarify once and for all what the EU understood as constituting state aid, as well as the scope of the criterion of regional selectivity within a context of member States that are politically decentralized with respect to the direct taxation of the companies operating within their borders. The Basque foral institutions were aware of this from the very beginning, and knew that it would eventually be necessary to submit the Economic Agreement to the acid test of a confrontation with the Court of Justice of the European Union (CJEU) of Justice (now the European Court of Justice). This despite the fact that, five years previously, those representing these institutions had done everything possible to avoid such a confrontation.[25]

However, the Spanish Supreme Court (just like the SCJBC in the previous case) did not issue any preliminary ruling. As a consequence, the defendants in the case, who felt that they were being harmed by this interpretation and by the application of European regulations, referenced the CJEU to issue a preliminary ruling. But this request was dismissed by the Spanish Supreme Court, and the consequent non-request led to the appeals to the Constitutional Court for legal protection on the grounds of the violation of the right to effective legal protection (Article 24 of the Spanish Constitution), appeals rejected via a Judgment of said court.[26]

The relevance of this 2004 Spanish Supreme Court judgment, in addition to its intrinsic importance, is reflected in later declarations in which the SCJBC repeatedly cited it in cases involving those foral provisions that had been enacted to fill the void left by the revocation of those previously in effect.[27] The SCJBC, in its announcement enforcing the said ruling, declared without effect those foral provisions that reinstituted the previously revoked tax rate (i.e., 32.6 percent). These new foral norms were also appealed by bordering Autonomous

Communities. However, in the meantime, the "Azores Case," with its "triple test" of autonomy,[28] had been presented. Thus, in the face of the uncertainty regarding any forthcoming Judgment on the part of the CJEU regarding the issue of state aid that would presumably be applicable to the historical territories of the SCJBC, chose instead to reference the corresponding preliminary rulings, which in turn led to the famous preliminary judgment of the CJEU of September 11, 2008.

What was at issue here was whether territorial selectivity was occurring. The answer to that question would in turn determine the legality of regulations generally applied within an infra-state territory—regulations different from that of the rest of the state. The applicable frame of reference to be applied in this case was of fundamental importance. This is because the very existence of any advantage can only be discerned relative to a tax requirement considered "normal" within the geographical zone of reference. For this purpose, the CJEU indicated that "the frame of reference does not necessarily have to coincide with the territory of the member State under consideration."[29] The same reasoning was applied to the preliminary judgment referenced by the SCJBC before the CJEU.

For these reasons, the measure under consideration resulted in an advantage in only one part of state territory, and only on the basis of the location of that territory, did not automatically constitute a selective measure under the terms of Article 107 of the TFEU. It was therefore obvious that the CJEU did not share the opinion pronounced by the Spanish Supreme Court in its unfortunate judgment of December 9, 2004.

For this reason, the preliminary resolution of the CJEU ended up serving as a "corrective" of the position stated by that ruling. The conclusions of Counsel General Kokott, which referenced the test of triple autonomy implicit in the "Azores Case,"[30] pointed out that the Spanish Supreme Court Judgment of December 9, 2004, did not necessarily constitute a definitive resolution of the issue of whether of national demands confer upon the historical territories sufficient material autonomy to define their tax systems, given that, at least apparently, the Constitutional Court (the Counsel General really meant the Supreme Court[31]) has delineated the boundaries of its competence beyond which the foral tax norms could be considered to constitute state aid.[32] In other words, before being able to assume that the measures under consideration are selective in nature, the Spanish Supreme Court should have established whether the authority from which such measures emanated had decreed them pursuant to an authority sufficiently independent from the central government—this for the purpose of determining the frame of reference needed in order to determine whether those measures were indeed selective.[33]

In relation to the negative reactions to the Spanish Supreme Court Judgment of 2004, it is important to note that Basque institutions, which were not in agreement with the interpretation of the Spanish Supreme Court in its Judgment of December 9, 2004, with respect to the challenged foral tax norms (i.e., considering them as constituting state aid) took two initiatives that applied EU regulations (Article 87 of the European Community Treaty) without prior pretrial consultation with the CJEU.

First, the Basque institutions lodged an appeal with the lower court judge determined by law (Article 24.2 of the Spanish Constitution) for legal protection against said ruling[34] on the grounds of violation of the right to effective legal protection that would assure a proper defense (Article 24.1 of the Spanish Constitution) as well as to a trial that would provide guarantees of due process (also in reference to Article 24.2). As is well known, jurisprudence in large measure views the appeal for legal protection before the Constitutional Court as a means for remedying a situation that has occurred when rights to effective legal protection have been violated as a result of failure to reference a proper preliminary legal ruling. The Basque institutions believed that these rights had been violated as a result of the fact that the Spanish Supreme Court, prior to issuing its verdict regarding the appealed ruling, did not reference the preliminary Judgment provided for in Article 267 of the TEC for the purpose of not applying the foral norms that had been revoked. In the view of the Basque institutions, this opened the door to lodging an appeal for legal protection in accordance with the legal precedent of the Spanish Constitutional Court Judgment 58/2004 of April 19—this notwithstanding the fact that the appealing party had not previously referenced a preliminary Judgment in the legal proceedings. Noncompliance on the part of the internal jurisdictional body with the requirement to reference a preliminary Judgment in accordance with Article 234.2 of the European Community Treaty constitutes (unless it occurs in the context of certain specified exceptional circumstances) a violation of EU law, and would therefore be subject to remedies via appeals for legal protection.[35] However, in the case of the Basque institutions, there was no permitted exemption from the requirement to reference a preliminary ruling, not in terms of the concept of aid that had been utilized in the judgment that was being appealed, nor with regard to the mechanical application of Article 88.3 of the European Community Treaty. This was even more the case in light of the fact that the judicial body interpreted and wrongly applied EU law.

It was thus the argument of abusive or improper use of the transparent action doctrine (i.e., which applies in cases when the EU regulation is so clear that its interpretation leaves no room for doubt[36]).

This is the doctrine that served as the basis of the appeal for legal protection filed by the Basque institutions with the Constitutional Court in protest of the Spanish Supreme Court Judgment of December 9, 2004. The reason for this justification was the fact that the foral provisions that had been revoked were characterized as state aid on the basis of their supposed "selective" nature—a characterization "that was not at all justified in light of all of the existing precedents that could be deduced from EU law (i.e., previous Commission decisions)."[37] In addition, although the interpretation made by the Commission of the requirement of selectivity had been corroborated by the International Criminal Court (now known as the General Court) in Rulings of March 6, 2002 (i.e., the Demesa and Ramondín cases), these rulings were ignored by the Supreme Court—despite the fact that it was aware of them. In the view of the Juntas Generales of Bizkaia, the Spanish Supreme Court did not have then and does not have now any precedent as regards "an issue that is materially identical, and which has been subject to a preliminary ruling" that could serve as the basis to justify its abrogation of a responsibility imposed upon it by Article 234.3 of the European Community Treaty. What this means is that the judicial body should have at least been given pause by the lower court ruling. It can thus be concluded that the actions of the Spanish Supreme Court involved the violation of both the fundamental right of the predetermined lower court judge[38] as well as the right to a trial with due process.[39] On the other hand, no evidence was adduced that could put to rest any doubt as to the manner of resolving the issue raised (i.e., the doctrine of transparent actions), which would constitute the other exception to the required referencing of a preliminary ruling.[40] Thus, given the fact that the Spanish Supreme Court eschewed the criterion of selectivity utilized by the Commission, it ended up introducing (from the standpoint of the plaintiff) at least one doubt as regards the application of EU law that, until that moment, did not exist, and this required it to reference a preliminary judgment in accordance with Article 267 of the TFEU. Despite all of this, the Constitutional Court decided not to consider the demand for legal protection.[41]

In addition, Basque institutions brought before the Spanish Supreme Court an incident involving the nullification of court proceedings[42] which was dismissed on April 4, 2005, by an official court document (which, in turn, was the subject of a new appeal for legal protection)[43]. The Spanish Constitutional Court resolved to not admit this appeal on the grounds of Article 50.1 a.), Article 44.1 (both of the Organic Law of the Constitutional Court) and the record of the case.[44]

Judgment of the CJEU of September 11, 2008

In this ruling, the European Court of Justice followed the same line of argument as that of AG Geelhoed in the "Azores Case," included by AG Kokott in her conclusions regarding the case in question, and which recognized the fiscal autonomy of the Basque Country. The Judgment delved further into the interpretation of the EU system governing state aid which had been initiated with the "Azores Case" which, for the first time, made the Community system of state aid compatible with the peculiar features of the tax systems of certain decentralized European states. On that occasion, the CJEU cited the asymmetry in competences and, to the extent that some infra-state entities are endowed with autonomy, insisted on the sufficiency of that autonomy, specifying in passing the criteria that comprised that sufficiency (i.e., the sum of institutional, procedural, and economic autonomy).

For the specific case involving the norms adopted by the Foral Deputations, the Judgment of the CJEU of September 11, 2008, followed that line of reasoning of sufficiency of autonomy, although the Court did not formally resolve the issue of whether regulatory competences regarding tax matters in the historical territories did or did not conflict with EU regulations (because this was not the issue brought before the referring Court). Thus, there are grounds to infer that the CJEU limited itself to simply referring the issue back to the SCJBC.[45]

In the first place CJEU confirmed that the only requirements for an infra-state entity to dictate its own fiscal regulations were exclusively those included in the "Azores Case": institutional, procedural, and economic autonomy. The Court categorically rejected the attempt of the European Commission to impose a fourth requirement (i.e., that the territorial entity in question exercise those competences needed to define the economic framework within which companies could operate in its territory).

These conditions of "triple autonomy" (i.e., institutional, economic, and procedural) were also cited in the conclusions of the General Counsel, which followed this classification with a number of terminological variations. For example, "procedural autonomy" was replaced with the term "configurative autonomy," which was further subdivided into formal configurative autonomy and material configurative autonomy. The AG argued that the CJEU clearly resolved the question of institutional and procedural autonomy (i.e. of "configuration" in both the formal and material sense) although it failed to clearly define the functioning of the quota, whose consideration as a possible compensatory instrument in the face of a possible loss of collected taxes on the part of the historical territories resulted in the economic and financial autonomy not being quite so total. In the end, the issue was referred back to the referring jurisdictional body (i.e., the SCJBC).

The CJEU addressed a total of five different issues: the admissibility of the preliminary ruling, the absence of a previous requirement, the infra-state entity to be considered, the relevance of jurisdictional control, and the three autonomy criteria established in the "Azores Case." We will not be discussing any of these issues here.

The judgment of the CJEU was made public on September 11, 2008,[46] and the header of the published judgment perfectly reflected its content:[47] judgment of the CJEU in consolidated cases C-428/06-C-434/06 (General Union of Workers of La Rioja, State Aid). The European Court of Justice specifies criteria allowing the verification, as regards state aid, of institutional, procedural, and economic autonomy of a territorial entity in relation to a central authority.

In this judgment, the CJEU stated that the Basque foral Treasury systems could a priori impose a corporate tax that was different from that which prevailed in the rest of the Spanish state because they were sufficiently autonomous in the exercise of their legislative competences as regards tax matters. However, the Court also indicated that the SCJBC was the entity responsible for definitively establishing if the Basque Country was in compliance with all of the requirements of tax autonomy. The CJEU made it clear that freedom of establishment is one of the fundamental principles of the European Union, taking into account the fact that the regulations that establish said principle attribute to those governed by those regulations rights that can only be limited in the event of the existence of particular interests that are considered preferential.[48] Only under those very strictly defined and exceptional circumstances of Article 52 of the TFEU (previously Article 46 of the TEC) are state regulations that might otherwise be considered discriminatory allowed, and these cases cannot be based on economic justifications alone (e.g., loss of tax revenues, combating against tax fraud, etc.) for the purpose of justifying the existence of restrictions of this fundamental European right. The Luxembourg Court in effect said the fact of the existence of a different tax system in a territory with financial and fiscal autonomy is not discriminatory for other regions.[49] Therefore, the Basque foral Treasury systems can stipulate a corporate tax (through which business owners can liquidate their revenues) that is different from that which is in effect in the rest of the state, because they enjoy sufficient autonomy as regards tax matters.[50]

Judgment of the SCJBC of December 22, 2008

On December 22, 2008, the SCJBC dismissed seventeen appeals against the foral tax norms regarding the corporate tax,[51] declaring that the level of autonomy of the Basque Country allows the dictating of tax provisions and measures that are differentiated from those of the state, "without prejudice to the fact that possible excesses might result in appropriate application of the characterization of State aid and thus require authorization of the Commission." In the cases it ruled upon, the SCJBC indicated that such a situation did not apply.

Although it is true that this judgment did not directly affect the appeals pending vis-à-vis the foral Treasury system (since they resolved a preliminary judgment that the SCJBC referenced to the CJEU regarding the appeals filed by the Autonomous Communities of La Rioja and Castile-León, and by the General Workers Union of La Rioja against the corporate tax rate of 32.5 percent that was assessed in 2005), it is also true that, in the resolution of this case, the SCJBC applied the judgment of the CJEU and, for the sake of consistency, will continue to apply the same Judgment in the appeals currently pending. This resolution of the CJEU does not affect the decisions adopted by the Commission with regard to "tax havens," which the Deputations are required to restore, given the fact that the Commission considers these to constitute state aid.

If, on the other hand, the CJEU had resolved that the reduced rates of the foral tax norms or regulations constituted state aid, taxation capacity would have been reduced to nothing more than a reproduction of state legislation. But this judgment does not definitively resolve the issue, given the fact that, on the one hand, the Commission already indicated at the oral hearing that it can continue to consider reduced rates as constituting state aid. The bordering Autonomous Community, as well as other Autonomous Communities that continue to feel harmed (unless the law is changed, as well as the active entitlement to try matters related to the foral tax norms, these complaints will be restricted to matters equivalent in status to laws) will probably continue insisting on the argument, which has not been brought before the CJEU, that the lower tax rates result in discrimination and advantageous market position[52] (Navarre tax rules are similar, and, curiously, have not resorted).

About Internal Jurisdictional Protection of the Foral Tax Norms and EU Effects: The Issue of So-called "Armor" of the Economic Agreement

On February 20, 2010, Organic Law 1/2010 of February 19, which modified the Organic Laws of the Constitutional Court and the Judiciary, was published in the *Boletín Oficial del Estado* (Spanish Official State Gazette). This law became effective as of March 12, 2010, and has since come to be known as the "armor" of the Economic Agreement.[53] This reform defines the proper jurisdiction of courts to hear appeals and challenges to the foral tax norms, removing those matters from the lower courts that had until then ruled on such issues and instead charging the Spanish Constitutional Court with hearing direct and indirect appeals against said regulations. The media has termed this change the "armor" of the foral tax norms, the purpose of which was to facilitate resolution of challenges to the nature of those regulations (which, as is well known, have the formal status of regulations, despite the fact that, materially speaking, their fiscal content is protected by the principle of legal reservation).

The fact of the matter is that, given the particular institutional configuration of the Basque Autonomous Community, the historical territories that comprise said community have historical competences that have been developed by their corresponding institutions. However, it is paradoxical that these institutions only enjoy regulatory capacity, despite the fact that issues such as tax matters ought properly to be formally regulated by laws (in this regard, it should be noted that only the respective Juntas Generales are able to maintain, establish, and regulate the taxes imposed under the terms of the Economic Agreement—a right which, in the rest of the state, is explicitly reserved by the Spanish Constitution and laws approved by the Spanish Parliament). This dysfunction in the nature of the foral norms (i.e., the fact that they are defined formally as regulations, while functioning materially as laws) means that those regulations which regulate particular taxes had been subject to appeal before lower courts (i.e., administrative law courts), while the tax laws of the rest of the Spanish state (which are laws in both the formal and material sense) can only be challenged before the Constitutional Court, and only by a relatively small number of parties entitled to do so.[54]

In this regard, Organic Law 1/2010, charged the Constitutional Court to hear matters involving appeals and challenges against the foral tax norms of the three historical territories (i.e., regulations enacted in the exercise of their exclusive competences as guaranteed by the First Additional Provision of the Spanish Constitution and recognized in Article 41.2.1) of the Autonomy Statute of the Basque Country), thus preventing administrative law courts from hearing and Judgment on direct and indirect appeals against those regulations in the future.

Reform Introduced by Organic Law 1/2010 of February 19, Modifying the Organic Laws of the Constitutional Court and the Judiciary Power

For some time, there has been a clear need to jurisdictionally "protect" the foral tax norms. As is well known, the Autonomous Community of the Basque Country comprises Foral Territories that hold Fiscal and

Tax Competences (First Additional Provision of Article 37 of the Autonomy Statute of the Basque Country). Given that such is the case, the Autonomous Community of the Basque Country is the Community that has the lowest tax capacity, and it draws upon the contributions of the historical territories (69.96 percent). It could even be said that its financing model is in line with those of federal States.

Despite all this, Article 31.3 of the Spanish Constitution includes the principle of Legal Reservation regarding tax matters, and this creates a problem regarding the competences of the historical territories within this sphere. This is because the Juntas Generales draft regulations that do not have the status of laws, at least not formally. This means, from the procedural and jurisdictional point of view, that the foral tax norms have the status of regulations, which in turn means that they are subject to appeals in the Administrative Law Courts, where anyone with a legitimate interest in the matter could lodge such an appeal. This situation has resulted in the foral tax norms enjoying less protection than the tax regulations of the rest of the Spanish State, including the Foral Community of Navarre.

The Preamble of Organic Law 1/2010 declares that "this difference has no material justification whatsoever: Materially, the regulation of the IRPF or of the Corporate Tax is the same thing, and they should therefore receive the same treatment in Navarre as in Bizkaia, Gipuzkoa, and Araba. Everything is reduced to a formal difference, a phenomenon which, in the case of the historical territories of the Basque Country, results in a lack of recognition of formal legislative authority in their institutions. This is a less than satisfactory state of affairs, given the material identity [of the regulations] emphasized previously."

In order to alleviate this situation that has resulted in so many conflicts, modifications were made of the Organic Law of the Constitutional Court (LOTC), Organic Law of the Judiciary (OLJ), and the Law Regulating the Administrative Law Courts (LRALC). The LOTC was changed to include within its competence the hearing of challenges to the Foral Tax Regulations. The other two laws were changed in order to redefine the scope of the Administrative Law Courts so as to include the hearing of matters related to "general provisions holding a status lower than that of laws," thus including foral norms in general.

Organic Law 1/2010, in addition to redefining the jurisdictional body competent to hear matters related to the Foral Tax Regulations, entitles as a consequence the respective Foral Deputations and Juntas Generales of the historical territories of Araba, Bizkaia, and Gipuzkoa to legally defend foral autonomy if they consider State legislation harmful. Thus, for example, matters concerning foral tax norms can no longer be heard in the lower courts and must instead be tried in the Constitutional Court.

For these reasons, it should be made clear that the reform changes the character of the jurisdictional protection of the foral tax norms, and redefines the body authorized to hear appeals against said regulations. Yet these Norms continue to hold the status of regulations, rather than of laws (an argument advanced by the Autonomous Community of La Rioja to appeal Organic Law 1/2010).

Scope of the Jurisdictional Protection of the foral tax norms ("Armor")

We should probably begin by pointing out that it seems more appropriate to talk of "the jurisdictional protection of the Foral Tax Regulations" rather than to use the term "armor" (like "immunization"), which the media is so fond of. This is because, as we shall see, the protections do not in effect "armor" anything—at least not in any absolute sense. As drafted, the reform has come to function as a solution to the litigiousness that has arisen regarding the foral tax norms within the internal context of the State, given that it limits the active entitlement to file appeals against those Norms[55].

But the situation is not quite so simple, given that fact that, because Spain is part of the European Union, it is subject to a regulatory frame of reference of broader scope, one in which supranational regulations need to be respected and internalized.

We should in this connection remember that national judges act also as European judges (i.e., in applying and safeguarding the laws of the European Union), and that it is EU law that limits the capacity of national legislators to act upon the competency of national judges—at least in matters concerning those competences established by the EU.

For this reason, we need to take into account the effectiveness of the jurisdictional protection of the foral norms at both the State and European levels. In this connection, it needs to be appreciated that the reform under discussion only considers the State level—an important level, to be sure, but not the only one that deserves to be considered.

The Need for Protection of the Foral Tax Regulations

The issue arises in relation to the legal nature of the foral norms in general, and the tax regulations in particular, and has to do with the body charged with jurisdictional control of these types of regulations. The reform under discussion has charged the Constitutional Court with jurisdiction of the foral tax norms (although this has been done without changing their fundamentally regulatory nature, and thus does not include them under Article 27.2 Organic Law of the Constitutional Court, with all the other regulations holding the status of laws, a state of affairs that creates significant problems).

At the State level, the Economic Agreement per se has not been challenged in quite some time, at least not in the courts (although it has been subject to challenge in certain media outlets, as well as among certain misguided political parties). Yet the same cannot be said as regards the foral norms that result from the Economic Agreement, given the fact that controversy prevails over their legal nature. It is the result of this ambiguity surrounding the nature of the Juntas Generales that draft these regulations that debates arise regarding both the legislative nature of this body and the regulatory status of the Norms. The problem fundamentally results from the particular characteristics of the Basque system of autonomy, which is foral in nature (and which is defined in the First Additional Provision of the Spanish Constitution, which protects and respects the Historic Rights of the Foral Territories. The Basque institutional structure thus is composed of both common institutions (i.e., Parliament and Government) and the foral institutions of each of the historical territories (whose scope of competences are significant, and which are exercised by means of a distinctive institutional organization that is binary in nature, in which the Juntas Generales exercise the function of a parliament or legislative assembly, while the Foral Deputations exercise the function of an executive body). Despite the existence of this defined sphere of competences (and especially of fiscal competences) which fall under the principal of legal reservation (Article 133 of the Spanish Constitution), the foral norms issued by the Juntas Generales that regulate such matters are formally regulatory in nature, and therefore have been subject to the jurisdictional control of the Administrative Law Courts. It is for this reason that they have been subject to so many challenges in the courts in recent times.

"Challengeability" of the Foral Regulations

The fundamental question in this regard is the aforementioned categorization of the foral norms, which are regulatory products of the Juntas Generales that, in a "formal" sense, do not conform to the usual parameters of the institutional structure of the Autonomous Communities.

The inclusion of foral institutions among public administrative entities subject to the jurisdiction of the Administrative Law Courts automatically supposes that the entitlement to legally challenge them before public bodies will be wide in scope, given the fact that all that is needed to do so is the claiming of a legitimate right or interest[56]. Doctrinal positions aside[57], this has resulted in the proliferation of appeals against the foral norms in recent times. It was necessary to put a stop to the chaos resulting from the large number of legal challenges that were being filed.

This is a problem that began to rear its head as far back as 1994, when the Autonomous Community of La Rioja lodged an appeal for a review of an administrative decision before the SCJBC[58] against the foral norms of the Basque Country[59] regarding "Emergency Fiscal Measures Supporting Investment and Promoting Economic Activity." The Basque defendants in this case filed a preliminary motion alleging that the complaint in question was inadmissible on the grounds of the lack of entitlement on the part of the Autonomous Community resorting to the court, and the SCJBC ruled in favor of this motion, upholding the view that the Administration of the Autonomous Community of La Rioja (the plaintiff in the case) was not entitled to present the appeal.[60]

When the case reached the Supreme Court, this body ruled in favor of the plaintiffs, upholding the legitimacy of the appeal against the orders of the SCJBC, revoking said orders.[61] The Spanish Supreme Court indicated that, in its view, the heart of the matter under consideration had to do with deciding if the Autonomous Community of La Rioja was actively entitled to challenge the foral norms in question before the administrative law courts,[62] all of which concerned "Emergency Fiscal Measures Supporting Investment and Promoting Economic Activity" (which were informally known as "tax havens"). The Court cited the arguments of the Autonomous Community of La Rioja to the effect that "said regulations established real privileges that ran counter to the essential principles underlying the functioning of the autonomic system: equality, solidarity, and market unity. These violations very directly affected the interests of La Rioja, given the fact that the latter bordered the Autonomous Community of the Basque Country, and which therefore was the party that was most directly harmed by the pernicious effects of such provisions, in terms of the loss of jobs and the reduction of its economic activity." At the same time, the court noted the arguments of the defendants (i.e., that Autonomous Communities were only authorized to challenge those regulations that affected the scope of their autonomy and that were enacted by the state administration—and not by another Autonomous Community, stating in this connection that none of the three foral norms that were being challenged affected the scope of the autonomy of La Rioja, and that the interest of the aggrieved Autonomous Community was therefore properly limited to a simple concern for the legality of the measures that did not justify their appeal[63]).

The reasoning of the Spanish Supreme Court focused on the distinction between so called *ad processum* entitlement and *ad causam*[64] entitlement. The former term refers to the authority to promote the activity of the body making the decision, and the Autonomous Community of La Rioja was recognized as exercising said entitlement. In the Supreme Court's view, this *ad processum* entitlement was sufficient to initiate proceedings against the foral norms that were being challenged, regardless of the fact that, afterward, the matter was resolved on the basis of entitlement of the Autonomous Community of La Rioja in the case. The plaintiff had not claimed *ad causam* entitlement, a matter that it conceded to the SCJBC once the litigation had commenced.

Because of this, even though the SCJBC had alleged in the prior litigation that bordering autonomous communities lacked procedural entitlement,[65] the Spanish Supreme Court, in reversing the earlier decision of the Basque Court, recognized La Rioja's entitlement, showing a tendency to acknowledge the active procedural (i.e., *ad processum*) entitlement, and without making any declaration regarding *ad causam* entitlement, of the Autonomous Communities presenting appeals in the administrative law courts against the aforementioned foral norms.[66]

The New Jurisdictional Control of the Foral Tax Norms

Given the particular institutional and competence structure of the Autonomous Community of the Basque Country, it is the Juntas Generales of each of the historical territories that are competent to regulate tributary questions through the foral tax regulations. There is controversy surrounding the question of the legal nature of these regulations—a controversy that has had problematic consequences, not only as regards the phenomenon of the continual litigation surrounding the foral tax norms but also the broad scope of parties legally entitled to challenge them, given their formal regulatory nature.

During this litigation regarding the foral tax norms—especially vis-à-vis European criteria and parameters—Basque institutions, both autonomous and foral, began making and reiterating a series of declarations that were officially promulgated and conveyed through media outlets. These declarations complained about the legal status of the foral tax norms (the issue is not new, and previous legal cases had addressed the matter over the course of many years[67]) and reviving the controversy surrounding the proper jurisdictional control of said regulations. The situation, both de facto and de jure, of the foral tax norms in recent years has once again made clear the need to change the procedural system governing them in a way that would place their jurisdictional control in the hands of the Constitutional Court, thus taking that control away from the administrative law courts, despite the fact that these regulations would formally retain their regulatory character.

In addition, there was also a call to remedy the other pending legal issues surrounding the foral tax regulations: the entitlement of foral institutions to have recourse to constitutional jurisdiction. This became a pressing issue because the historical rights of the foral territories, at least as regards their core essence, are not a matter of mere ordinary legality. Instead, "it is beyond question that they involve a constitutional issue in the same way as any Constitutional provision might involve, and this necessitates the facilitation of a practical and accessible means for their defense" that remedies the deficiency of protection of the foral institutions resulting from the lack of entitlement of said institutions to resort to the Constitutional Court in those instances in which it appears that either State or Autonomous legislators are invading the space that the First Additional Provision of the Spanish Constitution and Article 37 of the Statute of Autonomy of the Basque Country exclusively accord the foral institutions.[68]

The jurisdictional protection of the foral norms has received concrete expression in Organic Law 1/2010, which consists of two articles and a single additional provision. The first article modifies the Organic Law of the Constitutional Court by charging that court with controlling, and with hearing matters regarding, the foral tax norms (and, in addition, with defining a means for defending local autonomy). But it does so in terms far removed from those of Article 27.2 of the Organic Law of the Constitutional Court (where regulations can be found that hold the status of law for the purpose of control and declaring unconstitutionality), introducing a (new) Fifth Additional Provision, the contents of which establish the following:

> 1. The Constitutional Court will be charged with hearing appeals lodged against the Foral Tax Norms of the Territories of Araba, Gipuzkoa, and Bizkaia which are enacted in the exercise of their exclusive competences, which are guaranteed by the First Additional Provision of the Constitution and recognized in article 41.1.1) of the Statute of Autonomy for the Basque Country (Organic Law 311979, of December 18th).
>
> The Constitutional Court will also resolve challenges involving the reference for a preliminary Judgment on the part of jurisdictional bodies, and that deal with the validity of the aforementioned provisions, when the verdict regarding the primary matter under consideration depends upon such resolution.
>
> The validity parameters of the Foral Norms being prosecuted will be in accordance with article twenty-eight of this Law.
>
> 2. The filing and its subsequent consequences, as well as the entitlement, processing, and rulings with respect to the appeals and challenges referred to in the previous section, will be governed by the provisions of Title II of this Law for appeals and challenges involving unconstitutionality, respectively.

> The procedures regulated in articles 34 and 37 will, if applicable, be carried out by the corresponding Juntas Generales and Foral Deputations.
>
> In the procedures involving appeals and challenges which are regulated in the present additional provision, the attributive rules of competency will be applied to the Plenum and to the individual Courts stated in articles 10 and 11 of this Law.
>
> 3. The regulations of the State that hold the status of law may give rise to the filing of motions in defense of the foral autonomy of the Historical Territories of the Autonomous Communities of the Basque Country, an autonomy which is guaranteed by both the Constitution and the Autonomy Statute.
>
> The Foral Deputations and the Juntas Generales of the Historical Territories of Araba, Bizkaia, and Gipuzkoa are entitled to file such motions, by means of an agreement adopted for such a purpose.
>
> The above-mentioned motions will be processed and resolved in accordance with the procedures established in articles 63 ff. of this Law.

Article 2 of OL 1/2010 includes the corresponding modification of Organic Law 6/1985 of July 1, of the Judiciary,[69] while the Sole Additional Provision[70] accomplishes the same purpose as regards Law 29/1998 of July 13, which regulates the administrative law courts.

It should be pointed out that between the approval of the aforementioned legislative reforms (approved by Congress on December 17, 2009, and by the Senate on February 10, 2010) and the publication of the new legislation in the *Boletín Oficial del Estado,* in this small period (on February 5, 2010) which made official its entering into force, the Autonomous Community of La Rioja filed another appeal against the regulations of the corporate tax in the administrative law court of the SCJBC, which was accepted for consideration on February 16, 2010.

This appeal took advantage of the very limited time left to the bordering Autonomous Communities for filing appeals under the old system, and prior to the reforms taking effect. As in previous instances, the appeal focused on various foral provisions dealing with the corporate tax.[71]

Armor of Constitutionality versus Armor of "Europeanness"

It should be remembered that national judges that act also as European judges in fact are conducting two kinds of control (i.e., of internal legality and of the legality of the European Union), and that they utilize two different parameters (i.e., internal state constitutional legality and European legality), independently of the nature and range of the internal regulatory categories, as well as of the procedural mechanisms and the means or resources to control them, whether or not these are established by internal law, and in a manner that is always grounded in the principle of institutional internal legal autonomy vis-à-vis the laws of the European Union.

At the same time, we should also bear in mind that the contents of the control in question, as well as the internal parameters of prosecution, cannot determine the existence and efficacy of the control of European legality. The so-called "immunization" in internal terms does not imply an equivalent "immunization" in European terms. Thus, the fact that national lower court judges (i.e., of the administrative law courts) cannot control the validity and the efficacy of the foral tax norms in terms of internal law does not mean that they cannot control their applicability in European terms. It can therefore be predicted that national judges will continue to find themselves faced with the authority and obligation to refuse to apply those foral tax norms that are incompatible with EU law (i.e., when they rule on matters involving these laws, and when they control the application of these laws). However, national judges are not now in a position to revoke such laws (and administrative law courts can only revoke, when applicable, those foral norms that do not have to do with tax matters). This is something that, incidentally, the Constitutional Court does not do either (both because it doesn't see itself as functioning as an EU court, and because it does not have a procedural means to structure a control of European legality with *erga omnes* effects on internal law).

Summary

From an internal standpoint, the effect of the reform enacted in Organic Law 1/2010 is consistent with the idea that the foral tax norms can be immunized from lower court jurisdiction (i.e. from the involvement of national judges) in terms of the control of legality and constitutionality (i.e., "internal armor"). This reform is also consistent with adaptation of foral legislation involving tax matters with state legality, irrespective of the formal status of the regulations in question.

Yet from a more general standpoint that takes account of the fact that Spain belongs to the European Union, it needs to be appreciated that national judges are also judges of the conformity to EU law on the part of internal or state law (and therefore, in this same regard, also of the European legality of the Economic Agreement). All of the internal authorities, including the legislature itself (i.e., in matters in which competences are attributed to the European Union) are subject to the limitations of European law, when limiting the power of the national judge.

Internal competence as regards domestic jurisdictional application of European law is not, in regulatory terms, available to the state.

The Economic Agreement may "armor" in constitutional terms, but not in terms of the European Union (and the fact remains that the majority of the litigation that has taken place in legal venues in recent times has been within the context of EU laws). There can be an immunization for the purposes of internal legality (i.e., over and apart from European laws) but not for the purposes of European legality, which needs to be respected within the context of the Economic Agreement, and also when it comes to regulating judicial control with respect to the Economic Agreement.

For this reason, from the multinational standpoint (i.e., that of the European Union), the idea that the foral tax norms can be immunized or armored from the jurisdiction of lower courts (i.e., from national judges) is not sustainable, for this is a conclusion that directly contradicts the Simmenthal doctrine as well as original European Community Law. In this regard, it is clear that the legislative authority behind Organic Law 1/2010 did not intend to generate a second kind of "armor" (i.e., one in an external or European context). Furthermore, such an intention cannot be deduced from a literal reading of the text of the (new) Fifth Additional Provision that has just been incorporated into Organic Law 2/1979 of the Constitutional Court.

With the reform now in force, national judges who act also as European judges will continue to have the jurisdiction needed to control whether the foral tax norms (as well as the rest of internal Law, whatever status it holds) are or are not in accordance with the laws of the European Union and will be able to take appropriate action if such is not the case. It should of course be noted that the recent reform does not prevent national judges (i.e., of the administrative law courts) from continuing to hear matters regarding the legality or constitutionality of the acts of application of the foral tax norms (although they cannot hear indirect appeals against them[72]). They can therefore also, to that extent, carry out a control of the European legality of those regulations: an indirect control of the European legality of the foral tax norms through the hearing and control of their acts of application (e.g., the acts of application regarding taxes, or the imposition of sanctions on the part of the corresponding economic-administrative court, etc.) or a control that uses all of the powers and obligations that can be derived from EU law: the ability to refrain from applying particular laws, referencing preliminary rulings, injunctive relief, and so on.

In sum, the reform enacted in Organic Law 1/2010 generates an internal "armor" (i.e., in terms of constitutionality and the internal legality of the foral tax norms vis-à-vis the lower courts—and not, it should be noted of all of the foral regulations). But the same does not apply with respect to the control of European legality, which will continue to be in the hands of national judges, although it is also true that the way in which national judges can renew this kind of control will only be through the control of the acts of application of the foral tax regulations.

One cannot in any case speak of an "armor" in an external or European context. Once can conclude that the means of internal control and of control of European legality have been restricted, but it must still be recognized that national judges are also EU judges with respect to matters involving the foral tax norms (unless they are willing to act in ways that go against the Simenthal doctrine, or unless original European law is reformed) through the control of the acts of application of those regulations.

On the other hand, the reform also results in the Constitutional Court being charged with controlling the legitimacy of these foral tax norms. In this regard, we need to remember once more that, as long as the Constitutional Court continues to refrain from acting as an EU judge (i.e., as long as it takes the view that the application of EU law and jurisdictional control of the correct application thereof are questions that—because they do not touch on constitutional matters—are within the competence of lower courts), these foral tax norms (as is the case with the control of all regulations holding the status of laws, per Article 27.2 of the LOTC) will only be subject to an *erga omnes* control under the terms and within the parameters of constitutionality, and not of European legality.

Finally, it should also be noted that, within the context of the present discussion, the "impossible European armor" of the Economic Agreement vis-à-vis the lower courts does not mean that it is not feasible to identify some means of limiting or softening excessive control or excessive zeal when it comes to activating judicial control of the European legality of the foral tax norms or of the Economic Agreement, or the compatibility of their content with EU Law. Once such means might be in the currently effective orientation of the CJEU regarding the limits or requirements of the European legality of the Economic Agreement (in this regard, the Judgment of the CJEU, to which considerable attention has been devoted in section five of the present paper, has been vital).

An understanding attitude and a flexible view of the Economic Agreement on the part of CJEU jurisprudence—as shown in the previously cited ruling—could well ameliorate, at least partially, jurisdictional and pre-jurisdictional conflicts as regards the control of the European legality of said agreement.

* This work is part of the Research Training Unit (UFI), registration code: UFI11/05, General Coordinator: Juan Ignacio Ugartemendia Eceizabarrena, and of research group of the Basque Government IT 604/13.

Endnotes

1. There is a vast literature regarding the historical foundations of the Economic Agreement. The following two works of E.J. Alonso Olea supply basic background information: "Las haciendas forales vascas, 1500–2002: Una historia del concierto económico," *El Concierto Económico Vasco historia y renovación. Las valoraciones de la población de la C.A.P.V. al respecto*, Cuadernos Sociológicos Vascos, 12 (2002): 7–49; and *El Concierto Económico (1878–1937): Origen y formación de un Derecho Histórico* (Oñati: IVAP, 1995).
2. Assessed on the volume of business transacted (in the case of Spain, the VAT) or nonspecific kinds of consumption (i.e., special taxes, for both manufacturing ([hydrocarbon fuels, work with tobacco, etc.]) as well as the special tax on different kinds of transportation and as taxes on concentration of capital.
3. The Treaty of Lisbon (which modified the Treaty of the European Union and the Treaty Constituting the European Community), signed on December 13, 2007, and which went into effect on December 1, 2009, has brought about many changes, including those involving terminology. Thus, for example, reference is now made to "European Union law" instead of to "community law." In fact, the term "community" is no longer used. The names of jurisdictional bodies have also changed, as has the numbering of articles and other content. Still, even taking into account all these changes, we continue to make reference to the older terminology. This is because conflicts involving the foral tax norms arose and were conceptualized within a pre-Lisbon context. The new text modifies the EU and EC treaties, but does not replace them. The new treaty provides the EU with the framework and legal instruments necessary to confront future challenges and respond to citizens' expectations. See J. M. Faramiñan Gilbert, "El Tratado de Lisboa (un juego de espejos rotos)," *REEI* 17 (2009), online version. www.reei.org/index.php/revista/num17/articulos/tratado-lisboa-juego-espejos-rotos.
4. These approve the reformulated text of the corporate tax law and the regulation of the corporate tax, respectively.
5. Examples are Law 20/1990 of December 10, on the Tax System for Cooperatives and Law 49/2002 of December 23, on the tax system for non-profit entities and fiscal incentives for patronage.
6. Included in Law 20/1991 of June 7 and 19/1994 of July 6.
7. Economic Agreement with the Basque Autonomous Community, approve by Law 12/2002 of May 23.
8. Economic Agreement between the State and the Foral Community of Navarre, approved by Law 28/1990, of December 26, and modified by Law 25/2003 of July 15.
9. Articles 1 and 24 of the corporate tax law of Spain.
10. It should be remembered in this connection that Spanish territory, in accordance with Article 2 of the corporate tax law, comprises "the regions bounding the territorial waters over which Spain may exercise rights with respect to the land and subsurface, it's overlying waters, and its natural resources, in accordance with both Spanish legislation and International Law."
11. See B. Pérez Bernabeu, *Ayudas de Estado en la jurisprudencia comunitaria: Concepto y tratamiento* (Valencia: Tirant lo Blanch–Universitat d`Alicant,

2008).

12. It should be remembered that, before to the Lisbon reform, the system of state aid was included in Articles 87 and 88 of the EU Treaty. It can now be found in Articles 107 and 108 of the Treaty for the Functioning of the European Union. In addition, as we have indicated previously, reference is no longer made to the "Community" but instead to "Europe."

13. Alonso Arce, I. *El Concierto Económico en Europa* (Oñati: IVSP, 2010), 59.

14. Alonso Arce. *El Concierto Económico en Europa*, 60.

15. M. Sobrido Prieto, *Las Comunidades Autónomas ante el Tribunal de Justicia y el Tribunal de Primera Instancia de las Comunidades Europeas* (Valencia: Tirant lo Blanch–Instituto Universitario de Estudios Europeos, 2003), 417 ff.

16. Sobrido Prieto, *Las Comunidades Autónomas ante el Tribunal de Justicia y el Tribunal de Primera Instancia de las Comunidades* Europeas, 418–19.

17. The reference here is to the Judgment of the Second Section of the Third Court of the Supreme Court in appeal no. 7893/99, filed by the Foral Deputation of Gipuzkoa and the Juntas Generales of Gipuzkoa; the Foral Deputation of Bizkaia and the Juntas Generales of the historical territory of Bizkaia; and by the Federation of Business Owners of La Rioja, for reversal of the Judgment of September 30, 1999, decreed by the Administrative Law Court of the Supreme Court of Justice of the Basque Country. This case involved an appeal of court order no. 3753/96, which involved a challenge to Foral Norm 7/1996 of *the Juntas Generales* of Gipuzkoa of July 4; Foral Norm no. 3/1996 of Bizkaia of June 26, and Foral Norm 24/1996 of July 5 of Araba. Each of these three measures that were challenged regulated the corporate tax. The parties filing the subsequent appeal were the Juntas Generales of Araba; the Foral Deputation of Araba; the Juntas Generales of Bizkaia; the Foral Deputation of Bizkaia; the Basque Government; the Bilbao Chamber of Commerce, Industry, and Navigation; and the Federation of Business Owners of La Rioja.

18. For a far-reaching and detailed analysis see, for example, Alonso Arce, *El Concierto Económico en Europa*, 107 ff.

19. See a commentary on this controversial judgment, and an analysis of its consequences, in I. Alonso Arce, "Una crónica del Concierto Económico (1981–2005): Defensa de nuestros derechos históricos," *AVD-ZEA* 8 (December 2005): 31–93. See also J.W. Rodríguez Curiel, "La autonomía fiscal de las autoridades intraestatales no excluye la calificación de ayuda de Estado (Sentencia del Tribunal Supremo de 9.12.2004)," *Gaceta Jurídica de la Unión Europea* (March–April 2005): 84–91. Another analysis is provided in A. Orena Domínguez, "El Impuesto sobre Sociedades de Gipuzkoa tras las últimas sentencias del TS" *Revista Quincena Fiscal Aranzadi* 17 (October 2008): 45–56

20. Alonso Arce, *El Concierto Económico*, 111.

21. Thus, on December 9, 1999, the Foral Deputation of Gipuzkoa and the Juntas Generales of Gipuzkoa each filed motions requesting a favorable Judgment that would partially overturn the appealed Judgment by declaring article 26 of Foral Regulation NF 7/1996 to be in compliance with the Law. On November 12, 1999, a motion was presented to the Foral Deputation of Bizkaia requesting a favorable judgment that would overturn the appealed Judgment and declare inadmissible, on the grounds of lack of proper legal standing, the administrative court appeal that had been filed and, in its

place, declare in compliance with the Law Article 26 of Foral Regulation 3/96 of June 26, regarding the corporate tax of the historical territory of Bizkaia. On December 2, 1999, an appeal was lodged by the Juntas Generales of the historical territory of Bizkaia requesting the following: (1) in consideration of the first reason for the present appeal, and in accordance with article 88.1.c of Law 29/98, the overturning and revocation of the appealed judgment, declaring the inadmissibility of appeal via the administrative law courts filed by the Federation of Business Owners of La Rioja on the grounds of lack of proper legal standing; (2) Pursuant to the previous consideration: (a) confirmation, on the one hand, of the aspects of the judgment of the lower court that were expressly accepted by the appellant, given that their conformity with the laws of the foral regulation being challenged were recognized, and a dismissal of the entire contents of the appeal lodged by the Federation of Business Owners of La Rioja; and (b) acceptance of the full contents of the motion for appeal, including revocation of the judgment of the lower court and the issuing of another in its place that dismissed the appeal lodged by the aforementioned entity, declaring Article 26 of the challenged foral regulation in conformity with the law. Finally, on December 10, 1999, the Federation of Business Owners of La Rioja presented their final appeal motion requesting a Judgment that would overturn the appealed Judgment and uphold the legitimacy of the appeal in the administrative law courts which had previously been lodged, thus declaring the following foral regulations null and void: 7/1996 of July 4 of the historical territory of Gipuzkoa; 24/1996 of July 5 of the Historical Territory of Araba; and 3/1996 of June 26 of the historical territory of Bizkaia. Concomitantly, a request was made to declare null and void the following articles of the aforementioned foral regulation: 5, 11, 12, 13, 14, 15, 19, 24, 26, 29, 34, 37, 39, 40, 41, 42, 43, 44, 45, 49, 50, 52, 53, 54, 59, 60, and 177. Judgment of the Supreme Court of Justice of the Basque Country of September 30, 1999. Statement of Fact Number 3.

22. This opposition took the following form: (1) The Juntas Generales of Araba (July 1, 2002) requested dismissal of the appeal that had been filed by the representatives of the Federation of Business Owners of La Rioja; (2) The Foral Deputation of Araba (July 10, 2002) requested dismissal of the appeal that had been filed by the opposing party (i.e., the Federation of Businessmen of La Rioja) declaring the Judgment issued by the Lower Court in conformity with the law; (3) The Juntas Generales of Bizkaia (July 10, 2002) requested that its opposition be noted for the record, and that the appeal filed by the Federation of Businessmen of La Rioja be dismissed; (4) the Basque Government (July 16, 2002) requested that its opposition to the appeal filed by the aforementioned Federation be noted for the Record, and that said appeal be dismissed after proper legal procedures had been duly that the appellant followed; (5) the Chamber of Commerce, Industry, and Navigation of Bilbao (July 12, 2002) requested the dismissal of the entire contents of the appeal filed by the Federation of Business Owners of La Rioja, along with a demand assume all legal costs; (6) the Federation of Business Owners of La Rioja (September 18, 2002) requested both the dismissal of the alleged grounds and the declaration that the appeals filed by the Foral Deputation of Bizkaia and the Juntas Generales of Gipuzkoa were without grounds. Supreme Court

of Justice of the Basque Country of September 30, 1999. Statement of Fact Number 5.

23. Falcón emphasizes that this formal declaration of revocation is based on the fact that the corresponding provisions would constitute (in accordance with the judgment discussed in the text) aid that had not been reported to the Commission, and thereby automatically constitute a violation of the prohibition of lower fiscal pressure required within the system of the Economic Agreement and by particular constitutional regulations. It is important in this regard to note that the existence of aid, and the noncompliance with the obligation to provide notification of said aid, is the only grounds of the verdict, which is based on consideration of the first reason for the appeal, without considering any of the others. Considerations regarding the violation of constitutional regulations can thus be considered of secondary importance. See R. Falcón y Tella, "En torno a la STS 9 diciembre 2004 relativa a las normas forales de 1996 (I): Los efectos de la declaración de nulidad y el papel del Tribunal Supremo en el control de las ayudas de Estado," *Revista Quincena Fiscal Aranzadi* 2 (2005): 5–10.

24. J.G. Rubi Casinello, "El Concierto Económico a la luz de la sentencia del Tribunal de Justicia de la Unión Europea de 11 de septiembre de 2008," *Revista Aranzadi Unión Europea* 1 (January 2009), 24. This was also made clear by AG Geelhoed in his "Conclusiones en el Asunto Azores, C-88/03," present on October 2, 2005, in paragraph 43, although he recognizes that "the conclusions of Advocates-General Saggio; the *Juntas Generales* of Gipuzkoa; and the Foral Deputation of Gipuzkoa (accumulated issues C-400/97 to C-402/97) addressed this issue, which had to do with the compatibility of the Treaty with certain fiscal measures that support investment and promote economic activity within the Basque Country. However, the Advocates-General declared that these were nothing more than *ad hoc* regulations designed to promote competitiveness among the companies to which they were applied and that, therefore, they did not constitute general principles that could be used to analyze geographically limited tax differences. This Case was dismissed without the Court of Justice issuing any definitive judgment" (note 28).

25. Alonso Arce, *El Concierto Económico en Europa*, 117.

26. Official Constitutional Court documents of December 18, 2005, and May 17, 2006.

27. The foral regulations that were challenged were 7/2005 of June 23 of the Juntas Generales of Bizkaia, which modified Foral Regulation 3/1996 (for the Corporate Tax) of June 26); the Emergency Foral Fiscal Decree 2/2005 of May 24 of the Board of Deputies of Araba (which modified Foral Regulation 24/1996) of June 5 (and which regulated the corporate tax); and Foral Decree 32/2005 of May 24 of the Foral Deputation of Gipuzkoa (which modified Foral Regulation 7/1996 of July 4, and which regulated the corporate tax).

28. It was in what has come to be known as the "Azores Case," that the CJEU first addressed the question of whether a reduction in State tax rates restricted to a particular geographical area of a member state constituted state aid (i.e., "territorial selectivity"). As Urrea Corres has written, "In fact, the core legal Case of the Azores Case was nothing more than a demand to specify whether the acknowledgement of the capacity on the part of a infra-state entity to set

taxes that are lower than those in the rest of the state constitutes the kind of geographical selectivity characteristic of a legal system of State Aid or if, on the contrary, it is possible to accept a sub-national fiscal system as a normal tax system." M. Urrea Corres, "La autonomía fiscal del País Vasco a examen por el Tribunal de Justicia de la Unión Europea. (Comment on the Judgment of the European Court of Justice of September 11, 2008, General Workers' Union of La Rioja et al. vs. *Juntas Generales* of the Historical Territory of Bizkaia et al.) (As. ac. C-428/06 a C-434/06)," *Revista General de Derecho Europeo* 17 (2008), 2.

29. CJEU, Judgment of September 6, 2006, Case 88/03, *Azores Case*, paragraph 57.

30. Institutional, procedural, and economic autonomy.

31. A clear reference to the Spanish Supreme Court, which the AGs confused with the Spanish Constitutional Court.

32. Conclusions of AG Kokott regarding consolidated cases C-428/06 to C-464/06, presented May 8, 2008, paragraph 101.

33. J.G. Rubi Casinello, "El Concierto Económico a la luz de las sentencia del Tribunal de Justicia de las Comunidades Europeas de 11 de septiembre de 2008," *Revista Unión Europea Aranzadi* 1 (2009): 26.

34. Appeal for legal protection no. 1206-2005.

35. It should be remembered that those instances in which the obligation of referencing a preliminary Judgment does not apply are as follows: (1) when the appeal filed is irrelevant to Community law; (2) when the appeal to be resolved internally is materially identical to another that has already received a preliminary judgment from the European Court of Justice (the *Da Costa* case); and (3) when the application of Community Law can be imposed in manner that is supported by evidence that eliminates any reasonable doubt regarding the manner to resolve the appeal being filed (CILFIT case).

36. This is the so-called "CILFIT Doctrine," by virtue of which national courts of last resort may be exempted from the requirement to submit a matter for preliminary judgment when the proper interpretation is obvious, seems to have reached a critical point. Judgment of European Court of Justice of October 6, 1982, Case 283/81.

37. Page 35 of text presented on February 22, 2005, by the Juntas Generales of Bizkaia.

38. Constitutional Court Judgment 50/1994 and Constitutional Court Judgment ("auto") 254/1982.

39. Constitutional Court Judgment 173/2002.

40. In fact, in accordance with the doctrine enshrined in Constitutional Court Judgment 58/2004, the existence or non-existence of a doubt "cannot be understood in terms of the subjective conviction of the judge regarding a particular interpretation of EU law (i.e., a subjective evaluation), but instead in terms of an objective, clear, and categorical non-existence of any doubt whatsoever as to its application. It is thus not a matter of there not being any reasonable doubt, but of there not being any doubt at all."

41. Official documents of the Constitutional Court of December 18, 2005, and May 17, 2006.

42. Under the terms of Article 241 of the Organic Law of the Judiciary.

43. Appeal number 3951-2005.

44. Official Constitutional Court document 225/2007 of April 20, 2007.
45. See J.G. Rubí Cassinello, "El Concierto Económico a la luz de las sentencia del Tribunal de Justicia de las Comunidades Europeas de 11 de septiembre de 2008," *Revista Unión Europea Aranzadi* 1 (2009): 23–42.
46. Court of Justice, Third Court, presided over on that occasion by A. Rosas (Reporting Judge), President of the Court, as well as J.N. Cunha Rodrigues, J. Klucka, A.Ó. Caoimh, and A. Arabadijiev, Judges. Coincidentally, Rosas had also been the reporting judge in the "Azores Case."
47. Judgment of the Court (Third Chamber), September 11, 2008 (State Aid—Tax measures adopted by a regional or local authority—Selective nature), in Joined Cases C 428/06 to C 434/06. See http://curia.europa.eu/es/actu/communiques/index.htm (last accessed October 7, 2013).
48. Such as the reasons of public order, safety, and health included in Article 46 of the TEC.
49. It should be remembered that EU member nations currently impose more than twenty different corporate taxes.
50. The summary of the Judgment makes this very clear: European Community Court, Judgment of September 11, 2008. SUMMARY: Special territorial-based tax systems. Foral Treasury systems. Basque Country. Corporate Tax. TEEC, State Aid:

> Article 87.1 of the TEC should be interpreted as meaning that, in order to determine the selective nature of a measure, and therefore know if it constitutes State aid, one has to take into account the institutional, procedural, and economic autonomy enjoyed by the authority that adopts said measure. It is the responsibility of the referring judicial body (i.e., the SCJBC), which is the only body competent to identify applicable national law and interpret it, and to apply Community law to litigation that it hears, to verify whether the historical territories and the Autonomous Community of the Basque Country enjoy such autonomy. If such is the case, then the regulations adopted within the limits of the competences granted to said infra-state entities by the Spanish Constitution of 1978 and other provisions of Spanish law are not selective in nature, in the sense of constituting State aid, as defined in article 87.1.

See Supreme Court Judgment of December 9, 2004, appeal no. 7893/1999 (NFJ018721) and CJEU Judgment of September 6, 2006, Case no. C-88/03 [NFJ023663].
51. The SCJBC dismissed eight appeals against the corporate tax of Bizkaia, five against Araba, and four against Gipuzkoa. Among the appeals rejected are those made against the setting of corporate tax rates at 32.6 percent, 32.5 percent, and the currently effective rate of 28 percent.
52. The Supreme Court had already accepted this thesis, revoking the foral tax rates for the corporate tax of 32.5 percent (rates identical to those currently appealed before the SCJBC and referenced to the CJEU).
53. Despite its being called an Organic Law, it is only so to the extent that it modifies the Organic Law of the Constitutional Court (LOTC) and the Judicial Power Law (JPL). The part that modifies the Law of the Administrative Jurisdiction (LAJ) is not organic.

54. Article 162 of the Spanish Constitution: "Those entitled: a.) To appeal on the grounds of unconstitutionality—the President of the Government, the State Ombudsman, Fifty Deputies, Fifty Senators, the executive bodies of the Autonomous Communities and, if applicable, the Assemblies of those bodies; b.) In order to make an appeal for legal protection—any individual or legal entity claiming a legitimate interest, as well as the State Ombudsman and the State Prosecutor. 2. In all other cases, the Organic Law will determine which persons and bodies are entitled."
55. It is also not the only one, given that, as a number of authors (such as Muñoz Machado) point out, a more appropriate method might be the reform of the Statute of Autonomy of the Basque Country in a way that strengthens the foral institutions in general and the Foral Tax Norms in particular. See www.abc.es/20101119/local-la-rioja/rioja-201011190743.html, www.finanzas.com/noticias/economia/2010-11-17/382294_pedro-sanz-inaugurara-estejueves.html, www.abc.es/agencias/noticia.asp?noticia=59 4220.
56. Art 19 Ley Reguladora de la Jurisdicción Contencioso-Administrativa (LRJCA):

> 1. The following parties are entitled before the Administrative Law Courts: a.) Individuals or legal entities who claim a legitimate right or interest; b.) Corporations, associations, unions, groups, and entities referred to in article 18, and which are affected or which have the legal requisites for the defense of legitimate collective rights and interests; c.) the State Administration, when it has a legitimate right or interest, for the purpose of challenging acts or provisions of the Administration of the Autonomous Communities, and of public Bodies affiliated therewith, as well as local entities, in accordance with the provisions of legislation in the local system, and public bodies of any other entity not subject to said Administration; d.) The Administration of the Autonomous Communities, for the purpose of challenging acts and provisions that affect the sphere of their autonomy, and which have been issued by the Administration of the State, or by any other Administration or public Body, or by local entities, in accordance with the provisions of legislation of the local system; e.) Local territorial entities, for the purpose of challenging acts and provisions that affect the sphere of their autonomy, and which have been issued by the State Administration and Autonomous Communities, or by Public Bodies with their own defined legal status that are affiliated with either of the aforesaid Administration, or the public Bodies of other local Entities; f.) The Public Prosecutor's Office, for the purpose of intervening in legal proceedings required by Law; g.) Public law entities with their own defined legal status that are either affiliated with or dependent on any of the public Administrations, for the purpose of challenging acts or provisions that affect the scope of their defined activities.

57. Some authors, such as R. Ciprián de la Riva, maintain that the joint consideration of legal provisions of such a fundamental nature (i.e., of the LRALC and the civil code themselves make inevitable the possibility that the foral regulations of the historical territories might become subject to an appeal in the administrative law courts. R. Ciprián de la Riva, "El enjuiciamiento de

las Normas Forales de los Territorios Históricos," *Forum Fiscal de Bizkaia* (May 2000): 9–15.

58. Appeal no. 2684/93 against Foral Regulations 5/1993 of July 24 (Bizkaia); 11/1993 of June 26 (Gipuzkoa); and 18/1997 of July 5 (Araba), all related to "Emergency Fiscal Measures for Supporting Investment and Promoting Economic Activity," resolved in accordance with the formal truth inherent in the Supreme Court Judgment of October 31, 2000.

59. Specifically, against Foral Regulations 5/1993 of July 24 (Bizkaia); 11/1993 of June 26 (Gipuzkoa); and 18/1997 of July 5 (Araba), all related to "Emergency Fiscal Measures for Supporting Investment and Promoting Economic Activity."

60. Official court document of July 15, 1993.

61. The Supreme Court, in considering the appeal for reversal filed by the Autonomous Community of La Rioja, requesting the revocation of the resolutions being appealed (Official documents of Section 1 of the Administrative Law Court of the SCJBC of July 15, 1994, and January 2, 1995) issuing another Judgment in response thereto which dismissed the previous allegations of inadmissibility which had been formulated by the codefendant—the Foral Deputation of Araba—and ordering that the proceedings continue (Supreme Court Judgment of October 31, 2000).

62. We should recall in this connection the following Foral Regulations: 5/1993 of July 24 (Bizkaia); 11/1993 of July 24 (Gipuzkoa); and 18/1993 of July 5 (Araba).

63. Supreme Court Judgment of October 31, 2000, Court Consideration 1, paragraphs 2 and 3.

64. In this judgment, the Supreme Court established that the *ad processum* entitlement assumed a general suitability to participate in any proceeding (in accordance with the Supreme Court judgment of May 19, 1960), which "is the same as legal authority or legal status, because every person, by virtue of being a person, has rights and obligations, and may thus need to defend said rights and obligations." On the other hand, *ad causum* entitlement is limited to suitability for participating in a particular proceeding (in other words, it depends on the actor's purpose in participating in the proceedings or, as stipulated in the previously cited judgment, it consists of entitlement as such and "implies a special relationship between a person and a legal situation being litigated, by virtue of which it is that person who, according to the Law, must take part as either an actor or a defendant." In addition, this doctrine indicates that "this specific suitability grows out of the substantive problem to be addressed in the proceedings. Therefore, that problem is more closely tied to material Law, since it addresses a matter of substance and not one that is merely procedural"). See J.L. Monasterio, "La legitimación de las Comunidades Autónomas en los recursos contencioso-administrativos contra Normas Forales Tributarias de los Territorios Históricos," *Forum Fiscal de Bizkaia* (February 2001) (Ref. 015.028): 15–20.

65. In the previously mentioned official documents of the SCJBC of July 15, 1994, and January 2, 1995 (the latter containing a dismissal of an appeal filed by the Autonomous Community of La Rioja).

66. Supreme Court Judgment of October 31, 2000, granting procedural em-

powerment to the Autonomous Community of La Rioja.

67. For more on this topic, see R. Jiménez Asensio, "La "Norma Foral" en el sistema de fuentes . . . ," 143–71. In this same work, see M. Carrillo López, "Las Juntas Generales de Gipuzkoa: carácter representativo y potestad normativa," 131–42; M. Castells Arteche, "Las Juntas Generales en el entramado institucional vasco," 115–28; E. Cobreros Mendazona, "Las Juntas Generales y la Comisión Arbitral," 99--114; M.M. Razquin Lizarraga, "Las funciones y las competencias de las Juntas Generales," 75–97; G. Jáuregui Bereciartu, "Las Juntas Generales como institución de democracia representativa y participativa," pp. 37–54; and A. Saiz Arnaiz,"Las Juntas Generales: ¿Parlamento contemporáneo?," 55–71. Although these works deal exclusively with the historical territory of Gipuzkoa and its Juntas Generales, they are completely applicable to the other two historical territories as well, and therefore serve as important sources of the present paper.

68. Etxeberria Monasterio, "En defensa del "Blindaje" de las Normas Forales Tributarias," 23.

69. "Administrative Law Courts will hear matters related to the actions of public administrative entities subject to administrative law, pertaining to general provisions holding a status inferior to that of laws, or to legislative decrees as specified in article 82.6 of the Constitution, in accordance with what the Law establishes in that jurisdiction. They will also hear appeals related to the inactivity of an administrative entity, and those challenging its material actions which constitute matters of fact. What these courts will not hear are direct or indirect appeals concerning matters over which the Constitutional Court holds exclusive jurisdiction, under the terms of the Fifth Additional Provision of its Organic Law."

70. "Direct or indirect appeals filed against the Foral Tax Norms of the *Juntas Generales* of the Historical Territories of Araba, Gipuzkoa, and Bizkaia will be under the exclusive jurisdiction of the Constitutional Court, under the terms of the Fifth Additional Provision of its Organic Law."

71. This involved appeals against the proposed budget for 2010 contained in Foral Regulation 14/2009 of December 17 of the Deputation of Araba; against the tax reforms introduced in Foral Regulation 4/2009 of December 23 of the Deputation of Gipuzkoa; and against the General Budgets of the Historical Territory of Bizkaia for 2010. Specifically, the claims once again referred to corporate tax credits.

72. In other words, application cannot be revoked due to the illegality or unconstitutionality of a foral tax norms (i.e., in terms, or within parameters, of internal legality).

Bibliography

Alonso Arce, I. *El Concierto Económico en Europa*, IVAP, Oñati, 2010.

——— "Una crónica del Concierto Económico (1981–2005): Defensa de nuestros derechos históricos," AVD-ZEA. Bilbao, Diciembre 2005, nº. 8, pp 31–93.

Alonso García, R. *El juez español y el Derecho comunitario: Jurisdicciones constitucional y ordinaria frente a su primacía y eficacia*, Tirant

Monografías, nº 295, Tirant lo Blanch, Valencia, 2003.

———. La cuestión prejudicial comunitaria y el derecho a la tutela judicial efectiva, Tirant lo Blanch, Valencia, 2003.

———. "La (in)aplicación judicial del Derecho comunitario ante el Tribunal Constitucional: Falta de motivación, cuestión prejudicial comunitaria y derecho fundamental a la tutela judicial efectiva" en Jurisprudencia Constitucional sobre Trabajo y Seguridad Social, Tomo XI, Ed. Civitas, Madrid, 1994.

———. y Baño Leõn, J.M., "El recurso de amparo frente a la negativa a plantear la cuestión prejudicial ante el Tribunal de Justicia de la Comunidad Europea," REDC, Vol. 29, mayo-agosto 1990, pp. 193-222.

Alonso Olea, E.J. "Las haciendas forales vascas: 1500–2002. Una historia del concierto económico," en AAVV., El Concierto Económico Vasco historia y renovación. Las valoraciones de la población de la C.A.P.V. al respecto, Cuadernos Sociológicos Vascos, nº 12, 2002, pp. 7- 49.

———. El Concierto Económico (1878–1937). Origen y formación de un Derecho Histórico, IVAP, Oñati, 1995.

Conclusiones del Abogado General GEELHOED en el Asunto Azores, C-88/03, presentadas el 2 de octubre de 2005.

Conclusiones de la Abogado General KOKOTT, relativas a los Asuntos acumulados C-428/06 a C-464/06, presented May 8,2008.

Falcon Y Tella, R. "En torno a la STS 9 diciembre 2004 relativa a las normas forales de 1996 (I): los efectos de la declaración de nulidad y el papel del Tribunal Supremo en el control de las ayudas de Estado," Quincena Fiscal Aranzadi, nº 2/2005.

Faramiñán Gilbert, J.M. de, "El Tratado de Lisboa: Un juego de espejos rotos," REEI, nº 17, 2009, on line.

Fraile Ortiz, M. "Negativa del juez nacional a plantear una cuestión prejudicial ante el Tribunal de Justicia de la Unión Europea," REDE nº 7, 2003.

Orena Dominguez, A. "El Impuesto sobre Sociedades de Gipuzkoa tras las últimas sentencias del TS," Revista Quincena Fiscal, Aranzadi, nº 17, octubre 2008.

Ortiz Vaamonde, S. "El Tribunal Constitucional ante el Derecho comunitario," REDC, nº 61, Vol. 21, 2001.

Pérez Bernabeu, B. *Ayudas de Estado en la jurisprudencia comunitaria: Concepto y tratamiento*, Tirant lo Blanch - Universitat d`Alicant, Valencia, 2008.

Rodríguez Curiel, J.W. "La autonomía fiscal de las autoridades intraestatales no excluye la calificación de ayuda de Estado: Sentencia del Tribunal Supremo de 9.12.2004," Gaceta Jurídica de la Unión Europea, marzo-abril 2005. pp. 84-91.

Rubi Casinello, J.G. "El Concierto Económico a la luz de la sentencia del Tribunal de Justicia de la Unión Europea de 11 de septiembre de 2008," Revista Aranzadi Unión Europea, nº 1, January 2009.

Sánchez Legido, A. "El Tribunal Constitucional y la garantía interna de la aplicación del Derecho comunitario en España (a propósito de la STC 58/2004)," Derecho Privado y Constitución, nº. 18, 2004.

Serrano Gazteluurrutia, S. El Concierto Económico ante el Juez europeo. La judicialización de las Normas Forales tributarias en el ámbito jurídico europeo. Situación vigente (ayudas de Estado) y perspectivas de futuro. Premio José Mª Leizaola 2011, IVAP, Oñati, 2012, 978-84-7777-379-5.

Sobrido Prieto, M. *Las Comunidades Autónomas ante el Tribunal de Justicia y el Tribunal de Primera Instancia de las Comunidades Europeas*, Tirant lo Blanch-Instituto Universitario de Estudios Europeos, Valencia, 2003.

Ugartemendia Eceizabarrena, J.I. "El recurso a la prejudicial (234 TCE) como cuestión de amparo (a propósito de la STC 58/2004)," REDE, nº 11, 2004.

Urrea Corres, M. "La autonomía fiscal del País Vasco a examen por e Tribunal de Justicia de la unión Europea: Comentario a la STJUE de 11 de septiembre de 2008, Unión General de Trabajadores de la Rioja y otros c. Juntas Generales del Territorio Histórico de Vizcaya y otros (As. ac. C-428/06 a C-434/06)," Revista General de Derecho Europeo, nº 17, 2008.

List of Contributors

Dr. Joseba Agirreazkuenaga Zigorraga is full professor of contemporary history at the University of the Basque Country (UPV-EHU) and head of the University Research Group on Biography & Parliament (www.prosoparlam.org) for the period 2013–2018; member of the Commission for Research and Innovation since 2005 (UPV-EHU). His recent books include *The Making of the Basque Question: Experiencing Self-Government, 1793–1877* and *Euskal herritarren burujabetza: Euskal herritarren autogobernu auziaren bilakaeraz (1793–1919)*; *Foruen bidezko erakundetzetik Autonomia Estatutura*.

Dr. Eduardo J. Alonso Olea is permanent researcher (2011) and professor of history in the Department of Contemporary History in the Faculty of Social Sciences and Letters at the University of the Basque Country. He has published research on the Economic Agreement as well as on company history (Mutua Vizcaya Industrial—today's Mutualia, Centro Industrial de Vizcaya—today's CEBEK, and Santa Ana de Bolueta). His recent publications include *El Concierto Económico. Desde la abolición foral hasta su recuperación (1839–1981).* "El Concierto Económico como herramienta: Crisis económicas y políticas anticíclicas de las Diputaciones vascas, 1867–1936" in *Boletín de Estudios Económicos.*

Jose Mª Iruarrizaga Artaraz is a graduate in economic sciences at the University of the Basque Country and holds a master's degree in company management. From 1980 to 1987 he worked as an auditor (external and internal) at KPMG and Caja Laboral. From 1987 to 2002 he held different posts in the Basque government including director of services in the Department of the Interior, director of the quota and vice-councilor of the Economy, Budgets and Economic Control. Since July 2003 he has held the post of Foral Deputy of the Treasury and Finances of the Foral Deputation of Bizkaia.

José Luis Bilbao Eguren is a graduate in economic sciences at University of the Basque Country. Elected as a representative in the Representative Assembly of Bizkaia in 1983 for the Basque Nationalist Party. His political activity has since then been developed in the Foral Deputation of Bizkaia. Director of Budgets and Finances (1987),

Deputy of the Presidency, General Secretary of the General Deputy, Deputy of Agriculture and of Economic Promotion, and President of the Transport Consortium of Bizkaia. Since 2003 he has been General Deputy of Bizkaia.

Pedro Luis Uriarte was, between 1980 and 1984, Councilor of Economy and the Treasury in the Basque Government and President of the Negotiating Commission on the Economic Agreement (1981). Vice-president and Delegate Councilor of the BBVA bank (1994–2001). In July 2007, he created Innobasque (Basque Innovation Agency). Currently he is the Executive President of Economía, Empresa y Estrategia, a strategic consultancy, a member of the Councils of the Deusto Business School, of the University of Deusto, and of the CEIT (Centre of Technical Studies and Research, Gipuzkoa). He is a member of the Board of Trustees of UNICEF. See: "Pedro Luis Uriarte" in, Historia del Gobierno Vasco contada por sus consejeros (1980-1998). Oñati: IVAP, 2001, pp. 295-353

Mario Fernández Pelaz was professor of mercantile law in the Law Faculty and the Faculty of Business Sciences of the University of Deusto (1966–1997). Vice-president of the Basque Government (1985), and President of the Basque Council of Finances and member of the Arbitration Commission of the Autonomous Community of Euskadi until 2009. General Director of the Grupo BBVA, member of the Management Committee from 1997 to 2002. Since July 2009 President of the BBK (Bilbao Bizkaia Kutxa), and since January 2012 President of Kutxabank. His recent publications include *Esparru ekonomiko tixikiak: Euskadi esparru ekonomiko gisa / Los espacios económicos menores: Euskadi como espacio económico*.

Dr. Ignacio Zubiri Oria has a Phd from Princeton. He is full professor of public economics at the University of the Basque Country. He served as editor of the Spanish Public Finance Review (*Hacienda Pública Española*) and the journal *On Public Economics*. He has published more than 120 papers in academic journals and several books, including *The Economic Agreement between the Basque Country and Spain*.

Dr. Victor Urrutia Abaigar is full professor of sociology at the University of the Basque Country. He was director of EUSTAT (Instituto Vasco de Estadística [Basque Institute of Statistics]) (2009–2010) and the Sociological Prospection Cabinet of the Basque Government (2010–2012). His recent publications include editing *Las dimensiones sociales de la ciudad* with Amaia Izaola, Imanol Zubero, and Alberto de la Peña.

José Gabriel Rubí Cassinello is a member of the Senior Body of Controllers and Auditors of the State by civil service examination

(1981). Economic-Financial Sub-director in the Treasury and Finances Department of the Foral Deputation of Bizkaia, 1983, 1987, and at present, General Technical Secretary since October 1995, and member of the Negotiating Commission for the Renovations of the Economic Agreement in the years 1997, 2002, and 2007. In 2011, he was appointed representative of the Basque Institutions in the D–5 Work Group on the Code of Company Conduct, dependent on ECOFIN. Since its constitution in 2001 he has presided over the Board of Directors of the Ad Concordiam Association for the Promotion and Diffusion of the Economic Agreement. He has published "El encaje del Concierto Económico en el nuevo orden tributario internacional" in the *Boletín de estudios económicos*.

Dr. Santiago Larrazabal Basañez is professor of constitutional law in the Law Faculty of the University of Deusto and director of the Institute of Basque Studies. Researcher in Foral Public Law and European Integration. Since 2012 he has been the director of the Government Secretariat and of Relations with the Basque Parliament of the Basque Government/Eusko Jaurlaritza. He has a published *Statute Law in Bizkaia* and *Derecho Público de los Territorios Forales: De los orígenes a la abolición foral*.

Dr. Aitor Esteban Bravo is professor of constitutional law in the University of Deusto. Secretary of the Presidency and Spokesperson of the Foral Deputation of Bizkaia (1991–1995). He served as president of the Representative Assembly of Bizkaia (1995–2003). In the 2004 elections he was elected as a member of parliament for the EAJ-PNV in the Spanish Congress (Bizkaia constituency). In the November 2011 elections he renewed his seat and is currently the Principal Spokesperson of the Board of Spokespersons for the Basque Parliamentary Group in the Spanish Congress.

Dr. Miguel Martorell Linares is senior professor in the Faculty of Political Sciences and Sociology at UNED (Universidad Nacional de Educación a Distancia [National University of Distance Education], Madrid). Previously served as chief of staff of the Minister of Education Mercedes Cabrera between 2006 and 2009. He is the author of the books *Historia de la Peseta: España contemporánea a través de su moneda* and *Palabra de Liberal: José Sánchez Guerra (1859–1923)*.

Aritz Ipiña Bidaurrazaga holds a master's degree in contemporary history (2010) and is a contracted researcher in the Documentation Centre for the Economic Agreement at the University of the Basque Country. He has published different works on the purge of civil servants in Bizkaia in1937, especially in Bizkaia.

Dr. Susana Serrano Gazteluurrutia holds a law degree from the University of Deusto and received the title of doctor in 2010. She is a professor of financial and fiscal law in the Law Faculty of the University of the Basque Country. She is the author *El Concierto Económico vasco ante el juez comunitario* and winner of the Jesús Mª Leizaola prize for the year 2011.

www.ingramcontent.com/pod-product-compliance
Lightning Source LLC
LaVergne TN
LVHW010053110826
845155LV00028B/313